THE ICEWATER OF
THE NORTH ATLANTIC
WAS THEIR SHROUD

Few escaped these iron coffins that still contain so many of Hitler's navy. They were brave men, heroes in a wrong cause. They believed that they were all that stood between their country and disaster. Expecting death, most of them found it. This is their story, a terrifying tale of Germany's U-boat service as told by a survivor.

THE BANTAM WAR BOOK SERIES

This is a series of books about a world on fire.

These carefully chosen volumes cover the full dramatic sweep of World War II. Many are eyewitness accounts by the men who fought in this global conflict in which the future of the civilized world hung in balance. Fighter pilots, tank commanders and infantry commanders, among others, recount exploits of individual courage in the midst of the large-scale terrors of war. They present portraits of brave men and true stories of gallantry and cowardice in action, moving sagas of survival and tragedies of untimely death. Some of the stories are told from the enemy viewpoint to give the reader an immediate sense of the incredible life and death struggle of both sides of the battle.

Through these books we begin to discover what it was like to be there, a participant in an epic war for freedom.

Each of the books in the Bantam War Book series contains illustrations specially commissioned for each title to give the reader a deeper understanding of the roles played by the men and machines of World War II.

IRON COFFINS

A personal account of
the German U-boat battles
of World War II

by HERBERT A. WERNER

BANTAM BOOKS
TORONTO · NEW YORK · LONDON · SYDNEY

This low-priced Bantam Book
has been completely reset in a type face
designed for easy reading, and was printed
from new plates. It contains the complete
text of the original hard-cover edition.
NOT ONE WORD HAS BEEN OMITTED.

IRON COFFINS

A Bantam Book / published by arrangement with
Holt, Rinehart and Winston

PRINTING HISTORY

Holt, Rinehart and Winston edition published June 1969
2nd printing .... October 1969
3rd printing ..... January 1970
4th printing ...... March 1970
5th printing .... June 1970
A selection of the Book-Of-The-Month Club January 1970
Bantam edition / October 1978
2nd printing .. November 1983

Drawings by Tom Beecham.
Maps by Alan McKnight.

ISBN 0-553-23347-5

Published simultaneously in the United States and Canada

Bantam Books are published by Bantam Books, Inc. Its trademark, consisting of the words "Bantam Books" and the por-
trayal of a rooster, is Registered in U.S. Patent and Trademark
Office and in other countries. Marca Registrada. Bantam
Books, Inc., 666 Fifth Avenue, New York, New York 10103.

PRINTED IN THE UNITED STATES OF AMERICA

H   11 10 9 8 7 6 5 4 3 2

DEDICATION

To the seamen of all nations who
died in the Battle of the Atlantic
in World War II, and especially to
my U-boat comrades who lie entombed
in their Iron Coffins

There are no roses on a sailor's grave,
No lilies on an ocean wave,
The only tribute is the seagulls' sweeps,
And the teardrops that a sweetheart weeps.
　　　　　　　　　　　　　　—German song

Contents

Atlantic U-boat, Type VII, World War II

1. Superstructure
2. Pressure hull
3. Main deck
4. Forward hatch
5. Officers' quarters
6. Tower compartment
7. Bridge
8. Sky periscope
9. Direction finder
10. Attack periscope
11. Anti-aircraft guns (2 cm.)
12. Anti-aircraft guns (3.7 cm.)
13. Rudder
14. Rear hydroplanes and twin screws,
15. Motor room and aft torpedo tube
16. Diesel room
17. Galley and washroom
18. Petty officers' quarters and Battery I below deck
19. Control room and rear bulkhead

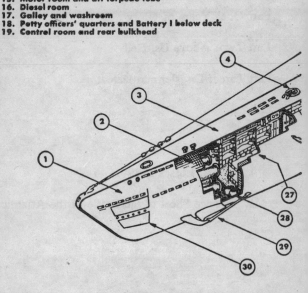

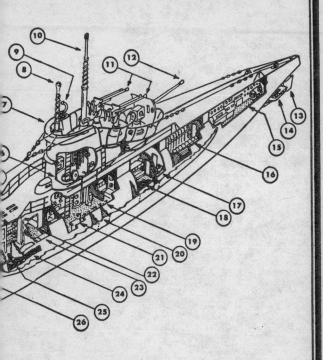

20. Saddle tank (fuel oil and ballast tanks)
21. Control room and forward bulkhead
22. Radio and sound rooms
23. Captain's nook
24. Battery II below deck
25. Chief Warrant Officers' quarters
26. Forward washroom
27. Bow compartment and men's quarters
28. Four torpedo tubes and spare
    torpedoes below deck
29. Forward hydroplanes
30. Outer torpedo tube doors

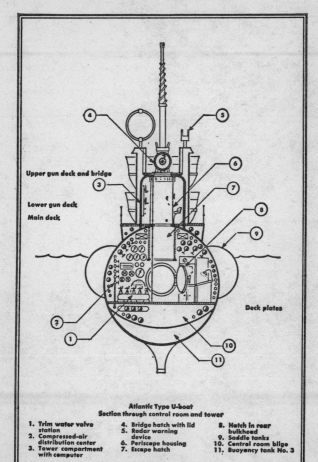

Upper gun deck and bridge

Lower gun deck

Main deck

Deck plates

Atlantic Type U-boat
Section through control room and tower

1. Trim water valve
   station
2. Compressed-air
   distribution center
3. Tower compartment
   with computer
4. Bridge hatch with lid
5. Radar warning
   device
6. Periscope housing
7. Escape hatch
8. Hatch in rear
   bulkhead
9. Saddle tanks
10. Control room bilge
11. Buoyancy tank No. 3

Foreword

An Appreciation by an American Contemporary

It is unusual for someone to have the opportunity, as I have, to write an introduction to a book by a member of a foreign and once enemy service whose personal history is so nearly a carbon copy of his own. Both of us were members of our naval academy classes of 1939; both of us finished submarine training and reported to our first submarines in 1941. Both of us served on board submarines throughout World War II, beginning in subordinate capacities and finally concluding the war in command of our own boats. Each of us has heard depth charges detonate alongside our boats, but not so successfully as others aimed at some of our good friends; and it is evident that depth charges sound surprisingly similar whether they be British, American, or Japanese. We have both participated in attacks on warships and merchantmen, and we have each seen great ships sink, sometimes gracefully and sometimes ignominiously, after the bottomripping burst of our warheads. The German submariners employed what I now recognize as nearly identical tactics to our own and both Werner and I have hurled futile imprecations upon our enemy for only doing his duty as well as he was able.

So Herbert Werner and I have a close bond in common, even though I had never heard of him until I read his story. But granting all this, there are two traps to be avoided in any objective evaluation. The first is the trap of shared professionalism which may obscure important differences stemming from contrasting environment and objectives. The second is that the inevitable intrusion of feelings and attitudes from the war could, if unrecognized, influence the objective attitude we should seek today. A fine line of demarcation ensues, for we can admire the men who fought for Germany even as we must condemn Hitler and his Nazis. It is important for the proper appreciation of this book that this divergence of feelings be kept in mind and maintained in its proper place on both counts.

In his own preface, Werner tells why he felt impelled to write *Iron Coffins*. It has been an obligation of long standing, he says, and he wants to honor the thousands of his comrades who lie forever entombed in their steel graves at the bottom of the sea. The political passions of the war have no place in either his narrative or his professed objective; he does not indulge in invective against his enemies, even though it is clear that he, like all of us, had his moments of vituperation. What he does say, however, merely by the telling of it, carries deep dramatic force, and the brutalization of all life touched by the war stands out in his book. It may sound strange, but ponder on this: the periods at sea—cramped in mold-ridden, diesel-hammering, oxygen-lacking, urine-reeking, excrement-laden, food-rotting, salt encrusted steel cockleshells, firing torpedoes in exultation, searching for convoys in frustration or receiving depth charges in stoic fear —these periods were the wholly admirable ones, regardless of who received the torpedoes or the depth charges, our side or theirs.

On the other hand, the times ashore were the times of degradation, and Werner does not spare us these. The picture of Germany in the spasm of defeat, infected with the moral destruction produced by war, appears ever more starkly as the ruin wrought by Hitler and his crew is played out to an inescapable and bitter end. Indeed, not the least contribution that Werner makes to the history of the second world-wide war is the personal picture of what war—total war— must inevitably mean to the decent men and women caught up in it.

None of this was totally unknown to the Allied

side, even though we won the war and they lost it; but
it was heightened in Germany. Through Werner we
see lovely girls giving freely because men might soon
die; we see civilians cowering in bunkers, afraid and
hesitant to extend the hand of help to persons in worse
condition than they; we see the profiteers—whatever
the commodity, be it sex or food—and the hierarchy
of superior staff echelons, protected from battles, having the best food and the prettiest girls, and giving
desperate, unrealistic orders to an ever-dwindling cadre
of fighting men.

But the war on the home front is not what this
book is about. Its theme is a life of incredible hard-
ships, terrifying warfare, absolutely fantastic determination, and unceasing dedication on the part of the
German submariners. At the end of the book one can
only survey their losses—fully ninety percent of those
actively at sea (as compared to the usual count
which included those in shore billets)—and one must
lift one's hat in tribute. One thing stands out clearly;
toward the close of the war, when only two out of ten
submarines leaving port were expected to return, they
still went out in accordance with orders, and with high
morale, knowing that most of them would not return.

It is the sad, terribly ironic truth, movingly faced
by Werner, that toward the end most of them knew
that their cause was lost. The heroism of the warrior,
who is generally naïve, young, honorable and incor-
ruptible, can never make up for a bad cause. Yet, in
reviewing the post-war decades, it is manifest that this
indomitability has been one of the assets upon which
Germany has rebuilt her national honor.

Allied records for the submarine war in the Atlantic state that the turning point came about March
1943; the full weight of the escort aircraft carrier,
improved radar, and new weapons were then thrown
against the U-boats. Nowhere have I read a more
dramatic account of how this all-out effort must have
seemed to the men who were on the receiving end of it
than in Werner's story. The story is told without he-
roics. It can be fully appreciated only by another submariner of the war, but anyone can get the message.

Take this passage: "Despite the dye marking our submergence, the Captain ordered an attack on the convoy before the escorts could attack us. Chirping Asdic pings, bellowing detonations (of depth charges) and the grinding roar of a hundred engines provided grim background music for our assault."

Tenacity was the strong point of these men, perhaps tenacity beyond logic or reasonable return for the risks taken—not that they individually had much choice in the matter—and the book ends, as it had to, on a note of demoralization and despair. But we have seen Werner grow into a tough-minded, cool, confident skipper. His was the last submarine to leave France during the retreat after the Allied invasion of 1944. Half a dozen predecessors died in the attempt, but he dared the gauntlet and brought his boat out safely with a load of people and equipment saved for a Germany which was too far gone to know or care. With his world cracking all around him, he was no longer the boy who went to sea five years before. He was now a man, although only twenty-five years old, able to see and record the breakdown all about him, note and yet stay above the danse macabre; recognize what had happened when the only reality left to him and his crew at the end was the reality of the leaky, obsolescent, damaged submarine to which they returned in relief from a shore leave too tragic to bear.

"Madness!" cries Werner from every page of the latter part of this book where he begins to question his country's policies. He still records his amorous affairs between patrols, but it is worthy of remark that as the danse macabre became worse, the amours became less important to him. It was not that there was greater reticence, nor that the demands of a young fighting man were any the less compelling. He was simply drained far more than he is able to tell, drained soul and body, nearing the limit of his life-force. There was no more Germany as he had known it—it had vanished long before, something he had begun to understand when his father was imprisoned for befriending a Jewish girl. There was no more German Navy; that part of it, the sea-going part, which had held value for him was all destroyed. Only a gargoyle remained, a façade around headquarters by day, drinking and womanizing at night.

"Madness!" cries Werner, and it was madness. But there were heroes, too, who deserve admiration even though their cause was wrong and, therefore, their sacrifice was worthless. No one can fault the warrior who believes in his country so strongly that he dies for it. This ought to permit these brave spirits to lie in peace, secure in the world's regard for them and their memory. Madness though it was, these were the flower of young German manhood, unfortunately— but not to their own discredit—early imbued with a warped ideal of how to achieve German destiny. They ought not to bear too harsh criticism, considering that the Treaty of Versailles is now hardly considered an ideal document. Furthermore, they were as a group unsullied by the cancer which afflicted the leading body politic. Because their leaders told them so, they believed that if they fought desperately, they might save their country from the disaster plainly grinding in from every side. They expected death, and most of them found it; but they fought hard all the same, and they carpeted the ocean floor with their bodies.

Edward L. Beach
Captain, U.S. Navy (Ret.)
U. S. Naval War College, Newport, Rhode Island

15 February, 1969

Introduction

This book, which tells of my personal experiences in the German U-boat Force in World War II, fulfills an obligation of long standing. Since the end of that destructive war, the role of the U-boat Force has at times been distorted and underestimated, even by military historians who should have known better. Because I was one of the few U-boat commanders who fought through most of the war and who managed to survive, I felt it was my duty to my fallen comrades to set the record straight. Very much to the point, duty was the first and last word in the lexicon of the U-boat men; and, remarks to the contrary notwithstanding, we did our duty with a correct gallantry unsurpassed in any branch of service on either side. We were soldiers and patriots, no more and no less, and in our dedication to our lost cause we died in appalling numbers. But the great tragedy of the U-boat Force was not merely that so many good men perished; it was also that so many of our lives were squandered on inadequate equipment and by the unconscionable policies of U-boat Headquarters.

In retrospect, the crucial importance of the U-boat Force is unmistakably clear. Whether or not Germany could have won the war, she was certain to lose it if the gigantic production of American factories reached England in sufficient quantity. On this proposition the lines were drawn for the epic "Battle of the Atlantic," in which the U-boats served as the vanguards of Germany's defense. No less an authority than Winston Churchill declared, "The battle of the Atlantic was the dominating factor all through the war. Never for one moment could we forget that everything happening elsewhere, on land, at sea, or in the air, depended ultimately on its outcome, and amid all other cares we viewed its changing fortunes day by day with apprehension." It is significant that Churchill, who knew all too well the ravages of the Luftwaffe and of Germany's V-1 and V-2 rockets, also wrote: "The only thing that really frightened me during the war was the U-boat peril." As viewed from the other side, Germany's fortunes in the war closely paralleled the rise and fall of the U-boat Force. The connection grew ever more obvious to me each time I came ashore after a long patrol.

The outbreak of hostilities in September 1939 surprised the German Navy; the U-boat Force in particular was caught fully unprepared. This state of affairs was dictated by a treaty, entered into between Germany and Great Britain in 1935, which limited German naval strength to 35 per cent of Britain's in order to maintain the tenuous balance of power that existed at the time. Germany in 1939 had just 57 commissioned U-boats, of which 52 were of small displacement and capable of only short coastal missions. The other five U-boats were larger craft designed for long-range patrols lasting eight weeks. Out of the total of 57, however, 18 U-boats were set aside for the training of new crews. Thus only 39 operational U-boats were available to take on the mighty British Navy, the huge British merchant fleet, the navies and merchant fleets of England's Allies, and an inexhaustible number of neutral ships that sailed under contract to the Allies.

Nonetheless, the first year of the U-boat war was extremely rewarding for Germany. Though the Force lost 28 boats, it destroyed one British aircraft carrier, one battleship, five cruisers, three destroyers, two submarines and 438 merchant vessels totaling 2.3 million gross-weight tons. Moreover, in the summer of 1940, after the surrender of France, our U-boats were gradually relocated southward to French ports on the Bay of Biscay. This move shortened our routes to and from the Atlantic and signaled a new phase of the war at sea—the great battles of the convoys.

Simultaneously Admiral Karl Doenitz, Commander-in-Chief of the U-boat Force as of 1935, launched an ambitious program to construct the largest fleet of submersibles that the world had ever seen. The most preferred U-boat of that time, Type VII, became the standard Atlantic U-boat; it had a displacement of 770 tons and a cruising range of 9,000 nautical miles. In the course of the war, 694 boats of this type were built and up-dated periodically with new improvements; they accounted for some 60 per cent of Allied shipping losses. In addition, more than 200 larger U-boats were constructed to lay mines, to attack Allied shipping lanes in distant areas, to transport critical war materials and, most important, to resupply the combat U-boats at sea with fuel oil, torpedoes, and provisions.

Great Britain soon felt the sting of this stepped-up building program. Unrestricted U-boat warfare against the North Atlantic convoy routes resulted in the destruction of 310,000 tons of shipping in one four-week period in the fall of 1940. Allied losses rose to 142 vessels totaling 815,000 tons in a two-month period in the spring of 1941, and a year and a half of U-boat warfare cost the Allies more than 700 ships totaling 3.4 million tons. Churchill wrote of England's darkest hour: "The pressure grew increasingly, and our shipping losses were fearfully above our construction. . . . Meanwhile the new 'wolf-pack' tactics . . . were rigorously applied by the redoubtable Prien and other tip-top U-boat commanders."

In May 1941, when I saw the first of my U-boat battles, our attacks on the shipping lanes were one-sided triumphs; Allied countermeasures—the use of radar, aircraft surveillance and new-type destroyers and convoy escorts—were still in their infancy and posed no serious threat to our raiders. This situation was not changed by the addition of 50 U.S. destroyers to the British fleet as part of the Anglo-American lend-lease agreement. By the end of 1941, our confident assumption of total victory seemed to lie within easy reach: combined Allied losses that year alone amounted to over 1000 merchant vessels totaling over 4 million tons.

Shortly after the United States entered the war, the U-boats extended their activities to the American east coast and raided shipping there with devastating results. During the first six months of hostilities against the United States, our boats sank 495 vessels totaling 2.5 million tons. Besides patrolling our North Atlantic and Caribbean hunting grounds, U-boats prowled the South Atlantic, the Mediterranean, and the Black Sea, and a few even showed up in the Pacific. In 1942, the most successful year in U-boat history, more than 1,200 Allied ships—nearly 7 million tons—were sent to the bottom.

But March of 1943, which brought the U-boat war to the peak of success, also heralded disaster. That month the U-boat Force sank over 650,000 tons of Allied shipping—and suffered a sharp and puzzling increase in losses. This unexpected turn of events was the opening gun of a carefully prepared Allied counteroffensive. The Allies had developed many new weapons, including fast escort vessels, small aircraft carriers, and a much-improved radar device. They had produced and assembled great numbers of escorts, carrier-based attack aircraft, and long-range land-based bombers. Bringing all of these elements into conjunction in April, the Allies struck back with such overwhelming numerical and technical superiority that fully 40 per cent of our U-boat force was destroyed within a few weeks. The Allied counteroffensive permanently reversed the tide of battle. Almost overnight, the hunters had become the hunted, and through the rest of the war our boats were slaughtered at a fearful rate.

The U-boat Force tried desperately to counter the counteroffensive, but to no avail. In 1943, when I was Executive Officer of *U-230* we were losing boats faster than we could replace them. By the summer of 1943, our toll of Allied shipping had fallen to a monthly average of 150,000 tons—this at a time when the Allies' shipbuilding capacity reached 1 million tons per month.

The plain fact of the matter was that the U-boat had become obsolete. Too long she had remained essentially a surface vessel that submerged only occasionally to remain unseen while launching an attack or escaping a pursuer. Headquarters did develop the Schnorkel, a device that permitted the U-boat to gape for air and recharge her batteries while staying submerged throughout her patrol. But the Schnorkel did not come into general use until March 1944, 10 fatal months after the Allied counteroffensive; and five more months passed before the life-preserving device was installed in all older U-boats. It was not until August 1944, when I sailed on my fifth U-boat, the second under my command, that a Schnorkel relieved me of the constant life-or-death game of surfacing for air, only to crash-dive minutes later before sophisticated attacks by Allied airplanes and destroyers. Moreover, the Schnorkel alone was far from an adequate answer to the Allied aircraft and hunter-killer groups. The U-boat was still dangerously slow and highly vulnerable in general, and deaf and defenseless in particular while using the Schnorkel.

The only real solution was a radically new U-boat. Several such types had been on German drawing boards for years: they were designed to sail submerged for hours at higher speeds than a destroyer, to shoot from a safe depth, and to carry twice as many torpedoes as the conventional U-boat. These underwater wonders were constantly promised to the Force. But they were not put into production until the collapse of the U-boat war, and very few of them were commissioned in time to see action.

So the U-boat Force fought with what it had and, in the last year of the war, it accomplished little but self-destruction. One by one, our crews sailed out obediently, even optimistically, on ludicrous missions that ended in death. The few veteran commanders still in action were decimated despite their experience in the arts of survival. New captains, even with veteran crews, stood virtually no chance of returning from their first patrols.

When hostilities finally ceased in May 1945, the ocean floor was littered with the wreckage of the U-boat war. Our boats had destroyed 2,882 merchant vessels totaling 14.4 million grossweight tons; in addition, U-boats had sunk 175 Allied warships and damaged 264 merchant ships totaling 1.9 million tons. In return, we had paid an incredible price. Our total of 1,150 commissioned U-boats met the following fate: 779 were sunk, two were captured, and the rest were either scuttled or surrendered as ordered at war's end. Out of a total enlistment of 39,000 men, the U-boat Force lost 28,000 men killed and 5,000 taken prisoner. This represents 85 per cent casualties.

Yet even these figures do not reveal the full extent of the U-boat disaster. Since only 842 U-boats saw battle duty, and since 781 of these were lost, 93 per cent of the operational U-boat Force was wiped out. In concrete terms, the toll seems even more shocking. Our tremendous U-boat Force on the Atlantic Front was reduced to a mere 68 operational boats by the time that the Allies invaded France in June 1944, and only three of these boats were still afloat at war's end. One of the three survivors was *U-953,* which I commanded as her last captain.

My account of the U-boat struggle was written with the aid of notes I took during the war, along with photographs and letters that I managed to save from the holocaust on the Continent and the disaster at sea. Though I relied heavily on memory, my recollections are still uncomfortably vivid and will remain so, I am afraid, until their pressure is lifted by my demise. In addition, I insured the proper sequence of events by referring to a brochure published by Heidenheimer Druckerei und Verlag GMBH, which lists the fate of every U-boat. All boats are referred to here by the actual U-number. The dates and hours of events are very close to correct and sometimes accurate to the minute. The radio messages, including signals sent by

Headquarters as well as by U-boats, have been reconstructed with care. The three lengthy transmissions from Admiral Doenitz are exact translations.

No less authentic are certain startling episodes in the book—episodes which are little known or which have been long suppressed. More than a few American naval officers can attest to the fact that U.S. warships, including the destroyers *Greer*, *Reuben James*, and *Kearney*, made attacks on U-boats as early as the summer of 1941, thus waging an undeclared war on Germany. I have yet to see any published reference to a shocking order issued by U-boat Headquarters just before the Allied invasion of Normandy. It ordered the commanders of 15 U-boats to attack the vast invasion fleet and, after their torpedoes were spent, to destroy a ship by ramming—i.e., by committing suicide.

Every individual mentioned in the book was a real person. The two commanders under whom I was privileged to serve are called by their actual names. So are other U-boat captains and distinguished flotilla officers, many of whom I knew as friends. So, too, are my closest comrades in the battles at sea and the escapades in port; sadly, almost all of them are dead. To protect the living, I have changed a few names; it would have been less than gentlemanly to reveal women I knew who have long since become the faithful wives of other men. But this book belongs to my dead comrades, stricken down wholesale in the prime of youth. I hope it pays them the honor they deserve. If I have succeeded in handing down to the reader the ancient lesson that each generation seems to forget —that war is evil, that it murders men—then I consider this my most constructive deed.

Herbert A. Werner
January 1969

U-boat Captain Herbert A. Werner

PART ONE

YEARS
OF
GLORY

1

"Ensigns," the Admiral began, "you have been called together to receive your first important assignments. You will be sent to front-line units today. Wherever there is a ship of our Navy, be it in the Baltic or the Atlantic, in the Mediterranean or the Arctic Ocean, there your services are needed. The time has come for you to show what you have learned. You will prove yourselves for the sake of your country. You will take on England wherever you find her ships, and you will break her power at sea. You will win victory."

The Admiral, a lean, tall man, gazed around to catch our eyes. We Ensigns had formed a horseshoe around him in the large square of the Naval Academy at Flensburg. The time was mid-morning of a day in late April 1941. The occasion was our graduation.

The Admiral went on to tell us of our great naval tradition and of our patriotic obligations as Germans. He spoke of honor and the cause. All of us had heard such speeches often before, and yet for most of us the call to glory or death had lost none of its exciting challenge.

For me, this moment was especially satisfying because I had awaited it for so many years. The decision that I was to become a naval officer was made for me when I was still in the crib. My father, whose nautical ambitions had been frustrated by family and business responsibilities, resolved that I would one day wear an admiral's stripes. And so I was pledged to the sea. My childhood and youth, spent in two towns in the Black Forest of southern Germany, conditioned me for my career aboard ships. Fascinated by the windjammers, merchant vessels, and luxury liners that carried men to every conceivable shore, I read countless books about sea battles, explorers, conquerors, and naval heroes. Before I reached the age of 17, I gained much practical experience sailing on Lake Constance, where I learned to handle nearly every kind of sailboat from a nutshell to a 60-foot, two-masted yacht. At 18 I served a six-month hitch as an apprentice aboard a schooner sailing the Baltic and North Sea. During my last year in high school I passed the rigid tests required for admission to the Naval Academy. Thereafter I served my compulsory term with the National Labor Service, regulating mountain streams and building roads. Then, in September 1939, the outbreak of the war changed everything. The blitzkrieg conquest of Poland provoked Great Britain's entry into the hostilities, and as a result I was called into the Navy sooner than expected. On December 1, 1939, I moved into the barracks of the officers' training center located on a small island in the Baltic. Here I joined my class of over 600 enthusiasts.

When I put on blues that first day of December, I was 19 years old. During that cold, harsh winter, we were exposed to the most rigorous military training program. Our intensified schooling and strenuous drills in snow and mud had been devised to eliminate all but the fittest. The rough training on land was followed by three months of sailing aboard the square-rigged windjammer *Horst Wessel*. Then came an exhaustive tour aboard a mine-laying training ship roaming the Baltic.

After the fall of France, I was given my first command. It was only a small ship in the 34th Mine-Sweeper Flotilla, based in Den Helder, a key port on the Dutch coast. But I became acquainted with death while serving with this very active flotilla. On duty clearing the English Channel, I daily escaped British, French, Belgian, and Dutch mines, and survived heavy British air attacks on sea and in port. I also shot down a Bristol Blenheim bomber with an old watercooled machine gun from World War I; suffered my first and last seasickness; won a promotion to cadet and a medal for sweeping up a great number of those round, black, explosive monsters from the infested waters; and participated in the trials of Operation Sea Lion, a plan for the invasion of the British Isles which never got offshore. All in all, I had earned my medal and promotion the hard way; and I expected to be put in charge of a larger ship after another term in school.

Bristol Blenheim

Shortly before Christmas of 1940, I rejoined my class of '39 at the Naval Academy in Flensburg. I discovered that a few of my classmates had already been killed in action. All the rest were promoted to Ensign, which entitled us to change into double-breasted blues. The following five months were extremely rough. We lived under constant pressure, with but a few hours of sleep a night. A rapid succession of classroom lessons complemented our education in navigation, naval tactics, marine engineering, naval architecture, and oceanography. We also polished up our English. In sports we exhausted ourselves in gymnastics, boxing, fencing, soccer, sailing, and even in horseback riding and jumping. The tough requirements had been designed to separate the boys from the men. Well before graduation day the weakest had been eliminated. Now that the great moment had come, I realized that this was the last time my class would meet as a complete unit.

The Admiral closed his little speech with Nelson's classic words, moderately altered to suit the situation:—"Gentlemen, this day Germany expects every man to do his duty." Then he and his staff left the square, and the officers who had guided us during the past months took over.

As we waited in tense expectation, the officers disclosed our new commands. Some of us had been selected to serve on destroyers, others on minesweepers. A few were assigned to capital ships. The majority, however, was ordered to report to the U-boat Force. This was a service that none of us had as yet experienced. To my surprise, I was ordered to join the 5th U-boat Flotilla in Kiel. That naval base was the largest on the Baltic coast. It was common knowledge that most of our U-boats, which had been so successful during the preceding months, had sailed from Kiel for their rewarding missions.

We dispersed exultantly. After lunch, the dormitory bustled with activity—the emptying of closets, the packing of luggage, and the bidding of farewells to all our friends. That evening we departed from the Naval Academy in various directions to meet with our individual destinies.

The crowded train rolled monotonously through the night. I sat in a corner of a third-class compartment of a sooty car and dreamed with open eyes. My classmates slept in impossible positions, pressed together tightly or suspended in luggage nets. I tried in vain to sleep. I was thinking about too many things at one time, about the present, the future, and the past changes that the war had forced upon us and the world. An eternity seemed to lie between the school years and that night, yet time had passed so fast, too fast to understand. I knew only that youth had vanished, that comfort and security were things of the past. I wondered what would happen in the weeks and months ahead, how it would feel floating below surface, and how I would be affected by the first battle aboard the mysterious U-boat. I thought of the possibility that my first engagement might also be my last. But if I survived the first encounter, how many more would I endure before fate struck? And I wondered how the depth charges would sound, whether the first one would crack the hull, or whether it would take 10, 50, or 100 to sink my ship. I caught myself trying to picture the horrifying last minutes when the boat went down. Would death come slowly at a depth of 500 meters? How long would my life preserver support me if I should be lucky enough to be left floating on surface?

And as I thought, my memory flashed back to my parents and my sister. I knew that they were, at that hour, in lasting security while I was traveling toward a questionable tomorrow, and I realized that everything was limited. The glory, the dreams of a successful life, the kisses of warm and longing women—all could be over soon and unfulfilled. My body could be entombed in an iron hull or float somewhere in the ocean as bait for hungry sharks. If I were lucky, someone might find my remains and give me a decent burial.

These thoughts accompanied me throughout the night. I felt closer to death than to the life I had just begun to enjoy. What did I know of life and love? I had to admit that I knew very little indeed. But I was prepared to leave this world whenever it should happen. We had been told many times over that sacrifice would bring us closer to victory.

It was still dark when the train arrived in Kiel. Only a handful of us left the old-fashioned compartments; the rest had departed en route to other ports.

Since it was still too early for streetcars to travel, we spent about an hour in the station cafeteria sipping sour *ersatz* coffee. When the first tram rang its bell, we stormed aboard it with all our baggage and headed for the Wik, the large Naval Base of the northern end of the city. The streetcar lumbered through the awakening suburbs. The sky slowly turned purple in the east, but the street lights were still burning when we dismounted at our destination.

I stood in front of a high brick wall that surrounded the naval complex. At the gate, the sentry examined my papers, then moved aside. When all of us had passed through the iron door, it closed with a shriek. Our hollow steps on the pavement echoed against the walls of the barracks as we walked toward the waterfront. The barracks and yard were a familiar sight. Here, almost three years before, I had gone through the tough exams that the Navy imposed on each prospective officer. I had returned again as a cadet aboard the schooner *Horst Wessel,* and had paid another visit the previous fall, after my service in the English Channel. This was the fourth time that I was drawn to the revered place of the Navy, and I would come back many times again during my career.

In the half-light before reveille, the Bay of Kiel presented itself in all its natural beauty. The water was calm and silvery, with the opposite shore reflected in dark green. Morning mist touched the several warships that rode at anchor, their gray superstructure shining almost white in the hazy air.

Directly ahead was the Tirpitz Pier, named after the founder of the modern Germany Navy, Admiral Alfred von Tirpitz. It reached far out into the Bay of Kiel. At that long jetty, many a British warship had fastened her lines for a friendly visit during the internationally famous "Kieler Week" of the Kaiser's era. During the First World War, parts of the German Fleet had sailed from that pier to fight the British cousin in the greatest sea battle of capital ships at Jutland. It was from that same pier that our U-boats had launched their attacks in 1914. During the peaceful years, the Tirpitz Pier had seen the beginning of many new careers for men and ships. A new history had begun on that pier in late summer of 1939, when our U-boats launched their second assault on Britain within 25 years.

The tide was low and the water splashed against the pier's wooden poles. The odor of tar, salt, and oil mingled with the smell of fish, seaweed, and paint. Numerous U-boats were moored here in rows of two and three. Guards on their decks leaned against conning towers or 8.8 cm. cannons, submachine guns hanging indolently from their necks. They examined us critically and seemed amused as we paraded down the planks.

We reached the end of the jetty where two ships were tied to either side of the wooden pier. An old steamer of about 10,000 tons rested at the north side, while at the south side the tender *Lech,* the command ship of the flotilla, was tied up. We presented our papers to another guard, then crossed the gangway to the *Lech* and piled our suitcases alongside her starboard railing. As we searched for the officers' wardroom, the scent of freshly brewed coffee led us to the mess hall. We received an excellent breakfast and soon felt reborn in our new environment. The room gradually filled with officers of all ranks. They wore snow-white jackets and looked relaxed and satisfied. Evidently they had found an ideal Navy life here; they worked and slept on a ship, saw water all day long, but were never far from the city and its hectic night life.

Around 0800 we prepared ourselves to report to the Commandant of the 5th U-boat Flotilla. His *Adjudant,* a young and arrogant *Leutnant,* made us wait for more than an hour before he let us know that the Commandant would not be available. Free to do as we pleased, we left the tender to acquaint ourselves with the U-boats and their crews. We learned that some of the boats had just returned from a patrol, others had completed their training in the Baltic and were about to be fitted out for their first mission. Large quantities of cans, boxes, and fresh foodstuffs were carted onto the pier by trucks and piled up alongside the boats.

Shortly before noon, we met again in the *Lech*'s

wardroom in expectation of lunch. Small standing parties discussed the latest "Special Bulletin" which had been broadcast minutes before. U-boats had attacked a British convoy in the North Atlantic and had destroyed, so far, eight ships totaling over 50,000 tons. It was the greatest success recorded on a single convoy operation, and with the U-boats still in pursuit of the enemy, more sinkings could be expected. A feeling of pride took possession of us, although we were not yet a part of the U-boat Force. Enthusiasm was high when the Commanding Officer stepped into the wardroom. He went to his traditional chair, waited until all of us had found a place, then addressed the assembly: "Gentlemen, we have received numerous radiograms from our commanders, who are presently chasing a British convoy across the Atlantic. According to their reports, the number of ships sunk has reached 14, with a total of approximately 85,000 tons destroyed. One escort vessel has been torpedoed. This is by far our most rewarding hunt. The battle in the Atlantic has become our battle. Our U-boats are dictating the terms."

We toasted the success, then sat down for dinner. The news was the prime topic of discussion. With a steadily increasing number of U-boats cruising the seas, the toll of British shipping was reaching unprecedented proportions.

Indeed, we had reason to believe that our hunger blockade against England would soon result in her downfall. On land, moreover, our armies had driven deep into enemy territory. Following our seizure of Poland, Norway had been defeated almost overnight; Holland, Belgium, and France were overrun within a few weeks and Denmark occupied. Our capital ships controlled the European waters far into the Arctic region. It seemed to me one thing remained to be done: intensify the U-boat offensive against England, starve the British and force them to surrender. Once we held the British Isles, the war would end.

After lunch we newcomers congregated on deck to await orders. Finally, at 1430, the *Adjudant* passed our crowd waving a few white papers. We followed him into the officers' mess hall and formed a ring around him, drawing nervously on our cigarettes while he sorted his sheets. At last the *Adjutant* began to speak. He called our names in alphabetical order, specified our boats and the port where each was to be boarded. Since my name was at the end of the list, my patience was put to a severe test. Some of us were lucky and were assigned to a boat moored at the pier. Others had to travel to faraway ports. My classmates Ahlers, Busch, and Faust were ordered to Bremerhaven. Goebel, Gerloff, and my best friend Fred Schreiber were sent to the Baltic U-boat base of Koenigsberg; they happily clicked their heels and raced off to the office to ask for their orders in writing. The *Adjutant* concluded by saying, "Those who have to report to Bremerhaven, Danzig, or Koenigsberg must leave with the next train. There is no time for a tête à tête with your sweethearts, gentlemen. Ensign Werner stays aboard the *Lech* for special duty."

I was stunned, bewildered. Hopeful that this was all a mistake, I approached the young *Adjutant* and asked why I had been left stranded aboard the *Lech*.

"Don't you worry," he said disdainfully. "You will get to the front fast enough. Your boat, *U-551*, is still on mission. You have to wait until she returns."

"When will that be, sir?"

"I can't tell exactly. But if it makes you feel better, I've heard the boat has radioed that she has broken off her patrol."

I was relieved to hear that I was to join an experienced crew, but I was a disappointed, envious ensign as I shook hands with my departing classmates. Later that afternoon I was told to place myself at the *Adjutant's* disposal. My main duty was to take officers aboard motor launches and shuttle them across the Bay to Kiel and the shipyards. I had expected responsibilities; instead I was asked to perform a minor duty that any petty officer could have done as well. I tried in vain to convince the *Adjutant* that I had never handled a small craft. "We shall see," he said, taking me aboard one of the launches. "If you haven't done it before, you will learn." Despite my best efforts to do the job poorly, the *Adjutant* seemed satisfied. To my displeasure, I found myself in charge of the motor-boats.

Several days passed. *U-551* had not returned from patrol. From time to time I went to see the radio officer in search of news. I became ever more restless as I watched my classmates prepare for their first war patrol. Then came the day that shattered my hopes for an early sailing. The *Adjudant* brought me the bad news that *U-551* would never return. She had been lost in the North Atlantic.

I expected to be transferred aboard another U-boat immediately. But when nothing materialized after several more days, I became uneasy. I suspected that the *Adjudant* had intentionally failed to arrange a new assignment. One day at breakfast I contrived to sit next to the Flotilla's Chief Engineer, whom I had regarded as a personable man. After a casual conversation about unimportant matters, I discreetly explained my awkward situation. The Chief promised to do something in my behalf. Though I was not quite sure he had made the promise in earnest, results came abruptly. The next afternoon I was told to see the *Adjudant*. Expressionlessly, he handed me a sheet of paper. In a second I realized that it was my new order. I clicked my heels in sudden joy, saluted, and left his office quickly. Outside, I read the order in detail. I was to report aboard *U-557* in Koenigsberg.

At 2100 the same evening, my express rolled into Stettiner Station in Berlin. The platforms were bustling with traffic despite the late hour. Soldiers from many fronts and all branches of the Armed Forces were changing trains. Carrying my two suitcases, I transferred to the S-bahn, the rapid transit system, for Station Friedrichstrasse. Before I left Kiel, I had managed to send a wire to my blond Marianne in the Capital. I had not seen her since the previous December and a reunion was long overdue. I was supposed to meet her in a small café near the Scala, where we had been accustomed to wait for each other. I knew Marianne was as reliable as she was beautiful.

She was but five minutes late, remarkable for a pretty

woman. Her face and blue eyes glowed as they had
when I had first met her before the war on Lake Constance. We sat and talked happily for a few minutes,
and when we left the café, there was the unspoken
agreement between us that we would not separate that
night. Only a few steps to the east was Friedrichstrasse,
the pulsating vein of Berlin. It was enveloped in darkness, but an occasional faint street light allowed us to
orient ourselves. Despite the late hour, Friedrichstrasse was jammed with people—soldiers, sailors, and
pairs of lovers like ourselves, all struggling to find their
way in the darkened city. Marianne and I walked north,
past the Station, into a dark, quiet section. Occasionally we saw a lonely soul or a car passing with headlights dimmed. We had assumed we would find asylum
in a small *pension,* but we rang dozens of bells and
still no door opened for us. We walked up and down for
almost an hour before we found a little place and a tiny
room to stay. However, it was big enough for the two of
us, and we did not require much space to be content.

Long after midnight, the sirens began to scream. I
had forgotten that there was a war on, and that the
Tommies occasionally slipped through our air defense. After some hesitation, we decided to remain
where we were and not seek shelter. While the flak
hammered sporadically, we heard the howling of falling
bombs accompanied by muffled explosions. The building vibrated slightly. When the raid was finally over, we
had learned that defiance sometimes can be sweet.

We had our breakfast in Café Wien on Kurfuerstendamm. There was no sign of the attack. The world
looked as peaceful as always on that April morning.
Stores, cafés, hotels were doing business as usual. Berliners mingled with soldiers in gray, green, blue and
brown; the famous avenue was the stage for a splendid
spectacle. When the church bells rang the hour, it was
like any sunny Sunday before the war.

Time to separate always comes too early, especially
when duty calls one from a shared hotel room. But that
day I was not quite sure whether I would have preferred
a further delay on my departure. Although I felt quite
comfortable in my love for Marianne, I regarded my

love for the Navy as being of a more permanent nature. It was near sunrise when we kissed good-by at the station, and we promised to see each other as soon as the war would allow.

The Pommeranian Plains stretched endlessly alongside the tracks. Heather gave way to woods of pine. Before the war, a traveller had to cross the German border twice en route to Koenigsberg; he showed his passport when leaving West Prussia for Poland and presented it again a few hours later when leaving Poland for East Prussia. Now, to the Poles' sorrow, the crossing of the border had become a very simple affair.

I traversed the battlefields of the war with Poland and arrived in Koenigsberg at dusk. I was astonished to see the station fully illuminated, as if in peace time. Streetlights, neon signs, storefronts, and windows were ablaze with light. Despite the vague directions given me by a policeman, I found the Navy yard where I was to board *U-557*. Several U-boats swayed alongside a granite jetty; for a moment I paused at the pier and stared at the black stilettos in the murky waters, wondering which one would carry me into battle against England.

Some distance away lay an ocean liner; it was painted blinding white and lighted up like a Christmas tree. Assuming that the white ship was the flotilla's headquarters, I dragged my baggage across the gangway and reported to the officer on watch. He referred me to the mate on duty and the mate sent me to the purser. He in turn arranged for a cabin. I eventually fell into a soft easy chair, hungry and exhausted. At last, I had arrived.

It was late when I went on an expedition through the ship to find the dining room and something to eat. In passing the bar I recognized my classmates, Guenter Gerloff and Rolf Goebel, who had departed from Kiel some two weeks before me. Approaching them from behind, I tapped their shoulders and said, "How come you are not at sea?"

They spun around. Chubby-faced Goebel replied, "It's not for you to ask, you land rat. We just came back from a long training trip."

Gerloff, tall and blond, added smilingly, "You see the salt crusts on our lips? They don't dissolve with water, we have to use alcohol. That's how long we've been at sea."

"I'll match that soon," I countered.

"Not if they keep you in port to run their motorboats, you won't," snapped Goebel.

"Don't worry about me. This time I've made it. I am ordered aboard *U-557*. Do you fellows know where I can find her?"

"She happens to be ours," Gerloff said, "and the Captain will have a fit when he hears of your addition."

The talkative pair began to tell of their first experience aboard a U-boat. Their enthusiasm for the weapon, for the Captain and the crew, seemed sincere and not the result of increased consumption of alcohol. I forgot my hunger and listened carefully, washing down their tales with a few more drinks than I was accustomed to. It was past midnight when I finally lay my spinning head on a pillow.

2

Next morning at 0800, I boarded *U-557* to report for duty. The boat was weatherbeaten. The conning tower looked like a surrealistic painting. The protective red undercoat showed in streaks through the splintered gray surface paint. Rust had formed everywhere, even around the barrel of the heavily greased 8.8 cm. gun on the foredeck. There was a light green shine of algae on the wooden deck that covered the steel hull. Her rundown appearance was obviously the result of months of drills in the Baltic, and I found it very appealing.

I presented my transfer orders to the Captain and said, "Herr *Oberleutnant,* I beg to report aboard."

He glanced at the paper, then hollered, "What the devil is wrong with Headquarters, sending me another ensign? They've already punished me with two just like you—beginners who haven't smelled real U-boat stink." Then, with a vivid oath, he expressed the hope that I might be useful as extra ballast.

I was disappointed by my welcome, but not by the Captain. *Oberleutnant* Ottokar Paulssen was a short, stocky man in his early thirties; he had blond hair and blue, witty eyes that sparkled under the peak of his white Navy cap. The cap, which only the commander had the right to wear aboard, showed traces of verdigris on its brass ornaments. He wore a long jacket of light gray leather; its seams at the shoulders and pockets had been expertly hand-stitched with a heavy yarn. An artistic seaman's braid was fastened at his left epaulet with thread bleached almost white; and his feet, cased in large leather boots, stuck out beneath his wrinkled pants. In short, Paulssen fitted my picture of the ideal U-boat commander.

With no regard for formalities, the Captain bluntly ordered me to change out of my dress uniform, then turned me over to his second officer. This slim and trim fellow, possibly two years my senior, introduced himself as *Leutnant* Seibold, watch and radio officer, and shook hands heartily.

Seibold answered many of my questions before I asked them. He told me that *U-557* had just completed a strenuous seven-month shakedown cruise in the Baltic. The boat's company totaled 48 men, not counting us ensigns; it consisted of 4 officers, 3 warrant officers, 14 petty officers and 27 seamen, machinists, and technicians. Some of the men had already seen action, and with them as a hard core, Paulssen had forged boat and crew into an effective war machine, ready and eager for the gruesome work that lay ahead. Paulssen himself, Seibold continued proudly, was a veteran of the underseas force. He had served aboard a U-boat in 1937 in the international control organization during the Spanish Civil War, cruising the Mediterranean and the Bay of Biscay. Later, as commander of a home-based U-boat, Paulssen trained many of the crews now manning U-boats on the Atlantic front. At the end of his little history, Seibold ordered the first seaman's mate to take care of my immediate needs.

The mate led me back to the liner. There I was equipped with three sets of fatigues, a complete leather suit, an oilskin outfit for foul weather, two blue sweaters, blue knitted underwear, rubber boots, felt-lined leather boots, thick gloves, binoculars, and a multitude of small items. To secure all this gear I had to make three trips from the supply room to my cabin in the liner.

I was putting on my fresh fatigues when Goebel rushed into my cabin, almost demolishing the door. "Hey sailor, pack your bags!" he cried. "We are sailing at 1400, destination Kiel."

"Damn it," I snarled, "I just came from there!" But I packed in a hurry, carried all my belongings aboard *U-557*, and threw them into one of the narrow berths.

At exactly 1400, *U-557* separated from the pier. The boat slid away in complete silence, powered by electric motors. She maneuvered into navigable waters, then her diesels took over the drive. *U-557* headed for the open sea.

When the silhouette of Koenigsberg had sunk below the horizon, the Captain ordered the third seaman's watch to the bridge. The boat followed a westward course. Hard, short breakers hit her from starboard; fine spray showered the superstructure. The smokers threw their cigarettes overboard and slipped through the conning tower hatch. I followed them down the vertical ladder into the long, narrow boat. Here all was peaceful. Each man had taken his proper place. The only sound I heard in the forward compartments was the knocking of the diesels.

Oberleutnant Kern, the Executive Officer and First Watch Officer, intercepted me in the center aisle and gave me a stern lecture on my immediate duties. I was to be a lookout with the second seaman's watch when the boat was surfaced; when it was submerged, I would do various jobs, assisting at the electric helm or the hydroplanes, helping Wiesner, the navigator, to calculate our position and helping Second Officer Seibold to decode top secret messages. I was also to spend time with him, Kern, and with Feder, the engineer; they would acquaint me with the boat's construction, machinery, equipment, tanks, valves, computer, torpedoes, and artillery armament. Kern urged me to spend my spare time studying the engineering manuals, so that I would catch up with the rest of the crew as soon as possible. He then took me on a tour through the pressure hull.

The trip soon turned into a sobering experience. After a few steps, I lost my bearings completely. I banged my head against pipes and ducts, against handwheels and instruments, against the low, round hatches in bulkheads that separated the compartments. It was like crawling through a bottleneck. Most annoying of all, the boat rocked vigorously in the increasingly rough sea. In order to keep my balance, I frequently had to reach for support as I staggered over the floor plates like a drunk. Apparently I would have to duck my head, walk softly, and ride with the boat or I would not survive one day in the tube.

As we passed through the control room, I bowed under the extension of the conning tower. Then, without warning, a heavy breaker came rushing down the hatch, drenching me to the skin. The old veterans laughed loudly. The Exec, who had obviously timed the baptism for my inauguration, hid his smile and continued to explain the construction of the underwater wonder.

The ship was divided into four pressurized compartments. The aft section contained all the machinery and electrical equipment, air compressor, and one torpedo tube. The two powerful diesel engines were capable of driving the boat at 19 knots on surface. Two electric motors, operating on gigantic storage batteries, ran the ship when she was submerged; they could propel the boat for one hour at the top speed of nine knots, or for three days at a cruising speed of one or two knots. However, these batteries had to be recharged under normal conditions every 24 hours. This could be done only by surfacing, for the batteries that ran the electric motors were charged by generators driven by diesel engines.

Between diesel compartment and midships were a tiny galley, a washroom, petty officers' quarters, and below the deck plates, one half of the 50-ton storage batteries. In the center compartment midships was the heart and brain of the boat, the control room. It was overloaded with pipes, ducts, valves, wires, handwheels, gauges, switches, meters, control mechanism, and a gyro compass. Its major equipment included pumps, fresh-water producer, lower periscope, magnetic compass, chart closet, and table, as well as electrical gear to control rudder and hydroplanes.

The forward section contained a radio room, a listening room, bow torpedo compartment with four tubes, and also men's quarters, officers' and warrant officers' wardrooms, the Captain's small corner, a hint of a washroom and, again below deck plates, the second half of the storage batteries. The three pressure compartments were subdivided into seven watertight rooms, each equipped with watertight doors that could withstand pressure equal to that at a depth of 120 meters.

The fourth and smallest compartment, the conning tower, contained the attack periscope, torpedo computer, and helm. Buoyancy tanks, trim cells, fuel oil, and fresh-water tanks were located throughout the boat and in the outboard tanks in strategic locations.

After walking the full length of the boat, I was overwhelmed by her complexity and throughly confused by the Exec's rather superficial explanations. I believed that it would take me years to gain his knowledge, the Chief's skill, and the Captain's qualifications.

I was at the navigator's small plotting table when the Captain called from the bridge: "Prepare for diving maneuver. Alarm for exercise!"

Moments later, the men on watch came tumbling down the aluminum ladder, hitting the deck plates with violent jolts. Then the alarm bell shrieked throughout the boat. To open up the ballast tanks to the sea, machinists grabbed the handles of leverage valves and hung from them, using the full weight of their bodies to speed the opening action. Others turned hand-wheels frantically. With a loud uproar, air escaped the tanks and water rushed in. *U-557* dipped so swiftly that I had to grab something to stop myself from falling to the metal deck plates. Again I was reminded that I had to remain constantly alert.

Suddenly there was a cry, urgent and piercing, "Outboard air induction valve doesn't close!"

U-557 sank fast, bow first, at an angle of 35 degrees. A machinist appeared in the round opening of the rear bulkhead, yelling, "We can't stop the leak! Head valve must be jammed!"

Paulssen shouted, "Blow all tanks—both planes up —surface, Chief!"

Within seconds, the depth-gauge needle gyrated to 60 meters, 70, 85, 110 meters. Then the boat briefly balanced out on even keel—and began to tilt down at the stern. I slid aft until I grabbed an overhead pipe. Now the boat tumbled rapidly toward the bottom of the Baltic, stern first. Her descent was so steep that everything not fastened—suitcases, boxes, food cans, personal belongings—rolled dangerously down the center aisle. The two men who operated the hydroplanes slid from their seats into the valve station. One man, flying through the round hatch in the forward bulkhead, clung to it in desperation.

The Chief yelled, "Stop blowing, boat is out of control!"

As *U-557* neared the ocean floor, a terrifying roar came from the diesel compartment. Tons of water rushed through a leak. Then the boat hit with a shuddering jolt. The lights went out. I lost my grip and landed on top of the navigator, who himself had fallen over somebody else. Then there was silence.

A hollow voice drifted up from the stern: "Inboard air induction valve is closed and secured."

The leak was stopped. But the boat, her stern buried in the mud, hung at a 50-degree angle, swinging back and forth gently like a pendulum.

"By auxiliary lighting, all men to the bow room!" This was the Captain's encouraging voice. At once, some lights came on, and shadowy figures began the climb uphill. Taking stock hastily, I noted that the depth gauge read 142 meters; *U-557* seemed to be stuck solidly in the mud beyond reach of rescuers from above. Her electrical circuits were out of order. The batteries had lost much of their acid, and poisonous chlorine fumes were escaping. There was also the possibility of an explosion.

My appraisal was interrupted by someone shouting through the voice tube: "This is the diesel room. Mechanic Eckstein is dead!"

It flashed through my mind that Eckstein might have gotten the best of a bad bargain. If the deadly gases did not burn away our lungs, we would die of suffocation as our oxygen supply was used up.

We continued struggling uphill on hands and knees, bracing our feet against a pump, a valve, a convenient pipe. As I dragged myself along the deck plates, I looked into the faces of men I hardly knew. Soaking wet, smeared with oil and grease, dirty and sweating, they followed Paulssen's order without showing emotion. We had all become important ballast, putting our weight on the scale of our fate. It was indeed ironic that the Captain had called me surplus ballast when I reported aboard.

Eventually, the men reached the forward torpedo room. But the bow of the boat lowered only slightly. She seemed to be locked in her position, the tremendous weight in the aft bilges acting as an anchor. I heard the Captain conferring with the Chief in the control room. I could see the two through the round opening of the hatch in the sparsely lighted section. It was as if I were standing atop the stairwell of a 10-story building, looking down into the lobby.

Paulssen ordered 25 men to form a bucket line to transport the water from the flooded engine rooms into the bilge of the bow compartment, thus equalizing the weight and putting the boat on even keel. I joined the group and descended the steep grade, sliding on my seat along the floor plates through the aisle. Arriving in the diesel room, I saw dark, oily water covering most of the rear torpedo room. Out of reach, caught in the mechanism of the aft torpedo tube, hung the dead mechanic. His head was split open at the right temple; blood streaked his yellow face.

The pool of black liquid seemed too wide and deep to move with buckets and cans. I calculated that our efforts to bale the water to the bow would serve only to use up our oxygen at a much faster rate. Nevertheless we baled. We worked in near silence, passing the full buckets from man to man up the elongated tomb, spilling the oily, salty substance over ourselves. Unable to hold any position for long, we skidded over the plates while trying to hand the full buckets uphill. Sometimes an empty can came flying past our heads like a projectile. Some men groaned under the load. Others uttered curses when the ugly water was spilled into their faces.

Three hours passed. We counted the buckets and cans in agony and in hopelessness: "Four hundred and twenty, four hundred and twenty-one, twenty-two . . ."

Four hours passed. With enormous effort we fought against fatigue and resignation. The water level in the stern had fallen only a little. But the containers passed from hand to hand in an unbroken chain, "Five hundred and eighty-two, eighty-three . . ."

After we had put in six hours of hard labor, the second half of the crew took their turn. The air had become thick; it stank of oil, sweat, chlorine, and urine. Our breath grew short, our movements weak. And still we continued to pass the containers in agonizing sluggishness. Now everyone was half suffocated, half drowned.

Nothing changed until we had been submerged for over 14 hours. By then the first bucket brigade had long since commenced its second shift, and *U-557* still had not lowered her bow appreciably. But then Paulssen made a new attempt for survival. He ordered the bucket line to quit work and all men to return to the bow compartment.

Gasping for air, we struggled uphill toward the tip of the boat. As I forced myself in between the torpedo tubes, the impossible occurred. Very slowly and gently, the hull began to sway. Air bubbles suddenly escaped the forward buoyancy tanks with a guttural sound. Then the bow descended and hit bottom with a thud.

Somehow the men drove themselves into action. The dead mechanic was carried to the Captain's nook and covered with a canvas; the Captain closed the green curtain and separated his corner from the traffic. The bilge pumps were out of order, but the excess water in the after bilges was distributed with buckets to balance the boat. The water damage in the electrical compartment—damage that could not be repaired at sea—had disrupted our cooking facilities, but the cook handed out cans of peaches, pears, and strawberries. Spirits rose as hunger and thirst were assuaged. But the fact remained that we were trapped. Some 40 tons of water kept the boat pressed to the bottom.

The Chief went to work to free us. At his command, compressed air shot into the buoyancy tanks with a hissing sound. The boat remained glued to the bottom. More air rushed into the tanks. Still no sign of a lift. Then the stream of air diminished, stopped. We had exhausted our compressed-air supply. We were still doomed.

But the Chief did not give up. Spinning around, he yelled, "All men to the bow!"

Everybody pushed and stumbled forward. As we crowded into the forward compartment, the Chief ordered us to turn around and run aft. We tumbled and tripped in the opposite direction, ducking through the hatches in the bulkheads, slipping and sliding along the wet deck plates. Arriving in the aft compartment, we heard the Chief calling us back, and again we turned around and started forward blindly, like mad steers in a stampede. We gasped and coughed and ran and ran. Almost imperceptibly, the boat began stirring. Then, as we poured into the bow torpedo room, the stern suddenly lifted. *U-557* had worked herself free.

The men ran to their stations. Then, unbelievably, the bow lifted and the boat floated gently upward in complete freedom. As I stepped into the control room, the needle of the depth gauge had already reached

140 meters. It swung to 130 meters and moved steadily along the dial. Excitedly the Chief shouted the figures to the Captain in the conning tower: "Eighty
meters. Forty meters. Twenty meters. Tower comes
free. Boat has surfaced!"

Paulssen flipped open the lid of the bridge hatch,
ending 20 hours in our underwater tomb. Fresh,
crystal-clear air streamed through the hull, reviving
every man but one.

U-557 resumed her voyage to Kiel on surface. Calm
routine replaced the hectic ordeal. An inspection soon
disclosed that a wrench was jammed in the outboard
air induction valve just below the cigarette deck. No
one knew how it had gotten there.

During the next two days and nights, I adjusted
gradually to my new way of life with its complex procedures and the boat's perpetual rocking and listing. I
became acquainted with most of the crew, made myself useful wherever possible, and took my place on
the second watch every eight hours. I learned how to
ride with the boat, to climb up and down the aluminum ladder in the tower without injury, to keep my
balance while swaying through the center aisle in
heavy seas, to duck through the circular openings in
the bulkheads, to eat my meals between the extremes
of the boat's motions, to acquire skill in using the
pump in the washroom by operating its various valves
in proper sequence. I also learned that the Captain's
harshness was only a shell around a congenial character, that he was married and had a baby son, and
that—to our mutual surprise—we had practically
grown up together. We had attended the same high
school and studied with the same professors, had
drunk from the same water fountain in the courtyard
and learned to love the sea while sailing on Lake Constance. These discoveries, however, did not change
Paulssen's attitude toward me. On the contrary, I felt
that he put even stricter requirements upon my training. While my two classmates, Gerloff and Goebel,
escaped his constant observation, he developed a
strange habit of catching me in my narrow bunk after

an exhausting day and sending me back to work in the engine compartment instead of allowing me to rest. Nonetheless, I managed to stay awake on duty.

On the fifth day of our near-fatal trip, we approached Kiel Lightship at around 0700. One hour later we sailed past the Navy's War Memorial, which pointed like an admonishing finger into the morning sky. The Bay of Kiel opened beneath the rising mist, and the boat maneuvered cautiously through the mounting traffic toward the Naval Base. At 1030 on April 26, *U-557* finally came to rest at the Tirpitz Pier.

Our rusty boat berthed near the stern of the tender *Lech*. The lines were not yet fully secured when Kern, the Exec, crossed to the liner to arrange for the crew's lodging and for Eckstein's last journey to his hometown. For the next two hours, every hand was kept busy transporting damaged suitcases, soaked seabags, and trunks from the U-boat to the steamer. The ship's comfortable cabins contrasted sharply with our tight quarters aboard *U-557*. I established myself in a third-class cabin, then returned to *U-557*, which was being stripped down for repairs and a new fitting-out. Seven months of rough training, climaxed by our recent damages, had left deep scars throughout the boat. But the men had already forgotten their brush with death; they were relaxed and cheerful as they worked. A radio blared out the latest popular tunes.

I was in the petty officers' wardroom when Gerloff came rushing down the aisle asking "Have you heard the bad news?"

"Haven't heard anything," I said. "What are you talking about?"

"Kretschmer and Schepke are supposed to be sunk. I can't believe it."

But the news was confirmed by *Leutnant* Seibold. *U-99*, with Kretschmer in command, and *U-100*, under Captain Schepke, had indeed been destroyed while attacking a convoy in the North Atlantic. Both great captains had been considered indestructible, and their loss—the first to be admitted publicly in 18 months of U-boat action—reminded us that the sea war was increasing in intensity as the British built up their de-

fenses. Kretschmer, our tonnage king, had sunk close
to 325,000 tons of enemy shipping, including three
destroyers. This was equal to the entire tonnage of a
medium-sized seafaring nation. Schepke, with more
than 250,000 tons to his credit, was killed when his
boat was rammed by the destroyer that had blown her
to the surface. Kretschmer, on the other hand, was
captured and spent the rest of the war in imprisonment
in Canada.

The double tragedy, which had occurred on March
17, stunned and baffled the country. Had the British
introduced new weapons or techniques of anti-submarine warfare? So far, hunting had been relatively
easy. U-boats were fast, maneuverable on and beneath
the surface, and were also capable of diving below the
British depth charges. Our losses were negligible compared with the casualties U-boats had inflicted upon
our adversaries. We were without an explanation. Supreme Headquarters, to soften the bad news, issued a
statement declaring that U-boats had, since the outbreak of war, sunk well over 4 million tons of enemy
shipping, as well as one battleship, one aircraft carrier,
and 18 lesser vessels of the Royal Navy.

U-557 was taken to the shipyard for complete
overhaul, including diesels, batteries, and electric motors. For one week the crew shuttled daily between the
Tirpitz Pier and dry dock. For me, new experiences
followed in rapid succession. The first day I was sent
to the Admiralty to complete our navigational file with
charts of the Atlantic. The second day I helped the
Exec round out our library of artillery and torpedo
manuals. On the third day, Seibold made use of my
modest administrative skills and my four-finger system
on the typewriter. Feder, the Chief, assigned me the
task of drawing diagrams of our stowing arrangements
in plan and elevation; I also assembled lists of all
government property that had to be accounted for—
tools, spare parts, seaman's gear, even jars of medicine. The officers displayed a tendency to unload their
work on us ensigns, and the nights as well as the days
were filled with chores.

Finally the weekend brought relief. On Saturday, I

drove into Kiel with Goebel and Gerloff, and we browsed through the bookshops searching for reading material for the long weeks at sea. We had Viennese cake in a café and steak for dinner in the Rathskeller, our favorite restaurant. We drank quantities of Moselle wine, toasting each other and a successful mission. It never occurred to us that our first battle might be our last.

On Monday, May 5, *U-557* sailed out of the shipyard fully overhauled. She had received a fresh coat of gray paint, and looked and smelled newly commissioned. We spent the day in the Bay making trim dives and other maneuvers, checking instruments and engines for proper function. I was amazed by the crew's high standards and the ship's great maneuverability. Although she displaced 770 tons and was 75 meters long and about six meters in diameter at the beam, she responded to the Chief's commands with speed and precision. *U-557* was ready to join her many sister ships in action.

On May 8, we sailed to the arsenal, where we loaded the boat with 14 torpedoes. Most of them were of the newest design, electrically powered and equipped with magnetic detonators. After the last two torpedoes had been secured in their racks on the floor, wooden decks were fastened over the sleek metal fish, leaving just enough room for the men to crawl to their bunks and to the torpedo tubes.

On May 9, *U-557* took on food and ammunition. Cans, barrels, and cartons were carefully sorted out and stowed away. While shells for our 8.8 cm. cannon and our 2 cm. anti-aircraft gun were lowered into special compartments, the provisions were distributed throughout the boat. I was astounded to see the food supply for eight weeks disappear between pipes and valves, ribs and machines, closets and ducts. Huge smoked hams were hung in the control room. Staples such as whipped cream, butter, coffee, and tea were locked up for distribution by the Captain. The fueling of *U-557* was accomplished on May 10. On May 12, we received loads of fresh vegetables, eggs, bread, and fresh water. We squeezed the crisp loaves

into the last unoccupied crannies and filled three ham-
mocks with the rest, letting them swing free in the bow
and aft compartments.

As these days of preparation ended, our carefree
mood turned serious. Retiring to the cabin on the old
steamer, I packed my surplus gear into suitcases, registered their contents, and labeled the luggage. In case
I did not return my belongings would be sent back
home. Then I wrote a last letter to my parents and
another to Marianne. Now I was ready to face the unknown.

3

On the morning of May 13, *U-557* was finally ready
to sail. As a last ritual, we brought aboard our clothing
and a few personal belongings—writing materials,
books, a toothbrush, snapshots of the family and of
one or more girls. Shaving implements were prohibited; our beards would have to grow because the boat's
limited supply of fresh water was to be used only for
cooking and drinking. *Leutnant* Seibold, in charge of
stowing procedures, kept a watchful eye on our comings and goings. His frequent checks turned up a few
forbidden bottles of liquor, an excess of clothing or
cigarettes. He eventually achieved a proper balance
between supply and demand.

At 1130 the boat's company assembled in the liner
for an extraordinary farewell dinner. The staff of the
5th U-boat Flotilla turned out to wish us Godspeed.
We were suddenly important—the center of attraction.
After a Lucullan lunch, the Flotilla's Commandant
toasted Captain and crew and expressed his best
wishes for a successful mission. Then he added, "Since
one among you has his birthday today, this makes the

13th of May a good day to sail. Let it be a sign of luck which shall prevail throughout your patrol. Happy birthday to Ensign Werner." The surprise was on me. I suspected that the leak came from Seibold, who knew my vital statistics.

Our spirits were high as we emptied our last glass of champagne and as we poured out of the steamer onto the pier. A Navy band was playing a resounding march, and a large crowd gathered. The moment we crossed the narrow gangplank onto *U-557* we were caught up in shipboard routine. A last head count, a few commands, and the ropes were removed from the pillars.

U-557 slid away in reverse, silently. Very slowly she separated from the pier, cleared her submerged hydroplanes, then increased speed. Fifty meters off the pier, the Exec swung the boat around and ordered the diesels started. A strong vibration traveled through the hull, and for a moment dark fumes escaped the exhausts. The twin screws beneath the stern thrashed the water into a foamy whirlpool.

"Both engines half ahead together, steer nine five."

U-557 turned sharply to starboard and thrust forward toward the center of the Bay. The music faded; the crowd lining the waterfront dispersed.

One hour later we maneuvered through the locks of Holtenau into the North-East-Sea-Canal. For the rest of the day and the following night we sailed at reduced speed through the narrow waterway. At dawn the next morning we reached its western end, the locks to the Elbe River at Brunsbuettelkoog, where two other U-boats had been waiting for our arrival.

At 1000 a pack of three wolves headed for the open sea. The low shore soon faded to a very thin line, then it sunk below the smudgy horizon. The pack sailed in line, with *U-557* up front. I was on watch until noon; as part of my regular duties throughout this mission, I mounted the bridge at 0800 and at 2000 for four-hour stints under *Obersteuermann* (Warrant Officer) Wiesner, our navigator and Third Watch Officer. After a quick lunch, I returned to the bridge to help keep a lookout for drifting mines. Be-

fore long, the island of Helgoland appeared on portside. A rain squall came down like a curtain, however, and blotted out the view.

The pack made good headway. To the east, beyond
the horizon, was Denmark and the Continent. To the
west, only a few miles away, huge minefields loomed
just below surface. After sundown I mounted the
bridge again for my regular watch. The four of us on
duty scanned the sky for enemy planes, searched the
waters for drifting mines. Dusk came slowly, gradually turning the sea darker and darker. I had plenty of
time to make my peace with God.

At midnight Gerloff relieved me from watch. I fell
through the hatch and lowered myself into the black
hull. The conning tower was illuminated only by a
feeble shimmer from the phosphorescent face of the
compass. The control room was dimmed; I could
barely make out the round of the hull, the dials,
wheels, switches, valves, and equipment. A small lamp,
well shaded, distributed a soft light over the chart table. With the boat listing and swaying beneath me,
I staggered into the chief petty officers' small wardroom where I had a tiny locker and a narrow upper
bunk. I jackknifed up into the tight berth, closed the
aluminum guard rail, and wedged myself between
closet and wall. For long hours I was kept awake by
the diesels' rhythmical knocking and the splashing
of water against steel, and by my thoughts of sailing
against the enemy.

Around 0600 I became aware that the boat was
rocking vigorously. We had left the German Bay and
entered the Skagerrak. At 0800 I mounted my watch,
packed in heavy oil clothes. The sea had gone mad.
Sheets of foam and spray slashed across the bridge.
When hard breakers crashed against the conning tower, the boat shuddered violently. The two companion
boats had been lost during the night. *U-557* was
alone in the vastness of the turbulent water desert.
We on the bridge were silently scanning the sea, the
horizon, the sky.

When *U-557* stood due east of the Shetland Islands, plowing her way through heaving mountains of

water and foam, we changed course to west-northwest, toward the Atlantic. Then at 2300, the Captain ordered another course-change—due west. We had reached a point about 70 miles north of the Shetland Islands; here we would break through the British air and sea blockade. *U-557*, her diesels throbbing reliably, made 14 knots through a lashing sea. The moon occasionally appeared from behind the flying clouds. The four of us on watch squeezed behind the superstructure, but cascades of water periodically turned the bridge into an icy pool. The towel that I had wrapped around my neck was soaked with water, which ran down my back and chest. As I stood there with the binoculars up to my eyes, water sloshed into my sleeves and coursed down into my boots.

Suddenly the third mate said, "Shadow bearing three-oh-oh, looks like freighter."

I snapped around, pointed my glasses into the given direction. Six or seven thousand meters ahead a faint shadow was about to cross our path at an obtuse angle. The ship was heading west-northwest.

"Captain to the bridge," Wiesner called into the tower with a controlled voice. The summons was repeated twice in the hull. Moments later the Captain emerged from the hatch. Wiesner pointed out the target.

Paulssen, adjusting his eyes to the darkness, spotted the vessel and said, "I'll take over, go down and plot the attack." Then he shouted into the hull, "On battle stations—Right full rudder—Steer three-two-oh—Both engines full ahead together."

The hunt was on.

Paulssen focused on the shadowy ship. The three of us scanned intensively to all sides. The Exec reached the platform and fastened the strong night binoculars atop the Target Bearing Transmitter (TBT). Two seamen on the bridge were exchanged. The second seaman's mate adjusted his computer in the tower. The torpedo gang rushed to the tubes. The crew was on battle stations.

Meanwhile, the freighter had veered to port, showing us her stern. We were now at a disadvantage. Paulssen turned into the wind, which brought waves crashing against the tower from dead ahead. Then a black cloud blotted out the moon; for a long minute we almost lost our target. But when the moon reappeared, there was our prey, running westward under full power.

Paulssen, displeased with the progress of the chase, shouted through the voice tube to the radio room, "Tune in on six hundred meter wavelength and monitor international traffic. If we've been detected, her skipper may stir up the neighborhood calling for help."

As he gave his order, the target turned to starboard, settling on her previous course. The Exec took fresh bearings, relayed his findings into the conning tower: "What's the target's speed and course?"

After a moment, Wiesner's voice came from below: "Target speed fourteen knots, course two-six-oh."

The vessel was a fast new cargo ship trying to make it across the Atlantic as a loner. But during the first 70 minutes of our chase we had reduced the gap distinctly, and it seemed certain that she was never going to reach the shore. The chase went on. Hunting fever had taken possession of us; we could not feel the waves slapping our faces, nor the water streaming down our skin. Ahead lay our first target—nothing else counted. Keeping in sight of the doomed vessel, but invisible to her with only the tip of the conning tower above water, we raced on a calculated path into the night. At 0215 we had the target on port, bearing 270 degrees, and we plowed forward relentlessly with ringing diesels into attack position. By 0300, when Paulssen corrected course slightly, we had managed to gain bearing ahead of the shadow and remain unseen. The freighter's radio had been silent. She had changed course at regular intervals, almost guaranteeing the success of our attack.

At 0325 the Captain told the Exec to prepare for the shot. Kern moved behind his TBT, trained it on the enemy, and yelled into the tower above the racket of the diesels: "Tubes one to four ready for surface attack. Open tube doors. Target angle left fifty, speed fourteen, range one thousand, torpedo depth seven. Stand by!"

"Tubes one to four ready for firing," came the report from below.

The next move had to come from the vessel; it would be her last if our calculations were correct. They were. The freighter made her turn exactly to the minute, swinging her bow toward us and racing straight into the trap Paulssen had set for her. The Captain threw his boat around into attack position, exposing the smallest silhouette to the enemy.

The ship bore down on us like a monster out of the darkness, closing to 1,000 meters.

"Shoot, Exec!" Paulssen shouted.

Kern aimed once more, then barked, "Tube one, fire! Tube two, fire!" He simultaneously activated the lever at the TBT permitting the release of the torpedoes. With two distinct shocks, two torpedoes shot out of our hull and churned toward the vessel.

We focused our glasses at the shadowy mass of steel, which grew bigger by the second. Someone

counted, "Thirty-five . . . thirty-six . . . thirty-seven . . ."

Suddenly a huge fire column rose from the freighter. The hard crash of the explosion hit our ears a moment later. This was the death of a ship.

Seibold's excited voice came through the tube: "Report from radio room. Vessel broadcasts as follows: 'German submarine, torpedoed, sinking, fifty-nine north . . .' Message was not completed."

Almost at once, the freighter listed to port. I saw her crew lower a few lifeboats; other boats dangled absurdly askew in the davits. The great broken hull stood out black against the red, yellow and golden flames. It was gruesomely beautiful.

Paulssen turned U-557 away from the sinking mass of debris; tube doors were closed and the men secured from battle stations. The mortally wounded ship slipped away and gently sank deeper. Then, convulsively, her bow tilted upward and she plunged, stern first, beneath the surface. Nothing was left but life rafts tossed by high waves.

Our first kill had come at 0410 on May 19. This swift victory, won in an area that most U-boats tried to avoid, was an extraordinary feat and gave us at least 7,000 tons to our credit. The pressure which had been building up for days was released. U-557 proceeded on her new course at maximum speed. The Captain put as much distance as possible between us and the scene of the sinking on the correct assumption that there would soon be a concentration of enemy power in the area.

I was drenched and shivering after nine hours on the bridge. The water in my boots spilled over at every move as I hurried down the aluminum ladder. Peeling off my sopping-wet fatigues and underwear, I hung them up to dry in the aft torpedo room, then ran through the boat in the nude and crawled into my narrow bunk.

For several days U-557 proceeded on surface, both engines half ahead. The wind was rough and the sea mountainous. The motion of the boat was a perpetual swinging, swaying, rocking, rolling, and listing. Inside, the humidity was intolerable. Moisture condensing on the cold steel hull, ran in streaks into the bilges. Food turned rotten and had to be thrown overboard. Bread became soggy and mildewy. Paper dissolved. Our clothes were clammy and never dried, and whatever we touched was wet and slimy. For days we had no proper navigational fix. We could not shoot a single star, nor did we see the sun or the moon. Only the daily trim dive brought relief from rocking and spray. Down in the quiet depth we finished the work we otherwise could not perform, had a meal without losing it on the deck plates or in the bilges. And for an hour or two we recuperated while waiting for the next assault of water and wind. These routine dives were never long enough, and surfacing always came too soon.

During those days of fighting the weather, we received from Headquarters a radio message of greatest significance. Our largest capital ship, the battleship *Bismarck,* was reported to be on a hit-and-destroy mission in the North Atlantic, accompanied by the heavy cruiser *Prinz Eugen.* On May 24, all U-boats at sea were informed of *Bismarck*'s quick victory over the British dreadnought *Hood,* His Majesty's mightiest ship. U-boats were advised to stand by for orders relative to *Bismarck*'s future operation. We considered the sudden appearance of these German surface vessels in the Atlantic a major achievement. The North Atlantic had become our front yard and sailing there would be deadly for the British Home Fleet as well as Allied merchantmen. Our conviction was strengthened by radio messages we intercepted from other U-boats. *U-556* had sunk vessels totaling more than 30,000 tons on her latest mission. *U-203* and *U-93* and others had destroyed almost 100,000 tons of Allied shipping the previous weeks.

On May 25, between sundown and dusk, we of the third watch saw smudge darkening a large section of clouds on the westerly horizon. A few minutes later we realized that the smudge was smoke rising from many stacks; then we spotted the heads of countless masts. We were on collision course with a convoy.

Wiesner reacted promptly, calling, "Captain to the bridge!"

Paulssen arrived, sighted and issued a string of commands. The alarm shrieked. We jumped into the hatch, *U-557* cut into the waves, and within 20 seconds she had submerged. As the boat balanced out, the crew hustled on to battle stations.

"To periscope depth," the Captain demanded.

U-557 glided up to the designated elevation. The Exec climbed into the tower, I assumed the helm. The humming noise of the periscope motor filled the small room. Paulssen had difficulty with the scope and worked it up and down between the rise and fall of the rough seas. The operator on the sound gear reported that the convoy was approaching fast. Soon we heard the grinding of a multitude of screws with the naked ear. The soundman then detected an escort group ahead of the convoy. The throbbing noise of turning screws covered the entire westerly horizon. Then we heard the sharp, metallic ping-ping of the Asdic impulses that the destroyers sent out to track us down. It was a new sensation for most of us on board. Each high-pitched sound struck the boat like a hammer hitting a tuning fork; then it traveled through the hull, escaped and spread across the entire horizon. Meanwhile, the low thumping knock of many piston engines and the chirping song of turbines grew steadily louder and more distant. The soundman reported that the convoy had turned in a southerly direction.

Suddenly, we distinguished the fast-rotating propeller of a destroyer. The Captain, turning the scope quickly around its axis, called, "Three destroyers, bearing three-two-oh, distance three thousand meters. Rudder full left, new course due south."

We could have attacked the menacing destroyers, but Paulssen wisely chose bigger, safer game. Soon he cried exultantly, "What a view! All five tubes ready for firing. Target speed ten, angle left thirty, depth seven, range twelve hundred. Hey, Exec, take a look at the parade!"

Kern bent forward and pressed his forehead against the rubber cushion of the eyepiece. Then he gasped, "There are at least thirty of them, rocking like elephants."

The Captain resumed his circular sweep, but before long he gave a start and retracted the scope. "Both full ahead!" he shouted. "Dive fast, Chief, bring her down!" The screws rotated wildly, the boat vibrated strongly, and plunged toward the ocean floor.

"Prepare for depth charges! Level off at one-seventy."

The nerve-wracking swish-swish of an approaching escort grew louder, drowning out the groaning noise of the 30-odd cargo ships. The destroyer crossed our track astern, then hurried away into a northeasterly direction. Feder gradually brought *U-557* up again to periscope depth, a maneuver that took almost 20 minutes. Meanwhile, the convoy had zigzagged again, and a quick sweep with the scope told Paulssen that he was in a disadvantageous position—too far north for a perfect shot.

At 2115, with nightfall only 45 minutes away, Paulssen decided to wait until dark, then surface and seize the convoy from astern. In the conning tower, oilskins were handed out to the assault watch, whose members made ready to mount the bridge. As part of the watch, I was relieved of the helm. Thirty minutes passed in silence, with the Captain still hunched over the scope. Then the soundman reported that the convoy had again changed course. The noise of many piston engines and throbbing propellers, magnified by the clear ocean water, made our hearts pulsate faster.

At 2245 Paulssen jumped off his seat and commanded, "Blow all tanks!"

As *U-557* broke surface, Paulssen flipped the lever of the hatch; it opened, and the howling wind swept spray into our faces. Five of us followed the Captain onto the bridge. The night was moonless and black—perfect for the attack. The boat lay low, her deck awash. *U-557* gained speed and surged after the targets.

"Shadows bearing two-five, distance five thousand," a lookout reported.

"Shadows bearing three-five-oh," called another.

We had the convoy dead ahead and gradually closed the gap. Cleverly Paulssen had the boat slip in 300 meters astern of a freighter. Incredibly, there were no escorts; they were searching in the wrong direction. The wolf was in the middle of the flock.

"Both engines one-third ahead!" shouted Paulssen. Then, to the Exec: "I am going to steer between the two columns. Take one shot for one ship. Take the farthest and fattest target first, the nearest last. Shoot to both sides and hold dead center."

Our distance from the shadowy monsters ranged from 400 to 700 meters. It was a stunning situation, sailing undetected amid an armada of enemy ships, selecting at leisure the ones which had to die.

The Exec repeatedly assured himself that all target values were correct: "Angle right seventy, distance five hundred, speed eleven knots . . ."

The Captain shouted into the wind, "Fire, Exec, let them have it!"

The Exec yelled above the roaring of the sea: "Tube one, ready—fire! Tube two, ready—fire!" Then he looked to the portside and gave the firing command to tubes three, four, and five. Time was 2340. Five torpedoes sliced toward the swaying phantoms. We waited tensely, unable to change course until the first torpedo struck home.

The first explosion came on starboard. Another hit on port, then another. A new flash—and the savage salvo of detonations rocked the air. Red and yellow flames and a lava of molten steel were hurled into the air. We heard the hollow boom of collapsing bulkheads and the piercing shriek of falling masts. Hell reached a climax. Our faces glowed in the glare of the wild fire.

The convoy fired a dozen flares which surged skyward in huge sweeps. One of the stricken vessels, a 7,000-ton cargo ship, rolled over to her side, extinguishing her flames in the floods. Keel up, she lifted her stern in her death agony, displayed rudder and screw in the flickering light, and slipped under fast. The second vessel broke amidships, collapsed like a pair of scissors; with a bellowing explosion she sank. As the third freighter floated in flames out of her column, an explosion ripped off her bridge and sent a new fiery streak skyward. Huge chunks of steel and debris splashed into the water around us. We took cover behind the superstructure and waited until the rain of steel stopped. It was the vessel's last agonizing motion; she went down in less than a minute. A few burning planks were all that remained of three of Britain's ships. The toll would have been heavier if the convoy had not made a drastic turn to the northeast after our first torpedo struck. Because of this change of course, two of our torpedoes had missed.

In the aftermath of the attack, I stood leaning against the periscope housing, scanning the seas astern. Two escorts rocked along some distance behind us, their lookouts unable to spot our low silhouette in the heaving sea. Paulssen maneuvered us toward the convoy. *U-557* fell in again a safe distance behind the last shadowy vessels and followed in their wake. Kern left the bridge to supervise the recharging of the tubes. Siebold transmitted a radio message telling Admiral U-boats of our contact. We on the bridge kept up our watch on the zigzagging convoy and made ready to renew our attack.

At 0230 the Exec reported all tubes reloaded. The Captain closed in on the freighters with the idea of repeating our successful penetration. We began our second assault with both engines at highest revolutions. There was no escort in the immediate vicinity; in any event, we were too close to the convoy for destroyers to operate safely.

Siebold appeared in the hatch; he shouted to make himself heard above the storm. "Sir, radio message from Headquarters: DO NOT ATTACK FURTHER, TRANSMIT BEACON SIGNALS, KEEP CONTACT UNTIL NEW ORDERS."

Paulssen cursed through his teeth. The order forced

us to play a waiting game until our beacons had brought other U-boats to share our prey. Angrily he ordered our speed reduced. *U-557* fell back to the end of the columns, then headed north-northeast using the dark horizon as cover for our escape. But as I routinely scanned the seas ahead, I saw a shocking sight. To our port, just 1,000 meters away, a destroyer was bearing down on us fast, her bow raising a white mustache of waves. Two other escorts followed at a short distance. For a moment my tongue was glued to the roof of my mouth. Finally I shouted, "Destroyer, bearing three-forty, angle zero!"

Paulssen reacted at once. "Right full rudder—both three times full ahead!"

U-557 swayed and listed while swerving in a bold arc; then she ran away westward at maximum speed straight into the onslaught of the waves. The three attackers, now astern, rocked strongly in the foamy sea, their bows dipping deep into the waves, their keels showing as they rode high up the crests. But despite their wallowing they were closing the gap. I kept staring at them as if I alone had the power to hold them at bay. If we could only speed up by one or two more knots we eventually would be able to out-distance them. The diesels hammered loudly, the boat vibrated strongly, but—as I realized with a sudden chill—they were still gaining.

"Alarrrmmm!" The Captain's cry cut into the night. We plummeted down the hatch, through the tower, and onto the deck plates. Paulssen shouted above the commotion, "Go down to one-seventy meters! Down into the cellar fast!"

As the Chief bellowed into his microphone, the Captain reversed our course. We swung toward the destroyers even as they rushed toward the foamy wake of our descent. In our frantic effort to undercut the attack, *U-557* nosed down toward the ocean floor at a sharp angle, but her stern still hung dangerously close to the surface. The escorts' swishing propellers came menacingly closer. Every man looked upward in expectation of the inevitable.

Then came a terrific explosion. A giant force lifted

U-557 by the stern and shook her violently, slamming the crew to the floor plates and throwing the boat into darkness. A second detonation burst moments later. Low rolling thunder followed.

Feder shouted, "By emergency lighting, blow tank three and five! Both planes up!"

Some lights flickered. The impact of the well-placed spread had forced the boat down to 185 meters, but the Chief had kept her well under control. It was the fastest dive he had ever made.

Paulssen ordered silence. He spoke in a low voice, almost whispering, "Rig for silent running, port motor seventy revolutions, starboard sixty."

All auxiliary motors were stopped. All instruments not needed were shut off. *U-557* floated at an incredible depth, noiselessly. Came the report from the soundman, "Target in one-two-oh, second target in two-two-five."

We did not need the sound operator to tell us what was happening on the surface. Asdic pings hit our hull like arrows. The destroyers above us set themselves up for a new barrage. We heard their pumps and their auxiliary motors; we even heard someone drop a hammer accidentally. For a moment all three hunters stopped. Then one destroyer started her turbine, threw her propellers into high gear, and began her run. The swishing noise was accompanied by high-pitched Asdic impulses that penetrated the steel plates and hit every man's heart. As the destroyer crossed over our boat, we heard one—two—three distinct splashes— depth charges.

Three deafening explosions astern to our port. The boat moaned under the impact, then shook off the salvos with a violent motion. At once a second pursuer began her assault.

"Both full ahead together!" yelled the Captain. "Hold your breath, sailors!"

Three more abominable detonations. *U-557* trembled, deck plates jumped, air hissed, but the boat remained watertight. The latest spread had exploded astern to starboard. It seemed that the hunters had no clear picture of our position: high seas and our extreme depth had saved us. *U-557* slowly floated away, leaving the destroyers far astern. For three hours we kept up our silent running and the destroyers continued exploding their charges. Then Paulssen reckoned we had put a safe distance of five thousand meters between us and the hunters.

At 0500, *U-557* surfaced. Fresh air streamed into the hull. The night was still black. We proceeded eastward with one diesel full ahead, while the other recharged our exhausted batteries. The regular watch took over. We had escaped the hunter-killer group and resumed our pursuit of the vanished convoy.

Shortly after dawn, May 27, our radio operator received an urgent directive from U-boat Headquarters: EMERGENCY ALL U-BOATS WITH TORPEDOES TO PROCEED AT ONCE AND AT FULL SPEED TOWARD BISMARCK GRID SQUARE BE 29.

Paulssen was given the decoded message on the bridge at 0635. By then the order was some eight hours old; it had first been issued at 2115 the previous evening, while we were submerged and unable to receive it. Since we had been under attack most of the night, we had no information on *Bismarck*'s predicament. But we guessed that the battleship must have crashed into a superior enemy force after her companion ship, *Prinz Eugen,* had been dismissed.

Paulssen was on the spot. Should he continue to chase the convoy or hurry to help the big ship? *Bismarck*'s position was more than 350 miles southeast of *U-557,* too far to be reached that day. While Paulssen worked toward a decision, we intercepted a signal from *U-556;* the message said that the *Bismarck* was engaged in a losing battle. This forced the Captain to turn immediately toward the *Bismarck*'s last reported position. We did not realize it at the time, but as *U-557* raced southward, two enemy battleships, one carrier, two cruisers, and a number of destroyers had converged on the distant battlefield and were delivering the *coup de grâce* to the mightiest man-of-war afloat.

The ocean went high, the wind swept hard. Showers cut into our faces. At 0925 we sighted two escorts and had to make a half-hour detour to avoid them. But when we returned to our previous course, our mission had already become obsolete. At 1150 we received from Headquarters this sad message: BISMARCK VICTIM OF CONCENTRATED ENEMY FIRE. ALL U-BOATS IN VICINITY TO SEARCH FOR SURVIVORS.

All night and the next morning we raced southeast through quieting seas toward grid square BE 65, where the *Bismarck* had fought her last battle. We arrived over her grave at noon on May 29, two days and seven hours too late. The water was calm and covered with a heavy layer of oil and debris. While the regular watch surveyed sea and sky for the enemy, a few of us scanned the flotsam for survivors. We found none. Not a corpse, not a single raft or life preserver. We searched the area for a full day, then turned back toward the northern convoy routes.

4

Our short mission had thus proved quite successful; boat and crew had emerged from their baptismal fire with colors flying, and with torpedoes left over for another attack. After a day's westward sail of almost 200 miles, we removed the two torpedoes from our outboard pressure tubes and lowered them into the hull. That afternoon we received from Headquarters a new order: PROCEED AT ONCE INTO AK 50. HX CONVOY EXPECTED. ANTICIPATED SPEED NINE KNOTS. COURSE EAST-NORTHEAST.

At once Paulssen swung *U-557* around in a lazy sea. Spring had returned to the North Atlantic. For the first time since our departure we enjoyed being on the bridge. Bearded, paleraced machinists stole a few minutes to look at the sun and the sky, to fill their lungs with clean, fresh air. Inside the boat conditions were quite different. The stench of 51 sweating seamen, diesel oil, rotting food, and moldy bread mingled with the noisome odors that emanated from the galley and the two tiny washrooms. The overbearing smells and the never-ending rocking made the men in the narrow drum dizzy and numb. Only the daily trim dive brought partial relief from the perpetual swaying.

On our march back into the northern region not a single ship crossed our track, but Paulssen was far from relaxing the rules. In fact, he made it a matter of routine to plunge his boat into a crash dive "for exercise" at the least expected moment when all was calm in the boat. He gave his deputies—Exec Kern as torpedo and gunnery officer, Seibold as radio officer, Feder as Chief, and Wiesner as navigator—a tight schedule of lessons designed to make us three ensigns good submariners before we returned to port. We were already employed to capacity: we mounted our four-hour watches every eight hours, Gerloff taking the first, Goebel the second, and I the third watch; we serviced the torpedoes, took turns in the diesel and motor rooms, crawled into the narrow battery compartments to control the acid level and to test the air for possible escaped gases, relieved the mates in the control room and made calculations to establish our position from bearings taken whenever the horizon was clear at dawn or dusk. Nevertheless, despite this workload, Paulssen himself gave us instructions on diving and attack procedures at any hour of day or night as he saw fit. Concerned that we might not meet his high standards, we regularly swung ourselves into our bunks with an engineering manual and studied until overpowered by fatigue. The head lamps were still burning when we were awakened for a turn on the bridge. As a result, we never opened those books we had purchased in Kiel for our anticipated "leisure" hours.

After a journey of several days, we arrived in our

assigned grid square. Visibility was excellent, but neither binoculars nor listening equipment disclosed an enemy ship. We spent a frustrating week criss-crossing the area in various search patterns. Then Paulssen informed Headquarters of his findings—or lack of findings.

It was an afternoon in early June when we were ordered into another square. According to intelligence reports, a convoy had assembled before Halifax Harbor, and its path was to bring it into an area six hundred miles south of Greenland. *U-557* set out to intercept.

We made an unexpected contact the following day. I had just finished lunch and was smoking a cigarette on deck when the port lookout pointed forward and called, "Mast ahead, bearing three-five-oh!" It was then 1250.

The Exec swung the boat around and called for Paulssen. When *U-557* completed her turn, the target was located astern, its masts sticking up like toothpicks in the distance. Paulssen hastened on the bridge to discover that the target, steering a westerly course, was about to disappear below the horizon. The Captain cursed angrily and yelled into the hatch, "Right full rudder, both engines emergency ahead!"

This was the signal; the hunt had begun. Our sleek boat split the choppy surface, leaving a foamy wake. After 15 minutes we determined that we had a large freighter before our tubes. Kern sent a constant stream of information into the conning tower, allowing Wiesner to plot the enemy's course and speed. Constant bearings established the fact that we had a slight speed advantage over the vessel. Paulssen raced his boat just behind the horizon, at the limit of visibility, attempting to get ahead of the target for a submerged attack. Suddenly, the ship made an abrupt change of course; her three masts melted into one and sank into the sea. For 20 minutes it was touch and go. But she crept back over the sharp, blue horizon in the south, then turned to display her masts and funnel.

Soon thereafter, at 1415, Wiesner climbed onto the

bridge and presented his chart to the Captain. "Sir, the target zigzags clearly around a mean course of 260 degrees, speed fourteen knots."

Paulssen was satisfied. The two plotted the attack and determined the course that would intersect the freighter's track. We took a coffee break while the doomed freighter hastened to a rendezvous with her executioner.

At 1610 the Captain changed course to cross the target's path. *U-557* reduced her speed momentarily and turned east toward the zigzagging ship. We proceeded slowly under a very blue sky, carefully scanning the sea. First we saw a smoke puff, then recognized the mastheads.

"Alarrrmmm!" The dive went like clockwork.

The soundman reported, "Propeller noise in zero zero, getting louder fast."

Paulssen, swinging himself onto the seat of the scope in the tower, gave his order: "Prepare tubes three and four for firing fan shot." He took a sweep all around the boat, then advised, "No more reports, I have her well covered. Rudder left ten, right so, steer seven oh. Attention computer: target speed sixteen, angle left twenty-five, depth eight . . ."

Using these values, the computer worked out the exact gyro-angle, transmitting it simultaneously to each of the torpedoes in the tubes. The periscope motor hummed continually. Paulssen maneuvered into attack position, held the boat steady, reduced her speed, then rapped out his final orders: "Correct distance eight hundred, angle left thirty, tubes three and four ready— ready—fire!"

Two light shocks indicated that both torpedoes had left their tubes. A swishing sound came from the bow compartment, accompanied by an increase in air pressure. The compressed air, which had activated the large pinlocks that expelled the torpedoes, was released into the boat instead of the water, thus avoiding the bubbly swell on the surface that had revealed the position of submerged U-boats during World War I. Meanwhile the torpedoes, examples of a new type powered by batteries, followed their fixed course toward the doomed ship without producing the sparkling streaks of older, faster models, propelled by compressed air, which were reserved for use in night attacks. The two steel fish and the British ship headed steadily toward their intersection.

Two powerful detonations from the freighter rocked our boat.

"She's hit, she's sinking!" shouted Paulssen. He leaned back, allowing the Exec to take a quick look. The second mate was the next to witness the kill. I followed and was struck with amazement. The vessel was sinking on even keel. There was no fire on board. Her super-structure was painted brilliant yellow, her hull fire-engine red. A beautiful ship.

She had settled with her deck about one meter above water, and she showed no inclination to sink further. The freighter's crew was abandoning ship. Since the sea was calm, disembarking went without panic. As the lifeboats left the vessel, Paulssen sailed among them, training his scope on the stunned men. Again he let me take a look: in one of the rafts the freighter's captain waved his white cap at his dying ship.

Paulssen decided that it was necessary to administer a *coup de grâce*. He sailed clear of the lifeboats, pointed our bow toward the stricken ship, and released another torpedo. It took 32 seconds to hit. With a long, hollow explosion, the proud vessel went down to the ocean floor.

Thirty minutes after sundown we surfaced. In three hours we had put nine miles between our boat and the rafts. To insure rescue of the survivors, we released a standard SOS signal on the 600-meter international wave length. Minutes later, Paulssen transmitted the following radio message to Admiral U-boats: SUNK FIVE, TOTAL 30,000. ONLY FIVE TORPEDOES. LOW ON FUEL. U-557.

Traveling at high speed for two days, *U-557* took up the assigned position in grid square AJ 94. On our arrival, heavy fog was rolling in; it reduced our chances to spot the convoy. At times the milky fog banks were so dense we could not even see our own bow or stern

from the bridge. We dived often for a sound check, but in order to survey our large area, we had to cover great distances between our dives. These dangerous dashes reduced our fuel supply to such a point we could not attack the convoy and return to base without refueling. Paulssen put through another message to Headquarters explaining the urgent need for supply. We waited six hours for the answer. It instructed us to proceed to a location approximately 80 miles off the southernmost tip of Greenland and refuel from the German tanker *Belchen,* which had eluded British raiders since the beginning of the war. We turned our boat around and chased with both engines full ahead toward the rendezvous. The weather grew rapidly colder, and we slipped into our blue knitted underwear.

Two days on this course took us into the iceberg region. We changed course often to skirt the small icebergs. Soon immense 'bergs appeared, and we sailed a respectful distance from these mountains. No one aboard had seen such a spectacle, so the Captain permitted the crew to observe the scenery. Between the azure sky and the light green ocean, hundreds of icebergs, splendidly white and of all sizes, floated majestically southbound. The sun reflected a millionfold in the glassy surfaces of these swimming islands.

"Smoke clouds on port!" yelled a lookout.

He had sighted three gray vessels—warships of a large class and of unknown nationality.

"Alarrrmmm!" We jumped into the hatch and *U-557* left the surface in a rapid fall. Feder balanced the boat, then brought her up to periscope depth, but Paulssen's view of the ships was blocked by the menacing icebergs. He frantically rotated the scope in his search for the enemy and his attempt to avoid hitting the submerged portion of the mountains, then finally caught sight of the three ships. He identified them as British cruisers of the *London* class. Focusing the scope on the targets, he ordered all tubes made ready for firing. He corrected his findings and changed course several times, then waited for the one second when all values would be in perfect coordination. But that second never came. The targets changed course abruptly and steamed away at 24 knots, far in excess of our top speed.

Paulssen shook his head in dismay. After a short waiting period, we surfaced and set a new course to meet with the tanker.

The icebergs gradually diminished as we sailed closer to Greenland's southwest coast. Early on the third day after our encounter with the British cruisers, we found the lonely *Belchen* at the designated place. Approaching slowly, we identified ourselves, exchanged courtesies through the megaphone, and caught the line to which the oil hose was fastened. Paulssen maneuvered *U-557* into the near-invisible wake of the tanker. She was a low, long ship of approximately 15,000 tons and probably carried enough fuel to supply our boats for months or even a year.

One of our machinists attached the hose to an outboard valve and secured the rope on deck. Then *U-557* began to suck the much-needed oil into her empty tanks. Foodstuff was shuttled from *Belchen* by rubber boats. At noon we received company; another U-boat had found her way to the supply ship and made her fueling connection with the tanker. At 1500 the assembly grew to three U-boats. *U-93,* with Korth in command, arrived and stood by at some distance in the icy waters. It was a rare and strange congregation, four German vessels in a lost corner of the North Atlantic. Pleasantries circulated from boat to boat, and also our warning of the three British cruisers. At 1700 we removed the hose, transferred it aboard *U-93,* wished each other good hunting, and separated from the group.

U-557 took on a southwesterly course, running at high speed toward an evening sky. Four hours later, during a dive to trim the boat, we heard three hollow detonations far astern. A whole series of booms followed; the bombardment lasted ten minutes. It came from the exact position of the *Belchen.* We were certain that the British cruisers had finally located their target.

At 2300, *U-557* surfaced, made radio contact with Admiral U-boats, reported refueling accomplished and the probable fate of *Belchen.* Sometime between midnight and dawn, our radio operator intercepted a confirming message: BELCHEN WITH CAPTAIN SUNK BY BRITISH SURFACE WARSHIPS. RESCUED CREW. FUELING NOT COMPLETED RETURN TO BASE WITH 93 MEN. U-93.

We proceeded toward grid square BB 90 to operate on the convoy route between Halifax and St. John's. Passing through the area where the icy Labrador Current meets the warm Gulf Stream, we were enveloped in heavy fog, but the curtain rose the moment we crossed the 47th Parallel. The radiant sunshine surprised us after several days of blindness. The sea was choppy, but the air was mild. We slowly patrolled the routes for two days with only one diesel working at a time.

It was mid-June and the summer season was about to reach its peak. On each watch, my thoughts wandered back across the Atlantic, some 3,500 miles east, to where Marianne was awaiting some sign of my safe return. I recalled for the hundredth time our last tête à tête and dreamed about a *wiedersehen* on the beaches of the Wannsee in Berlin. Love and life seemed so long ago, so far away—almost unreal . . .

At 1600 on one of those flawlessly sunny days, I was released from my watch after sitting on the rim of the bridge for hours, skimming the horizon. I went below and had a sandwich garnished with rancid butter and green mold. I sweetened it with a heavy portion of strawberry jam and washed it down with strong coffee. But at 1815 the meal ended abruptly.

A cry arose from the bridge, electrifying, bloodcurdling: "Both full ahead, right full rudder! Torpedoes on starboard!"

I leaped through the control room and up the tower. Reaching the bridge as the diesels began to howl, I spotted three sparkling streaks rushing toward us with insane accuracy. The horrifying sight of death coming closer paralyzed us. During those very last seconds, I braced myself to meet eternity. In a moment, the foamy streaks would hit the boat. . . . Now . . . now!

But there was no detonation, not even the sound of

steel hitting steel. Astonishment at our survival overcame us. As we spun around to portside, the ghostly wakes of the torpedoes revealed to us that two of them had underpassed *U-557* midships and one had shot by the rudder astern. Still not quite sure that we were alive, we inhaled deeply—and our hearts began to beat again.

U-557, in agonizing sluggishness, had finally turned to starboard and achieved greater speed. Ahead of us was the launching point of the enemy's torpedoes, a swell clearly visible on the choppy surface. Within moments we reached the spot. Paulssen, who mounted the bridge only seconds after death had brushed us, shouted out determined orders: "Battle stations, clear the bridge!"

The crew eagerly prepared for a duel between U-boat and submarine. The alarm shrieked and *U-557* plunged after her attacker into the black depth. The Captain ordered all tubes flooded and made himself comfortable in the control room, where he could concentrate on both the sound gear and the torpedo computer. This was a different kind of fighting; our boat sailed in almost total soundlessness. Our listening gear located the enemy sub in a westerly direction, but as soon as we had her dead ahead, her propellers' swishing gradually diminished. The enemy was on the run. We chased her with all our power, but to no avail. The enemy submarine was faster.

Paulssen became suspicious. "I'll bet that sub is going to surface. Chief, prepare for surfacing. Have diesels ready for immediate high speed." I followed the Captain into the tower.

The soundman's voice came through the tube: "Enemy blows all tanks."

Paulssen countered: "Surface—blow out tanks with both diesels full ahead!"

Moments later the boat cleared the water, and we stormed to the bridge with our glasses trained dead ahead. There she was, no more than eight thousand meters before our tubes. With "three times full ahead," we chased the sub. Her fuming diesels made it obvious that she, too, was under full power to avoid our coun-

terattack. She began to zigzag. Her erratic dashes gave
us views of her superstructure to compare with diagrams in the international naval catalog. Paulssen and
Kern discovered that she was a British submarine of
the *Thames* class.

We realized that the British submarine was our superior in size and speed. Since it was fruitless to chase
her, we changed course and followed the attacker with
our glasses until she disappeared behind the horizon
in the direction of Boston. We wondered what the
British skipper would say for failing to sink us with
three torpedoes. He had made a perfect approach and
had made an excellent fan shot. Two torpedoes out of
three would have been hits—if the torpedoes had been
set to run at proper depth. Whatever caused the failure,
it had saved the lives of 51 men.

At sunset and 25 miles later the Captain ordered
U-557 below surface to celebrate the survival of the
entire crew; we called it a "birthday" party. The same
night, after resurfacing, we informed Headquarters:
HAVE BEEN ATTACKED BY BRITISH SUB-
MARINE IN CC 36. COUNTER ATTACK.
ENEMY ESCAPED. U-557.

We remained in the general area for another five
days. The sneak attack prompted us to keep watch for
periscopes as well as smoke stacks. We saw neither.
For the second time in a short period, we had been
ordered into a specific square to attack a convoy
which was not there. The possibility of a leak in our security system occurred to some of us.

Following orders from Headquarters, we headed for
grid square BC 35. Here, together with two companion
U-boats, we were to form an advanced patrol line that
ran from the 48th to the 53rd Parallel, passing some
450 miles east of Newfoundland. We arrived two days
later. By now, six weeks had passed since we had left
port. We had become full-fledged submariners. However, our food supply, which was calculated to last for
two months, had shrunk considerably despite the few
cans we had received from *Belchen*. Much had landed
in the bilges or had turned bad. Paulssen quickly

solved the problem: he ordered Seibold to reduce the daily ration. As a result we tightened our belts every other day.

On the morning of June 20, we intercepted a radio signal from Commander Muetzelburg, whose U-boat was also hunting in the northern Atlantic: HAVE SIGHTED U.S. BATTLESHIP TEXAS IN BLOCKADE AREA. ASK PERMISSION TO SHOOT. U-203.

The appearance of the *Texas* was a remarkable challenge by the Americans, who knew that every foreign ship that entered our blockade area was risking destruction. What would be Doenitz's decision? We were all for shooting and sinking the *Texas. U-203,* still without an answer that afternoon, asked again for permission to attack. At dusk we finally intercepted and deciphered an important signal from Admiral U-boats, replying to Muetzelburg's pressing demands: BY ORDER OF THE FUEHRER ALL INCIDENTS WITH UNITED STATES SHIPS MUST BE AVOIDED IN THE COMING WEEKS. UNTIL FURTHER NOTICE, ATTACKS MAY NOT BE MADE ON BATTLESHIPS, CRUISERS AND AIRCRAFT CARRIERS UNLESS DEFINITELY IDENTIFIED AS HOSTILE. WARSHIPS STEAMING AT NIGHT WITHOUT LIGHTS ARE NOT NECESSARILY HOSTILE.

This order not only denied *U-203* the right to shoot, it was also eventually directed to all U-boats at sea and significantly limited our future method of operation, especially on guarded convoys. As we would learn, it was virtually impossible at night to distinguish a British destroyer from a U.S. escort.

On June 22, the broadcast of the latest Armed Forces communiqué rocked our boat like a depth-charge barrage. Our armies were on the attack against the Soviet Union, advancing from the Baltic to the Black Sea. This event caused great excitement on board. Our invasion of Russia, which dwarfed Napoleon's attempt in scale and scope, represented a basic and long-awaited German aspiration. We had been taught that there was no possibility of Germany

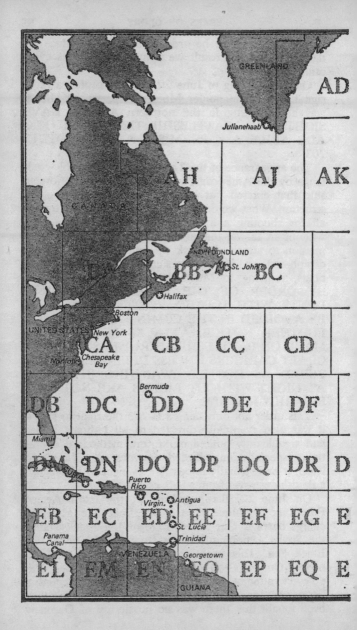

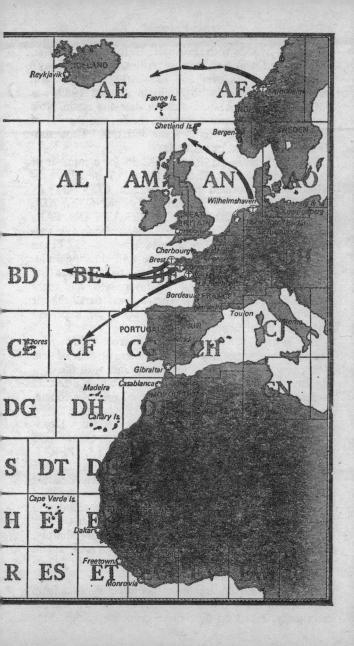

living side by side with the Soviet Union; Communism,
not England and her western Allies, was Germany's
mortal enemy. As everyone knew, the nonaggression
pact we had signed with Stalin in August 1939 was
but a temporary measure, a clever delaying tactic. Now
that our Eastern Armies were on the march, the fall of
Russia could be expected soon and our "Thousand-
Year Reich" would be assured.

We had been in grid square BC 35 for a number of
days without success. Then at dawn of June 23 we received a long-awaited radio message: CONVOY IN
BD 15 ON COURSE EAST TEN KNOTS. ALL
U-BOATS IN VICINITY TO OPERATE ON TAR-
GET WITH HIGHEST SPEED. Immediately, we calculated our chances. They were excellent. *U-557* began
pursuit. It developed into a tense and thrilling hunt.
We plowed southeast at 18 knots to intercept the
convoy in about 22 hours. The day passed, and night
promised a new encounter. The sky was dark, the air
was crisp, the sea choppy and black . . . a perfect
night for a surprise attack.

But not a single shadow appeared. When day
dawned we saw nothing but an endless stretch of sea.
According to our fix, we should have met with the convoy four hours before. Not knowing in which direction
to search, we ran huge zigzags on an easterly course,
trying to see beyond the sharp line of the horizon.

At 0915 we received new instructions from Headquarters: FIRST U-BOAT MAKING CONTACT
WITH CONVOY MUST REPORT ALL PERTI-
NENT INFORMATION BEFORE ATTACK. We
were also advised that four other boats were heading
toward the convoy. With eyes strained we scurried
eastward for the entire day without seeing a smudge in
the sky. It was as though the convoy had never existed.
The high-speed run reduced our fuel supply sharply,
and we knew we would not be able to go west again.

At 2135, a scream came through the hatch: "Captain to the bridge! Shadows ahead!"

Paulssen, wearing sunglasses to protect his eyes from
the lights in the hull and thus be ready for a nighttime
emergency, raced up the ladder onto the bridge. Mo-

ments later I heard his call, "Battle stations—prepare for surface attack!"

I bounded into position behind the Captain and realized that we had crashed into the rear of the convoy. The first thing I saw was a destroyer on parallel course, a faint shadow only. Paulssen outmaneuvered the threat, leaving her starboard astern. Visibility was but 3,000 meters. We clung to the fringes of the convoy only until the Captain had determined all target values. Seibold radioed our findings to base, then *U-557* surged ahead into attack position. Two giant shadows mounted on port. Another phantom appeared starboard ahead, mean distance only 600 meters. The vessels on port overlapped each other—excellent targets. Paulssen screamed a few commands. *U-557* slowed down. Eight, nine shadows lumbered closer through the long breakers. The Captain ordered Kern to shoot.

At that moment I spotted a destroyer—no, two destroyers—cutting through the curtain of darkness astern, angle zero. I waited for Kern to shoot until I could no longer contain myself, then I shouted, "Two destroyers in attack position!"

Paulssen swung around and faced the menace: "Holy Cross, Exec, shoot . . ."

From Kern: "Tube one and two, fire! Tube four, fire!"

"Close tube doors, both three times full ahead," the Captain yelled into the wind. *U-557* gained momentum only slowly. As our torpedoes sliced toward the masses of steel, we slipped into the deadly grip of the two escorts.

A hard detonation to our left. A second boom followed. I saw one of the shadows explode into two fire columns, and the ship ceased to exist. There was no third hit. Star shells and parachute flares drenched our boat in daylight. We saw we were trapped. The two hunters were closing in astern. A third raced up amidship from behind a freighter. There was no escape on surface. We were squeezed between a giant press.

"Alarrrmmm!" The Captain's call was drowned in the shriek of the bell. *U-557* dipped her bow into the inky sea. Simultaneously a thunderous explosion lifted the boat by the stern, shook her violently, and turned her wildly off her axis. *U-557* was out of control. She fell fast.

"Leak in diesel compartment!"

"Starboard motor out of order!"

"Rudder jammed!"

Four hellish eruptions threw the boat around like a toy, forced her deeper into depth, made her sway and tumble. Men skidded along the deck plates. In the flicker of emergency lighting, I saw the needle of the depth gauge waver at the 125 meter mark, then move rapidly to 140, 160, 180 meters. The thrashing sound of a destroyer came nearer, and the footsteps of its racing screws seemed to drum loudly against the steel of our hull. All eyes looked upward. The swishing of propellers reached a crescendo as the destroyer passed over our boat.

"Rudder hard-a-starboard!" shouted Paulssen. "Port motor half ahead."

Three charges exploded, seemingly just above the conning tower. After each shattering roar, the hull moaned, the floor plates jumped and kicked our feet, wood splintered, glass disintegrated, food cans flew through the boat; then all was black for long seconds until the emergency lighting came on again. But the hull itself held tight. Only the gaskets and the seats of many valves had loosened, letting water trickle into the bilges in countless little streams. The force of the detonations had pressed the boat deeper, and the influx of water drove her still closer to the limit of her design.

The escorts grouped for another attack, their Asdic chirping relentlessly. The minutes stretched into endless agony. We hardly risked breathing. Suddenly two distinct explosions came from the direction into which we had heard the convoy disappear. Other U-boats had arrived! But elation gave way to horror as the three escorts rapidly neared our position. One by one they churned over our coffin, each dropping a final depth charge like chrysanthemums upon our grave. The three fiendish bursts only deafened our ears, for *U-557* was now too deep for charges to damage her. Only depth itself could have collapsed her hull.

Two hours later we surfaced, shaken and exhausted. The fresh air speedily revived the crew, then we inspected the damages. They were greater than we first assumed. The starboard motor was knocked off its foundation, the aft ballast tank was ruptured, and the starboard shaft was bent. This meant the end of our patrol.

U-557 began to crawl 1,600 miles to her new home base, Lorient in western France. The spirit of the crew had been catapulted to the highest peak by our latest success. We did not mind the scars our boat had received. The 37,000 tons of British shipping we had sunk was a vital contribution toward the defeat of Great Britain.

5

Five days of cautious sailing brought *U-557* to the fringes of the Bay of Biscay. We had been warned by Headquarters to approach the Bay carefully, for the British had extended their air surveillance into that area. But here and elsewhere, as we learned with satisfaction from the intercepted reports of other U-boats, the Royal Navy was faring poorly. The messages indicated a sharp rise in Allied shipping losses.

One U-boat, leaving the Bay of Biscay on patrol, reported: PASSED EIGHTH LONGITUDE WEST. SUNK ONE DESTROYER.

Another boat informed Headquarters: SUNK FIVE TOTAL 28,000. ONE MORE DAMAGED. LIGHT DEFENSE. PUSHING AHEAD.

From a U-boat in the North Atlantic: SUNK SIX

42,000 TONS. ALL TORPEDOES EXPENDED. RETURN TO BASE.

And another boat reported: CONVOY AK 40— SUNK TWO 13,000 TONS. KEEP CONTACT.

But the heaviest toll was gaily reported by a larger-type U-boat operating in southern waters: SWEPT AREA CLEAN. SUNK EIGHT TOTAL 53,000 TONS. ONE DESTROYER. PLEASE SEND TORPEDOES AIR MAIL SPECIAL DELIVERY.

The battle in the Atlantic increased in intensity as new U-boats were able to break through the ineffective British defense between the Shetland Islands and Iceland. The noose around Britain was gradually tightening.

On the morning of July 10, exactly eight weeks after we had sailed from the cold, unfriendly North, we tensely watched and waited until the thin dark line of the Brittany coast emerged from the morning haze in the east. France presented herself in the most beautiful way. Ever higher the land rose out of the ocean. Soon we could recognize the green stripes of vegetation. Gradually, white houses with red, gray, and blue roofs came into focus. We looked forward eagerly to sampling the wonders of this exotic foreign world.

At 1300 we were met by a minesweeper, sent to a predesignated point to guide us through the mine-infested waters to Lorient. Some of our seamen prepared white pennants and hoisted them on a line fastened to the protruding periscope head. Each flag represented a sunken ship, the six totaling 37,000 tons. The crew was in a festive mood. Every hand changed into fresh fatigues and combed his long beard for the reception.

Sailing around the tip of a small peninsula, past the ancient fortress Port Louis, we saw Lorient dead ahead. Our arrival took on a dream-like quality. It was a hot midsummer day; the flowers were brighter, and the grass was greener, and the houses shone whiter, and everything contrasted sharply with the drab world we had left behind two months before.

U-557 reduced speed as she reached the inner harbor. Silently, we sailed and floated toward the large crowd lining a quay. Our comrades-in-arms stood by in

Victory Flags

gray-green uniforms, navy blues, and a variety of battle dress. Many girls—nurses from our military hospital—were waiting for us with flowers. How satisfying it was to be expected, how good it was to have survived!

A military band launched into a resounding march as *U-557* came alongside the quay and fastened her lines. The Commandant 2nd U-boat Flotilla shouted words of welcome, then walked across the gangplank and shook hands with Captain and company. The nurses followed with a smile, a kiss, and a bouquet of flowers for every man. Now we knew that we had jumped off the devil's shovel, that life was sweet and rewarding.

With the exception of a small watch, left aboard to guard the once-again rusty and weatherbeaten *U-557*, our crew assembled in one of the old halls of the former French Naval Préfecture. The homecoming celebration—this one for the men only—was about to begin. We cheered Paulssen for his promotion to *Kapitaenleutnant*, which had come through while we were at sea. There was champagne and lobster, followed by other rich courses. The Captain made a speech, and the Commandant of the base listened entranced to his tales of our adventures. When the last bottle of champagne was emptied, we received our mail. It was placed on the white linen tablecloth in bundles large and small, and each of us opened his packet in ceremonious silence. I sliced my letters open with a butter knife. Marianne had sent one anxious and loving letter a week, and several notes from my parents begged me for a sign of life. Their concern was comforting. Yes, I had returned. I was still alive and expected to remain so for a long time.

We were in a wonderful singing mood. Our heavy meal was followed by great quantities of good German beer. After four hours of eating and drinking, Goebel, Gerloff, and I had to help each other into our quarters in the old naval complex. There we found our baggage, which had been sent overland by truck from Kiel. After hanging out our double-breasted blues, we took our first bath, shave, and haircut in eight weeks. Hours later, all dressed up and with money in our pockets and pride in our hearts, we set out expectantly to explore the town. Our progress was embarrassingly unsteady; it was hard to navigate on solid ground after weeks of walking on a perpetually swinging and swaying deck. But we gradually got our land legs back as we proceeded along a picturesque avenue into the downtown district.

At twilight the streets were still bustling with traffic. Vendors displayed baskets of fruit and fish and shouted the virtues of these wares in their melodious tongue. Many of the women wore the colorful native costume of Brittany—embroidered blouses, white, starched headpieces, and fluffy skirts that reached down to their heels. But the military dominated the scene: everywhere we saw army vehicles and uniforms of gray and blue. Groups of sailors roamed boisterously through the narrow sidestreets searching for adventure or women or the usual packets of unusual "French" action photographs.

After sipping an apéritif in a sidewalk café, the three of us made our way in the dark to a restaurant on the fishermen's wharf. There we had a long, leisurely dinner. Lingering over our glasses of champagne, we stared out into the black lazy water, and memories of our first patrol rose up, silencing our conversation.

We spent the next three days awaiting a visit from Admiral Doenitz, called the Lion; he was to come down from his headquaters in Kernevel, a small town just north of Lorient, to meet the crews of *U-557* and two other boats that had also returned from patrol. On the appointed morning, we assembled in front of the Préfecture, the old command post of the defunct French harbor administration. We waited in the hot July sun, sweating profusely in uniforms too heavy for the climate; we cursed bitterly and longed to take cover under the acacias and palm trees that lined the square. Finally, a brass band struck up, and the Admiral marched into the square accompanied by a large retinue, including officers of his staff and high-ranking guests from the Army.

Doenitz was lean in appearance, brief in his speech, and stern in his demands. We men of the U-boats had three duties, he said: to pursue, to attack, to destroy. At the proper interval, the three crews joined in chorus and promised to fulfill his highest expectations. Then the Lion passed down our ranks, shaking hands with each man, pinning medals to blouses and coats. At that moment, we felt that most of the power of the U-boat command was concentrated in that square, and every man among us was convinced that he would do more than his share toward winning the last fierce battles of the Atlantic.

The day after Doenitz's visit, *U-557* was moved from her exposed pier to a dry dock sheltered in a new concrete pen that looked like a great cathedral. With the boat provided for, the crew was divided into three groups, to be sent alternately to the seaside resort of Carnac for a week at a time. Gerloff and Goebel, benefiting from their position in the alphabet, left port in the first group. Before my turn came, I had to struggle through huge piles of paperwork and assume responsibilities that my superiors ignored. I typed the final version of the Captain's logbook and the Chief's reports, wrote a full accounting of the disposition of each torpedo, and made detailed diagrams of *U-557*'s entire route and each of the attack patterns Paulssen had used. To escape the harassments of Kern, Siebold, and Feder, I also volunteered to type out the papers for their protracted leave in Paris.

But if the days were long, so were the nights. Our crewmen had inherited the local *établissements;* they enjoyed the girls who had served many a sailor before them, including comrades who now lay on the ocean floor. For those of us with a taste for gastronomy, there were several good restaurants offering exotic dinners and long wine lists; even meals of only fair quality were an inspiring experience for men who had survived for weeks on moldy bread and dissolving food. And it was a pleasure simply to walk alone on the streets of Lorient and look into the shop windows. In this region left untouched by the war, merchandise was unusually plentiful and of fine quality.

But the war was always with us. Our Armed Forces communiqués, broadcast regularly over German radio stations, kept us in a state of excitement over the dramatic progress of our troops on the Eastern front. German forces had already dealt the Red Army appalling defeats, and had taken close to 2 million Russian prisoners. Our soldiers were on the attack near Leningrad; they had seized Riga on June 29 and Minsk a day later. The eastern campaign promised to repeat, on a far grander scale, our sweep through much of the Balkans during the previous spring.

Special bulletins informed us of U-boats triumphs. In the month of July, more than 300,000 tons of Allied shipping had been sunk in the Atlantic, topping considerably the toll for June. Repeated successes were reported by U-boats operating against British convoys around Gibraltar and in the Mediterranean. These boats also guarded our supply routes to North Africa, where Rommel's Afrika Korps had launched a startling counteroffensive against elite British armored divisions.

Life, like the war news, ran at full tide for me at Carnac. I lounged on the shore in the torrid sun, swam with tanned French girls and consorted with one or another of then long into the night. After a few days of this summer idyll, I returned to Lorient with my group, and we were greeted with an order to assemble at once, in full battle dress, in the courtyard of the Préfecture. It was the first time in 20 days that the whole ship's company was together again, and Kern took the opportunity to advise us that the good life had come to an end. He told us that *U-557* has been transferred to the quay for fitting out, and that in the next several days we would work like slaves to load her with torpedoes, ammunition, fuel, and foodstuffs.

Our labors proved to be as heavy as Kern had promised, but the crew accepted them with a kind of satisfaction. For most of us, the glamor of life in port had already faded, and the desire for action at sea was mounting.

Suddenly, the work was done; our departure was scheduled for the following morning. Again we went through the ritual of severing our connections with life. In solitude, we labeled our surplus luggage and wrote last letters home and prepared our sea gear. Afterward, some of us emptied a bottle of wine. Others spent their last night in the arms of a sweetheart or a professional. But all of us wondered whether we would survive to go through these motions once again.

6

The month of August in '41 was but a few days old when U-557 sailed for her second patrol. At 1400 we removed the lines from the pillars. The obligatory band played a march, and a thunderous "hurrah" came from the Commandant of the flotilla, officers, and enlisted men. At the far end of the quay stood the public, including a number of girls who were waving tearful farewell to their lovers. The war had brought them together—the war separated them again.

U-557 sailed out of Lorient under electric power. When she had Port Louis on her left, the diesels began to mutter their old, intimate song. Half of the ship's company was standing on the cigarette deck or leaning against the railing, smoking, chatting, and enjoying a last hour of sunshine. Astern, picturesque Lorient and the Brittany coast slowly diminished. As our escort vessel departed, her skipper shouted through the megaphone, "A pleasant trip and good hunting!"

The men were ordered below. The watch and the Captain remained on deck, together with a newcomer who had embarked only 30 minutes before we had put out to sea. *Kapitaenleutnant* Kelbling, a classmate of Paulssen, had been assigned to us as a prospective commanding officer. He had no special function; his only duty was to round out his experience with one war patrol. Later, we passed through a fleet of fishing boats lying lazily in the blazing sun. Their yellow, red, and green sails pointed into the deep blue sky like colored sugar cones. As we approached the last of the trawlers, Paulssen ordered quietly, "Both full ahead. Set course two-seven-oh."

After the Continent had sunk into the sea, *U-557* submerged for her first trim dive. For three days we saw no enemy plane or smoke cloud. The Bay of Biscay was calm and deserted.

When *U-557* passed the eighth Longitude West, Paulssen opened the sealed envelope he had received from Admiral Doenitz. Our orders were to attack the convoy routes in the North Channel between Ireland and Scotland: Headquarters expected a heavy concentration of enemy shipping in that area. The envelope also contained details of the minefields near the Channel.

U-557 took on a northwesterly course. The diesels roared the symphony that made every man's heart beat faster. The next morning, at 0700 sharp, the men off duty were awakened by a blaring loudspeaker. This was not the first time that phonograph music had heralded a new day aboard, but it was the first time that a British song was played. Everyone recognized the wishful lyrics, put on a broad smile, and hummed with the British in chorus: "We are hanging our washing on the Siegfried line . . ." The British, far from being able to take our famous defensive line, had abandoned the record in Lorient, along with uniforms and war material, when they fled through France before our advancing troops in 1940.

On the sixth day of our patrol we sliced into a critical area, 120 miles southwest of Fastnet Rock, the lighthouse on the southernmost tip of Ireland. Here the southern convoy routes converged to a narrow path not more than 80 miles wide. We made no contact, however, and continued on a circular course approximately 250 miles west of the Irish coast to avoid detection by the British aircraft. Eventually, we arrived at the 58th Parallel, made a sharp turn to starboard, and went on an eastbound course toward the North Channel. Ten days after departing the French paradise, we reached a spot three miles northwest of the soaring cliffs of the Island Inishtrahull, which lay almost in the center of the shipping route. We tried to lurk there, for the island's lighthouse offered us an excellent navigational fix, but the strong current washing through the Channel forced us back into the Atlantic.

We cruised the area for several days without hearing a sound or spotting a ship. Obviously the British had redirected their convoy traffic. The fruitless search began to affect the disposition of the crew. Paulssen, frustrated, contacted Admiral U-boats asking to be relocated into better hunting grounds. The answer suggested that Headquarters was receiving excellent intelligence from Nova Scotia: PROCEED INTO AL 69. HALIFAX CONVOY EXPECTED GENERAL COURSE EAST-NORTHEAST ELEVEN KNOTS. LIGHT DEFENSE. GOOD HUNTING.

We raced westward at high speed for three days. When we arrived at our designated position it was night and the black sea breathed gently. *U-557* stopped her engines, and the sound operator began his watch. However, we spent the night without spotting the enemy. With the first morning rays we resumed our chase and crossed the square in irregular patterns. At 1510 the same afternoon, as I was plotting course at the small table in the control room, a man on the bridge shouted, "Smoke cloud, bearing three hundred."

The Captain dashed past me and leaped to the top. I heard him hollering at the man in unmistakable anger, "You call that a smoke cloud? It's a forest fire! Crew on battle stations!"

When I reached my place on the bridge, *U-557* had turned toward the black smudge. As we approached, the cloud expanded into a broad black curtain of dense smoke and fumes. Then we spotted the mastheads and stacks of the zigzagging destroyers preceding the armada. Five minutes later a forest of masts crept over the sharp edge of the horizon. We were on collision course with a huge convoy.

1535: "Alarrrmmm!"

1545: The parade of ships had not yet appeared in the eye of the scope; Paulssen relied solely upon the report from the sound room. The crew moved quietly on action stations. The torpedo gang flooded the tubes. The second mate adjusted his computer. I took the helm.

1610: Two sweepers came into view, sailing in erratic patterns.

1625: The sound gear picked up two destroyers, propellers whirring at high revolutions. Both hunters made their moves as if not quite sure in which direction to search for the silent enemy. Asdic impulses began to bounce against our hull.

1635: The sound mounted in volume and density. The hammering of piston engines, the thrashing of propellers, and the knocking and rumbling of many approaching vessels reached a fierce crescendo.

1645: Wiesner had calculated the convoy's speed and course; the rest was up to Paulssen, and he swung his boat into attack position. His hands were busy adjusting the scope to the ups and downs of the sea, training the cross-hair on the fattest targets. Suddenly he shouted the decisive order: "Tubes one to five ready!"

"Tubes one to five are ready," assured Kern.

Paulssen released five shots within 25 seconds. We in the conning tower counted the seconds until the torpedoes hit. Meanwhile the Captain kept turning, extending and retracting the scope, watching the cargo ships approach in orderly fashion. There they swayed in a sluggish sea, innocently carried away to their destruction. Within a minute this respectable parade of 45 rocking giants would be disrupted by fiery, breaking ships; the rest of the vessels would spurt away, their crews terrified by the horror of devastation.

Then came one—two—three hard explosions. The Captain, all smiles, shouted, "Exec, write down: hit on freighter, 5,000 tons; hit on second vessel, also 5,000 tons; hit on 4,000-ton freighter astern. Two misses. What's the matter with those damned torpedoes?"

1705: We in the tower were given a chance to view the holocaust. Three vessels lay heavily listing, shooting smoke and fire columns into the air. White lifeboats hung head down in their davits. Two destroyers raced toward the dying ships. It was a painting of rare and vivid colors.

1710: Depth charges detonated close by. Paulssen jokingly insisted that they were at least 1,000 meters away.

1720: Escorts disappeared. Sound contact with convoy was considerably reduced.

1800: Cook distributed coffee and battle sandwiches. Too much salami. The sweating torpedo gang hoisted up five steel fish and reloaded the tubes. The Chief balanced the boat like a juggler. The Captain sat at the scope watching the convoy flee toward the southern tip of Ireland.

2125: *U-557* surfaced. Only a very thin light line in the west indicated that the day—a successful one for us—had come to an end. Darkness hindered our sight. But the convoy could not run away—we were too close to its heels. With both engines full ahead we pursued the battered herd.

2205: We signaled Headquarters: CONVOY GRID SQUARE AM 71. COURSE ONE-TWO-FIVE. SUNK THREE 14,000 TONS LIGHT DEFENSE.

Midnight: We turned to starboard and proceeded south. No convoy.

0030: We dived to sound out the depth. Reported the operator, "Propeller noise bearing three-oh-oh to three-six-oh, estimated distance ten miles." Ten minutes later, *U-557* surged back to the surface. Once again, the song of the engines together with the swishing noise of the sea rushing alongside the hull produced the hymn which accompanied us into battle. A flare fell in the east.

0115: Destroyer 3,000 meters on port. We drew a big loop around the escort, swinging into the convoy's wake. It was as if we drove into nowhere: sky and sea formed a solid black wall.

0220: Two escorts shot out of the darkness, showing their white mustaches.

"Alarrrmmm!" shouted Paulssen. "Dive to one hundred and seventy. Hard left rudder."

The furious commotion of our crash dive covered up the propeller noise of the destroyers, which were closing in on us with terrifying speed. We clung to pipes and equipment to hold our balance—that was how steeply *U-557* hurtled into depth. Before the escorts could split her stern, she was already down to 90 meters.

Two charges erupted in our wake, flogging the boat like a gigantic whiplash. Total darkness enveloped us for long seconds. *U-557* fell and fell. It seemed to be the end. But the lights came on again, and Feder leveled the boat off at a depth of 200 meters.

0230: Both destroyers had stopped. Silence above, silence inside the hull. Our soundman reported other propellers approaching. The escorts had called for reinforcement. We braced for a long barrage.

0245: One escort began to run up on our port side. We veered at high speed to avoid her spread. Then we heard three splashes, soon followed by three infernal explosions. The well-placed cluster slammed our boat deeper. Hydraulic oil spouted across the control room. The steel groaned, motor relays tripped, planes and rudders jammed, deck plates jumped. As the echo of the booms subsided, someone threw the relays back in, the Chief reduced the speed to silent running, and all was again quiet inside the iron drum. The well-trained destroyer crews above had stopped for a new probe into depth.

0318: Another attack began: three cruel detonations came at close intervals. Then another run. We sat at our stations in the twilight of our emergency lighting, biting our lips and holding our breath as the Asdic pings grew unbearably loud. Some of the men lay on deck staring upward. Others were sitting and staring into an imaginary something. There was no talking, no coughing. The men showed no signs of desperation, only tiredness and stress.

Hour after hour, the attacks were renewed sporadically and inaccurately. Depth was our prime advantage, our only protection.

1200: Above us they were still searching. The Captain ordered fruit conserves and biscuits distributed. A healthy decision. The men relaxed a little as they took on nourishment.

1412: The latest barrage brought to 128 the number of canisters dropped upon us. But the soundman claimed that he heard two escorts leave the scene. We were hopeful.

1520: Not a single detonation for over one hour. Had the Tommies run out of depth charges? Had they abandoned their game? The sound operator turned his wheel with loving care. The entire horizon seemed to be free of hostile sound. Where was the third hunter?

Paulssen said, "Start up bilge pump, let's see whether they take that bait."

The impertinent grinding sound tortured us like a dentist's drill. Though it betrayed our position, it produced no response from above. The third enemy had also departed.

1610: *U-557* surfaced after being submerged for 14 hours. As the Captain opened the bridge hatch, I was literally thrown out of the hull by our internal pressure. Brilliant weather greeted us; we inhaled the fresh air gratefully, though a sudden abundance of it almost made us black out. The ventilators transported oxygen to the sweating hands inside the drum. For us on the bridge, the sun was never so red nor the sky so blue. Since the convoy had fled safely beyond our reach, *U-557* raced west in search of new targets.

We traveled three days, covering 450 miles in a medium sea. On the fourth night, a U-boat operating in the extreme North flashed a signal across the Atlantic: CONVOY AJ 35 COURSE EAST TWELVE KNOTS. ATTACK.

Taking the cue, we changed course and dashed into old, faraway hunting grounds. Simultaneously, other boats deciphered the message and raced to intercept the convoy. However, Headquarters had other plans for *U-557*. We were instructed to proceed into a different area, leaving the loot to others. The boat's company cursed like pirates over spilled rum.

As it turned out, a large wolf-pack made contact with a Halifax convoy. One by one, their torpedoes crashed into its flanks and decimated it. Short signals came rushing in, proclaiming victory in one of the greatest battles ever fought in the Atlantic. Those messages, accumulating on the Captain's desk, reflected the ferocity of the assault which sent ship after ship to her grave. The radiograms were as precise as the shots the Captains fired: TORPEDOES EXPENDED. SUNK FIVE 24,000 TONS. SET FOR BASE.

SUNK THREE 18,000 TONS. DAMAGED TWO. KEEP CONTACT.

TWO VESSELS SUNK. DEPTH-CHARGE DAMAGES. RETURN TO BASE.

HAVE SUNK FOUR 21,000. CONTINUE HUNT.

The battle went on cruelly for two more nights and days. Through those hours of ruthless sinkings, we stayed tuned in on our German radio stations and listened to the special bulletins that informed the nation of our victory at sea. Then the wolves lost the convoy in the northern fog, leaving the bottom littered with 20 battered hulks.

As one of the triumphant U-boats headed home, it crashed into another convoy, and at once a new hunt began. This time U-557 was ordered to operate against the target. As we approached the northern region, the sea rose higher: cold spray and foam and a slashing wind mauled me during my watch on the bridge. Visibility quickly dropped from 16 miles to 4. The typical North Atlantic weather caught up with us once again. U-557 beat the waves head-on and listed strongly in the long breakers as the chase went into its second day.

"Alarrrmmm!" It was exactly 1730.

The boat tilted immediately and submerged fast. Paulssen, racing into the control room, called into the tower, "Exec, what's the matter up there?"

Kern replied through frozen lips, "Destroyer bearing thirty, distance four thousand meters."

As soon as the Chief had the boat under control, the soundman reported that high-pitched propellers were slowly disappearing; we had not been detected. The operator made another discovery: "Wide soundband port ahead. Must be a convoy."

We had run into the starboard flank of an unreported convoy. Paulssen ordered the crew on battle stations and the boat on periscope depth. The scope revealed nothing, so the Captain brought us to the surface.

As soon as the tower was clear, we rushed through cascading waves onto the platform. Visibility was only two miles. A thick layer of clouds hung just above the boiling sea. We immediately pushed after the source of the sound band. Forty minutes later we again sighted an escort and quickly outmaneuvered her. The sea, rolling from west to east, drove us violently ahead as huge, long waves lifted our boat at her stern and carried her forward high on their crests.

While in hot pursuit through a violet twilight, we informed Admiral U-boats of our discovery. It soon became apparent, however, that the convoy made drastic changes of course. We continued eastward for two hours in a huge zigzag pattern, but detected no convoy. Reluctantly, Paulssen ordered the Chief to dive to take a new sound check. The soundman reported a faint disturbance on starboard 40.

We surfaced at once. Dusk had closed in and visibility was reduced to less than a mile. *U-557* swayed and listed in a tumultuous sea. Sheets of water broke over the superstructure, lashing our faces and burning our eyes. I sought cover in a squatting position, with my glasses leveled over the rim of the bridge; but the fierce spray split my skin and lips, drenched the Turkish towel I had wrapped around my neck, and ran down my back into my boots. I shivered in the chill of the night despite my triple layer of clothing, topped by a one-piece diver's suit of thick rubber.

U-557 kept thrusting toward the enemy. It was almost midnight when a shadow moved into my glasses. Then there were two . . . three . . . four. Paulssen saw them, and the Exec also saw them. Two escorts flitted nervously at the tail of the starboard column, and one zigzagged ahead of our boat, all of them unaware of our breakthrough. Huge shadows—giant cargo ships—pitched about unperturbed, their broad flanks inviting a shot.

U-557 gradually swung into attack position. An escort broke toward us through the wall of darkness, but we eluded her by sneaking close to a huge freighter. Paulssen pushed into the herd from astern. No enemy eye could spot our boat in the high windswept whirlpool. As Paulssen steered tenaciously in between two columns, the fat shadows grew monstrous. The Captain shouted into the raging storm, "Exec, pick your targets, make it quick, we can shoot only once!"

"Have them all on a string. Tubes one to five ready ... ready...."

"Hard right rudder!" Paulssen screamed. "Shoot, Exec!"

Seconds later two torpedoes leaped out of their tubes. Quickly another fan shot left the boat against an overlapping target. Finally the last torpedo churned toward the nearest shadow in the column. Then there was breathless waiting.

Three hard explosions bellowed into the night. Three volcanoes erupted almost simultaneously. Three sharp shocks rocked the boat. Dozens of star shells climbed into the sky and countless parachute flares hung in the clouds, illuminating the wild seascape with a ghastly green and yellow glare.

We had long since escaped the scene of disaster when two escorts arrived to rescue survivors. The impact upon the enemy was so severe, the confusion so great, that no serious counteraction followed. As a result, we risked staying on the surface to reload the tubes. We clung to the convoy, carefully holding our distance behind the shadows. The stricken convoy had made a sharp turn to the north, but the wolf was still within the flock. Some distance to the south, three vessels lost their struggle, and the last flickering flames were swallowed by the violent sea.

Forty minutes after the attack, our last two torpedoes were ready for use. U-557 closed the gap. Minutes later we had the targets before our tubes—dead ahead. With the rudder turned hard, our boat surged in an arc into proper position. Then two brief commands, two light shocks, and the last torpedoes sprang from their tubes.

The Captain said, "That's all, gentlemen. Both engines emergency ahead, hard right rudder. Set course one-eight-oh."

U-557 turned away and escaped at top speed. We watched the targets for 60 seconds . . . 70 seconds . . . we counted and waited and hoped. But the two torpedoes were failures.

During those moments between life and death, I pictured the seamen on their doomed vessels—riding the huge waves holding onto life rafts. I felt sorry for those courageous men who had to suffer and go down with their ship; it was a terrible ending of a hopeless struggle. I could understand why the British seamen persisted; they were fighting for the very existence of their country. But I was bewildered by the stubbornness of the captains and crews from foreign lands. Why did they continue sailing for the British, defying our torpedoes and the growing ferocity of the battles? Whatever price the British had paid for their services, it could not have been enough to compensate for their risks and very lives! I was astounded that His Majesty's Admiralty was still able to recruit any number of foreign ships.

Thirty minutes after our last attack, we informed Headquarters of our night's encounter and advised that we would be sending beacon signals to home other wolves toward the herd. For three hours, we remained in cautious proximity to the convoy, transmitting the beacons vital to the continuation of the battle. Then two detonations, accompanied by two fire fountains in the front half of the convoy, indicated that another U-boat had arrived.

Our mission was completed. At 0530, *U-557* dived into secure depth. There the Captain had a surprise for us. The sinking of six ships called for the opening of some "medicine bottles" that had been kept under lock and key. With cup in hand, each man filed through the narrow aisle, halted at the Captain's tiny corner for as long as it took him to pour a rare shot of Cognac. Then we retreated to our stations or bunks sipping the potent liquid.

After 20 hours of running submerged, *U-557* surfaced and set course for the Bay of Biscay.

7

Our second patrol, which ended on September 18, had produced a different kind of crew. We were now seasoned warriors in the powerful force that had re-shaped Europe in just two years. Our hit-and-destroy operation against the major convoy we had discovered had been an important contribution to the inevitable defeat of England. We ourselves had sunk three ships of the convoy, bringing our total to six and 32,000 tons. Our attack was continued by other U-boats, which sank six more vessels in less than four days. Moreover, this engagement broadened into a great 12-day battle against three convoys crossing the North Atlantic in staggered pattern. Altogether, our U-boats had hit the incredible number of 20 ships out of the first convoy, four out of the second, and nine out of the third, making a toll of 33 ships totaling at least 165,000 tons—all sunk within two weeks. These extraordinary sinkings proved again the great potential of our wolf-pack tactic which left the British defense helpless and turned the Atlantic and the waters around England into a grave-yard for Allied shipping. We had, indeed, reason to feel proud.

As victorious veterans, we took for granted the hearty reception that greeted us at the quay in Lorient. The cheering crowd, the flowers, the brassy band music, the respectful salutes of the Flotilla's Commandant and his staff—all this was our due. The only unexpected bonus was the bold appearance of the girls from the *établissements,* who could not resist the temptation to welcome home their best customers. A night filled with warm embraces made a pleasant prospect for our crewmen, but even this had become just another routine part of the sailor's life.

Our first duty after landing was to attend the usual ceremonial dinner at the Préfecture. The meal was a long and rich one, laced successively with champagne, red wine, and German beer. When the speeches ended and the men dispersed to their respective quarters, I was sent back on board *U-557* to take charge of the watch the first night in port.

The boat lay like a phantom in the low tide. My three guards stood on deck enjoying the lukewarm night. I went below, into the stifling stench of oil, grease, sweat, and decaying food. The sudden calm and motionless state of the boat that had rocked and pitched and had spread death and destruction for almost 50 days was a new sensation. I realized how important this delicate instrument had become to me; its power was now a vital part of my life, if not a part of myself. Knowing that I would have very little time later, I sat down on the Captain's green leather mattress, switched on a small headlamp over his narrow desk, and wrote my letters home.

My night watch ended early; it was barely morning when workmen came aboard and began stripping *U-557* of all moving parts in preparation for her transfer to dry dock for refitting. The crew, the majority just back from the *établissements,* set themselves up in the old naval complex in quarters that had been greatly improved while we were at sea. I found that my living conditions were even better. The flotilla had assigned me a large room in the local Hotel Beausejour, and my luggage was already there when I arrived. For the first time since we sailed, I was able to take a shave and hot shower. After washing away my filth and smell, I rolled myself in white, fresh-smelling linen, spread out in my huge bed, and fell into a long sleep.

Our first three days in port gave us just enough time to recuperate and prepare ourselves for the obligatory meeting with Admiral Doenitz. Again, the ceremony took place in the sun-drenched plaza in front of the

Préfecture, with the band playing a march and a large number of high officers in attendance. Doenitz showered us with Iron Crosses and took time to pin a medal on my chest.

That day in late September was significant for another reason. After the ceremony on the plaza, my classmates Gerloff and Goebel were informed of their immediate transfer to U-boat school. The day had started out as a happy one, but this news dampened our enthusiasm. In the evening, the three of us had a fine dinner in town to celebrate our decorations and their new assignment as well. We toasted one another and promised to sink many more enemy ships before the war would end.

My friends departed on the morning train. I never met them again. Both found their graves in different places in the Atlantic. For each, the first patrol after school became the last.

The departure of my friends was not the only bitter pill to swallow. About the same time, the good news from the Atlantic and Eastern fronts was mixed with word of two important U-boat casualties. Long after it actually happened, Headquarters reluctantly announced that *U-47*, with her famous Captain Guenther Prien in command, had been attacked while pursuing a convoy and sunk by a British destroyer. Prien was known as the "Bull of Scapa Flow" because he had dared to enter the British Home Fleet's sanctuary in '39; here he had sunk the battleship *Royal Oak* and damaged the seaplane carrier *Pegasus*. Prien was stopped after having sunk almost 200,000 grossweight tons of Allied shipping. Also lost was *U-556* under the command of much-decorated Captain Wohlfahrt. She had been wrecked by a heavy depth charge series, but her Captain and most of her crew had been rescued by the three attacking British destroyers. Wohlfahrt, too, was one of the aces with more than 100,000 tons to his credit. It seemed to me that men like Wohlfahrt and Prien could not be replaced; yet the U-boat war was creating aces much faster than it destroyed them.

Now that I was the only ensign aboard *U-557*, triple duty fell upon my shoulders. As work on the boat proceeded rapidly, my days were filled with responsible tasks. I got no help from the Captain, who quickly departed for Lake Constance and home, or from his classmate Kelbling, who left our company four days after our return, or from the Exec and Seibold, who hurried off on a two-week leave. But my labors were not without reward. In the evenings, I walked through the streets of Lorient, enjoying my solitude; or retreated into a cozy restaurant, supplementing the sailor's ration at the base with a delicious dinner; and some of those lukewarm nights made perfect covers for my escapades. By the time the crew began to reassemble, however, I had my fill of the pleasures of liberty in port.

On October 8, *U-557* set out for the third time, again heading for the North Atlantic. After a few days of calm sailing we left the Bay of Biscay astern and encountered high seas. Summer had ended, and the first gale winds of autumn lashed the waves to tremendous heights. Under a sky thick with dark clouds, the mountainous waves toyed with our boat, tossed her wildly, and kept the bridge half-filled with water. *U-557* worked frantically to stay on course and make headway.

On the sixth day of our patrol, we reached a position approximately 300 miles west-southwest of the North Channel. That afternoon, as we traversed our old hunting grounds, I was put in charge of the third watch —part of the greater responsibilities that the Captain now entrusted to me. The watch was a harsh one. The gale whipping the water to a milky froth crusted our eyes and noses with salt. Our binoculars were useless.

After three hours on the bridge, I spotted a destroyer moving into our starboard aft quarter. I immediately pointed our stern toward the grey menace, increased speed, and informed Paulssen. I assumed the ship was a part of the convoy's defense. The Captain arrived in a hurry, secured his steel belt to a clamp at the superstructure, and put both diesels into high gear. Following orders to concentrate on supply bearing freighters, Paulssen wasted no torpedoes on the destroyer but sped away from her. Within minutes the bouncing ship had fallen back to the horizon.

For two hours we tracked the escort's evasive maneuvers, hoping she would reveal the whereabouts of the convoy. At 1520 Wiesner, who continually plotted the enemy's zigzags, identified a general westward path. The convoy had to be south of the escort. After another hour of battling giant waves, we saw a smoke-blackened cloud on port. Once again we began the hunt, keeping contact with the steaming herd at a distance of ten miles.

When Wiesner relieved me on the bridge, I lowered myself into the tower, then dropped into the hull. Here, in humidity of 100 per cent, with the waves showering salt water through the hatch onto the metal deck, I went to work feverishly at the chart table, plotting course. Condensing moisture dripped from overhead plates, pipes, and ducts onto charts and paper. My parallel ruler did not slide nor my pencil write. Water sloshed around my feet to the rhythm of the boat's rocking.

At 2000, I again took my place in the starboard front nook of the bridge. The Captain was at my back. Suddenly a searchlight, very faint, beamed into the dusk in the southwest. For seconds only. We chased after the clue. Forty minutes later, shadows loomed ahead, feeble, unreal. A quick correction of course and we surged forward on a parallel track with the convoy. Our powerful glasses revealed the classic picture of dim freighters wallowing in the blackness. We counted 17 cargo ships, but there had to be more behind the rain squall. We detected an escort, port astern, and kept her under close surveillance. The Captain held his boat at a constant distance while we established all target values for a midnight attack.

We charged forward, spreading foam and spray, breathing air full of smoke and soot. The wind howled and the waves thundered above the clatter of our engines as we raced past the shadows and outmaneuvered two escorts with ease. The sea swallowed our small steel drum; only the tip of the bridge protruded. Now we stood in the horseshoe up to our necks in water, tied

to the boat with wide steel belts. The phantoms rocked
in several columns westward, their broad flanks exposed temptingly. Through the savage wind and throbbing engine noise, I heard shouted commands and bellowing reports from below. The Exec clung to the
TBT to hold himself erect while aiming through it at the
numerous targets. The final moment had come for some
of the giants, and for those who manned them.

"Open fire!" screamed Paulssen, the storm tearing
his order from his mouth.

"Fire . . . fire . . . fire!" shouted the Exec.

"Hard left rudder, steer two-fifty," hollered the Captain and slammed the cover of the voice tube shut.

Long seconds ticked away. A blast, a fire ball, then
a loud detonation. A huge fountain rose over the dying
vessel. A second bolt, a boom, a terrifying shriek. Then
a third explosion, a flaming jet. Large chunks of steel
hurled into the illuminated clouds. The bow of a 7,000-
ton freighter broke off; the ship drifted, burning furiously, amid the convoy, and was avoided only with
difficulty by hard rudder maneuvers of the vessels following. Erupting star shells and the roaring of heavy
guns mingled with exploding cargoes and unfolding
parachute flares to turn the night into a bright inferno.
A destroyer, rushing north to the aid of the three victims, threatened to cross our track at close range. *U-
557* swerved, showing her tail, and was carried away in
long lifts, lashed at by the waves. The unexpected interference caused us to lose sight of the two dying vessels,
and we were unable to witness their demise.

One hour of pursuit revealed no trace of a ship. It
was as if the convoy had sprouted wings. We dived for a
sound check, but adverse water conditions swallowed
every sound. After surfacing again, Paulsssen followed
a hunch and directed the boat into a southwesterly
track. Dawn arrived, and with the new day came a stiff
breeze. It chased the clouds low and pitched the spray
high. Visibility changed rapidly from zero to three miles
and back to zero again. We hunted all day without
spotting a trace of a ship. But at dusk, there was a
sudden detonation in the port quarter ahead. A second
one followed. Typical torpedo hits. Another wolf had

found the herd. Sweeping star shells showed us the way to the targets.

One hour and 16 miles later, we detected the first shadow. We followed the phantom for 20 minutes, allowing the Exec to obtain new target values. Suddenly heavy fog rolled in, and the target dissolved. Just as suddenly, a freighter appeared and bore down on us.

"Shadow bearing two forty!" cried someone.

The ship's huge bow moved toward us, so close that we could only shoot and run. The command came, "Tube five, fire!" and our boat turned to starboard just in time to avoid ramming the freighter. We waited 40 seconds, 60 seconds. The torpedo was a miss.

Three vessels, spewing black clouds of soot, rose like mountains in front of our tubes. I could almost hear the throbbing of their piston engines. Paulssen shouted over his shoulder, "Exec, let them have what they deserve!"

Kern rapped out his orders in short spurts. Three torpedoes fanned out. Two explosions ripped the night, then the pressure waves hit our faces. Two flashes blinded us for seconds; the scene was drenched in daylight as two cargo ships sent flames skyward. One ship turned wildly in a circle, her rudder jammed. Both listed and sank within minutes, before their crews had time to lower the life rafts. A flash came from one of the shadowy cargo ships. We had sailed too close to her in our excitement, and a few ant-like figures on the aft deck had manned a cannon and were shooting at us. Two, three, four tall fountains rose around our boat. Several shells screamed over our heads. Speeding away from the spitting freighter, we hid behind a curtain of smoke and dropped to the end of the wounded herd.

One hour later torpedoes were hoisted into the tubes. *U-557* reduced the distance to the convoy, then raced into it again, splitting it open from astern. Two merchantmen, still unaware of our presence, continued on their rigid course.

"Sink those monsters, Exec!" shouted Paulssen.

Two shots were fired in an instant. *U-557* swung into a loop, quivered under the hard waves, then raced away. After two minutes we realized that the torpedoes had missed. Paulssen curbed his anger and steered his boat into a fresh assault.

"Destroyer, bearing two twenty!"

The high ship came charging out of nowhere, her bow rising knife-like in the blackness. Paulssen bent over the hatch and hollered, "Attention, Chief, give us full power or an escort is going to bite off our stern!" He squeezed his boat between two cargo ships, but the destroyer clung to our tail, a mere 200-odd meters astern. There was no chance to dive with safety. The Captain made quick maneuvers around a few bows and sterns, then a fast dash into the night through the furious seas. Death did not claim us; the Good Lord had put His thumb between the hunter and the hunted.

After our escape, we returned to the attack but found no trace of the convoy. Dawn came at 0615, and we were alone in a water desert. The men, tired and disappointed, dozed or ate on battle stations. Food tasted awful. Bread had become mildewy, salami had turned green and slimy, and we washed down the battle sandwiches with a coffee that the Café Berger in Frankfurt could not have reproduced. Sweat, condensate, and salt water had soaked our clothes, diluted the food, and made everything clammy and sticky. We were drowsy from the boat's perpetual motion, weak in our knees, numb from cold, and almost deaf from the everlasting thunder of the diesel engines, the wind and ocean. But the hunt went on.

"Smoke clouds on port!" The cry from the bridge excited the last man in the farthest compartment. Aching bodies rose and were instantly ready for action.

As dusk closed in, we took on the convoy expecting nothing but success; it was the giddy sensation we always felt before an attack. Soon the misty, dirty night limited our vision, but we saw a ghostly escort moving across our wake at high speed. Then three, four cargo ships materialized on starboard, all in perfect position for our attack.

A fast command, a hard rudder maneuver, then came Paulssen's call, "Shoot, Exec, I can't hold this course much longer!"

Kern swiveled the TBT, his aim hampered by the rampaging sea.

"Hell, get the eels out of the tubes!" the Captain slammed his order into Kern's face. The Exec, his hands clamped around the steel support of the TBT, and his head pressed against the rubber cushion of the night binocular, swiveled again, focused, then screamed the orders that released two torpedoes.

U-557 listed sharply as she described a short curve to port.

An explosion—a hit. One ship broke instantly behind the bridge. The second torpedo hit; the second victim listed to starboard, feverishly burning, her deck slipping closer to surface. The gale wind carried to us the stench of the explosions, the stink of burning cargo, the smoke of coal-fired boilers.

The tubes now had to be recharged. U-557 dropped astern of the convoy, secured herself from a surprise attack, and wallowed incapacitated for an hour while our last torpedoes were hoisted into the tubes. Afterward, we resumed the chase. At dawn the convoy was still far ahead.

With the day came the rains. All morning and half of the afternoon they whipped our faces and washed away the salt crusts. The convoy, meanwhile, had disappeared behind the low-hanging clouds. At 1845 a destroyer floated into view. We kept her under careful surveillance and tenaciously followed her course. Two and one-half hours after nightfall we again sighted freighters, three shadows listing in the turbulent waters. U-557 closed the gap. A 7,000-ton vessel became Kern's target, and the torpedo hissed out of the tube.

The ship nosed under instantly with a crashing boom, and as her stern reared up, we saw the propeller turning its last dying revolutions. Immediate counteraction. Long-lasting flares hung in the dirty sky, their glare so brilliant that I could count the whiskers on the Captain's face. And there, not far on port, the breaking ship shrieked in her last convulsive agony.

Paulssen maneuvered through the columns cleverly and soon reached the dark section of the parade. The flares attracted an escort; she stopped near the sinking ship and began taking aboard survivors. She was an easy target, but an unwritten law prohibited attacks on ships engaged in rescue operations. And so Paulssen broke into the herd again. He was in high spirits. This battle went his way, he dictated the terms.

After 90 minutes of pursuit, run-off and re-entry, we managed to break into the center of the remaining ships. A 10,000-ton monster was Paulssen's target. We had but one precious torpedo left in the aft tube. U-557 slammed against the waves as she struggled into attack position. Somehow the Exec's order to fire was heard above the raging gust. The last torpedo streaked toward the phantom.

A quick getaway, a run into the wall of the night. But as hard as we listened and strained our eyes and hoped, there was no hit.

The battle had come to an end. U-557 left the convoy the same hour, our course set for the Bay of Biscay and port. Later, we dived to give the crew a well-deserved rest. Only a few hands stayed awake to keep the boat afloat. For hours there was absolute peace. The only sounds heard aboard were the soft humming of the electric motors and the tiny thuds of the condensate drops hitting the deck plates.

Our latest toll, harvested from a single convoy, was six ships sunk and two more possibly destroyed. These triumphs were matched and surpassed by several other U-boats, whose radio reports we picked up on our way back to Lorient. U-107, a somewhat larger boat, had cost enemy shipping over 100,000 tons on a single operation. All told, ships totaling more than 160,000 tons were destroyed in October, and 200,000 grossweight tons had been sent to the bottom in September. In London that fall of 1941, a record amount of tonnage had to be stricken from Lloyd's Register. It was a hard time for the maritime insurance business.

8

On October 27, *U-557* sailed into Lorient harbor. A gay crowd awaited us. This time, however, the girls from the *établissements* were not among the well-wishers; as we learned later, the naval complex had been fenced off against unauthorized personnel. But after our usual welcome-home dinner and a thorough washing, a good portion of our men found their French girls holding open house in the downtown bordellos. Most of the men were not seen on the base before reveille the next morning.

On the afternoon of November 3, the crew again assembled in the large square of the Préfecture. Admiral Doenitz had come from his command post to greet us. Again he dispensed medals with a lavish hand. I watched proudly, unaware that these were my last minutes as a member of the crew of *U-557*.

After the affair, Paulssen broke the news that I was transferred to the 1st U-boat Flotilla in Brest, the largest port on the coast of Brittany. It was a hard blow. Only reluctantly did I accept the order that separated me from my many friends, and from the boat on which I had found my cause. The wonderful camaraderie that had united enlisted men and officers was suddenly, for me, a thing of the past; I no longer belonged. As I said good-by to Captain and crew, I saw traces of moisture in several eyes.

That day was the last time that I shook the hands of those men, those dear comrades who had escaped death with me so often. *U-557* left Lorient on November 19 for the Mediterranean. She succeeded in breaking through the Strait of Gibraltar, where the British had set up a tight blockade, and crowned her career with the sinking of the British cruiser *Galatea* near Alexandria. But *U-557* met her fate on December 16 in the ironic form of an Italian destroyer, the *Orione,* a ship of a friendly nation, which accidently rammed her in the Sea of Crete. *U-557* went to the bottom, carrying her whole crew down into eternal entombment.

On November 5, I was chauffered by a Russian immigrant driver across the sun-drenched landscape of Brittany. As our Citroen chased down the highway, the needle of the speedometer often crept over the 120-kilometer mark. Speed and sun and the beautiful countryside soon changed my mood. It was exhilarating to come back from the inferno at sea and find myself flying across a foreign world full of marvels. Nonetheless, I was relieved to step out of the car when it careened to a stop at the gate of the 1st U-boat Flotilla in Brest.

Before me, overlooking the bay, lay a sprawling granite complex. Some of the buildings were not yet completed. The stately structures had been built to house the French Naval Academy, but our conquest of France had put a halt to the college program. Instead of French enthusiasts, German U-boat aces had moved into the quarters.

I reported briskly to the *Adjudant* of the Flotilla. He told me that I would soon have to attend U-boat school; the winter term was about to begin. This was disappointing news. However, I had no objection to a few days of idleness after six months of extraordinary activity. I established myself in a room with a breathtaking view of the harbor and Crozon Peninsula. Then I went out to explore the town.

Brest, I had been warned, was a hotbed of espionage and sabotage; occasionally, too, members of the French resistance abducted or murdered our men. But the city was busy and peaceful; its cafés, bistros, and shops were gay and thriving; and the presence of countless Germans in uniform offered added reassurance. It was a sunny November day, the scent of fall was in the air, and I resolved to enjoy myself to the fullest.

After a delicious seafood dinner, I walked through

the picturesque streets, stopped at this café or that, and browsed through every bookstore I passed. In one of these shops I saw Yvonne. She worked there. Her blonde hair and blue eyes attracted me at once. I asked her for some books that she could not possibly have, and managed to engage her in a conversation that ended with a dinner date for the following evening.

The next day, fearing that sudden transfer orders would spoil my plans, I left the base early and spent another pleasant afternoon wandering through Brest. Well before the time to meet Yvonne, I was waiting impatiently for her in a bistro across from the City Hall. She was graceful, fragile, and afraid. Her only contact with a German, she said, had been an occasional remark over the counter on the subject of books. But soon she found herself in an unpatriotic tête à tête with one of the intruders in the obscure light of an exclusive restaurant. Dinner was excellent; desert was sweetened by her promise to see me again. The evening ended, much too soon and, to my great disappointment, at the fence surrounding her house on the other side of town.

I met Yvonne again the following evening, not during daylight, for she did not wish to be seen in public with me. At her gate after sunset, under the protection of the growing darkness, she was not so afraid anymore. From then on I was a regular guest at Yvonne's home. Whenever I went to her, I secured my gun at my belt, determined to meet Yvonne and not my executioner, a member of the Maquis, in a lonely alley of Brest. Whenever I slipped out of Yvonne's home it was sunrise, never before—for I wanted a clear view of anyone who might be following me through the streets of Brest. I never asked Yvonne more than I needed to know. She said that she loved me, and that was all I wished to hear. In turn, I promised her everything for the love she so graciously spent on me.

I enjoyed these days of sunshine and autumn flowers, but after two weeks came the task of telling Yvonne about my new command. We vowed to see each other again as soon as I would return: I hoped

to be back in the spring, when the cherry blossoms
would be in bloom. The last I saw of her was her
bright scarf disappearing in the night as my train pulled
out of the station.

Arriving at the Gare de Montparnasse, I decided
impulsively to stay in Paris that day and take the evening train to Germany. I rushed through the Louvre,
walked down the Champs Elysées, stood at the Place
de l'Etoile, surveyed the city from the top of the Eiffel
Tower, and sat in the Café de la Paix watching a brilliant new world go by. When the church bells rang out
the day, I had barely sampled the pearl of all cities.

Next morning, it was cool and misty as my train
crossed the Rhine. But the sun had burned off the fog
by the time the express hurtled through the pine
woods south of Frankfurt. No one greeted me in the
Main Station, for I had not announced my arrival.
This was the way I wanted it. I was no friend of sen-
timental receptions in public.

Not far from the station plaza was my parents' home
in a quiet, tree-lined street. As I turned into the familiar avenue, I saw a pair of pretty legs not far ahead. I
looked again, then realized they were my sister's. I said
but one word, "Trudy."

She spun around and clutched me; her tears mois-
tened my cheeks. "Why didn't you let us know that you
were coming? We would have been at the station.
You look good. You have lost weight, though, haven't
you?"

"I don't think so. It's only because you haven't seen
me for a year. Tell me, how is Father, how is Mother
doing?"

Trudy tried to tell me all the news in the few minutes it took to reach home. Mother was full of joy.
One year and 100 imagined deaths lay between us and
my last leave. She did not ask about my war. Her
interest was aimed at my health and my appetite:
"You could have sent us a telegram and I would have
a cake for you today."

That morning the cake was baked anyhow. I talked
to Father on the phone. He closed his office for the rest

of the day and made the short walk home in a hurry. His welcome was hearty and we pressed each other's hand like two old soldiers. "Hello, son, how long does your leave last this time?"

"I am not on leave, Father, just passing through on the way to the Baltic. I have no more than thirty hours to spend."

"That's unfortunate. Let me see how we can make these few hours most comfortable for you." Then he began asking me questions. How had I earned my decoration? What is a convoy battle really like? How do depth charges affect boat and company? He was eager to hear my view of our progress against the British, and he wanted to know all I could tell him about my patrols. Gradually our discussion veered to a point that seemed to be of great concern to him: "Don't you think we are spreading our forces rather thinly over the Continent?"

"It seems to me we have sufficient manpower to cover the occupied areas."

"But how many more fronts can we possible afford?" he asked cautiously.

There was no answer, and the question made me vaguely uneasy. I steered the conversation back to happier subjects.

That evening at home and the next were deeply satisfying. Home meant security, an island of rest and intimacy amid the disorder of war. Despite my father's persistent queries, I said little about the U-boats and my feelings in combat. I wished to leave them with the impression that my work was not deadly and tragic, that I would always return.

When my train arrived in the Capital, icy and violent gusts were blowing in from the northeast. Marianne was at the station, punctual as always. We walked through the almost deserted streets to the plush Hotel Fuerstenhof, where I had chosen to stay. The hotel was far better and costlier than the modest accommodations we had to put up with during my last stop, but with my increase in pay I could afford it. And Marianne was different too—somehow less reserved. Her caresses made me forget that there was war and that I had been in battle all summer and fall. The brutal world ceased to exist in her embrace and an air-raid warning went unheard.

During the two days of my visit we rushed from one entertainment to another. To the dismay of the critics, the war had curtailed Berlin's cultural life and lowered the standard of theatrical and operatic performances. Another notable casualty was the quality of the meals offered in restaurants on Kurfuerstendamm. No, Berlin was not the same. But my warm Marianne made the cold city beautiful, and I was sorry—perhaps too sorry—to pack up again and kiss her good-by.

The temperature was minus 15 degrees centigrade when I arrived in Koenigsberg on the last day in November. Shivering in my light uniform, I caught a local train to Pillau, a small port on the Baltic. The compartment was like an icebox, and when I reached my destination I was almost frozen stiff. It was midnight when I boarded the luxury liner *Pretoria,* the residence of the 1st U-boat Training Division.

At breakfast there was a grand reunion. I shook hands with many a classmate and celebrated many a *wiedersehen* at the bar. We had come from all over Europe; we had fought far-flung battles and sunk a gratifying number of Allied ships. Seven months lay between our graduation party in April and this bitter cold first day in December. For most of us, seven months of U-boat war had passed without serious injury. This was reason enough to celebrate.

Our rigorous training began under severe handicaps. Pillau Harbor was covered with ice, in some places up to 30 centimeters thick, and icebreakers worked continually to keep a channel open to minor traffic, giving our U-boats access to the Baltic. We went to sea day and night, with each of us alternately assuming the duties of engineer and captain. Our teachers, experienced commanders, taught us all the new tricks of surface attacks at night and submerged assaults by day. Diving maneuvers were deliberately fouled up, so that we sweated blood to keep the boats afloat. Soon we could perform routine and emergency drills in our sleep. Some of us almost did, for we never had enough rest to recuperate from the harsh exercises of the previous day.

But there were also easy days. The Commandant of the flotilla, Schuhart, a decorated U-boat ace who had sunk the British aircraft carrier *Courageous* in 1939, was a superior teacher whose lessons were attended eagerly. The weekends I spent aboard the *Pretoria,* enjoying a book, playing cards, or discussing Japan's reasons for attacking the American Fleet at Pearl Harbor. The Japanese advances in the Philippines and in the Pacific were too far away to be of any great interest to us. I was aware, however, that events in the Pacific would profoundly influence the U-boat war in the Atlantic. With the full involvement of the United States in the hostilities, and particularly in our fight at sea, the outlook for the future changed almost overnight. I prepared myself for a long war.

Nonetheless, the battle in the Atlantic still went well, and we had reason to be confident of ultimate victory. Our radio networks sounded frequent fanfares and kept public count of enemy ships sent to the bottom. Almost 3 million grossweight tons had been sunk in 1941. The British were still unable to counteract our mounting pressure; entire convoys were virtually abandoned to our wolves. We continued to suffer losses, though. In December another ace was lost around Gibraltar. *Kapitaenleutnant* Endrass and his *U-567,* destroyers of more than 200,000 tons of enemy shipping, had been sunk without survivors.

Our tough training in Pillau went on through January of 1942. Early in February I was sent to the Naval Academy in Flensburg to attend torpedo school. Six weeks of classes and practice shooting taught me the latest secrets. Courses in U-boat tactics and radio communication followed as winter slackened its grip. With the arrival of spring I was promoted to *Leutnant* while attending gunnery school. As spring came, I eagerly awaited orders to return to combat. Remembering Yvonne with some complacence, I hoped to be sent back to Brest.

Admiral U-boats, however, had other plans for *Leutnant* Werner. I was in instructed to go to Danzig and report aboard *U-612* as Executive Officer. I read the teletype twice before I comprehended. It was indeed a fact that I was to become the first officer—second in command only to the Captain—aboard a new submarine. The dim prospect of becoming a U-boat commander had suddenly moved within my reach.

I arrived in Danzig on May 19 and reported aboard *U-612*. My boat, new but already weatherbeaten, swayed alongside an old stone jetty. A guard told me that the Captain was below. I lowered myself into the ship; its familiar and obnoxious smell was suddenly inspiring. I found the Captain in his nook and said, "I beg to report for duty, sir."

"Welcome aboard. I am *Oberleutnant* Siegmann. I have been waiting for you since yesterday. We are ready to clear port. Come over here, please, I wish you to meet the other gentlemen of *U-612*." The Captain, a stocky officer with reddish-blond hair, had the look of an old seafarer and seemed to be about seven years my senior. I followed him into the tiny officers' wardroom and was introduced to the Chief and the Second Watch Officer. We traded a few pleasantries, and they told me of the boat's history. She had been commissioned in Hamburg, the Captain's hometown, in the previous December, and had been in hard training since then. Siegmann expected to finish the mandatory shakedown exercises within three months, which would qualify boat and crew for battle. I learned that the previous First Officer had been relieved of his post due to poor health. The black-haired Chief, *Leutnant* Friedrich, was a married man one year my senior. Surprisingly, the Second Watch Officer, *Leutnant* Riedel, was a classmate of mine. Both men lacked battle experience and that was the chief reason for my transfer. Although the Captain had served as a prospective commander on a U-boat patrol in the Atlantic, only one-third of the ship's company had tasted combat; the rest had to be trained for their first mission. I introduced myself to the chief petty officers, who had long service records. Then I retreated with my new Captain into his corner, and he gave me a brief but firm idea of what he expected.

As Executive Officer of *U-612*, I was to be her torpedo and artillery officer; I was to shoot when attacking on surface and to oversee firing when submerged. I was also to attend to the crew's well-being as the Captain's deputy. The fact that I was given the Exec's position in preference to my classmate Riedel was based solely upon my war experience, nothing more. Riedel and I had a frank talk later in the wardroom. We agreed to respect each other's position and to fight the enemy, not each other. The chat initiated a long friendship which ended, as usual, with a death.

U-612 sailed that day for the Hela Peninsula. There I made accommodations for the crew in the neat one-story barracks that were spotted among the evergreens in the white sand dunes. *U-612* continued her rigid training with six weeks of torpedo practice. Day after day we put to sea as early as 0700, and one hour later I was shooting at targets. We changed the routine in the afternoon, and Siegmann emptied the tubes, simulating a submerged attack. Stripped of torpedoes, we raced into port to take on a new load. Then we repeated the entire program in the dark, releasing the last torpedoes around midnight. The crew worked zealously, almost without rest or interruption, six days a week. During those six weeks, I compiled a sound record: I learned to shoot the torpedoes at the targets and not out to sea.

Early in July we wound up our most taxing exercises. *U-612* soon was attached to another division, and an easier routine replaced the feverish activity at Hela. We sailed to a pier in Gotenhafen, a port in the Bay of Danzig, and I moved the crew into solid masonry quarters. Our interests now turned in a different direction. Summer had arrived, and I had not seen a girl for six weeks or more. However, women were plentiful only a 20-minute trainride away, in the famous sea resort of Zoppott across the Bay. I spent the weekends in Zoppott's luxurious Casino, in the cafés, and on the beaches. I arranged and attended parties, won and lost girls, and generally harvested the good life before death could harvest me.

While *U-612* and her crew were preparing for battle, our armies drove ever deeper into enemy territory. Leningrad had been surrounded, though it still held out stubbornly. Sevastopol in the Crimea had capitulated; our fast-moving divisions had reached the Caucasus, had occupied Rostov on the Don River, and were storming toward the rich oil fields near Maikop. In North Africa, Rommel had led his Afrika Korps to victory after victory over the Tommies; he had taken El Alamein in the Libyan desert and was pushing hard against the Nile. In the Atlantic our U-boats ravaged Britain's convoys with increasing ferocity, despite the entry of the United States into the war. Our U-boat operations were extended to America's east coast against little or no opposition. From Nantucket to Hatteras, from Florida to the Windward Islands, our torpedoes shattered the silence of peaceful commerce. Between Boston and New York, before Jacksonville, Miami, Havana, New Orleans, and Corpus Christi, near Baranquilla, Maracaibo, and Port of Spain, Barbados and Guadeloupe, U-boats attacked the Allied shipping routes, burned, torpedoed, shelled and sunk a fortune of ships. During those months some 2.5 million tons— over 500 vessels, including 140 tankers—were sent to the bottom. The golden age of U-boat war had arrived.

The spirit of our crews in training soared to new heights. I myself, however, was in a state of constant irritation over our long, drawn-out exercises. I wanted to go back to the attack, to sink my own ships, to revive the victory celebrations. But my limited patience was to be put to further tests.

The disastrous August 6 almost sank my ambitions. As always, *U-612* cleared port by 0800. The Bay was flat and reflected the sun like a mirror. The day promised to be another hot one. Well over 20 U-boats in their light gray paint headed into their designated squares, their wake sparkling in the clear air. The city of Danzig lay on starboard, its many old steeples and towers pointing into an immaculate blue sky. Our navigator Prager continuously took bearings from points on land. After two hours of small talk—most of us having returned late from our pleasures in Zoppott—Prager informed me that we had arrived in our square. The Captain was called to the bridge and we began our daily routine. The seamen, divided into three watches, took turns exercising on the heavy gun while we made simulated diving maneuvers and surface attacks. At 1100, U-612 dived. We cruised at three knots at a depth of 25 meters. I was in the forward compartment teaching torpedo science to a large part of the crew, plus 12 prospective U-boat men who had been taken aboard to get their first feeling of being submerged.

At 1142, the boat was suddenly struck astern. The force of impact lifted her high up, then flung her to starboard. Instinctively, I knew that we had been hit by another submerged U-boat. I hollered, "Don life preservers—all men into the control room!" and ran aft until I was stopped in the diesel compartment by a tremendous water jet.

U-612 was sinking. I saw some men trapped in the stern torpedo room and shouted, "Get out of there or you will never get out alive."

They hesitated for a moment, then all of them surged through the waterfall. The boat filled fast and tilted down strongly astern. I managed to clear the rear compartments, slammed the doors in the bulkheads water tight, then raced into the control room, closing the round hatch behind me. Meanwhile, Siegmann had ordered the Chief to surface. Friedrick kept the lines blowing, allowing compressed air to flow into all buoyancy tanks to hold the boat afloat and permit the men to escape the hull. The Captain on the bridge directed his wounded boat toward the coast, four endless miles to the south. I ordered life preservers distributed and pushed the guests up the aluminum ladder. For a second I could see the round opening in the tower and the blue sky above. I felt a desperate urge to race up the ladder, but duty condemned me to ride it out below with the Chief—and probably to die with him. With one eye I watched the swinging depth-gauge needle, with the other I watched the men abandon ship. Soon the boat would be too heavy astern and fall away like a rock, taking all of us down to the bottom. I muttered angrily, *"Verdammt,* in a minute more we could all get out of this coffin." Then I spun around and yelled into the tower, "Get the lead out of your feet, the men behind you have to get out too!"

U-612 suddenly slipped away tail first. A cry from the bridge, "Boat sinks! Get the hell out of there . . ."

The last two machinists hoisted themselves up the ladder. Friedrich leaped across the valve station and ducked under the extension of the tower, then climbed up the ladder to the hatch. I followed. A sudden heavy influx of water almost tore me off the ladder. I pushed against a ton of water, wedged myself through the opening, and was pulled to safety by the Captain. Then the sea swept me off the bridge. At that moment, the bow of *U-612* reached far out of the water like the hand of a drowning man. Then the boat sank rapidly. I was shocked by the suddenness of her destruction.

As we floated in the Baltic I realized I was without a life preserver; I had given mine to one of the guests. The water, however, was calm and warm and only a gentle breeze ruffled the surface. Some distance away, Siegmann's white cap was gleaming in the sunshine. It was still neatly set on his head as he floated comfortably in his yellow life jacket. He was shouting across the water, "Keep close together, boys, they are going to pick us up momentarily!" Then he turned toward me and called, "Did you get all the men out, Exec?"

"There is not a soul aboard, I was the last to leave."

Black figures in yellow life jackets were bobbing up and down over a wide area. Beyond, far to the hazy south, I recognized the vague stripe of coast where the Vistula River emptied. Its grey waters were forcing us ever farther out to sea. Knowing the current, I calculated that it would be impossible for us to swim to shore safely.

But about 20 minutes later, the bow of a U-boat sliced to the surface. Within seconds the boat was fully exposed and gaining speed in the direction of the scattered black and yellow spots. The boat that had struck the fatal blow was about to make the second mistake. I stretched out of the water and waved both arms in a frantic attempt to signal her Captain to stop the engines. Fortunately, someone aboard understood. The engines were cut off and the boat floated slowly toward us. As she came to a full stop, a second U-boat surfaced nearby and drew cautiously closer. Our men swam to the two metal islands and were hoisted aboard, coughing, puffing, and sneezing. Helping hands put blankets around their shoulders.

I climbed aboard the ship that had sent ours to the bottom. Siegmann accepted the Captain's apology, but his anger mounted as the culprit explained that he had not even realized his boat had hit a submerged object.

Our men fell in line on the aft deck for a roll call. I counted 37 heads, including some of our guests, who had made an excellent showing. Calculating that 22 men had to be with Friedrich on the other boat, I established contact by lamp and signaled, "Please report your final count."

"Twenty men taken aboard," was the Chief's reply.

"Does that include you also?"

"That does include me," he flashed back.

"Please count again. You are supposed to be twenty-two."

"Sorry, cannot make it twenty-two since we are only twenty."

We were missing two men. I was positive I had not left them aboard *U-612*.

Siegmann became ever more furious. "That's just about what we need. Look here, Exec, didn't you tell me that you were the last one to leave the boat?"

"Yes I did, and I made damn sure that I got all the boys out. There is not a soul in there," I pointed helplessly at the spot where our boat had been an hour before. But our search revealed no men in the sea, only two drifting lifejackets. They were the last items we fished from the Bay as we sailed homeward—aboard the boat that had put us in this miserable predicament. Her navigational fix had been incorrect at the moment of collision. Running submerged, her Captain had miscalculated or overlooked the strong current of the discharging Vistula River, and had continued blindly on his course without precautionary use of his sound gear or periscope. Human error had thus destroyed two lives and a costly submarine.

The sinking of *U-612* affected our lives profoundly. Just how profoundly became obvious the next morning when Siegmann held our roll call in the compound yard instead of aboard our boat: we were a highly trained crew with no ship to sail. The Captain announced an officers' meeting in his quarters to discuss our uncertain future. Everyone was depressed. We assumed that we would be assigned as a company to a new U-boat, but the process of readying a new boat would set us back many months. Meanwhile, the fattest convoys would be raided by others and we would be left with the remnants, if we were not too late altogether. There had to be a quicker solution. So we explored the possibility of raising *U-612* from a depth of 48 meters.

The idea of salvaging our boat quickly took on concrete form, and Siegmann submitted his detailed plan to the High Command. Two days later we received the answer: raise *U-612*. Without any delay we swung into action. I located a diving company with the required experience. Friedrich secured two large floating cranes. A tugboat with Friedrich, myself, and a diver aboard left harbor one day later. The weather was perfect for our ambitious enterprise. The two cranes arrived the same day over the grave of *U-612*. Positioning took up the better part of the following day. While Friedrich and I devoted our time to the salvage operation, Siegmann and Riedel took our crewmen to Danzig where they were billeted aboard an aged passenger ship of the Hamburg-America Line.

On the fifth day of the operation the diver finally managed to tie heavy cables around the hull. When the two cranes tried to lift the boat, they almost toppled under the load and the cables snapped. Replacements had to be shipped in from Danzig. The work was in its seventh day when the diver once again secured the steel loops. One of the cranes succeeded in lifting the bow of our boat one meter off the bottom. Having eliminated the suction effect, the second crane then heaved the boat's flooded stern out of the sand. That was as far as she could be raised. The two cranes weighed anchor and crept slowly toward Danzig. After traveling two days to cover 16 miles, they dragged *U-612* through the shallow harbor until her conning tower appeared above surface. Another day was spent patching up the hole in the hull from the outside. On the 12th day, a hose was finally lowered through the tower hatch and a tug began to pump the oily water out of the boat. The water level sank rapidly, revealing instruments and equipment. After three hours the entire midsection was sucked empty. Curious as I was, I hurried down the aluminum ladder. The control room was a shambles. Fine sand, mixed with black oil and grease and algae, covered all parts. Then I made a crushing discovery: also flooded was the compartment containing the radio room, the officers' and warrant officers' quarters, as well as the forward batteries. In the excitement of the accident, we had forgotten to close the voice tube leading from the conning tower into the radio room. While the boat lay on the bottom, water had flowed in through the narrow pipe and ruined the entire section.

I inspected *U-612* fully the next morning, after she had been pumped out completely and towed into dry dock. The hole in the hull was as big as a bucket. The only section that had not been flooded was the forward torpedo room; its bulkhead had held absolutely tight. The two missing men were not found aboard. An inspection by a commission disclosed that the boat would take from eight to12 months to repair. My hope for an early return to the battle was shattered.

For two days we were kept in suspense. Then Headquarters instructed us to commission a new boat, *U-230,* which was nearing completion in a shipyard in Kiel. The crew was to have an extended leave before we assumed our new duties.

The sinking of *U-612* with the loss of two lives was not our only calamity. During the salvage operation it was discovered that Messner, our cook, had hoarded a large quantity of coffee, tea, and butter. Interrogated by Riedel, Messner confessed that he had sold similar lots on the black market. Crew members said that the cook's dealings had been going on since his arrival aboard; it was inexplicable to me that no one had reported his activity before. In any event, Messner had to be brought to trial. He had a hearing and was convicted.

But on the day of sentencing, the cook disappeared. I vainly searched his quarters for a clue to his whereabouts. While I was there, two seamen approached with angry faces, claiming Messner had stolen a camera from one and the other's best uniform. A quick check of the officers' luggage revealed that the cook had escaped with the navigator's Luger. Before issuing an alarm,

Navy Luger

I let one day and one night pass, to give Messner a chance to return. However, he stayed away and the matter became a case of desertion. Learning that Messner was noted for his collection of women, I assembled a list of addresses where he might have tried to hide. I decided hopefully to apprehend Messner myself and save him a court-martial, which could have cost him several years behind bars. Requisitioning a chauffeur-driven car, I loaded two of my men into the rear seats and set out on a private manhunt.

I found the first address in a suburb of Danzig. A decent neighborhood. The girl said that the cook had not been there for weeks. We then drove to a house on the shore road to Zoppott. The mother of another "fiancée" opened the door hesitantly. I was on the right trail, but had come too late: the cook had slept there the previous night, then had disappeared—for home, so he had said. Next we raced to Gotenhafen, where another female was known to be awaiting Messner's hand in holy matrimony. I found the girl but not the fugitive. The last address was a shack surrounded by pines on the Hela Peninsula, a perfect place to hide. The shack proved to be empty. Thoroughly frustrated, we returned to the liner late at night.

Early next morning, the fourth day after Messner's desertion, I received a telephone call from the Danzig police saying that a sailor had burglarized a home in a suburb. I was convinced that this was my man. The case was now out of my hands; the cook had gone too far. The same afternoon, I was informed by the Zoppott police that a seaman fitting Messner's description had been seen leaving the scene of a robbery in a grocery store. I stayed awake until late that night expecting further developments, but no new reports came in.

Two days later, the chapter Messner was finally closed. The military police called from Zoppott and informed me that Messner had been found lying in a ditch on the road to Danzig. He had tried to take his own life with the Luger, but had succeeded only in blinding himself for life. If I were interested in questioning the suspect, I would find him in the Municipal Hospital.

The Captain suggested that I interrogate Messner while he was still in shock. I left at once for Zoppott. The day was hot and humid, and storm clouds were thick when I arrived. Lightning flashed across the Bay; it was followed by rolling thunder as I entered the hospital. The smell of disinfectants and ether, the silent movements of interns in white, the nurse's wordless understanding of the reason for my coming, the lightning and thunder and sticky humidity—all these made me believe that I myself was embarking on the last leg of life's journey. The nurse guided me upstairs to the cook's room. The window was open and the stiff wind blew the curtains into balloons. The sound of the storm echoed from the walls of the white room. Messner lay in the thin linen like a dead man, stretched out, completely apathetic. He was fully conscious. His blind eyes were bloodshot, his lids swollen. A small white bandage was wrapped around his head covering a tiny hole in each of his temples. I felt a sinking pity for the man who had the nerve to attempt suicide but not the courage to stand up for his mistakes.

While I was sitting next to him, waiting for him to speak, the raging storm seemed to send lightning and thunder into the room. The booms struck in relentless repetition, as if a convoy battle were being fought out on land. For a long time Messner remained silent. I saw his useless eyeballs move behind the swollen lids. I saw tears coming through the slits slowly, only a few and very small at first. But then he could not hold back his sorrow any longer, and the mistaken warrior cried. His tears dissolved the man into a boy.

Lightning and thunder reached their peak while the boy in the pillows cried for forgiveness and his mother. I was unable to help the cook, and from now on he would be unable to help himself. Never again would he see the flash of lightning, the clouds accumulate, the rains come down, the sun rise or set; he would never again see his mother or a girl smile at him.

When the thunderstorm had moved away, I asked the doctor on duty for a stenographer. She sat down at the foot of the white bed, her pad on her knees, bewildered and shy. Messner could not see her, not her bleached hair nor her beautiful blue eyes. He answered my questions willingly. At the end of my interrogation, he blurted out, "Sir, I am not a criminal, I did not want to steal."

"Why, then, did you have to take all the food and sell it on the black market? Why did you steal you friend's camera, the uniform? Worse, why did you break into the house and the store?"

"Sir, you won't believe it, but it's the truth—I wanted to be caught. I thought it was the only way to escape the war. I don't like this war, Exec."

"What you say doesn't make any sense, Messner," I said, astounded. "Why, then, did you run away from sentencing? And why did you steal again afterward?"

"My buddies are lying, sir. They traded the camera and the uniform for coffee, chocolate, and cigarettes. And the food I took in Danzig and Zoppott, believe me sir, I did it only because I was hungry."

"So, why did you want to kill yourself? I cannot understand your action, Messner."

"I guess I was confused. I didn't want to steal or kill myself. I lost my head. I am finished."

"You're right. Nobody can help you now. You better pray for your soul."

"Sir, I don't pray—not even now. I don't believe in God. I believe in communism. My Father was a Communist and he was killed for his belief during the Spartakus revolution. That's why I condemn this war, Exec, it's no good."

I looked at him with amazement. I was shocked by this kind of talk and was sure that my man had lost his mind. Since I had enough testimony, I told the girl not to include his last statements and send the typewritten copy to the liner. I did not wish to make Messner's life more miserable than it already was. I closed the window, drew the curtains. I was convinced that the man had indeed lost his senses.

Days of activity followed the incident. I wound up my administrative work, and the Captain sent the rest of the crew on furlough. We were to meet again in Kiel. By then summer would be over and the disaster a thing of the past.

Before my departure, tragedy struck again. On September 2, a distress call reached land: late that evening, U-222, on a training mission, had been rammed on surface by another U-boat. With the exception of three men, who had been on the bridge at the moment of impact, the entire ship's company had gone down with the boat to the bottom of the Bay of Danzig. When I heard the bad news it was close to midnight. I boarded the tug that had helped to salvage U-612 and rushed to the spot where U-222 had sunk. Other boats were scanning the black surface with searchlights. Immediate help was out of the question. U-222 lay 93 meters below the surface. The men had to help themselves, provided they were still alive. The crews aboard several

U-boats, their sound gears tuned in, listened carefully for a faint sign of life from the sunken boat. All surface vessels near the scene lay with their engines stopped to make the silence complete. The leading rescue ship tried for hours to establish contact with our friends in the tomb. They never answered the calls.

I returned to Danzig convinced anew that we must have been under the special protection of the Fellow Upstairs to have escaped our floating coffin.

Four days later I became the last member of our crew to bid farewell to extravagant Zoppott where the traditional customs created the illusion of eternal peace. I boarded a train and started a long journey halfway across the Continent to the southern border of Germany. I had received the news that Trudy was to be married on the coming weekend and I planned to make an unannounced appearance.

A day later, I arrived in paradise. Lake Constance unfolded beyond the evergreens; its silvery waters mirrored the white peaks of the Alps which rose majestically into the azure southern sky. The train halted in Ueberlingen, a small medieval town where I had spent many years of my youth. It was so peaceful that I hesitated before stepping off the train; it was as if I would be contaminating the tranquility of the place with my warlike presence. As I walked into town, I recognized the old pine and chestnut trees that had stood there for centuries. I gazed at the ancient houses, the neat flowerboxes. I recognized the stores, the people. Everything was as it had been when I left town seven years before.

My sudden return, and my promotion to *Leutnant*, caused a commotion for an hour or so, then all attention focused on the bride. The next day the wedding took place in a small country chapel. The bridegroom gave his greatest performance in uniform. An anti-aircraft gunner who did most of his fighting in the orderly room, he was a safe risk for Father and Trudy, and stood a good chance to survive the war.

The blitz-wedding did not change my sister's life. Five days after the ceremony her husband had to return to duty. My parents departed from the Lake, taking Trudy with them. As they left, I gave them my promise to write more often, but I knew—and they knew—that there would not be much letter-writing.

I lingered on for two days more under the Alps and the blue satin sky. The air was rich with the scent of asters, roses, hay, and southern pines. The water was soft and warm and the swimming was excellent. I walked along the shore promenade, and when I passed the bench beside the old chestnut tree, I remembered sitting there with Marianne and watching a midsummer night's fireworks before the war; and it was as if the war had never happened. And when I stood at the old stone quay where I had fed the seagulls after school, I was—briefly—a boy again.

9

I arrived at the Tirpitz Pier in Kiel late in September of 1942. One year and six months had gone by since I had departed from the pier for my first war patrol aboard *U-557*. Things were not exactly the same. The long jetty where the U-boats moored had been screened against air surveillance. As I was told by one of the white-jacketed stewards aboard the old steamer, the Tommies now flew quite frequently over the Bay of Kiel. First a lone airplane would come by daylight to take photographs of the activities in port. Then a few bombers would come the next night and drop bombs and flares—"Christmas trees" we called them. I was pleased to hear that our anti-aircraft kept the planes high, and that the attacks had only a harassing effect. But the increased activity caused me no little concern for the safety of *U-230*. Should our new boat be damaged by a stray bomb, our long delay in reaching the front would be extended indefinitely.

One by one, our men came back from furlough. Three days after my arrival, I mustered the crew on the pier and found them eager to go to sea. But as it turned out, we were far from taking possession of our new boat! Siegmann told us that *U-230* would not be ready for another four or five weeks. We had to accommodate ourselves in an antiquated cruiser, the former *Hamburg,* which had been stripped to serve as quarters for "crews in waiting." Nonetheless, it was gratifying to be back in my daily routine of training and teaching our men.

Early in October I left for the Belgian seacoast to attend a course in electronics. Our boat was to be equipped with radar, which would enable us to locate the enemy at night and even in heavy fog long before we could spot him with our glasses. The device had been used for years on capital ships and had been instrumental in the sinking of the *Hood;* now it would revolutionize U-boat warfare, permitting us to circumvent cordons of escort destroyers and attack targets without seeing them. I returned from radar school excited by the potential of our fine new weapon.

Back in Kiel, I was promptly overtaken by my demanding love affair with *U-230*. Overseeing her completion, inspecting special installations, reading technical manuals, and keeping the crew in good trim consumed most of my time.

On October 24, we commissioned *U-230,* which had just been moved from the shipyard back to the Tirpitz Pier. Wearing our best uniforms, we stood in closed ranks on the aft deck, and the Commandant of the 5th U-boat Flotilla ordered the flag raised. It was the same flag that had flown from the ill-fated *U-612,* and we believed superstitiously that it would somehow extend the life of our new boat. The ceremony was followed by a rather meager dinner, which reflected our noticeably shrinking food supply in the fourth year of the war.

U-230 was received by her crew with gratitude; she restored to us our status as seamen. Eager to rejoin the great Atlantic battles, we plunged into a long, hard series of drills, tests, shakedown cruises, and battle maneuvers. On these short trips, we used our radar at every opportunity, detecting buoys as well as ships. The instrument was not yet perfected, however. Because its sensing apparatus was mounted rigidly in front of the conning tower, it would pick up targets only when they lay ahead of the boat, and when they moved out of the forward section, they disappeared from our oscillograph. Thus, if we wished to scan the horizon, we had to sail in a full circle—a procedure that was time consuming at best and would be impossible under battle conditions.

It was early in November when *U-230* left for the shooting grounds in the eastern Baltic. Not far from the spot where we had lost *U-612*, we released a few dozen torpedoes to check the new firing equipment and polish up our routine. Crash dives and simulated attacks alternated with exercising on the 8.8 cm. gun and the new anti-aircraft automatics, with trim and deep dives in exhaustive repetition. The climactic test of this shakedown period was a week-long war at sea. A mock convoy of some 20 cargo ships and several escorts was sent to hide in the northern Baltic, and a Luftwaffe squadron was held in readiness to fly anti-submarine missions. One bitter cold day in December, *U-230*, along with other U-boats assembled in Pillau harbor, crept through the ice floes and headed north to find and "destroy" the convoy. As *U-230* reached the open sea, a Siberian wind blew frozen spray against her superstructure, coating it with heavy ice. Sixteen hours later, we located the convoy in the dark and "attacked" at once. Our assaults continued day and night. The captain tried every attack pattern; I fired my dummy torpedoes from every angle and decimated the convoy many times. Constant "air attacks" conditioned our watches to stay on guard against death from the sky. The war games ended five days before Christmas, when *U-230* sailed around Kiel Lightship, through the narrow waterway cut by icebreakers, and came to rest at the Tirpitz Pier. Boat and crew had performed with high efficiency and were declared fit for her first patrol, but we still had not reached the end of our exasperating delays.

Early on the day before Christmas, with the thermometer reading 17 degrees below zero centigrade, I transferred the boat into the shipyard to be equipped with an extension to her bridge and a second deck for an additional anti-aircraft gun. These and other adjustments were finished on New Year's Eve, and departure on our first patrol was set for January 9, 1943. But on January 8, a serious leak was discovered aboard the boat, and our sailing was rescheduled for the following Monday.

These last two weeks of waiting put a strain on us all. The weather was frigid and blustery, excellent for U-boat operations but miserable for marking time in our drab, depressing quarters aboard the stripped-down ocean liner. Our meals were poor and skimpy even on Christmas Day, which would have passed without notice but for the parcels from home. We listened eagerly but impatiently to radio broadcasts of our Armed Forces communiqués. It did not help our disposition to learn that Rommel's Afrika Korps had suffered a setback at El Alamein and was forced to retreat, or that the Russians and the Russian winter were proving formidable adversaries on the eastern front. But the temporary difficulties of our conquering armies were easier to accept than the glowing accounts of U-boat triumphs in which we did not share. According to year-end reports, U-boat attacks had cost the Allies more than 6 million tons of shipping in 1942, including at least 500,000 tons each month from July through October, and 117 ships totaling some 600,000 tons in November alone. The hunger blockade that the U-boats had established around England seemed to be near its ultimate objective. The ghost of starvation and of a lost war was marching across the United Kingdom and knocking at the door of No. 10 Downing Street.

The U-boats' phenomenal record had been compiled despite the steady improvement of Allied air surveillance over the crucial defense area between Scotland and Greenland, and also over the Bay of Biscay. The enemy had developed a new kind of radar which permitted bombers to detect a surfaced U-boat even in heavy seas. But to counter this threat, our boats were equipped with an ingenious device, the Metox, that intercepted radar waves, warning us of an imminent attack and giving us time to crash-dive before the planes zeroed in on us.

Allied air activity had also increased annoyingly overland. Hamburg, Duesseldorf, and other cities were subjected repeatedly to harassing raids. We experienced a minor attack in Kiel, and I went out of my way to get caught in a more serious one in Berlin.

After *U-230* was found to have sprung a leak on January 8, Siegmann took the opportunity and left for Hamburg to see his wife and children for the last time before sailing. I decided to use this latest delay to make a quick trip to the Capital to see Marianne. We were reunited on Saturday night. It was then that I realized that the solid ribbon of our friendship was stronger than my volatile affairs in port.

The bombers appeared while we were having Sunday lunch in the Café Wien on Kurfuerstendamm. With the air-raid sirens screaming and Marianne tugging my arm, I paid for our unfinished meal and ran for shelter in the nearby U-bahn station. We were working our way down into the subway through the jostling throngs when the first distant explosions shook the foundation walls. Marianne led me through the crowd filling the platforms. Women sat on suitcases or on cartons containing their valuables. Others stood in groups holding bags and rucksacks. Old men and women lined the rear walls or rested on small folding chairs. Children played unconcerned, oblivious to the tremors and thunder of bomb hits and the staccato bellowing of anti-aircraft guns. Whatever prompted the British to fly on Sunday and disturb the afternoon strollers and make war on civilians—their raid only strengthened my desire to meet them in open battle at sea.

The attack lasted a little over an hour. When we reached the surface, the streets were littered with mortar, glass, bricks, and debris. The air was filled with the stench of cordite and smoldering fires. The blue sky was distorted by dirty black and gray clouds rising and falling over the tortured city. Some distance away

I heard the bells of fire brigades and the long sighs of police-car horns.

My train to Kiel was scheduled to leave from Stettiner Station at 1730, but the raiders had destroyed the tracks in a northern suburb. I stood helpless in the rubble of crumbled façades and broken glass from the roof of the station house. *U-230* would not be able to leave on patrol because her Executive Officer had valued love more than duty. I investigated the possibility of boarding a train to Hamburg; that route was still open and it promised a roundabout way out of the trap. I was told that the train would leave at 2000, six hours late.

Farewell was not a heart-rending ceremony. Marianne was a good girl and had long been accustomed to my brief appearances. We promised each other that we would be careful and that we would preserve our love. As the train left the darkened station I heard the air-raid sirens wailing again.

At 2030 the following evening I finally reached Kiel, and 40 minutes later I knocked at my Captain's door. He had heard of the air raid, and before I could make an excuse he said with relief, "You could have been killed in Berlin, you would have done better staying here."

I too was relieved, for it seemed that I was not responsible for delaying our departure. I asked, "When are we sailing, sir?"

"A few minor adjustments must be made. It should take another day or so to put our boat in combat order. I want to leave port Wednesday after lunch. I expect you to have boat and crew ready by then."

We sailed from Kiel at 1400. The farewell party had been brief, and the traditional last dinner was a mere shadow of the Luccullan meals that had been served on such occasions in the past. A fierce snowstorm had prevented the band from playing at the pier. But the crew did not care. Nothing mattered but that we were sailing. We were convinced that victory was only months away and that we had to hurry to sink our share of enemy vessels.

U-230 fought strenuously with the winter storm. Strong gusts drove snow and hail into our faces. Short, hard waves hit the superstructure and the spray froze in midair. Couse was due north. Visibility was zero; we used our radar to "feel" our way through the heavy storm. The Danish Sea was deserted, for surface vessels seldom risked traveling in these difficult waters during a blinding blizzard. *U-230* picked her way through the narrow passages between the many islands, proceeding cautiously from buoy to buoy.

The snowfall ceased around 0400, and by daybreak we were on our way toward Norway at high speed. We crossed the Skagerrak on surface, sailed around the heel of Norway, and slipped into Hardangerfjord with its grandiose, snow-covered peaks. The scenery was spectacular all the way through Bjornefjord and into the harbor of Bergen. We remained in port for a little over a day, made some minor repairs, filled the tanks and bilges with diesel fuel, supplemented our food supply with greens and four barrels of fresh eggs. *U-230* was now equipped for a trip that could have easily carried her to the United States and back to France.

The sun was shining the day we sailed, but untamed winds swept through the fjord at 60 miles an hour. As we approached the open sea, I saw it rising like a giant wall in front of the fjord. I secured the antenna of our new radar detection gear, placing it behind the superstructure of the bridge, and had a seaman rotate it continually. The antenna was a bulky wooden cross with cables across its top. We called it the Biscay Cross because it was first used by our boats in the bay of that name.

The moment we left Bergenfjord astern, the ocean hit us with shattering impact. The only thing that suffered damage was the Biscay Cross. I lowered the broken wooden mess into the conning tower and ordered it repaired in a hurry. For the hours we were without a warning device we could be detected by an enemy using his radar before we could see him. Fortunately, visibility was excellent and the watch could concentrate on scanning the sky.

Biscay Cross

U-230 followed a northwesterly track toward the strait between the Shetland Islands and the Faeroe Group. We assumed that the British had been alerted to our approach: a U-boat sailing could not be kept secret in hostile Norway. However, the first day of our patrol ended without anyone spotting a single plane. Darkness descended upon the rough sea, and the Biscay Cross, again operable, became a powerful eye in the sky as *U-230* drove ever deeper into enemy waters.

At 0220, the operator on the radar detection gear indicated a contact. The gear sounded the alarm by emitting a beeping tone. The radio man came alive, "Contact, volume two, getting louder fast . . ."

Siegmann leaped from his bunk, ran through the round hatch into the control room, and hollered up to the bridge, "Down with the cross! Alarrrmmm!"

The engines went into high gear; the cross came falling into the control room, and one by one, the watch fell on top of it, smashing it to pieces. The boat dipped her bow. After 20 seconds, she was submerged. Within thirty seconds, the depth gauge needle crept to 40 meters, but the boat's stern still hung close to the surface. At 50 seconds, the hum and whine of the electric motors was drowned out by four hard explosions astern. Four times *U-230* was shaken by violent concussions. Her stern was lifted to the surface, tilting her bow downward at a severe angle. Then she catapulted into the depths, flinging everyone to the deck plates and throwing those with slow reflexes through the hull against the next bulkhead.

Friedrich stopped the boat's rapid fall at 125 meters. The crew was shaken; these were the first bombs for most of the men. But *U-230* had remained tight and withstood the first test. At 0430 we surfaced. The empty sea glittered peacefully in the moonlight. Our Biscay Cross had again been repaired. One of the men on watch rotated the fragile instrument while the operator down in the hull listened with apprehension.

We crash-dived once more that night and four times the following day. Each time the aircraft presented us with a bouquet of bombs. We had developed a healthy respect for the enemy above and kept scanning the sky most of the time. Between the air attacks, we passed between the island groups, putting the unfriendly area quickly behind.

As we pushed through heavy seas toward our assigned position 600 miles east of Newfoundland, conditions worsened rapidly aboard *U-230*. Water that poured in through the open hatch sloshed around our feet, and the high humidity within the hull caused food to rot, the skin to turn flabby, and our charts to dissolve. The smell was brutal. The extra fuel we carried in our bilges sent out a penetrating stench; our clothes reeked of it and our food took on the taste of oil and grease. The perpetual rocking and swaying of the boat was too much for those unaccustomed to the Atlantic or unequipped with cast-iron stomachs; most of the men lost their appetite and often more than that. This left only a small group of indestructibles to eat up the four barrels of eggs before they turned bad. To assist in the consumption, I ate eggs all day in all styles: raw before I climbed to the bridge to mount my watch, scrambled when I was relieved from duty, poached or turned over for lunch, sunny-side up for dinner, and soft-boiled whenever I felt like having another.

We were now battling our way through the February storms, the severest of the winter. The sea boiled and foamed and leaped continually under the lash of gales that chased one another across the Atlantic from west to east. *U-230* struggled through gurgling whirlpools, up and down mountainous seas; she was pitched into the air by one towering wave and caught by another and buried under tons of water by still another. The cruel winds whipped across the wild surface at speeds up to 150 miles an hour, whistling in the highest treble and snarling in the lowest bass. When we were on watch, the wind punished us with driving snow, sleet, hail, and frozen spray. It beat against our rubber diver's suits, cut our faces like a razor, and threatened to tear away our eye masks; only the steel belts around our waists secured us to boat and life. Below, inside the bobbing steel cockleshell, the boat's violent up-and-down motion drove us to the floor-plates and hurled us straight up and threw us around like puppets. And yet we managed to survive the furious wind and water, and to arrive in our designated square in one piece.

The war at sea had increased greatly in scale since I last took part in it. Our U-boats no longer operated loosely or in small wolf-packs of three or four. Instead, we now patrolled the North Atlantic in groups of 20 to 40, covering vast areas with mathematical precision under close coordination by Admiral U-boats. Approximately 100 U-boats of a contingent of about 250 on active duty now lurked in ambush in all parts of the seven seas. In our large group, *U-230* was on advanced patrol in the extreme north; and twice within ten days we were moved on orders from Headquarters to locate a reported convoy. Curtains of sleet and snow limited our vision to one mile at most, and our chances of detecting a convoy shrank to a bare minimum. Nevertheless, luck was with us.

I had just been relieved from watch, and was pouring liters of salt water from my diver's suit, when the Captain stuck his head into the control room. His ruddy face was framed in a three-weeks' growth of red beard, and his white teeth gleamed as he called, "Let's have some action, Exec, one of our boats reports sighting the convoy. Both engines emergency ahead."

The news traveled swiftly through the hull. I hung up my wet underclothes in the aft torpedo room, walked naked through the tumbling boat to my berth, slipped into fresh clothes, then joined the small conference in the Captain's nook. We bent over a mildewed chart on which Prager had marked the convoy's reported position; and despite the rocking and listing we managed to plot our best approach.

As the hammering diesels turned the shafts in high revolutions, and as the boat careened over the giant waves, the torpedo gang serviced their weapons, the machinists oiled their engines, and the radio men decoded a string of messages—all of them performing well even though most of the crew was experiencing the magic of pursuit for the first time. The wind came from astern and blew the men on the bridge against the superstructure like wet leaves against a wall. Mighty waves lifted and pressed our boat forward. Only when the evening descended did the sea lose some of its violence; but as soon as the new day broke, the raging storm reached a new high and the waves rose into the sky. At the end of the second day of the hunt, we drew close to the convoy and braced ourselves for the furious encounter.

2138: The first detonation of a torpedo released our tensions. Now the competition for tonnage began.

2143: Another explosion, a flash. Flames divulged the convoy's position. We corrected our course and stormed ahead, northward, on parallel course with the waves. Visibility was close to zero in the trough between breakers: the flames were swallowed up by the huge waves.

"Flood tubes one to five, prepare for firing!" I screamed, anxious to shoot and fearful that my order would be lost in the wind.

2215: Two destroyers entered our glasses, zigzagging in the port forward section. While U-230 with her low silhouette remained hidden in the watery mountain range, the escorts presented their high black profiles in shameless arrogance. Their erratic movement forced us to change course several times. We finally turned to port to break through the cordon, cutting into the onslaught of the waves, riding more below than above the sea.

Seventy minutes passed in relentless pursuit, with our boat driving through snow squalls, darkness, and a lashing sea. Suddenly three escorts appeared on port. With a quick move to starboard, U-230 dipped into the trough of a wave; we escaped unseen, leaving them 600 meters astern. Five minutes later we turned again to the north. Then . . .

A fire column dead ahead. In the moment of the flash, we spotted the armada. Soon I had a string of shadows in my glasses. Five minutes more and they had grown to giant cargo ships. Two destroyers zigzagged on starboard 90, one escort on port. We had smashed into the starboard column of the convoy. The concentration of enemy forces was enormous. A breakthrough into the heart of the convoy was now said to be an impossible task. But things had not changed that much.

The violent rocking and listing made it difficult for me to aim with the TBT and shoot with accuracy, so I decided to apply two fan shots. I screamed to the Captain, "Sir, I take the four coffers port ahead!"

Siegmann understood, changed course slightly, and U-230 surged into attack position flanking a column of shadowy phantoms. At my order to fire, the boat shuddered four times. Time was 2320.

Four torpedoes fanned out. The Captain swung the boat around to let me shoot once more, but U-230 smashed into the soaring sea, denying me any further action. A fireball, a hit! A second lightning! A third. The three huge blasts sent fountains of fire and sparks into the sky. Then the flames collapsed and the three freighters burned quietly with their derricks grotesquely pointing into the night. The convoy lobbed distress signals. Star shells rose and fell, but the storm carried the fireworks away like sheets of burning fabric. Parachute flares unfolded, but were hurled into the water. Darkness soon covered the battlefield. Far astern, the three stricken vessels slipped slowly beneath the surface.

There was another explosion, somewhere in the northeast. Other U-boats had slashed into the convoy, cutting the escort forces in two. Walls of water and fire erupted. While the battle raged, we separated from it to reload our tubes. The men below began their toughest job, heaving the torpedoes on trolleys and chains into the empty tubes. To make their work easier, the Captain changed course to east, running ahead of wind and sea.

Then we spotted an escort, a black silhouette in violent motion. Our eastward course was a fairly easy one compared with the destroyer's westward track. As she ran against the sea, her bow dipped into mountainous waves, scooping up pools of water. The towering breakers smashed against her superstructure, making her list so dangerously that her guns touched the ocean's surface. I had the distinct feeling that I was safer aboard a submarine, that I would not change to a surface vessel for any price. With the winds now blowing at hurricane force, our crew labored and sweated, charging the tubes, keeping the engines running, and maintaining the boat's buoyancy.

By the time that our tubes were reloaded, we had lost the convoy. By daybreak, we searched through skyhigh seas. *U-230* climbed the peaks with terrible effort, careened on their crests, then blustered down the slopes and buried herself in the trough of the waves. Those hours of precarious existence on the bridge offered us moments of fierce beauty. When the boat topped a prodigious wave, we could briefly see across the Alpine mountain range of water, down into deep valleys 50 or 60 meters below. And when the boat tumbled into the depths, burying herself in a foaming

whirlpool, it seemed that the waves met above us,
blotting out the sky. And when the walls of water
surged to 70 meters high, their crests collapsed and
cascaded down upon us forcing us on the bridge to ride
for long seconds far below surface, pressed to the deck
by towering columns of 30 and 40 meters of ocean. By
0900, the waves were so monumental that our search
for the convoy became a mockery. The Captain's order to dive was greeted with satisfaction and soon we
floated at 140 meters, still gently heaved by the raging
sea.

Sometime in the afternoon, as I lay dozing in my
bunk, I heard a voice speaking as if from another
world, saying, "Propeller sound, bearing three five." It
was the soundman, and he had whispered only.

That had to be the convoy, freighters or escorts.
Siegmann ordered the Chief to bring the boat up to
periscope depth. Once again I donned my diver's
gear and buttoned it up to my chin. As soon as *U-230*
rose to about 60 meters, a tremendous upsurge hurled
her out of the water like a bouncing ball. The Captain
and I leaped to the bridge seconds later. We glanced
about as we fastened our cables, then at each other in
shock. We had surfaced amidst the convoy!

There, no more than 400 meters to the east, a damaged destroyer fought pitiably for survival under hurricane winds. Even closer, a cargo ship with a damaged bridge swayed helplessly. Six other vessels, their
screws exposed and turning slowly as they rode on top
of long cliff-like waves, were lined up in perfect position for the kill. Everywhere there were ships, most of
them in distress. Gigantic water walls, mercilessly
pounding against their hulls and superstructures,
cracked their railings like straw; battered their lifeboats and cut them off their davits; pinched funnels,
bent masts and booms, punctured hulls, split decks,
ripped loading hatches, tore cargo off decks and tossed
it overboard. Breaker after breaker smashed the vessels' rudders, bent their shafts, ruptured their spines.
They needed no torpedoes to sink them.

The crippled armada, driven from west to east
across the hurricane-whipped surface, was incapable

of controlling its course. Our boat, surrounded by armored ships with a destroyer in shooting range, was herself dancing so wildly on the waves that she was in no danger of being attacked by the enemy. I imagined the horror that our appearance had caused among the crewmen of the convoy; they were white with fear of being torpedoed ship by ship without being able to defend themselves or to escape. I enjoyed the thought and the moment fully. However, *U-230* could not attack either, for torpedoes released into the savage sea would never have reached their target. There was only one thing we could do; we dived away into the raging floods to ride out the hurricane in quiet depths.

Twenty hours later, a signal from Headquarters directed all U-boats to break off operations against that battered convoy and to report their positions. We were also informed that other boats had reported the sinking of six vessels out of the same armada. There had been 12 U-boats attacking steadily for three nights and days until the operation was halted by the weather.

U-230 broke her radio silence, signaling: SUNK THREE VESSELS 16,000 TONS. REQUEST NEW ORDERS.

However, three U-boats failed to make contact with Headquarters. The loss of *U-187*, *U-609*, and *U-624* was a high price to pay for our victory.

Through the rest of February we continued to patrol our storm-swept hunting grounds. Allied losses for the month were at least 60 ships totaling more than 350,000 grossweight tons—a toll considerably greater than in any previous February. The year 1943 promised us the best hunting ever; the only trouble was that the convoys were too few and far between to suit our ambitions.

Shipboard routine had replaced the excitement of the chase and the battle. And it was a maddening routine. The small ship rolled and slapped, listed and shuddered endlessly. Utensils, spare parts, tools, and conserves showered down on us continually; porcelain cups and dishes shattered on the deck-plates and in the bilges as we ate our meals directly out of cans. The

men, penned up together in the rocking, sweating
drum, took the motion and the monotony with stoicism. Occasionally, someone's temper flared, but
spirits remained high. We were all patient veterans.
Everyone aboard looked alike, smelled alike, had
adopted the same phrases and curses. We had learned
to live together in a narrow tube no longer than two
railroad cars. We tolerated each other's faults and became experts on each other's habits—how everyone
laughed and snarled, talked and snored, sipped his coffee and caressed his beard. The pressure mounted
with the passage of each uneventful day, but it could
be relieved in an instant by the sight of a fat convoy.

One raw, foggy day in early March, the Captain
joined me on the bridge. "Tell me, Exec," he began,
"what's the matter with the English? Don't they go to
sea anymore?"

"I guess they have a pocketful of problems," I answered, keeping my glasses on a sweep of the horizon.
"Maybe they're reshuffling their forces, who knows?"

"Something has to happen soon, this idling can't go
on much longer." Siegmann was about to light a cigarette when a heavy breaker crashed against the superstructure, showering him and washing away his cigarette. He snarled, "Goddam, the Fellow Upstairs won't
even let me have a cigarette," and he left the bridge
to smoke in the conning tower.

"Convoy in AK 79, course east, nine knots!" Riedel
shouted.

Minutes later the Captain was back on the bridge
wrapped in heavy oil clothes. "Exec, I'll tell you what's
the matter with the Tommies. They don't send out any
small convoys lately. They wait until sixty or seventy
ships have accumulated in port before they chase them
out to sea. This convoy—it's reported to be 120 miles
to the south—has sixty-five vessels. Let's have them!
Both full ahead, right full rudder, new course one-
four-oh."

This day, March 8, a hunt began. The boat that had
made contact with the enemy sent beacon signals at
regular intervals. Snow squalls reduced visibility to
zero and forced us to sail blind at times. After 14

hazardous hours, we had made well over 150 miles and we were still racing southeast, searching, sniffing, probing.

In the dark at 1910, we brushed the convoy for the first time. Borchert, a keen-eyed man on my watch, spotted a destroyer. I leaped to the starboard aft quarter and saw a typical broadside behind a snow curtain. The ship was sailing on parallel course, and I assumed we had had her company for quite some time. We veered to port, pointed our stern at the shadow, and ran away. But we had been detected. The escort swung majestically around until she had us dead ahead. Siegmann raced up the engines and sent his boat into a snow drift ahead on port. We followed the movement of the squall and stayed hidden in the falling snow. When we noticed the odor of smoke and fuel oil, the Captain ordered the crew on battle stations.

At 2130, the sky cleared suddenly. Brilliant stars shone between scraps of clouds and the moon, emerging from behind the snow curtains, drenched the surface in silver. Not far away, a destroyer changed course in a normal screening pattern. As we escaped the shadow, I saw that the entire eastern horizon was studded with black spots. But the moon disappeared and the curtain went down in front of us. Two minutes later we spotted another escort on port as she emerged from a cloud bank. We raced to starboard into a white, fluffy wall.

2335: A double explosion ahead. We sped toward the blast. Thirty minutes later we veered to outmaneuver a destroyer on starboard. Then Siegmann swung his boat back in the direction of the explosion. However, the convoy seemed to have dissolved.

0240: Bold shadows ahead—cargo ships. I began attack procedures. Two, three minutes, and U-230 was in a perfect position. Suddenly a move by the columns. Soon the entire parade showed us its rear. From starboard ahead came a sweeper, forcing us to withdraw. After a daring run of two miles in hail and sleet, we almost hit the towering stern of a freighter. A hard rudder maneuver, a turn to starboard, a surge ahead alongside the ship, distance but 400 meters. I aimed and launched a torpedo.

The vessel split in front of her bridge. Then the convoy began signaling furiously. Star shells spurted into the clouds, flashed briefly across the sky, and were extinguished in the white sheets of sleet and snow. As the merchantman collapsed, we raced forward to launch another shot.

However, day dawned with sudden brightness, catching us between convoy and destroyer cordon. We criss-crossed the boiling sea, kept in contact with the escorts while playing hide-and-seek in snow squalls and inhaling the stinking exhaust from some 60 fuming funnels. We made seven or eight contacts with destroyers that day and dived briefly in the afternoon to sound out the convoy. At 2000 Headquarters ordered all U-boats to report their positions. By counting their replies, we learned that 18 wolves were biting into the flanks of the convoy.

2215: Low shadow on starboard. Destroyer, distance 1400 meters. Red light on top of mast. Probably rescuing survivors.

2240: Huge shadow port ahead. A smaller one, an escort, emerged from behind it, then crossed our path —and the merchantman disappeared. We pursued the frighter but encountered another destroyer instead. Siegmann shouted angrily, "How many of these tin cans can they have on this convoy?" We made an evasive move and passed the sweeper's wake unseen.

2310: Two silhouettes on port, high and bulky, one low on starboard. As Siegmann drove his boat into attack position, his voice trailed off in the wind, "Now it's your turn, Exec."

I aimed and bellowed, "Tubes one and three, fire!"

The doom of the ship was sealed at 2325. While the torpedoes streaked toward the target, *U-230* raced straight ahead. I lined up three shadows and prepared to release the rest of my torpedoes in a quick salvo. Before I could pull the lever, the first torpedoes exploded and sent a fire column up from the target. That was the end of the vessel—and the end of my shooting. Two destroyers had swung toward us. The Captain yelled, the boat described a sharp arc—and away we sped. We passed the dying freighter some 70 meters astern, putting her between us and the pursuing destroyers. But then the sea cleared—the vessel had sunk. *U-230* charged into the wind, cutting through the waves head on, then zigzagged to shake off the escorts. A quick move to starboard, and within minutes we slid behind a curtain of hail. Once again contact with the convoy was cut off. Midnight passed, no shadows. We searched for three hours in a northerly direction, then plowed to the east. Aside from a few contacts with sweepers, we detected no ships.

March 10. 0640: The Captain released the exhausted crew from battle stations and went below to take a nap. I remained on the bridge to finish my turn on watch. Green, dirty waves with long white streaks of foam rose and fell; they looked like marble. A thundering wind drove gray clouds low overhead; snow and hail came showering down upon us.

0710: I began to sniff. A distinct smell of smoke and burned fuel.

0713: The smell became more intense. We broke through a wall of clouds and saw six ships wallowing in a golden patch of sunlight.

"Captain to the bridge, crew on battle stations!" I yelled into the conning tower. Then came a shattering boom. The nearest vessel, a 10,000-ton cargo ship, exploded and began blowing herself to bits. The pressure wave hit us with such force that our lungs almost burst. Siegmann's head appeared in the hatch, but he ducked back into the tower as the gigantic fireworks sent chunks of steel hurtling through the air and tons of debris raining down. I took cover behind the bridge with the others on watch. Long seconds later, when I dared to peer over the rim of the bridge, I saw five vessels sluggishly riding the waves and there, 1,000 meters on starboard, two destroyers leaping toward us from behind a freighter. A third escort darted from astern. Desperately I shouted, "Clear the bridge, both emergency ahead—alarrrmmm!"

We had but one course—to dive to great depth and take the punishment meant for the U-boat that had done the shooting. But huge swells held our boat in an iron grip; though *U-230* struggled violently to disappear in the floods, surface tension held her as if in a sea of glue. All free hands stumbled into the forward torpedo room. Their additional weight slowly tilted the boat downward while the menacing cadence of the escorts' propellers drew closer fast. With maddening laziness, *U-230* churned into the depths. A series of eight depth charges whipped our boat wildly and sent her straight down. Friedrich managed to stop her fall at nearly 200 meters and leveled her off. *U-230* floated silently in a great, deep, evasive arc. As the convoy wandered eastward, Asdic impulses hit our hull piercingly, threateningly. Fifteen minutes after the first attack, a spread of 16 canisters exploded above the conning tower in a hellish concert. Under the impact, our steel groaned and wooden cabinets splintered. We changed course drastically to evade the next charge, but the enemy above was no novice. Another series of 24 cans splashed on the surface, floated down, then detonated just short of our stern. The third salvo shook us off the deck plates. Bearded faces turned toward the ceiling and bloodshot eyes searched fearfully for a break in the hull. The relay man at the aft bulkhead whispered, "Propeller packings leaking heavily."

The Chief tried in vain to trim the boat and level her keel. The leaks had filled the aft bilge and tilted the boat down at the stern. *U-230* floated downward at an ever-increasing angle, with slowly increasing speed. Depth charges exploded every 20 minutes sharp. Nine hours passed, and the escorts were still throwing their cans. The cold crept through the steel and made us shiver. Moisture condensed on the hull, pipes, and ducts, and dripped on us and drenched us to the skin. *U-230* tilted astern at a 30-degree angle, with stern and bow planes in rise position, and struggled desperately to halt her descent. She had fallen to 245 meters. Unless the pursuit stopped, permitting us to raise the boat, our destination was the ocean floor, 5,000 meters below our keel. But as the day came to an end, the three escorts turned away and sped after their convoy. We remained submerged for another two hours at a more comfortable depth, then surfaced.

I promised myself to find the U-boat Captain whose torpedo had brought the escorts down on us. Weeks later, I learned that it was Trojer, commander of *U-221*, who had sunk the ammunition carrier. However, I never had the opportunity to tell him how he had made us suffer. *U-221* failed to return from a later mission.

We cleared the foul air, drained the bilges, and charged our exhausted batteries. Then we informed Headquarters of our unreported triumph and chased into the night at high speed. In the early morning hours, Riedel decoded a vital message from the Lion. It said that in three days and nights of fighting, our group had sunk six Allied ships totaling over 50,000 tons. More important, the signal ordered us to break off our pursuit of Convoy SC 121 and to take position in a new patrol, formed to intercept another convoy which was expected from Halifax. From the various radiograms we intercepted, I concluded that something very special was in progress. At least 40 U-boats had been deployed throughout an 80,000 square-mile area which included the major convoy routes in the North Atlantic.

U-230 took up her position and cruised for three days in extremely heavy seas. On March 16, one of our boats crashed into Convoy SC 122 and reported contact. Promptly 40 U-boats received Headquarters' order: ALL U-BOATS PROCEED WITH MAXIMUM SPEED TOWARD CONVOY GRID SQUARE BD 14. OVER SIXTY SHIPS COURSE NORTHEAST NINE KNOTS.

We calculated that we could reach the enemy in 12 to 14 hours and raced with new vigor toward the new targets. Despite the enormous strain of battling blizzards and enemy for seven weeks, the crew's morale was at its peak. Somewhere in the east, where the night had already settled on the ocean, rocked the convoy, its officers and seamen constantly alert to the threat of being spotted, attacked, decimated, mutilated, killed. That threat grew with every mile and was the greatest in the center of the Atlantic. And that point was reached the following night.

Two hours after the sun had sunk into the water, the moon rose behind fast-moving clouds. Its pale yellow light was no help to us—in fact, it hindered our shooting at close range. As the night grew older, the violent winds abated slightly.

Borchert, our man with the magic eyes, saw the shadow first: "Destroyer heading north, distance four thousand."

"Keep her covered, son, tell me when she turns," said Siegmann quietly without leaving his quarters. We had no way of knowing if we had been detected: our Biscay Cross had long since been stored away because it was of no use during attack or in the center of the Atlantic where no enemy aircraft had yet appeared. Soon the shadowy escort dropped out of sight. Time was 2130. For the next two hours we cut through a wild night of howling winds and brief snow squalls. We beat the sea to spray and foam, creating a large whirlpool aft of our half-sunken conning tower. The white water would divulge our presence to any enemy in close proximity.

2240: It was again Borchert who spotted the convoy: "Shadows on port, distance 6,500. It's the whole herd!"

The shadows, dots the size of bugs, moved along the indistinct moonlit horizon. Long rolling waves hid the ghostly parade periodically. We approached the fleet from the southwest, trying to cut into its starboard column. Soon we reached a point 4,000 meters south of the last row of ships and rode parallel to them, ahead of wind and sea, to establish all target values.

2330: The first destroyer of the inner cordon shot out of obscurity. For a few minutes she cruised at high speed between us and the convoy; then she turned 120 degrees, sped right into our wake, changed course again and closed in fast on the last column of slow-moving targets. Racing along their southern side, U-230 advanced far enough for Siegmann to swing into attack position. But as soon as we turned, the boat began to rock hard, causing our treacherous white wake to spread wider and glisten in the moonlight like a thick torch. A shadow separated itself from the black background and the silhouette of a destroyer loomed up sharply. She was not alone; a second escort emerged from behind her. We turned and chased away into the valleys of the long waves, saw the escorts dash south, kept them covered for 60 seconds, then swung around again and resumed our assault.

Though *U-230* was continually shaken by hard breakers, she moved inexorably into firing position. Far on port, three sweepers patrolled rigorously, while two escorts swept the surface astern. Ahead of us steamed one of the largest convoys ever to sail the Atlantic. Shadow after shadow crawled through the lenses of my TBT, and their masts stuck up along the horizon like a heavy picket fence.

"Destroyers astern, closing in fast," our first mate muttered.

Without using my binoculars I saw the monsters darting at us. White foam leaped from their foredecks and bridges. *U-230* made no evasive move; we had to fire at the shadows first.

"Exec, select your targets!" Siegmann howled into the storm.

"Tubes one to five, stand by!" I shouted into the hatch. "Ready ... ready ..."

"What are the fellows astern doing?" That was the Captain again.

Before the mate could answer, I thumped him in his ribs, told him to keep quiet and reported, "Holding steady." It was not the truth; the escorts were gaining. I corrected my values, then lined up the shadows before our bow for execution. One by one they wandered through the cross hair of the TBT, I aimed carefully at the fattest targets.

"Time is up, Exec, shoot!" cried the Captain.

I pulled the lever five times. Immediately, Siegmann turned his boat toward the tail of the convoy to shake off the pursuing destroyers. We smashed head on through the giant waves, a feat the escorts could not duplicate. Then we heard the terrific rumble of three hard explosions. Blinding flashes revealed innumerable cargo ships, destroyers, and trawlers. Three of the vessels careened out of file, floating torches. The armada made a sudden turn to port, firing its distress flares into the sky. *U-230* thrust her sharp bow west-ward and raced into the black wall of another winter storm. Confusion, excitement, and the fireworks sub-sided. Silence followed. Two of the stricken vessels broke apart in the heavy sea. The third victim had drifted out of sight; we never saw her sink. The convoy disappeared in the stormy vastness of the ocean.

U-230, barren of torpedoes, retreated from the battlefield. Throughout the night, we observed more flashes and heard the bellowing of more detonating torpedoes. When the morning sun rose, dispelling the fog and sending red and gold clouds into the light blue sky, when the snow banks melted over the steaming and chaotic sea—the Allies had lost 14 ships—over 90,000 tons. Six more vessels were drifting damaged in the choppy ocean.

U-230, low in fuel and short on food, started on her way to port. We transmitted a summary message to Headquarters: SUNK SEVEN FREIGHTERS 35,000 TONS. TWO MORE DAMAGED. SET FOR BASE.

As we proceeded southeast through the blizzards, the battle with Convoy SC 122 went on with dramatic fury. When March 17 came to an end, eight more cargo ships had sunk into their graves. As the night of March 18 closed in on the hunters and hunted, the thunder of depth charge explosions and torpedo deto-nations erupted anew and the convoy's desperate fight against annihilation continued. Throughout the follow-ing day U-boats were still pursuing the enemy, biting and shooting their way through the shrunken fleet. Then the U-boats suddenly detected another convoy in the wake of SC 122; they hacked their way through screens of escorts, blizzards, and mountainous waves and pushed into the flanks of eastbound Convoy HX 229. New fighting erupted. Soon the two stricken con-voys fused in a gigantic holocaust where over 130 cargo ships, over 30 destroyers and corvettes clashed with 38 U-boats. The battle raged for another two nights and three days; great tracts of ocean echoed to the sharp reports of torpedo hits and the sound of crushing hulls.

When the U-boats ran out of fuel and torpedoes, when new blizzards covered the stricken convoys with snow and sleet and fog, when their battered remnants finally reached the protection of British long-range bombers—only then did the infernal battle come to a halt. It had strewn the bottom of the Atlantic with Allied ships. A laconic report by U-boat Headquarters described the dimensions of our victory: *"In all 32 vessels of 186,000 tons and one destroyer were sunk and hits were scored on nine other ships. This is the greatest success ever achieved in a single convoy battle and is all the more creditable in that nearly half the U-boats involved scored at least one hit."*

While one of the largest naval engagements in history had claimed 32 British, American, Dutch, Norwegian, Greek, and Panamanian ships, we had lost only a single U-boat. *U-384* had fallen victim to the bombs of an aircraft of the British Coastal Command in the last day of the giant struggle.

Four days later, *U-230* approached the western fringes of the Bay of Biscay. Our rusty, dilapidated boat was making 14 knots. Siegmann announced that our destination was Brest, the port where I had left Yvonne. I was pleased by my prospects and overjoyed with our spectacular victories. Everything seemed to be right with the world.

PART TWO

ABOVE US, HELL

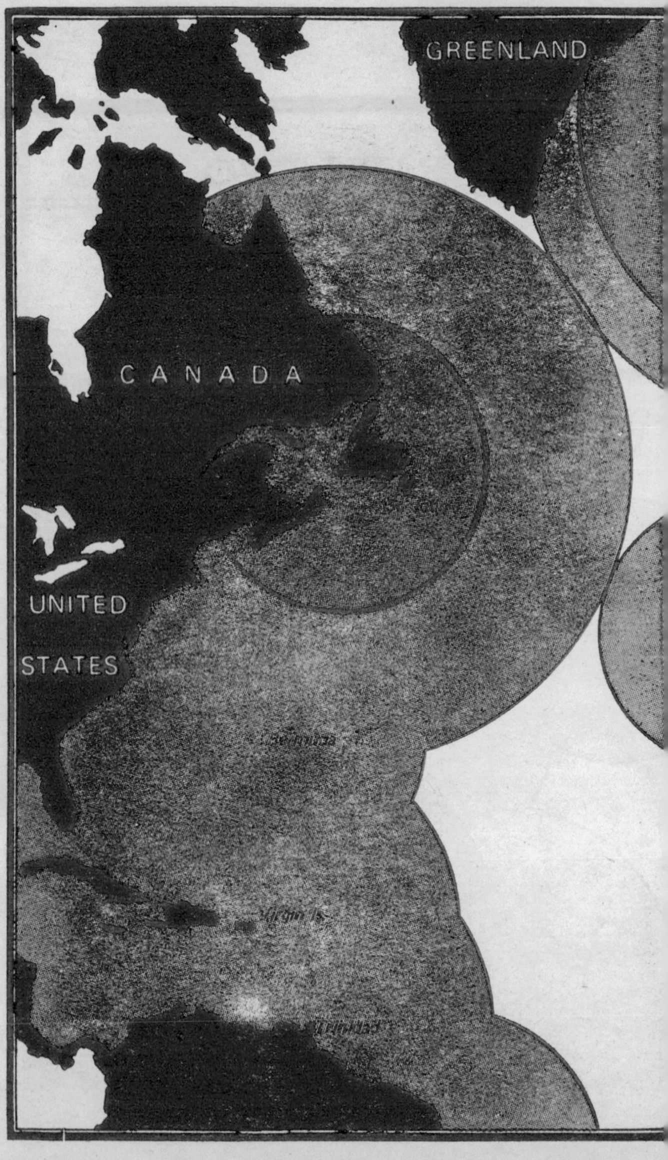
GREENLAND
CANADA
UNITED
STATES
Virgin Is.

ICELAND

NORWAY

GERMANY

Cherbourg
Brest
Lorient
St. Nazaire

Azores

Gibraltar

AFRICA

Dakar

ALLIED AIR COVER

September 1939 – March 1941

March 1941 – July 1942

July 1942 – May 1945

10

Unknown to us aboard *U-230,* our homeward journey through the Bay of Biscay was to be a harbinger of troubles to come. March 25, the fifth day after the colossal convoy battle, passed uneventfully. With ballast tanks preflooded, deck awash, and our Metox warning gear tuned in on the enemy above, we proceeded cautiously eastward into the growing evening. That night we made three radar contacts. Three times we crash-dived, and three times an aircraft dropped a cluster of bombs in our wake.

The next morning at 1012, Borchert with his magic eyes stretched his arms and yelled, "Aircraft!"

Spotting a tiny black fly diving at us out of the cloud cover, I tossed the Biscay Cross into the tower, and my men plunged after it. With our deck already submerged, I glanced at the aircraft and guessed that we might have a grace period of 30 seconds before its bombs exploded. Then I tumbled through the hatch and slammed the lid shut just as the sea crashed in upon me. *U-230* had dived in just 18 seconds, leaving a margin of safety of at least 10 seconds. As the boat churned into the depths at an angle of 50 degrees, the plane zeroed in on the foamy spot of our submergence. Four bombs detonated just short of our starboard aft ballast tanks. The explosions hurled our stern out of the water, giving the bombardier the impression that he had scored a fatal hit.

Down below, we were surprised, for no radar impulses had been received. We remained submerged for over a half-hour. Then we surfaced—but only briefly.

1225: Crash-dive before a two-engined aircraft. No radar impulses.

1250: *U-230* surfaced.

1332: Alarm. Aircraft. No radar detection. Four bombs exploded in close proximity, causing our rear planes to block in down position.

1405: We surfaced at high speed.

1422: Alarm. Four-engined Sunderland. Hard rudder maneuver. Four more bombs.

Short Sunderland

It could not be denied that the British had laid a tight screen of aircraft over the Bay of Biscay. Siegmann decided to run submerged during the day and to travel on the surface at night only, when the Tommies would be forced to resort to their radar to find us. Nevertheless, that night was no different from the day. We crash-dived three times, evading 12 more bombs by meager margins. We stayed submerged throughout the next day, floated at a slow speed of three knots through the depths, and listened to the threatening propeller sound of a hunter-killer group that the British had stationed in our front yard. We also heard the constant rumbling of faraway detonations. Surprisingly, the Bay was very much alive.

After dark the next day, we were forced to make six crash-dives, each time receiving the inevitable four charges. But each time we managed to escape and come up to surface again. The next day we spent sailing submerged at 60 meters, but not without spo-

radic and inexplicable explosions. At dusk we surfaced, and around midnight penetrated a large fleet of
French trawlers fishing for sardines. Their presence
saved us from further harassment. When occasionally
we heard the roar of aircraft engines, we drew close to
the trawlers, frightening the fishermen with our maneuvers. Soon after daybreak, we finally arrived at the
spot where we were supposed to meet our escort, but
the sea was empty. Everything seemed to be going
wrong. Our prospects of reaching port soon were not
exactly overwhelming, and they dimmed even more
when we learned from a distress signal that *U-665*
had been sunk by aircraft only one hour before she
was to be met by her escort.

We dived and waited. The Coast Guard vessel
eventually approached us just before noon, six hours
late. Siegmann waited until the ship was so close that
he could see the color of her skipper's eyes in his
scope. Then we surfaced. Pale-faced men poured out
of the hull, eagerly inhaling fresh air. Some of them
went about attaching cartridges to the guns, while
others fell on deck, taking their first insecure steps.
A faint violet strip starboard ahead announced our
approach to land. The first green patches, white walls,
and red roofs soon showed clearly in the sun. *U-230*
reached port without firing a single shot.

The Captain, looking like a Viking in his long red
beard, smoked his cigar with satisfaction. His men had
assembled on the aft deck, smoking and joking, their
faces yellow in the sun. An ovation burst forth across
the inner harbor as I maneuvered our boat toward a
concrete· pier overcrowded by welcomers. A band
played while those men on their first patrol stood
stunned by the attention they were receiving. Even our
handful of veterans found it a moving affair after eight
weeks of battling the storms, the sea, and the enemy.

Ahead of us rose a giant concrete structure at the
water's edge—the bombproof U-boat pens that har-
bored well over 40 wolves. *U-230* nosed into one of
the berths of this newly constructed bunker.

"Both half astern. Both full stop. Fasten all lines."

The shore party fell silent. The boat's company steadied into firm ranks. I presented the crew to the Captain, and Siegmann saluted the Commandant of the 9th U-boat Flotilla. As we palefaced, bearded celebrities teetered over the gangway and stepped cautiously on solid earth, we were showered with flowers and kisses from the always-enterprising girls of the administration.

Staggering on our shaky sea legs, we stowed our gear in one of the multistoried pastel buildings that housed the 9th U-boat Flotilla. I noticed that our compound was well maintained and closely guarded, and that large camouflage screens had been built over several structures to deceive enemy aircraft. The modern complex would serve well as a home for my stays in port.

Before I had a chance to shave, we were caught up in a round of homecoming receptions and celebrations that lasted long into the night. Proud of our accomplishments and almost desperately eager to enjoy ourselves again, we overdid everything. We gorged ourselves on the plentiful food of Brittany; we drank too much French wine; we sang and joked and laughed with loud abandon. No one objected to our excesses. It was comforting to know that others understood our needs after our weeks of anguish.

The next morning at 0800 I mustered the crew in a paved courtyard. Only a few men appeared for roll call; the rest were incapacitated. For the next few hours I was kept busy reviving the men, especially Riedel and Friedrich, and preparing papers for the Captain's report to Headquarters. It was only after 16 hours ashore that I was able to think of myself. I repeated the ritual of rejuvenation, remembered well from my returns to Lorient. I took a long hot bath, carefully removed my nine weeks' growth of black beard, put on a clean uniform, sat with eyes closed as a barber cut my hair. Then, as a new man, I sorted out and read my accumulated mail. First I opened the pink envelopes from Marianne. According to one of her letters, things did not look good in Berlin:

The English were here again, four nights last week and twice in one day. The raids are frightening. As you know, I work in the center of Berlin and last week we spent long hours in the air-raid shelter in the cellar of our office building. While I was there a bomb hit the building across the street and destroyed it entirely. There were no survivors. All were buried alive in the basement—so what good is it to seek shelter in a trap? When I finally left for home and saw the burning and destruction and the dead, I cried almost all the way. My best girl friend was buried in the rubble that day. I can't understand why we don't drive the Tommies away. This is the nation's capital and should have more protection. It's hard to say where we are going from here. Goering promised that no enemy plane would ever cross into Germany. We wonder what has happened to him and his pledge. We have not heard of him for some time.

Yesterday I listened to a news bulletin about our U-boats' new success in the Atlantic and thought of you. Darling, I pray that you always return from your missions to find my letters. I think of you constantly and want to be with you. Please, take care of yourself. When the war is over, everything will again be as it was on Lake Constance and under the chestnut tree on that long, hot summer night in '39. . . .

I was disturbed. I thought of urging Marianne to leave the big city and settle somewhere in the country —for the time being at least. The news from my parents was less dramatic. Mother wrote of a few unsuccessful air raids in the Frankfurt area. She said that people had organized to help each other extinguish small fires in their attics, that some English pilots had been shot down, that Father was working hard in his business and that Trudy, now a war bride of seven months, was still assisting him as his secretary. I was satisfied with the news from home, and in my letters to both Mother and Marianne, I wrote that all would change for the better very soon.

This I firmly believed despite growing evidence to the contrary. The air raids on German cities had increased steadily in size and frequency, passing the point of mere harassment. The radio and newspapers were vague in their reports of bomb damage and casualties, but I got the impression we were now taking severe punishment.

There were other bitter facts to be faced. Only reluctantly did I accept reports that adverse developments had taken place on the Eastern front while we were at sea. Apparently the Soviet winter offensive had resulted in our defeat at Stalingrad, where our 6th Army had been beaten. The news from the North African theater was not encouraging, either; the British were advancing more or less steadily in the desert. Nonetheless, these reverses seemed to me to be of local character and unlikely to affect the outcome of the war.

Actually, the only front where Germany registered dramatic gains was the one at sea. The battle of the Atlantic was going well for us. Our U-boats, now operating in large wolf-packs, were taking an incredible toll of Allied shipping from the Arctic Circle to the Caribbean Sea. This March of 1943 was the greatest month in U-boat history; our boats had sent to the bottom almost 1 million tons of Allied shipping. Currently, close to 250 U-boats were in action on various fronts, in training in the Baltic, in port for refitting, and in shipyards nearing completion. As for the future, our boat-building program bore the stamp of top priority.

Even in the sea war, however, our triumphs were now being wrenched from the enemy with a difficulty unknown in previous years. As the size of the convoys increased, the coordination of British and American naval units had sharply improved their convoy defenses. Escort vessels of a new type, the swift and highly maneuverable corvettes, increased the hazards of U-boat attacks. Most ominous of all was the plague of enemy aircraft. More and more planes were flying ever farther to sea and bombing our boats on the homeward run or outward bound with ever-deadlier accuracy. The threat from the sky had added a new dimension to the sea war, and we were hard put to keep abreast of rapidly changing conditions.

As I saw it, the whole war now hinged on our

U-boat effort in the Atlantic, It was obvious that the Allies had had time to recover from our early blows, and that they owed much of their new vitality to supplies shipped across the Atlantic from the United States. We of the U-boat Force had to prevent American food and ammunition and airplanes from piling up in British ports and on the docks of Murmansk and Archangel. We had to annihilate the enemy at sea before he could mass the material and manpower for an invasion of Europe. And we would do it.

With the help of all hands, *U-230* was quickly stripped for refitting, and at the end of our second day in port she was put in charge of the naval yard's engineers. Work on the boat was only a fraction of my hectic schedule in those first few days in port. I continued making charts and reports for Siegmann's meeting with Admiral Doenitz; the Captain was to go to Paris, where Doenitz had established his Headquarters after being elevated to Commander-in-Chief of the Navy in January. Also I made arrangements for sending one-third of our crew on leave.

Despite my heavy work load, I found time to think of Yvonne and, late one afternoon, to pay her a surprise visit. Armed with a bouquet of flowers, I entered the bookstore where she had worked. She was not there. I did not wish to involve the proprietor in our personal affairs, and so, thinking that Yvonne might have changed jobs, I began searching for her in the other bookshops in town. But Yvonne was nowhere to be found. I finally made the long walk to her house, where I had spent many nights. There was no Yvonne—or at least no one admitted to knowing her. On my way back into town I hurled the flowers over a stone wall, convinced that I would never see her again. Then, on a sudden impulse, I returned to her bookshop and addressed the old proprietor behind the counter: *"Pardon, monsieur, où est-ce-que je pourrais trouver Yvonne?"*

"Yvonne? Oh, Yvonne." He peered at me over the rim of his spectacles and then informed me of the obvious: "She isn't here."

I repeated my question. "Tell me, please, where can I find her?"

"Young man, all I can tell you is that she left eight, nine months ago. To live in Toulouse with an aunt, so she said. But"—he gave me a significant glance—"she had to leave the city. Didn't you know she was persecuted for her association? Things like that can't be kept a secret." The old man's look was not one of hate. There was only sadness in his eyes.

This was the last I heard of Yvonne.

Two days later, the Commandant of the flotilla arranged a party to celebrate our successful patrol. At lunch in the officers' mess hall, he revealed his plans and invited everyone to attend the affair, which was to be held at the flotilla's country resort, Chateau Neuf. At the end of his announcement, the Commandant said with a smile, "I have provided the place, the food, the drinks, and a dance band. But you gentlemen will have to provide your own female companions."

This, I soon learned, was no easy matter in a town full of "regulars"—officers who never went to sea. When the bus came to take us to the party, the regulars had the company of pretty nurses and government employees. We womanless newcomers had no choice but to concentrate on the fresh, blooming landscape of Brittany.

Just after sunset, we arrived at the chateau, a seventeenth-century castle nestling among rolling hills. There was little time to admire the elegant architecture and lavish appointments; the hall filled up fast, and I soon found myself shaking hands with many old friends and classmates, including Fred Schreiber. To open the party, the band played "Tiger Rag," then continued with French, German, and English tunes. The food and wine were French, and of excellent quality. The eating started early and continued late. The dancing ended after midnight as the lucky couples disappeared one by one into upstairs rooms, where the drapery was velvet and bedding pure silk. The drinking, which was the lot of us dateless guests, went on until wine and weariness conquered all but a few diehards. I put Riedel and Schreiber to rest in a bed once used by lords. Then I found my own peace in an overstuffed armchair.

After this grandiose reception in his behalf, Siegmann, a staunch family man, departed for his home in Hamburg; en route he was to make his report to the Admiral in Paris. My fellow officers took their cue from the Captain and left to spend two weeks with their families. I remained on duty with a handful of our men in Brest. But duty was now a relaxed routine. The countryside was bountiful in these serene April days. I visited the chateau at will. I splashed in its huge sunken marble bathtubs, sampled its extensive library of old books, went pheasant shooting with the farmers of the neighborhood. I watched the buds open and unfold under the warm breezes from the sea. The scent of spring was everywhere.

One mild evening, I was introduced to the racy life in port by new friends who shared my fate. We had been sipping cocktails, playing cards, telling jokes and seamen's yarns in the bar at the base. Suddenly Forster had an inspiration: "Listen, friends, how about a nice little celebration in town? The night has only begun, let's end it at Madame's place. Shall we go closed ranks to the C.B.?"

His proposition was adopted by acclaim, and it had its appeal for me as a newcomer in officers' circles in Brest. As for the merry endorsement of Forster's suggestion, I asked my classmate Schreiber, "What's so special about this C.B., Fred?"

He finished his gin fizz and said with a broad smile, "The C stands for casino and the B stands for bar. The Casino Bar is a place where one can forget his griefs, drown his thirst in good French wine, and satisfy his appetites with Madame's beauties. All in absolute privacy."

"So this is a fancy *établissement*, is it?"

"Call it by any name you like, it is highly recommended."

We marched through the blackened city and came to

a halt at an inconspicuous door identified only by a
small light and the initials "C.B." The door was locked.
A young *Leutnant* rang the bell in a special way—a
signal that we, only we, were at the door. An old woman opened the door a crack, then recognized some of
my friends. As she swung the door wide open, I heard
the laughter of girls and a phonograph blaring the song
"J'attendrais le jour et la nuit." Inside, dim red lights
created a suggestive atmosphere. As we filed in, gay
greetings came from both sides of the entry to the bar,
and my friends answered boisterously, *"Hallo, hallo,
Suzanne, Janine, bon soir, Paulette, Simone. Ah, bon
soir, Madame!"*

The girls—nearly a dozen lively, pretty ones—welcomed us with exaggerated enthusiasm. Madame was a
fragile woman in her thirties, with full, strong black
hair. Fred caught me staring at her and advised me,
"You can't touch Madame, it's against the rules. Nobody yet has had the luck to conquer Madame, so you
had better concentrate on the girls."

Madame's exhibits, all of them in their twenties,
were unfortunately outnumbered by the men, including some officers of the 1st Flotilla. When the general
levity had subsided, the newcomers were introduced
and welcomed according to house custom—with a dig-
nified kiss from Madame.

Now the fete began in earnest. Champagne sparkled
in our glasses and the girls glowed in our embraces.
We danced to the soft music of the record player,
sipped the effervescent wine, and tasted the red lips.
We kissed the willing creatures as if we had never done
so before and might never have another chance.

As the evening lengthened, our songs became more
animated, our laughter more vociferous, and the girls
appeared ever more attractive. We drank the champagne in mounting quantities and soon our inhibitions
—and the girls' laces—fell away. I danced with Janine
most of the time. She was suitably ardent. I wondered
when the time would come to take her away from the
party.

However, the *établissement's* main offerings would
have to await another preliminary. Ballard, a U-boat

Chief, called out, "Madame, now please present us with one of those action-packed movies."

His request was greeted with cheers.

"But messieurs," Madame protested, "isn't it too late for a show? The girls have yet to perform. . . ."

"Never mind, dear," Ballard said, "the night's still young. We have forgotten too much of life at sea. First let's have a refresher course."

Bowing to pressure, Madame sighed, "I understand your wishes as any mother does."

I put one arm around Janine's slender waist, grabbed a fresh bottle of champagne, and followed the group into an upstairs room. The lights were turned off; the projector began to hum and the film to roll. The hour that followed was truly educational. The movie taught us graphically that love without art is like a racing car without a driver. I emerged from that show full of new ideas. Janine was the first one to benefit from the lesson.

It was morning when I paid the tariff to the old concierge and stepped out into the fresh sea breeze.

At the naval compound things went their usual way. I did my paperwork. I made frequent inspections at the shipyard to see that the overhaul of *U-230* progressed according to schedule. I met more old friends from the early days of the war and visited classmates at the quarters of the 1st Flotilla, where I had been in December of 1941. I repeatedly heard of U-boat aces who had not returned from patrol. The year that had been so highly successful had also been full of sacrifices. The expansion of the U-boat war had brought about losses among my friends, and many newcomers to the front had found watery graves instead of fiery triumphs.

The weeks in port passed like April showers. Our joys and amusements were but brief compensation for what we had endured in combat. The fires of life burned high and we stirred them ever higher. I frequented the meeting places of Brittany's gourmets, had unforgettable lobster dinners in the "See Kommandant," a local German restaurant, spent a peaceful evening at the fireside of our castle resort in the country. Then there were the nights in the Casino Bar with

Janine. These were the nights when our wild energies of youth were tamed by Madame's girls of pleasure, nights in which we disengaged from war and duty.

But during silent hours of solitude in my room, I was always reminded that the battle in the Atlantic was far from over. The memory of the fury and destruction we caused flashed vividly in my mind. The bellowing explosions of torpedoes, depth charges, and bombs rang loudly in my ears. These were the hours that forced me to think of how dangerously the battle was changing. The front had been brought much closer to shore; it now lay only two hours from port, where sky and water met in the west. That was the thin line between war and peace.

Our Chief returned from his leave in mid-April. I saw Friedrich, still wearing his beard, enter the mess hall during dinner and I went to greet him. "Hello, old sailor, how was the hero received at home?"

"With pipes and drums. You see I kept the beard. The kids loved it, so I let it grow." He told me that he had spent too much of his leave riding trains and visiting relatives, and he was glad to be back. I briefed him carefully on the status of our boat and related developments. I was less precise in describing our escapades. However, when Riedel, also a bachelor, returned on the evening express from Paris, I freely told him of the cheerful life and had no difficulty in introducing him to the paths of pleasure.

Soon all the crew members on furlough drifted back from their homes halfway across Europe. The Captain arrived positively relaxed. The stress lines of his first patrol had disappeared from his face. So had the flaming red Viking beard. Several days of intense activity replaced three leisurely weeks. The efficient shipyard had completed U-230 as scheduled, and the fitting-out would take but four days.

My last night in port was a quiet one. I was troubled by thoughts of what the next patrol might bring, and tried to concentrate on writing a few letters. I asked Marianne to be extremely careful and told my parents that I would be silent for a while. Around midnight, I finished packing my belongings for storage. A new order required us to file a testament together with the detailed list of the contents of our luggage. There was not much I had to give away. But when I signed my will in the somber seclusion of my room, I had the feeling that I had signed my life away. And I wondered whether I would ever retrieve that envelope again, or whether someone else would open it to execute my modest last requests.

11

April 24, 1943. *U-230* lay in the shadow of her concrete berth, lines removed from the pillars. Her company stood in closed ranks on the aft deck, facing the farewell party on the pier. The men had flowers fastened at their caps or in the buttonholes of their olive-green fatigues. Beneath them, the oily water was beaten up by our screws, which turned silently in reverse. *U-230* detached herself gently from the concrete wall and sailed, stern first, out of the shadowy darkness of the protective bunker into the blazing sun. At the same time a second boat, *U-456,* separated from another pier and followed in our wake. Her orders were the same as ours. On her bridge I saw Forster, a frequent companion at Madame's, and we waved to each other. Then our boat rapidly increased the distance to land and friends. Once we passed the center of the Bay, everything on board was at war: the actions, the spoken words, and the thoughts. It was as if there had been never a port, never a leave, never a jovial moment at the Casino Bar, never a night in the arms of a woman.

U-230 sped at 17 knots over a smooth surface, under a sky full of high clouds. *U-456* raced on parallel course 500 meters to starboard. Astern, the escort disappeared behind the horizon; ahead, the gray sky blended with the green of the sea. We ran along keeping a close watch on our radar detection gear. Our boat had been equipped with a new electronic instrument, an improved version of the Biscay Cross. The bulky cross had to be removed before submergence, but the new small antenna of the Metox was welded to the rim of the bridge and offered no interference with our emergency dives. Feeble impulses had been accompanying us ever since we left port. As they increased in volume, *U-230* made a perfect routine dive, with *U-456* following only seconds behind us. That was when we lost contact with *U-456,* which continued on her own track into our allotted area.

At nightfall we surfaced to try our luck and run for mileage. With a hull full of fresh air and both diesels charging her batteries, *U-230* thrust forward. The infinity of the night sky and the dark expanse of the sea fused in the distance and created the illusion that we were sailing through the universe. Alone between heaven and sea, our black boat sped along in the midst of the large, phosphorescent whirlpool that she whipped up—a perfect target for an alert pilot. While the diesels hammered their steady beats, I counted the minutes that we were allowed to travel on surface. Seventeen minutes passed. Then there was a screaming radar impulse—detection. We dived at once.

The nights became our days and the days became our nights. The hours inside the hull were spent in darkness lit by a few dim bulbs, and the nights on the bridge were as black as tar. We continued our advance with our ears tuned to the enemy above and our eyes glued to the black sea, always ready to duck the bombs that came hurling down from the sky with alarming frequency. And during daytime we floated at a depth of 40 meters, listening to the distant but intimate sounds of propellers, Asdic pings, and detonating depth charges and bombs.

As April gave way to May we reached the "Black Pit" area, where no enemy aircraft had yet penetrated.

Radar impulses had gradually ceased and we dared to stay surfaced under the sun again. After playing hide-and-seek for six nights and days, after being thrown into shock, dismay, fear, and anger by the British audacity, I considered the sun the guarantor of our survival. Its light enabled us to see clearly and far. By using our eyes and the Metox, I was hopeful that we would be able to spot the black flies at safe distance.

After we had passed the 15th Longitude West, we informed Headquarters that we had made safe passage through the Bay of Biscay. Four hours after base had acknowledged receipt of our message, Riedel received and decoded new instructions: PROCEED INTO GRID SQUARE BD 95. EXPECT EASTBOUND CONVOY.

The area of operation was far below the stormy northern region where we had been during the winter months. I expected better shooting conditions as well as a faster convoy hunt. The strain of the march through the Bay was soon erased by a series of beautiful days, undisturbed by enemy planes.

May 2. The weather was serene, the sea calm and iridescent. At 1408 Riedel spotted a fast-moving target behind the southern horizon, a loner. We raced at highest speed on a track that would intersect the vessel's mean course. After three hours of running, during which we left the cargo ship cautiously behind the horizon, we dived leisurely, having plenty of time before the vessel would become visible. One hour later, our hopes of shooting the first torpedo vanished. The ship was identified as a Swedish freighter traveling the "Philadelphia Route," which we had guaranteed as a safe path for neutrals.

After we had allowed the Swede to pass, we intercepted a signal from one of our boats: CONVOY IN AJ 87 COURSE NORTHEAST. SUNK TWO TOTAL 13,000 TONS. KEEP CONTACT. U-192. Grid square AJ 87 lay between Newfoundland and Greenland—far beyond our reach. We had to leave the convoy to wolves patrolling that area.

May 5. *U-230* charged toward her allotted square.

During the morning, we intercepted a signal that confirmed our worst fears. Riedel handed me the deciphered message in silence: DESTROYER. ATTACKED. SINKING. U-638. This report was the last act of *U-638*. Nothing was heard of her again.

Two hours later, a fresh distress signal was hastily decoded: ATTACKED BY DESTROYERS. DEPTH CHARGES. LEAVE BOAT. U-531. This second alarming call alerted us to the fact that the battle at that convoy had produced unusually fierce countermeasures by its defense.

May 6. It was still dark when another signal from the battlefield flashed across the Atlantic: ATTACKED BY CORVETTE. SINKING. U-438. This third death message angered and puzzled us. What caused this sudden stream of messages which told us of nothing but dying?

Now another was intercepted: AIRCRAFT. BOMBS. RAMMED BY DESTROYER. SINKING. U-125.

A fourth casualty! Our anger changed to shock.

May 7. *U-230,* cruising with extreme caution under a star-strewn sky, intercepted still another last report: AIR ATTACK. SINKING 47N 05W. U-663. I checked the victim's position on our mildewy chart and marked the spot of her destruction, in the center of the Bay of Biscay, with a black cross. She was the fifth boat to go to the bottom within three days. But seven hours later I had to revise the total when, after repeated requests by Headquarters to report their positions, *U-192* and *U-531* had not answered. They had met their fate while attacking that convoy southeast of Greenland.

May 10. It was a sunny day. We arrived in the designated square, a small area almost in the center of the Atlantic. Here we were supposed to intercept the convoy reported earlier. With us in ambush lurked six boats, and many more sailed between our patrol and the British Isles. *U-456,* our companion since our departure from Brest, hid somewhere behind the horizon. The trap was set.

May 11. Another obituary, again originating in the Bay of Biscay: ATTACKED BY AIRCRAFT. SINKING. U-528. We were outraged and determined to pay back the loss of our friends a hundredfold.

One hour later we received, as a consolation, attack orders from Headquarters: ALL U-BOATS IN GRID SQUARE BD INTERCEPT EASTBOUND CONVOY IN BD 91. ATTACK WITHOUT FURTHER ORDERS. At once we set *U-230* on a new course at high speed; her bow split the water ahead into two sparkling fountains. Preparing for action, I ordered a complete overhaul of all torpedoes.

May 12. At 0400, the tension was apparent throughout the boat as I mounted my watch. At 0540, as the new day dawned, Prager shot several stars and established our position. At 0620, he reported from below that we had arrived on the convoy's calculated mean track. I reduced our speed and turned *U-230* onto a westward course, toward the convoy, cautiously probing ahead. The eastern sky turned bloodred as the sun prepared to rise over the horizon; only a thin line in the west remained dark.

0615: The sun shot like a fireball out of the ocean. At that spectacular moment, I spotted a smear over the southwesterly horizon—the convoy! I called Siegmann to the bridge and said as he arrived, "I have a present for you, Sir."

"Thanks, Exec, encouraging news at last."

We watched the smudge grow bigger and wider. Soon the Captain turned the stern of the boat toward the gray and black fumes. Three mastheads crept over the sharp horizon in the west and mounted higher. Emerging fully, the three ships were seen to be escorts, the sweepers in front of the convoy. They zigzagged closer, moving jerkily like puppets on an empty stage. We proceeded slowly eastward, maintaining safe distance, to determine the convoy's exact course.

0638: Mastheads appeared over a wide section of the horizon. Then the funnels followed. These were the cargo ships, the targets we were after. A mighty display of masts and funnels rose ever higher out of the sea. We were almost dead ahead of the parade, in excellent position. Within one hour, I calculated, we would have plenty of targets at our disposal.

0655: Siegmann acted. "Clear the bridge! On diving stations."

I was in the conning tower as the alarm bell sounded the call to action. Five minutes later the boat was properly trimmed and floated just below the surface. The Captain, seated at the scope, informed the crew over our intercom system, "We have sighted an extremely large convoy, probably over one hundred vessels. We shall attack submerged. I need not remind you that this is no holiday cruise. I expect your utmost effort to make this attack a success." Then he activated the motor of the scope.

0705: No visible contact yet. Siegmann ordered all tubes prepared for firing.

0710: I reported *U-230* combat-ready as the convoy's thumping roar spread through the depths.

0716: The soundman conveyed news that ruined our plan for a submerged assault: "Convoy apparently has changed course. Sound band changed to three-one-oh."

The Captain, visibly annoyed over the unexpected change, raised the scope further into the air to catch a view of the parading fleet. The high-pitched spinning of escorts' propellers echoed through the water, and the grinding noise of the huge armada hit our hull like the beating of countless jungle drums.

"Damn dirty trick," muttered Siegmann. "The convoy zigzags to the northeast. There are at least a dozen corvettes spread over its starboard side."

The convoy steamed away at 11 knots while *U-230* floated undetected by the outer defense, unwilling to attack till she had passed through the cordon of destroyers. The rhythmical thrashing of a hundred propellers penetrated the heavy steel of our hull and bounced forth and back inside the boat. The Captain relinquished his seat at the scope, snarling, "Come over here, Exec, take a look. If I only had a faster boat I could roll up the convoy like a carpet."

I swung into the seat. Seven miles on port I saw an

amazing panorama. The entire horizon, as far and wide as I could see, was covered with vessels, their funnels and masts as thick as a forest. At least a dozen fast destroyers cut the choppy green sea with elegance. As many as two dozen corvettes flitted around the edges of the convoy. I said in awe, "Quite a display of power, sir. It's probably the largest convoy ever."

"You might be right. Once we are close to that wall of ships our torpedoes can't miss."

Before we could risk surfacing to race into a new attack position, we had to put distance between us and the convoy. The swishing of propellers, the pounding of piston engines, the singing of turbines, and the chirping of Asdic pings accompanied us on our clandestine run. For almost two hours we traveled diagonally away from the giants of steel.

0915: *U-230* surfaced. Mounting the bridge while the deck was still awash, I took a hurried look in a circle. Far to the northeast, mastheads and funnels moved along the sharp line which divided the ocean from the sky. *U-230* forged through the sea, parallel to the convoy's track, in an attempt to reach a forward position before dusk. Riedel flashed the message of our contact to Headquarters and the other wolves in ambush: CONVOY BD 92 COURSE NORTHEAST ELEVEN KNOTS. STRONG DEFENSE. REMAIN SURFACED FOR ATTACK. U-230.

0955: A startled cry at my back, *"Flugzeug!"*

I saw a twin-engined plane dropping out of the sun. The moment of surprise was total.

"Alarrrmmm!" We plunged head over heels into the conning tower. The boat reacted at once and shot below surface. At this moment of our maximum danger and minimum ability to act, our lives depended upon a miracle, an accident, or the good luck that had so far saved us from extinction.

Four short, ferocious explosions shattered the water above and around us. The boat trembled and fell at a 60-degree angle. Water splashed, steel shrieked, ribs moaned, valves blew, deck-plates jumped, and the boat was thrown into darkness. As the lights flickered on, I saw astonishment in the round eyes of the men.

They had every right to be astounded: the attack out
of the sun was a complete mystery. Where had the
small plane come from? It did not have the range to
fly a round-trip between the nearest point of land and
the middle of the Atlantic. The conclusion was inescapable that the convoy launched its own airplanes. It
seemed highly likely, though we did not want to believe
it, that the planes returned to convoy and landed on an
aircraft carrier. The idea of a convoy with its own air
defense smashed our basic concept of U-boat warfare.
No longer could we mount a surprise attack or escape
without meeting savage counterattacks.

1035: *U-230* came up to periscope depth. A careful
check with our "sky scope," an instrument similar to
the periscope, revealed no aircraft. We surfaced at high
speed.

The hunt went on. We pressed forward obstinately,
with that terrible constriction in the stomach. The diesels hammered hard and pushed the boat swiftly ahead.
I glanced only occasionally at the dense picket fence
along the horizon and concentrated on the sky. Thick-
ening white clouds scudded along at medium height
under a stiff breeze from the west. The wind pitched
the water up on deck and once in a while blew a sheet
of spray across the bridge.

1110: I detected a glint of metal between the clouds.
It was a small aircraft, and it was diving into the attack.

"Alarrrmmm!"

Fifty seconds later, four explosions nearby taught us
that the pilot was a well-trained bombardier. Shock-
waves rocked boat and crew. Friedrich, struggling to
prevent the boat from sinking, caught her at 180
meters, balanced her out, and brought her up to periscope depth.

1125: *U-230* surfaced. We drove forward and clung
to the fringes of the convoy with grim determination.
Instinct forced us ahead, kept us moving despite the
constant threat from above, made us numb to the
repetitive detonations. We raced in defiance of fear
and sudden destruction—always forward, toward the
head of the convoy.

1142: "Aircraft—alarrrmmm!"

U-230 plunged into the depths. Four booms twisted the hull, but the boat survived the savage blows. We waited for the plane to disappear with our hearts beating under our tongues.

1204: We surfaced in an increasingly choppy sea and surged ahead, the boat jolting and shaking. The convoy had slipped into a northwesterly position, and despite our constant harassment we had gained considerable headway on it. I spotted the escorts on the horizon but the real danger lurked above. The clouds had lowered and thickened, covering the last patches of blue sky.

1208: A call from below reached us on the bridge: "Message for Captain, signal just received: ATTACKED BY AIRCRAFT. SINKING. U-89." Again we were stunned. With a shudder, I pictured what would happen to us, once our own hull was cracked.

1217: "Aircraft dead astern, alarrrmmm!"

U-230 dived once more and descended rapidly. I bit my lip and waited for the final blast. At 45 seconds, four booms whipped the boat with violent force. Every second we were able to snatch from the pursuing aircraft brought us closer to the convoy and success. But if we dived a second too late, bombs would end our hunt with sudden death.

1230: We surfaced again. This time only three men went to the bridge, the Captain, the first seaman's mate, and I. We raced ahead stubbornly, plagued by the thoughts of being annihilated within the hour.

Lockheed Hudson

1315: A twin-engined plane dropped suddenly out of a low cloud, only 800 meters astern. It was too late to dive. After freezing for a horrifying instant, Siegmann yelled, "Right full rudder!" I jumped to the rear of the bridge to shoot while the mate manned the second gun. The small aircraft grew enormous fast. It dived upon us, machine-gunning the open rear of the bridge as the boat turned to starboard. Neither the mate nor I were able to fire a single bullet; our guns were jammed. The aircraft dropped four bombs which I saw falling toward me, then roared over the bridge so close that I could feel its engines' hot exhaust brush my face. Four bombs in a row erupted alongside our starboard saddle tanks. Four high fountains collapsed over the two of us at the guns. *U-230* was still afloat, still racing through the rising green sea. The aircraft, having used up its bombs, turned and disappeared into the direction of the convoy.

1323: Our radio mate delivered an urgent message to the Captain: ATTACKED BY AIRCRAFT. UNABLE TO DIVE. SINKING. 45 NORTH 25 WEST. HELP. U 456.

"Have Prager check position," Siegmann shouted back. "Maybe we can save the crew."

The Captain's impulse to rescue our comrades might well result in suicide. We were closer to death than to life ourselves. But help was imperative—we would have expected the same. Moments later, Prager reported that *U-456* was only 12 miles ahead, 15 degrees to starboard. Immediately, the Captain changed course.

1350: We spotted a plane circling four miles ahead. Then my glasses picked up the bow of *U-456* poking out of the rough sea. The men clung to the slippery deck and to the steel cable strung from bow to bridge. Most of them stood in the water up to their chests. The aircraft kept circling above the sinking boat, making it foolhardy for us to approach. Another danger prevented rescue: astern, a corvette crept over the horizon, evidently summoned by the plane. Now our own lives were in jeopardy. We turned away from the aircraft, the escort, and *U-456*, and fled in the direction of the convoy.

1422: "Aircraft astern!"

Again it was too late to dive. The single-engined

plane came in low in a straight line exactly over our wake. I fingered the trigger of my gun. Again the gun was jammed. I kicked its magazine, clearing the jam. Then I emptied the gun at the menace. The mate's automatic bellowed. Our boat veered to starboard, spoiling the plane's bomb run. The pilot revved up his engine, circled, then roared toward us from dead ahead. As the plane dived very low, its engine sputtered, then stopped. Wing first, the plane crashed into the surging ocean, smashing its other wing on our superstructure as we raced by. The pilot, thrown out of his cockpit, lifted his arm and waved for help, but then I saw him disintegrate in the explosion of the four bombs which were meant to destroy us. Four violent shocks kicked into our starboard side astern, but we left the horrible scene unharmed.

The downing of the aircraft must have upset the enemy's flight schedule. Minute after minute passed without a repetition of the attacks. Running at highest speed, *U-230* gained bearing ahead of the convoy. In about an hour, we approached the calculated intersection with the convoy's track.

1545: A report from the radio room put our small victory into proper perspective: DEPTH CHARGES BY THREE DESTROYERS. SINKING. U-186. This new loss was the 11th we had heard of since our patrol began. A naval disaster seemed to be in making. But we could not afford a moment of sorrow for all the men who died that one death that every submariner pictures a thousand times.

1600: *U-230* cut into the projected path of the convoy. I saw four columns of ships creep over the sharp horizon in the southwest, headed in our direction. We had to halt them, had to spread fire in their midst and blow gaps in the mass of steel and iron.

1603: "Aircraft, bearing three-two-oh."

We plummeted into depth. Four detonations, sounding like one, drove the boat deeper and caused rudders and hydroplanes to block in extreme positions. Minutes later, more explosions occurred in the vicinity, but in defiance of our attackers, Siegmann ordered his boat to periscope depth. He raised the scope but downed it instantly, cursing angrily, *"Verdammt!* The fellow has dropped a smoke bomb and has dyed the water yellow."

Despite the dye marking the spot of our submergence, the Captain ordered an attack on the convoy before the escorts could attack us. Chirping Asdic pings, bellowing detonations, and the grinding roar of a hundred engines provided grim background music for our assault.

1638: Up periscope. Then: "Tubes one to five stand ready."

"Tubes one to five are ready," I answered quickly, then held my breath.

Siegmann swiveled around to check the opposite side. Suddenly he cried, "Down with the boat, Chief, take her down for God's sake, destroyer in ramming position! Down to two hundred meters!"

I fully expected the bow of a destroyer to cut into the conning tower momentarily. As the boat swiftly descended, the harrowing sound of the destroyer's engines and propellers hit the steel of our hull. It grew so fast, and echoed so deafeningly, that we were all unable to move. Only our boat was moving, and she went downward much too slowly to escape the blow.

An earshattering boom ruptured the sea. A spread of six depth charges lifted the boat, tossed her out of the water, and left her on the surface at the mercy of four British destroyers. The screws of *U-230* rotated in highest revolutions, driving us ahead. For seconds there was silence. For seconds the British were baffled and stunned. After a whole eternity, our bow dipped and the boat sank—and sank.

A new series of exploding charges lifted our stern with a mighty force. Our boat, entirely out of control, was catapulted toward the bottom five miles below. Tilted at an angle of 60 degrees, *U-230* tumbled to 250 meters before Friedrich was able to reverse her fall. Floating level at a depth of 230 meters, we thought we were well below the range of the enemy's depth charges. *U-230* was speedily rigged to withstand pursuit. Once again we were condemned to sit it out in crushing depths.

1657: Distinct splashes on surface heralded the next spread. A series of 24 charges detonated in quick succession. The bellowing roar slammed against our boat. The explosions again pushed her into a sharp down tilt while the echo of the detonations rolled endlessly through depths.

1716: A new spread deafened us and took our breath away. The boat listed sharply under the shattering blow. The steel knocked and shrieked and valves were thrown into open position. The shaft packings leaked, and a constant stream of water soon filled the aft bilge. Pumps spouted, the periscope packings loosened, and water trickled into the cylinders. Water everywhere. Its weight forced the boat deeper into the depths. In the meantime, the convoy crawled in a thunderous procession over our boat.

1740: The uproar was at its peak. A sudden splash told us that we had 10 or 15 seconds to brace against another barrage. The charges went off just beyond lethal range. While the ocean reverberated under the blasts, the bulk of the convoy slowly passed the spot of our slow execution. I pictured the freighters making a detour around the escorts massed above to end our existence. Perhaps we should risk going deeper. I did not know where our limit was, where the hull would finally crack. No one knew. Those who had found out took their knowledge into the depths. For hours we suffered the punishment and sank gradually deeper. In a constant pattern, spreads of 24 charges battered our boat every 20 minutes. At one time we thought we had won. That was when the escorts departed and rushed to take their positions in the convoy. But our hope was short-lived. The hunters had only left the *coup de grâce* to the killer group following in the wake of the armada.

2000: The new group launched its first attack, then another, and another. We sat helpless 265 meters below. Our nerves trembled. Our bodies were stiff from cold, stress, and fear. The mind-searing agony of waiting made us lose any sense of time and any desire for food. The bilges were flooded with water, oil, and urine. Our washrooms were under lock and key; to use them then could have meant instant death, for the tremendous outside pressure would have acted in reverse of the expected flow. Cans were circulated for the men to use to relieve themselves. Added to the stench of waste, sweat, and oil was the stink of the battery gases. The increasing humidity condensed on the cold steel, dropped into the bilges, dripped from pipes, and soaked our clothes. By midnight, the Captain realized that the British would not let up in their bombardment, and he ordered the distribution of potash cartridges to supplement breathing. Soon every man was equipped with a large metal box attached to his chest, a rubber hose leading to his mouth, and a clamp on his nose. And still we waited.

May 13. Over 200 canisters had detonated above and around us by 0100. Several times we had used a ruse in an effort to escape. Through an outboard valve, we repeatedly expelled a great mass of air bubbles. These screens of air floated away on the current, reflecting the Asdic impulses like a large solid body. But our attackers were fooled into chasing the decoys only twice, and both times they left at least one vessel behind, directly over our heads. Unable to sneak away, we gave up the game and concentrated on conserving our power, our compressed air, and our dwindling supply of oxygen.

0400: The boat had fallen to 275 meters. We had been under assault for 12 hours and there was no sign of relief. This day was my birthday and I wondered whether it would be my last. How many chances could one ask for?

0800: No lessening of the attacks. The water in the bilges rose above the deck plates and splashed around my feet. The bilge pumps were useless at this depth. Whenever a charge erupted, the Chief released some compressed air into the tanks to assure the boat's buoyancy.

1200: The boat's down angle had sharply increased. Our compressed-air supply was dangerously low, and the boat slipped ever farther away.

2000: The air was thick, and even more so as we breathed it through the hot cartridges. The devil seemed to be knocking on our steel hull as it creaked and contracted under the enormous pressure.

2200: The barrage increased in violence as dusk closed in on surface. Wild attacks at shorter intervals indicated that the enemy had lost his patience.

May 14. By midnight, we had approached the limit for boat and crew. We had reached a depth of 280 meters and the boat was still sinking. I dragged myself through the aisle, pushing and tossing men around, forcing them to stay awake. Whoever fell asleep might never be awakened.

0310: A thunderous spread rattled down, but without effect. We were closer to being crushed by the mounting pressure than by the exploding canisters. As the echo of the last blast slowly subsided, something else attracted our attention. It was the thrashing of retreating propellers. For a long time we listened to the fading sound, unable to believe that the Tommies had given up the hunt.

0430: For over an hour there was silence. We spent all that time doubting our luck. We had to make sure, so we turned on our fresh-water producer, went high with the motors. No reaction from above. Using the last of our compressed air and battery power, the Chief managed to lift the overloaded boat, meter by meter. Then, unable to slow her upward movement, Friedrich let her rise freely and yelled, "Boat rises fast . . . fifty meters . . . boat has surfaced!"

U-230 broke through to air and life. We pushed ourselves up to the bridge. Around us spread the infinite beauty of night, sky, and ocean. Stars glittered brilliantly and the sea breathed gently. The moment of rebirth was overwhelming. A minute ago, we could not believe that we were alive; now we could not believe that death had kept his finger on us for 35 gruesome hours.

Abruptly I felt the impact of the oxygen-rich air upon my system. Almost losing consciousness, I sagged to my knees and slumped over the rim of the bridge. There I stayed until I regained my faculties. The Captain recovered quickly, and we congratulated each other on another miraculous survival.

Then the Captain called out, "Both diesels half ahead. Steer one-eighty. Ventilate boat. Secure from action stations." Siegmann had thrown the dice again.

The diesels coughed to life. Since the convoy had disappeared long ago, we traveled south, toward our last position. The engines muttered reassuringly, topping off our drained batteries and pushing the boat toward a new sunrise. The bilges were emptied, the foul air expelled, and the accumulated refuse thrown overboard. When the darkness dissolved and a new day dawned, *U-230* was again ready for combat.

Still numb from the murderous assault and stiff from the cold depth, we added up our account. Three U-boats in our group had been sunk. Well over 100 Allied ships had plowed past us, and we had not been able to sink a single one. We might now expect that some 700,000 tons of war material would safely reach the British Isles. It was not a pretty picture.

The day promised to become a good one. Prager lifted his heavy frame to the bridge and shot several stars before the sun wiped them off the sky. I lit up a cigarette and watched the sunrise. The sky changed from dark blue to violet, turned purple and then bloody red. I remembered an old saying, "Red sky in the morning, early death's warning," and wondered what the day might bring.

0710: "Smoke clouds dead ahead," reported the first mate. All glasses spun to bear on a smudge over the horizon in the southwest. There was no doubt about it, we had sighted a second convoy. At that moment, it occurred to me the escorts had left us knowing that we would sooner or later fall into the hands of destroyers in the following convoy.

0720: *U-230* dived. The crew, without sleep for at least 70 hours, manned their stations wearily. They had hollow cheeks, pale faces, red eyes. Their haunted glances told me they understood things had changed drastically, that they knew they were nearer to the ocean floor than to port. I walked through the compartments, clapped a shoulder here, made a joke there, and managed to say some encouraging words.

0745: A voice came through the tube. "From soundman to Captain, propeller noise wanders to starboard. Enemy's course must be east, not north."

The Captain muttered an oath into his beard, searched again with the scope, spotted nothing, then ordered the boat to surface. It suddenly struck me that the event had a certain similarity to the one we had experienced three days before.

0750: The two of us rushed through the hatch, surveyed the sky, and located the convoy. It was obvious that the parade had made its morning zigzag and was now traveling away from us, just as the previous convoy had done. What had seemed an easy catch was suddenly beyond reach. Without further consideration, we began the chase.

0822: "Aircraft from the sun!"

A rapid dive brought us well below the detonating bombs. The Chief raised the boat immediately and soon we floated at periscope depth. The sky was empty. Seconds later, Siegmann snapped up the periscope handles, stood up as the scope hissed back into its tube and cursed angrily, "The devil with these birds, that plane has dropped a smoke bomb. Let's get away from here, Chief, surface with high speed."

0832: U-230 raced east and away from the thick black fumes that marked our position. Far off, astern to starboard, the masses of ships revealed their masts and funnels. Corvettes and destroyers zigzagged in a striking display of coordinated power.

0855: A twin-engine plane attacked from behind. U-230 went down within seconds. Four bombs tore the sea.

0915: We broke surface and chased forward, always ahead. A distress signal was handed to Siegmann on the bridge: AIR ATTACK. SINKING. U-657. Again, every hand aboard wondered how long it would take until we, too, would be delivered to our Maker.

1005: "Alarrrmmm!" An airplane had materialized as if by magic. U-230 crash-dived in record time. When the thunder of the detonations subsided, the boat was still afloat.

We surfaced and crash-dived again and again. We

ducked the blows, we trembled, shuddered, and vibrated under the heaviest barrages. The boat broke slowly under the murderous attacks. Her rivets burst, her bolts cracked, her hull was dented, and her ribs bent, but she still obeyed orders and the Captain drove her mercilessly into firing position.

By sunset, Siegmann's tenacious pursuit seemed about to be rewarded: hidden from the escorts by the curvature of the earth, we had worked ourselves miles ahead of the convoy. But then one of the flying devils forced us below again. And as the convoy rocked and pounded through the sea, our men swiftly occupied their action stations, suspense carved into their faces. With stern determination I prepared torpedoes and crew for a battle on surface.

My hopes failed unconditionally. In the turmoil and uproar of the approaching convoy, three escorts had somehow managed to zero in on our spot of submergence. Siegmann yelled in surprise, *"Achtung! Dive to two hundred meters! Brace for depth charges!"*

Seconds later, the sweepers presented us with an extravagant gift. A thick layer of depth charges exploded in an enormous eruption that dwarfed all previous barrages. Darkness followed the terrible quake. I pulled myself up the steel ropes of the scope, aimed the beam of my flashlight at the depth gauge, saw with horror its needle swinging rapidly, saw the two planesmen dangling at their wheels in confusion, listened to the Chief's desperate commands, and heard the shocking sound of splashing water. This was how the curtain went up for another long siege, an exact duplicate of the persecution we had just endured. As dusk settled upon the hunters above, the wind faded with the day and the sea smoothed; and as a result their bombardment increased in violence. The fierce salvoes made the ocean roar and rumble. We shivered and sweated; we were both hot and cold as we neared the limits of human endurance. As the night wore on, deadly fumes escaped from our batteries; we were half poisoned and nearly unconscious. And when the sun rose for our assailants, they renewed their bombardment with over

300 charges by actual count. It was all in vain. *U-230* stayed afloat some 280 meters below.

In the afternoon, we faced the fact that we had absolutely no more leeway, no more air to breathe. We now had to choose between suicide and surrender. In a last effort to steal another hour from death or imprisonment, Friedrich released some compressed air into the midship buoyancy tank to raise the boat. The hissing sound attracted our assailants' attention. A ferocious blast pulled the boat upward. As the air in her tanks expanded, she rose with increasing speed. But then a battery of canisters detonated, violently slamming into her starboard side, sending her down again for the final crush. We crawled through the center aisle to distribute our weight even though we were sure this was our end. Then, very gently, *U-230* leveled off near the 300-meter mark and vibrated in her last convulsive shakes. The men bit the mouthpieces of their rubber hoses, drawing hot air through the potash cartridges, incessantly coughing. Eight minutes after the blast, six more depth charges exploded astern. Then all remained silent for a long while, for well over an hour. There was not a ping, not a beep, not a sound from above.

Having survived past the absolute limit of our air supply, we tempted the Tommies into a move with a hammer blow against the hull. There was no reaction. *U-230* began her slow ascent.

1955: The lid of the hatch to the bridge flew open. Siegmann and I were thrown up to the bridge by the tremendous overpressure that had built up inside the hull. Radiant sunshine. Air in overabundance. But no enemy as far as the eye could see. After a careful check of sky and sea, we assessed our damages. The starboard aft oil bunker was broken wide open. Diesel oil had washed away, leaving a long treacherous trail of iridescent colors in our wake. To the enemy, a large oil slick was an unmistakable evidence of a direct hit. That was why the British had departed.

However, the boat was a shambles. Two tanks were ruptured, the starboard shaft was bent, the starboard diesel foundation was cracked, and countless smaller damages were reported. A large amount of fuel had been lost. A continuation of the mission was impossible: even our return to base was highly doubtful.

At 2105, Riedel transmitted a message to Headquarters, advising Admiral U-boats of our condition and the massive air defense in the center of the Atlantic. He added that two convoys had gotten away without our being able to launch a single torpedo. But our many lost chances to add tonnage to our credit seemed insignificant when compared to our unexpected survival. Only a special providence had allowed us to live while so many others had perished in the sea.

On the evening of May 15, at the end of the four-day battle, it was confirmed that *U-456* had been lost, and that two more boats had followed her to the bottom. *U-266* and *U-753* had never answered Headquarters' summons to report their position. The result of the fight was that six U-boats had been sunk and the seventh was battered and unable to continue. It was a disaster of the greatest magnitude, and the second one in the month of May. The Allied counteroffensive at sea had struck with frightening power and accuracy.

U-230 limped east through the vastness of the Atlantic. Luckily, no aircraft was sighted for two consecutive days. However, the calm was punctuated by a string of desperate signals from boats in distress. Decoding the death messages had become a normal part of our shipboard routine. The messages piled up on the Captain's table, and in reading them I half-expected to see one from *U-230*.

BOMBED BY AIRCRAFT. SINKING. U-463

HAVE LOST CONTACT. ATTACKED BY AIRCRAFT. U-640

ATTACKED BY DESTROYER. SINKING. U-128.

DESTROYERS. AIRCRAFT. UNABLE TO DIVE. U-528

ATTACKED BY AIRCRAFT. SINKING. U-646

Nothing was ever heard again of these boats. The thought of our destruction haunted us as more of the death cries were intercepted. It could be only hours, days at the most, until the killers would catch up with us and bring us death in our iron coffin.

May 18. At dawn we were instructed to refuel at high sea from *U-634* in grid square BE 81 on May 21.

May 19. The British scored two hits. *U-954* and *U-273* were bombed and sunk almost simultaneously. Their signals were identical; only the place of their dying was different.

May 21. *U-230* cruised for hours at the spot of rendezvous. By 1315, we had begun to doubt the existence of *U-634*, but then Borchert with his magic eyes spotted the boat. Forty minutes later we sailed alongside her. I discovered that her Captain was Dahlhaus, an old friend from my mine-sweeping days in Holland. We strung rubber hoses from boat to boat while drifting parallel before the wind, and the pumps transferred 15 tons of diesel oil into our tanks. The fueling took almost two hours—two helpless hours of nervous waiting for airplanes to dive upon us. None appeared. With great relief, we separated from *U-634*, and both boats set course for Brest.

May 23. *U-230* crossed the 15th Longitude West, the door to Biscay Bay—and purgatory. We intercepted more bad news. A signal from *U-91* told us that they had seen *U-752* attacked and destroyed by aircraft; there were no survivors. At 1040 we crash-dived before a Sunderland airplane. No radar impulses. Quite obviously it must have attacked on sight. It announced the start of a six-day nightmare.

Under cover of darkness, *U-230* made her dash at a pitiful top speed of only 12 knots. We crash-dived seven times and shook off 28 attacks by bombs or depth charges. By sunrise, we were stunned, deaf, and exhausted. We disappeared in the floods for the rest of the day.

May 24. Apparently the British were aware that two U-boats were running for port; their aircraft seemed to be looking for us, including the land-based four-engined bombers. During that night we crash-dived nine times and survived a total of 36 bombing runs.

May 25. Three hours after daybreak we floated into the deadly range of a hunter-killer group. Running submerged in absolute silence, we managed to slip by the endless, cruel, ravenous pings. One hour before midnight, we surfaced into the inevitable air assaults. On the first attack, four ferocious detonations rocked the boat as she surged into the deep. Suddenly there was a flash in the rear of the control room. A stream of sparks shot across the narrow space and enveloped us in choking smoke. The boat was afire. It seemed impossible to bring her to surface before we died. The round doors of the two bulkheads were slammed shut, the compartments sealed. Several men fought the fire with extinguishers. *U-230* rose sharply toward the surface where only seconds before the aircraft had dropped its diabolic calling card. Thick fumes choked us. Fire leaped from wall to wall. I pressed my handkerchief against mouth and nose and followed the Captain into the tower. The boat leveled off, she had surfaced. We hastened to the bridge. Somebody threw ammunition magazines on deck. The port diesel began to mutter. Red light and fumes escaped the hatch. We drove like a torch through the blackest night until the men below managed to kill the fire.

That night we outmaneuvered seven attacks and outlasted 28 bombs.

May 26. It was the fourth day of our run for life and port. We floated at 40 meters, listening to a depth-charge barrage many miles to the west. It lasted all day. At 2230 we surfaced. The night was very dark. Over an hour passed without radar detection. Then we saw a huge spotlight hanging in the sky, growing bigger with insane speed, drenching the bridge in daylight, blinding us. A four-engined Liberator came roaring down, guns blazing. The boat swung toward the fast-approaching light. The giant roared over our bridge and catapulted into the night, showering the bridge with sparks and hot air Four bombs exploded, bellowing barbarously. My legs were jarred into my body at each concussion.

Moments later came the call from below, "Boat is tight, ready for dive."

When *U-230* was balanced in protective depth, Siegmann stormed into the radio room, up to the mate who had failed to warn us of a radar detection. "What the hell is the matter, Kaestner? Are you asleep? You nearly got us all killed!"

"Sir, there was no impulse," the mate protested. "And our gear is in order."

"Don't tell me any stories, Kaestner," hollered Siegmann, "the entire crew is in your hands. If you fail again, our skins aren't worth a penny."

May 27. We surfaced, low on power and air. Tension was at a peak. My nerves twitched and my tongue was hot and dry. I reckoned that we would have no chance for survival if another attack occurred immediately. But for long minutes the roar of our one diesel and the sigh of the air intake was the only sound we could hear.

After an hour of grace, time ran out again. A white shaft of light suddenly engulfed the bridge. The beam came at us from starboard aft. Again a giant Liberator swooped down, its guns emitting small red flames, its bullets missing our heads by only centimeters. Then the plane roared into the night, headlight turned off. Four bomb bursts sent geysers of water into the air. The boat was violently shaken, but emerged without further damage. We dived immediately.

As I passed the Captain in his nook, he was unbuttoning his salt-caked leather jacket. Looking up, he said, "I concede, Exec, there were no radar impulses. Our Metox seems to be in perfect order. The British must have invented a new kind of radar. It's the only explanation I can think of."

We were stunned. First the aircraft carrier. Now a new electronic trick that permitted British planes to locate us without betraying their own position. There was no longer a reason for traveling submerged by day and on surface at night. We had to reverse our tactic and travel the surface during the day, when we could see our adversaries with the naked eye. Shooting it out in daylight seemed better than being hacked to pieces at night.

At 0720 we surfaced. Our prospects of winning the

last 170-mile dash to port were not at all promising. We spotted four Sunderlands and five Liberators. Nine times we crashed into depth and received the blood-curdling baptisms. Nine times we surfaced and plowed ahead. We reached the Continental shelf that afternoon. At nightfall we informed Headquarters that we would be at the pick-up point the following morning at 0800. Then, taking no more chances in this new war at sea, we dived.

12

On May 28, at 1240, *U-230* sailed into the inner harbor of Brest. With her aft deck largely submerged and her superstructure damaged, she gave everyone on the pier a broad hint of what we had gone through. There was no band playing the military tunes; only the girls with the flower bouquets reminded us of the glorious past. The Commandant 9th Flotilla and his party showed signs of shock. We were hastily and unceremoniously transported to the compound. But once we were ushered into the reception hall, our landlubber hosts tried hard to make our homecoming a pleasant one.

After the party, I returned to my room, the same room that I had abandoned five weeks before. My belongings had already been delivered from storage. As I retrieved the envelope containing my testament from one valise, I felt an overpowering gratitude: I had survived. In my mail, I found only two letters from Marianne. A multitude of strange thoughts flashed through my mind. Then a small parcel from home distracted me. Mother had sent me a birthday cake. It was already four weeks old, and had hardened and broken into many pieces. But I wished to honor my mother's belief in her son's longevity, so I ate a piece of the cake anyway.

The strenuous routine of the two days in port—stripping our boat and bringing her into dry dock—kept me from brooding over our misfortune. But I was reminded of our wrecked mission the next morning; I was at the pier by chance when *U-634* finally sailed into harbor, three days late. I thanked Dahlhaus for his help, this time with a handshake.

Nevertheless, I managed to suppress my morbid thoughts, to forget that death had been my constant companion during the month of May. With the self-renewing vigor of youth, I went out to embrace the hot and fast life in port. I joined my friends—those who had made it back from patrol—in a turbulent night in the Casino Bar. We celebrated everyone's birthday and danced with all of Madame's beauties. Madame had replenished her staff with several exotic flowers, ranging in color from the white to yellow and coconut brown. Janine was as loving as ever. No matter that she gave her love to my friends in my absence. It might well prove their last hours of love and life.

In fact, the U-boat war was fast becoming one long funeral procession for us. The Allied counteroffensive at sea had struck with unexpected and unprecedented force. The British and Americans had quietly, steadily massed their forces. They had increased their fleet of fast corvettes, built a number of medium-sized aircraft carriers and converted a number of freighters into pocket-sized carriers, assembled squadrons of small planes for carrier duty as well as huge armadas of long-range land-based bombers. Then they hit with sudden power and, in 38 cases, with frightening precision. This was the count of U-boats they had sunk in that fateful May of 1943. In those U-boats many of my friends and classmates had met their end. Unless Headquarters produced dramatic countermeasures, all our proud new U-boats would be turned into a terrible surplus of iron coffins.

It was estimated that the overhaul of *U-230* would take at least four weeks. Since I was eligible for a pro-

longed leave, I made plans for a stop in Paris, a visit
at home, and a week with Marianne in the hot summer
sun on the beach of the Wannsee in Berlin. Yes, my
leave was a long one, but I was all too aware that my
time was limited.

One evening in early June, having turned over my
business to Riedel, I set off on an express to Paris.
As the train flashed through the French countryside, I
imagined hearing familiar sounds: hammering diesels,
depth-charge explosions, the detonations of bombs
and torpedoes, the breaking of ships, and the roar of
the ocean. But it was only the unfamiliar noise of the
train wheels as they clicked over the joints of the
tracks.

I arrived in Paris' Gare de Montparnasse while the
morning was still fresh and new. A cab took me to my
hotel near the Place Vendôme, which had been com-
mandeered for naval officers. I had decided to remain
unattached during my short stay in town, but the
abundance of aggressive girls soon tested my resolve.
I hurried into the cool halls of the Louvre and spent
most of the day strolling through the Galerie d'Ap-
polon, the Grand Galerie and the Salle des Cariotides
where, according to legend, many Huguenots had been
hanged from the rafters. In the evening I went to an
elaborate restaurant near the Opéra and dined in solitude and pomp. Then I wandered down the Boulevard
des Capucines, declined several offers of commercial
love, and retreated into the comforting silence of my
hotel room.

The next day, time stood still for me. In the morning I walked through the Place de Pigalle, consumed a
large breakfast in a small café in Montmartre, climbed
the long stairway to Sacré Coeur. I spent the afternoon
and evening in luxurious idleness in the streets and
cafés of the Left Bank. Paris, beautiful Paris—how I
hated to leave her! But at 2200 I boarded my train
for Germany.

The morning sun was riding high when my express
pulled into Frankfurt station. I noticed at once that
the huge glass dome spanning the tracks was badly
damaged. All the glass had been smashed in air raids,

leaving only a naked steel skeleton. The sight made a gloomy prelude to my visit.

As always, I returned home without notification, and when Mother answered the bell, she glanced at me as if I were a stranger. After a second I said, "Hello, Mother, you might as well let me in, it's good to be back."

I noticed that Mother was unusually nervous, and that she had lost considerable weight. I believed I also noticed a hint of grief in her face. But instead of asking her questions I tried to please her: "I'm really glad I can stretch my legs under your table again."

Naturally she asked me whether I had enough to eat, insisted that I had become too thin, and wanted to know all about my health. "Tell me, did you have enough underwear to keep yourself warm? You might not know, but we have given away whatever clothes we could spare to our soldiers on the Russian front. We have contributed all your shoes and your ski outfits as well as the skis. Tell me also, how is the war in the Atlantic? We don't hear as much anymore about the U-boats."

I told her that she would soon hear again of our successes; but, having made up my mind that I would not discuss the war, I changed the subject: "How is everybody? How is Trudy doing, has she seen her husband lately?"

"Trudy is fine, just fine," she said. "Hans was here on Easter. We had his parents too. They had some serious air raids in Duesseldorf and have left for the Black Forest to wait until things turn better. We also had some heavy attacks recently, but not as bad as they have been elsewhere."

Then I asked, "How is Father?"

And Mother burst out crying. With the tears running down her cheeks, she told me that he had been taken away—the Gestapo had arrested him three months ago. He was still imprisoned at the city jail in the Hammelsgasse. Mother sobbed, "I didn't tell you in my letters. I didn't want you to know."

Torn between disbelief and outrage, I managed to extract from her a vague account of what had happened.

Father had maintained a more-than-just-friendly-and-occasional relationship with a young woman. She had been one of his employees and he had kept her on the payroll for a long time. One day he had asked Mother for a divorce to marry the girl. But this was not the reason for Father's arrest. The trouble was that the woman he loved was Jewish, and that, according to the government's doctrine, was a crime. He had committed another crime by hiding her from persecution. Unfortunately, somebody had found out and reported that the girl was Jewish, and so the Gestapo had seized the girl and Father. They had put her into a camp and Father into jail.

I was shocked and angered by Father's imprisonment, but I was not surprised by the injustice of it. He had suffered before at the hands of our government. Back in the winter of 1936, Father's business, a finance company, had been closed down by edict, along with 36 similar firms. Simply because such companies no longer fit the policies of the leaders of the Third Reich, Father was deprived of his life's work without warning, explanation, or appeal; and he had to start all over again at the age of 46. It was only through ingenuity and hard work that he managed to build up a new business and provide for his family.

Soon afterward, the government's ideological nonsense produced far uglier results. I myself had witnessed the "Crystal Night" in Frankfurt in 1938, when the mob had raged through the streets, smashing the windows and plundering the stores of Jews while the police stood by and did nothing. The mob tossed furniture out of apartment windows, threw pianos over balcony railings, flung down china, books, lamps, and household utensils. And when everything of value had been stolen, the rest was piled up and burned in huge bonfires. I remembered how my Father had led me through the flaming wreckage to help a Jewish friend, only to find his apartment ransacked and vacant. It was then that I saw Father in anger and with tears in his eyes.

To us, the "Crystal Night" was shameful and tragic; but my father was not a rebel in search of hopeless causes, and neither was I. I knew that something was seriously wrong in the country I loved; but the war caught me up when I was 19, and I had neither the time nor the political interest to investigate. Now, however, I was inextricably entangled in an affair that made me feel like a flaming rebel; and I would have to see it through even if I damaged my position and my military career.

Immediately I walked to Gestapo Headquarters in the Lindenstrasse, a short distance from our home. My uniform and decorations got me past the guards without an interrogation. As I entered a large hall, a secretary at a desk near the entrance asked me whether she could help.

"I want to see *Obersturmbannfuehrer* von Molitor, please." I put on a pleasant smile and handed her my calling card, adding, "It will be a surprise for Herr von Molitor." I assumed he seldom saw a U-boat man, much less one whose Father was behind bars.

I had to wait just long enough to plan what I would say. Then the girl ushered me into a well-appointed room and introduced me to the chief SS officer in town. So this was a fearful SS man, whose snap of a finger could decide someone's life. The middle-aged officer in the light gray SS uniform looked more like a jovial businessman than a cold-blooded prosecutor.

Von Molitor's greeting was as genial as his appearance: "It's a pleasure to meet somebody from the Navy for a change. I know you serve in the U-boat force. Quite an interesting and exciting job, isn't it? What can I do for you, *Leutnant?*"

I treated him with quiet severity: "Sir, you are holding my father a prisoner. This is unreasonable. I demand his immediate release."

The expression on his fleshy face changed from a friendly smile to profound consternation. He looked at my calling card, read my name again, and then stuttered, "I was not informed that we had arrested the Father of an outstanding soldier. I am sorry, *Leutnant.* It must be a mistake, I shall investigate at once." He wrote something on a piece of paper, pushed a button. Another secretary came through a second door and took the slip from his hand. "You see, *Leutnant,* I am not informed about every single case. But I also realize that you would not be here if your Father weren't in jail."

"Obviously. And I consider the reason for his arrest and imprisonment . . ." Before I could make a serious blunder, the girl came back and handed von Molitor another note.

He took the time to read it carefully, then said in a conciliatory tone, "*Leutnant,* I am now aware of the case. You will have your Father back by evening. I am sure that three months in solitary have taught him a lesson. I am sorry that it happened. But it was strictly of your Father's making. I am glad I could help you and do you a favor. I hope you will now enjoy your furlough. Good-by, Heil Hitler!"

Rising quickly, I thanked him briefly—not that he had done me a favor, for he could hardly have denied my request. I left with a provocative military salute. After I had reached the street, I remembered the girl who had been sent away, and I was sorry that I was unable to help her also. It was not until after the war that I learned she had somehow survived.

Then I went to Father's office to see my sister Trudy for the first time since her wedding. When I told her that Father would be home for dinner, Trudy dissolved in tears. She said, sobbing, "We tried to free Father, but the Gestapo always refused to hear our pleas. You don't know how glad I am that you came home. Mother and Father's marriage is on the rocks. It's a terrible situation. Since he's been in the Hammelsgasse, I have managed the business all by myself."

I told her what a good girl she was, and that I was proud of her, and I proposed to close the office for the rest of the day and celebrate. She gave instructions to a female supervisor and we made the short walk home.

Mother was highly nervous and disturbed but full of forgiveness. She was ready to forget the whole affair as long as Father did not leave her. That possibility had been greatly reduced by the removal of the object of Father's affections.

It was almost dinner time when the key turned in the front door and Father, unaware of my presence, stepped into the vestibule. The moment he saw me, he realized that it was I who was responsible for his release from prison. We shook hands in silence. He wore a week-old beard. The Gestapo did not even have the decency to give him a shave.

The evening dragged on uncomfortably. It was difficult for us to concentrate on a subject and keep the conversation going. I talked briefly about the Atlantic front without telling the truth. The epic difficulties of our armies in the Russian theater and the complete defeat of Rommel in North Africa troubled Father more than his brush with the Gestapo. He also told me about the frequent air attacks on Frankfurt and spoke of moving his business out of town. We talked about many things, but Father never touched on the subject of his romance, never indicated whether he would stay with Mother. As far as I was concerned, nothing mattered but that Father was home. As for the marriage—well, that was something he and Mother had to work out between themselves.

One day and one night later, I arrived in Berlin. Emerging from the Anhalter Station, I was stopped in my tracks by the destruction. Broken glass, mortar, and rubble were strewn everywhere. And for the first time, Marianne was not at the station.

Intending to call on Marianne at her office, I boarded a streetcar bound for the center of the capital. That ride was appalling. Large sections of the city had almost been leveled by the saturation bombings, leaving rubble, dust, and a million tragedies. I felt as if the bottom were falling out of my world. I felt like running away and leaving the city on the next train. But I eventually reached the spot where Marianne had worked—that is, where her seven-story office building had once stood. Only a few walls had remained. Bricks were piled up two stories high.

I turned away from the devastation, searched for and found the nearest subway stop, then took the express train to the suburb where Marianne lived with her parents. Leaving the station on foot, I saw here and there a home burned to the ground, an apartment house collapsed. It seemed that death and destruction were following me. As I neared Marianne's home, I braced myself against a reality I already sensed. Then I was standing before the heap of charcoal that had been the house. Its chimney poked into the air like a warning finger. Around it lay smashed bricks and blocks, black with soot; steel beams bent in the heat of the fire; jumbled debris of all sorts. Then I saw the sign stuck in the rubble. Somebody had written in red: ALL MEMBERS OF THE HARDENBERG FAMILY ARE DEAD.

I read it two or three times before I turned away. I was unable to comprehend. Something acrid burned in my throat. I swallowed repeatedly. Then my heart suddenly hardened. At that moment all in me was dead—burned out like the homes. I was without emotion.

The next express carried me back home to Frankfurt. With Marianne's death preying on my mind, I spent four aimless days in Frankfurt. I also spent one night in the cellar of our apartment house, listening to the screaming sirens and the bellowing of the flak, shaking to the tremors of the exploding bombs and looking into the serious stony faces of people who accepted the raid as a routine event. When it was all over, the night was filled with the caustic stench of cordite, the moans of the wounded, and the bells of the fire brigades. This was what the war had come to: that my Marianne was an air-raid victim, that my family had grown accustomed to living underground in fear of their lives. After that night, there was nothing left for me at home. I had to return to my boat and fight the war at sea to a successful end for the sake of those who remained at home in anguish and dread.

After a night on a darkened train, I arrived in Paris. The city breathed peace, and the hot June sun gilded the trees and rooftops. The heat made my uniform uncomfortable and set me to thinking about the advantages of civilian clothes. How I would enjoy pretending to be a part of the sophisticated Parisian crowd which did not care about the war one way or the other. There I noticed that the most elegant Parisiennes paid no attention whatsoever to men in uniform. I realized how far I was from their lives of splendor, beauty, and charm; how deep was the gulf between the peaceful crowds in the city and us on the front, who had no choice but to sail and fight and die.

I arrived in the compound in Brest late in the evening, and found Riedel and my other friends in high spirits in the flotilla's bar. I joined their merry party, and we made the bar tremble with our rough exuberance and echo with our ribald sea chanteys. This was what we all needed to help us forget that our number would soon be called, that we all had but a short reprieve to sing and drink. This was what I needed to counteract the twin shocks of Marianne's death and Father's trouble with the Gestapo. I needed my friends, strong drinks, and the excitement of the wanton life to bring me sweet forgetfulness. I also needed duty and hard work. In the days that followed, I had all these and more in abundant supply.

I quickly adjusted to the old routine, made my daily trips to the shipyard, took a firm hold of the crew. Only one man caused me any real difficulty. That one, a seaman, used to jump the wall at night to join the fun in town. He had the bad luck to get himself involved in frequent fist fights, usually over girls, and I decided to send him away for eight days—into solitary that is. Otherwise he was an excellent man and reliable as soon as our boat left port.

During my short absence there had been a remarkable addition to the flotilla's staff. The importance of the flotilla's place in the Navy had been discovered, and with it the need for a staff photographer to record interesting events for posterity. The photographer turned out to be an attractive young woman. Her casual "Good morning" prompted me to issue an invitation to a drink. As soon as we sat down at the bar, I said, "You have a very familiar southern accent."

"Yours is not exactly Berlinish, either," she retorted with a smile.

"I admit that. I grew up on Lake Constance, on the north shore."

"What a coincidence!" she said. "I lived across the lake, in Constance. I am Veronica, everybody calls me Vera."

I invited Vera for dinner and she accepted without thinking it over. After my day's work was done, I took a swim in the pool, which was another new addition to the compound; then it was time for our rendezvous. I knocked at the door of the bungalow Vera had received in lieu of an apartment.

We left the compound and strolled through the narrow streets of Brest in the fading afternoon sun. For dinner, we had snails broiled in butter and herbs, shrimps and tartar sauce, a large lobster, and a bottle of Beaujolais. Then we went to a small secluded café and we danced to the music of a piano player who obliged us with all the tunes we requested. Soon we returned to the compound, and it was a strange experience to be admitted to the flotilla's closely guarded quarters with a female.

From that night on, I met Vera regularly after work. The evenings were ours. One Saturday I recalled my vow to buy a civilian suit, and invited Vera to join me in a search for material and a tailor. Despite the depletions of the long war, one tailor offered an amazing variety of fabrics—without ration tickets. I chose a plaid fabric, had my measurements taken, a price fixed, and a date set for delivery of the finished suit. I was not the least disturbed that I might never have an opportunity to wear it. With this purchase I somehow forced myself to be optimistic.

In those few remaining days in port, there was plenty of reason for pessimism. When a friend failed to return from patrol, when the truth about our losses in May was confirmed, when a boat crawled into harbor severely beaten, when reports of mounting losses circulated through the mess halls, then the memory of our watery hell came back to my mind, and a presentiment of disaster rose like a wall between the two lives I led. The worst of it was that our boys were unable to sell their lives dearly. For all of our casualties, we had sunk in April only one-third as many ships we sent down in March, and only 50 enemy vessels, totaling a mere 265,000 tons, had been sunk in the disastrous month of May. As of mid-June, the U-boat war had come to a virtual standstill. Sixteen more boats had been lost in a fortnight, and Admiral Doenitz had called for a temporary halt in our attacks on the shipping lanes of the North Atlantic. The surviving boats were redeployed but not withdrawn from the front. On the contrary, to offset our stunning losses, great efforts were made to refloat boats in dry dock and to finish those under construction in shipyards. The idea was that every boat we had, even the unsound and outmoded ones, should be put into action to show the Allies that our back had not been broken. Doenitz, in a speech he made in Lorient, assured us that our battle reverses were only temporary, that the tide would be turned by our countermeasures, but that in the meantime we would have to go on sailing. Our efforts, he said, would tie up Allied naval forces in the Atlantic and keep Allied bombers away from our cities.

At the end of June I took *U-230* out of dry dock and brought her to the pier, where her fitting-out was to be completed. With that one decisive movement, all our adventures in port came to an end. All that was real was the boat, the war, and the inevitable clash with the enemy. These were the facts. Everything else was merely a wishful dream.

In the afternoon of June 29, after the Captain had returned from a briefing at Senior Officers' U-boats West Headquarters, he asked me to see him in his room. Siegmann added, "Bring Friedrich and Riedel with you. I have some interesting news."

Twenty minutes later, we were there. The Captain said, "Have a seat, gentlemen, it will take a while for what I have to say. And what you are going to hear must not leave this room.

"Headquarters has selected us for a special mission. The prime objective of our next patrol will be the laying of mines. The target is the east coast of the United States. We will take aboard twenty-four magnetic mines of latest design and plant them in Chesapeake

Bay—more precisely, in front of the U.S. Naval Base at Norfolk. I do not have to point out the dangers of this undertaking, and I insist that our destination remain a secret until we are at sea. I would not like to arrive in the United States to find a reception committee waiting.

"One thing more. The waters of the Chesapeake Bay are too shallow to permit a submerged operation, so we will have to execute our mission on surface. I ask you, Exec, to secure all necessary charts of that area and keep them under lock and key."

The three of us had listened intently and greeted the plan as a welcome departure from a routine patrol. Concerned about our defense, I asked the Captain, "If we have to store twenty-four mines, that doesn't allow us to take more than two torpedoes."

"Two is correct, Exec. The rest of the space will be taken up by the mines, for which you will be responsible."

Friedrich asked, "How much fuel are we going to take aboard?"

"Just the regular amount. Everything is well organized. We will be supplied by one of our large U-tankers somewhere near the West Indies, our future area of operation. There we will receive plenty of food, fuel, and torpedoes. You, Riedel, will have the crew fitted out with tropical gear and arrange for that special diet for the tropics." And Siegmann concluded, "Gentlemen, I expect to stay at sea for the remainder of the summer."

On July 1, we took over the mines. The strange supply of elongated capsules stirred immediate speculation among the boat's company. Some of the men were positive we would mine an English port. Others thought that the place would be Gibraltar Harbor. The smart ones, however, believed we would travel as far as the important west African port of Freetown. I smiled at the heated discussions and was glad to see that the crew was as eager as ever to go to sea.

But the closer we came to the date of our seagoing, the more skeptical I became about any imminent betterment of our situation in the Atlantic. None of the

anticipated improvements had been installed aboard
U-230. The Metox, our radar detection gear, was still
said to be the ultimate in radar warning devices. Additional anti-aircraft guns had been promised, but had
not arrived in port in sufficient numbers. Rumors
about new inventions, such as a rubber coating around
the hull and superstructure to reduce radar and Asdic
detection, proved to be just that—messhall rumors.
The only real improvement was the installation of ar-
mored-plating around the bridge in lieu of our rigid
radar, which was as obsolete as the 8.8 cm. cannon
on foredeck that had also been dismantled. As things
stood, all the odds were against us. The British were
throwing in planes in such huge numbers that scarcely
a U-boat could traverse the Bay of Biscay undetected.
Within a six-week period, the Allies had reduced our
active U-boat Force by 40 per cent, and many of the
survivors had yet to break through the blockade and
reach port safely.

Notwithstanding the terrible attrition in our ranks,
we still believed that we would reverse the tide if we
held out long enough. We had to hold out.

Two days before sailing, I went to see my tailor
again. He had not completed the suit as promised. I
told him to have it ready in two weeks, and as an in-
ducement I paid him the balance of the price. I did
not wish to be indebted to him in case I did not return.

13

Monday July 5. The departure of *U-230* was scheduled for the evening. During the day we received an
additional passenger. Because of the anticipated length
of our voyage and the recent increase in injuries inflicted upon gunners and lookouts by aircraft gunfire,

Headquarters had added a doctor to our crew. He arrived at the pier laden down with several suitcases, as if he were embarking on a pleasure cruise. "Hello, Herr *Leutnant*," he said. "My name is Dr. Reche. I will try to take good care of your men. But I must admit I have never been on a ship, much less a U-boat. Would you please show me my cabin?"

Our boys, listening with broad grins on their faces, made some inappropriate remarks. I shook the doctor's slender hand and explained apologetically, "Doctor, there is no such thing as a cabin aboard a U-boat. Also, we have no room for all that luggage. Please take only what you really need, about one quarter of what you have there, and follow me below." After he had reduced his baggage, I managed to accommodate him in the warrant officers' wardroom, assigning him the berth above the navigator's.

At sundown we attended our farewell party in the compound, then went to man the boat in small silent groups. Everyone, from the Captain down to the lowliest seaman, said nothing of his thoughts about our imminent encounter with the deadly foe. It had become widely known, despite all efforts to keep it a secret, that the enemy was sinking three out of five of our boats as they made their runs through the Bay of Biscay. On June 24 alone, the Tommies had sent four U-boats to the bottom within 16 hours.

The night was stark and moonless when *U-230* sailed. No band, no ceremony, no cheering crowd betrayed our clandestine departure to French partisans or English agents. These days British Intelligence had its eyes and ears on us everywhere—in the compound, in the shipyard, in the restaurants, and even in the *établissements*.

At the tip of Brittany, where the rocks of the coast sink into the ocean, we were picked up by a coastguard vessel which guided us south along the shore to a rendezvous with other U-boats from Lorient. The night passed without incident and at dawn we joined *U-506* and *U-533*. We three had been ordered to travel together through the Bay of Biscay, using our combined firepower to ward off British air attacks.

As the boats converged, four escorts circled, the strange assembly on tense alert. The three U-boat Captains carried on a shouted conversation through megaphones, discussing the strategy of the group march. They were to travel at the high speed of 18 knots on surface during the day, to stay submerged but in close contact all night, and to surface at dawn upon command. If an airplane was detected at a safe distance, the Captain of *U-533* would wave a yellow flag, indicating that all three boats should crash-dive. But if he waved a red flag, the aircraft had already come too close for a safe dive, and all three boats were supposed to shoot it out.

This plan, so cleverly conceived by our staff officers in the security of their office, was faulty in conception and nearly impossible to execute. For lack of anything better, however, the three Captains agreed to try their luck.

At 0810, the three boats turned their bows westward and began their attempt to break through the enemy's heavy defense. The escorts steamed east, back into port, as we hurried off. It was a humid and hot day— a good day to spend at the beach. Clouds were high, haze lingered low. The Metox was quiet. Three strained hours passed without interference or contact.

1135: The yellow flag went up on board *U-533*. The same instant we spotted the aircraft about 10,000 meters on starboard. All three boats ducked. Thirty minutes later we heard *U-506* sending the signal to surface on her newly acquired underwater sound device. Like trained seals three U-boats broke surface simultaneously. They went to full speed and hammered westward, leaving three long foamy wakes.

1310: A Liberator shot out of the cloud cover, distance 3,000 meters. Too late to dive. The red flag went up at once, and on all decks the guns were manned. The big black bird dived down for attack. But before we had the range to open fire, the plane turned away and began to circle our group.

1318: A second Liberator appeared in the sky—a new variation on a familiar theme. Both aircraft kept circling at a respectful distance. I ordered more ammunition to the bridge and more stored in the conning tower; diving at this point was out of question. Trapped by the planes, the three boats dampened the Tommies' eagerness to attack by sending bursts of gunfire toward them. The diesels' thundering noise filled the air and from above came the low throbbing roar of the aircrafts' engines.

1325: A Sunderland dived through the clouds and joined the two Liberators in their circling. Its appearance reduced even further our meager chances for escape.

1332: With the arrival of a third Liberator, the fourth aircraft, our chances sank to zero. Our patrol, only a few hours old, seemed to have come to a premature end. We waited for the assault with only a small spark left of the confidence with which we had sailed.

1340: A Liberator plunged into attack. The guns of three U-boats blazed at the pilot, who seemed insane to fly into our concentrated fire. But quickly a second Liberator fell upon us from the opposite side, forcing us to divide our fire power. All three boats began wild zigzag movements to spoil our attackers' aim. One of the planes, diving down on *U-230* with flames spurting from its gunbarrels, dropped its bombs and roared by, missing our bridge by only three meters. Four explosions—four giant geysers. One man on our lower gun sagged and fell to the deck. Another replaced him. Moments later four more fountains erupted around the tower of *U-506* as the second plane cut through our firing line.

We lowered the wounded gunner into the boat and heaved fresh ammunition to the bridge. Suddenly *U-506* dived. The four Tommies, seeing their chances, flew a combined attack. Then something unexpected happened. *U-506* returned to the surface immediately and some men jumped to the guns. The boat made a sharp turn to port, avoiding the bombs dropped by the Sunderland. The explosions boomed between the bellowing of our flak and the planes' stuttering guns and the roar of our diesels and the thunder of aircraft engines. The sea fumed from multiple exhausts and foamed from bomb bursts. The air shrieked with shrapnel and bullets ricocheting off our armor plating. Rising from its dive, the Sunderland caught a burst, shuddered and fell slowly into the sea. After the Sunderland had crashed, its comrades retreated. That was the moment we acted. With racing engines, the three U-boats ducked in an instant and dived. We were not quite down in safe depths when the tremor of detonating bombs told us that the British had not yet given up.

That was the end of our plan to travel in a group through the Bay of Biscay. Our contact with the two other boats was soon lost. Neither of the two reached port again. *U-506* was sunk six days after the encounter, and *U-533* was destroyed twelve weeks later, both victims of Allied air attacks.

Dr. Reche, shaken by fear and seasickness, managed to treat our one casualty, who had been shot in the upper right thigh. Luckily, the bullet had passed without smashing any bones. Reche bandaged the gunner with greatest difficulty, and when he had finished he crawled into his bunk, himself badly in need of help.

Day and night the pursuers continued to bombard us savagely. We were hunted, persecuted, and almost driven insane. Dozens of times we crashed into the depths and the detonations reached after us, and yet day after day, for seven days in a row, we managed to escape. And when *U-230* reached the rolling prairies of the mid-Atlantic, where we were relatively safe, we rose from the depths astounded by our survival. As usual, others had not shared our luck. During the same period, *U-514* and *U-232* were hacked to bits on July 8, and *U-435* was sunk one day later. On July 12 the enemy scored two hits, destroying *U-506* and *U-409*, and the next day the British bombed *U-607*. All these boats were lost in the Bay of Biscay, perilously close to our route of march.

Passing from the Bay, out of range of the land-based bombers, we ducked only two or three times a day, gaining long hours on surface. The boat was cleaned of its mold and rot, the bilges scrubbed, and the refuse thrown overboard—a routine we had omitted in the Bay. We also prepared our mines for the drop and our torpedoes for use when needed. Now, on watch, we enjoyed bright days, and the blazing sun burned our skins deep brown. The crew began to show signs of appetite and some machinists came up into the conning tower to puff a pipe or smoke a cigarette. The only one who never saw the sun, who never even rose from his berth, was our doctor. Reche slowly dissolved on his mattress in seasickness. Yellow and thin, he rested quietly in his narrow bunk, accepted nothing, asked for nothing. It was only when we submerged for our regular trim dive, coming to rest for a while at 60 meters, that the doctor emerged from his leather bed, reminding us that he was still on board.

U-230 proceeded steadily toward her destination. On most days, we reduced the distance to Chesapeake Bay by approximately 160 miles, depending upon the severity of the harassment from above. The stream of signals from boats in distress never ceased. Around that time *U-509* reported that she had been heavily damaged by aircraft and needed parts urgently, but nothing was heard from her again. The radio mate not only deciphered distress signals, he also typed and multigraphed the Armed Forces communiqués he intercepted daily. We were startled by the news of swift Allied landings on Sicily and dismayed by word of continuing reverses in the Russian theater. The world was aflame and the flames blazed highest where they were the least expected—inside Germany. Our Luftwaffe, neglected by Goering and decimated by the Allies, could not prevent the Allied air flotillas from bombing our cities into ashes. Suddenly it struck me that the recent disasters of the U-boat Force bore alarming resemblances to the defeat of the Luftwaffe in the air. But despite the burnings and bombings, the retreats and defeats and the imminent danger of our own destruction, we kept our hopes high. We had been told that the war would be won, and we still believed it.

And still our U-boats continued to die. On July 20, a radio signal told us that the logbook of one of our friends of better days in Brest was closed forever. The message—AIRCRAFT. ATTACKED. SINKING. IMPRISONMENT. U-558—was his last report.

The following day we sighted a Catalina, a two-engined flying boat. We dived swiftly and stayed submerged for two hours, forcing its pilot to give up the

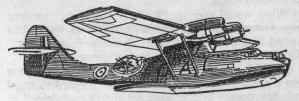

Catalina

chase. When we surfaced late in the afternoon, the sky was congested with heavy dark clouds. We took advantage of the storm front and raced at high speed into the evening. The night descended, but it was soon turned into day. Lightning flashed across the firmament; dozens of bolts at a time stabbed perpendicularly down from the sky to the ocean, rose from the surface in agitated zigzags to pierce the clouds. Hour after hour the lightning slashed forth and back, up and down, keeping the sky ablaze with the light of a billion torches, and the vast artillery of thunder burst and rolled and roared. The air reeked of phosphorus and made our eyes burn. After five full hours of lightning and thunder, the rains came. While the flashes kept lancing the clouds and the thunder echoed between sea and sky, torrents of rain beat the surface of the ocean flat. When the storm finally ended, a new day was born. It was clearer, brighter, more brilliant. It was the day we reached the continental shelf of North America.

Expecting heavy U.S. air surveillance, we dived at 0945 and put *U-230* on course at a depth of 110 meters. During the long submergence that followed, we planned our tactics. The crew rested undisturbed in total silence. Later the men were informed of the objective of our mission. At nightfall we surfaced; it was

2115 and Prager prepared to shoot several stars to determine our exact position. As he adjusted his sextant, I told him jokingly, "Make sure you get a good fix, so we don't find ourselves caught in the locks of the Panama Canal."

"What would you say, Exec, if I brought you into Lake Ontario," replied Prager, and we on watch had a good laugh that relieved our tension. Prager added, "Don't laugh, boys, we're on perfect course."

At 0140 we spotted a shadow on starboard. It grew into a merchant ship. Her skipper had a guardian angel with him on the bridge; we wanted to avoid detection, not to sink ships. The balance of the night was uneventful except for a false alarm about the time that Venus rose in all her brilliance. The air and surface proved to be empty; no aircraft or Coast Guard vessel came to disturb our stealthy approach. *U-230* continued undetected at 18 knots, Cape Charles dead ahead.

That night we received perplexing news. We heard on short-wave radio that a *coup d'état* had taken place in Italy, that Mussolini had been arrested and Marshal Badoglio had succeeded him as head of government. If the broadcast had not come from a German radio station, we would have derided the report as an enemy lie. Even so, it seemed unlikely, though not particularly important.

When the sun began to rise, we dived to maintain secrecy. Traveling westward slowly at a depth of 40 meters, we came within 30 miles of Cape Charles. Because we knew nothing of the U.S. defenses, we manned action stations and kept the aft tube ready to shoot in case of a surprise attack. Shortly after noon, the soundman reported increasing propeller noise. The Chief raised the boat to periscope depth for the Captain to investigate. To Siegmann's surprise, we were dead ahead of a small convoy—much closer than the gear indicated. There were four destroyers shepherding only seven cargo ships. Suddenly the Captain cried, "Boat is coming up, hold her down, bridge is breaking surface, down with her, Chief!"

Friedrich applied all emergency measures—no reaction.

"What the hell is wrong with this sloop, dive, dive fast!" hollered Siegmann.

Valuable seconds passed as *U-230* hung like a fish on a hook in full view of the escorts. Then, slowly, insanely slow, the boat drilled herself into a layer of heavy-density water. Just as her stern moved into the specifically heavier stratum of water, a spread of six charges detonated in closest proximity. The explosions propelled the boat below the thermal shift, and her screws, turning in maximum revolutions, drove her downward until she touched the sandy bottom. The Asdic pings released by the U.S. destroyers chirped through the shallow water, but did not hit our hull with the usual force; the sound waves were largely refracted by the dense layer of heavy water above us. For almost two hours the hunters nervously screened the depths, vainly seeking something to attack. Then they departed without spending one more depth charge on us.

We surfaced at nightfall. *U-230* pushed swiftly and relentlessly ahead. Three hours passed in apprehension and mounting excitement. Then, port ahead, a vague glow crept over the horizon—the lights of Norfolk. Minutes later, Borchert shouted, "America dead ahead!"

We had reached our destination. Time: 2325. Date: July 27, 1943.

As the thin line of the coast emerged from the water, Prager's voice drifted up from the darkness of the control room: "Boat is four miles east of Cape Charles. Suggest changing course to two-three-five."

"Very well," acknowledged Siegmann, "Exec, have the eggs ready for the drop."

"Right, sir," I said. "Do you wish them served sunny-side up?"

Everyone on the bridge laughed loudly. We were hilarious as we approached Fisherman's Island unmolested. One of the men imitated an Indian war cry, and we pictured ourselves as painted Indians attacking in a canoe.

I ordered the four front tubes flooded and the doors opened. *U-230* proceeded at high speed, leaving

Fisherman's Island on starboard. Our depth finder sounded out the water. Prager took constant bearings. Our presence was still a secret.

When we reached the halfway mark between Cape Charles in the north and Cape Henry in the south, Siegmann turned the bow of his boat into the shallow waters of the Chesapeake Bay. Surprisingly, not a single enemy vessel was there to stop us as the lights of Norfolk became clearly visible on port. The American soldiers must have been at a big party that night; they were surely not at sea. As we passed the Naval Base, the silhouette of the illuminated city rose sharply against the dark sky. Land rose all around us as we penetrated deeper into the Bay.

Two hours after midnight, we detected several cargo ships heading for the open sea. Their sudden appearance wrecked our plan to drop the mines that night. We had no time to dive and no alternative but to retreat into the darkness. For one long minute, our broadside was exposed unseen as *U-230* made a full turn. Then we sped ahead of the vessels out of the Bay. We saw one of them turn north and three veer south before they all dissolved in the night. We continued dashing eastward, covering 30 miles in two hours, then laid *U-230* aground in shallow water and waited for the next evening to arrive.

July 28. At 2145, when the last rays of the sun were extinguished, we surfaced and raced with highest revolutions back into Chesapeake Bay. Again we passed the line Cape Charles–Cape Henry. To the left lay Norfolk, and the American Navy was again celebrating in port. The Bay was deserted; only *U-230* made the sounds that disturbed the serenity of the night. It was near midnight when Borchert spotted a shadow suddenly mounting in the blackness dead ahead. We slowed down immediately. But the shadow grew so fast into a giant that Siegmann had to stop both engines to prevent our crashing into the stern of a merchant ship. Obviously, she was heading toward Baltimore. She sailed at a mere eight knots, rather slow for our timetable. But since we could not tell her skipper to hurry, we had to adjust our speed and follow in her wake. For several minutes we used our powerful binoculars to survey the American countryside.

July 29. At 0210, Siegmann reckoned we had proceeded far enough into the Bay. Swinging his boat on opposite course, he headed back toward the flickering lights of Norfolk. As *U-230* steadied on her course, I lowered myself into the darkened hull to activate and release the mines. Five minutes later, the first egg dropped from its tube with a soft splash. Three minutes later, egg number two followed, then number three—and the first tube was empty. As the mines were discharged in regular intervals the tubes were speedily reloaded. Fresh mines were lifted from their racks by trolleys and chains and cautiously moved into place. The hot bow room steamed with the sweat of half-naked bodies and resounded with the clanking of chains. The drop went smoothly and lasted one hour and 50 minutes. After it was all over, I hurried to the bridge and reported, "Twenty-four eggs dropped into Uncle Sam's front yard."

Replied Siegmann, "Since Easter is a long way off, let's not wait till the egg-rolling starts. Both engines full ahead, steer course nine-oh." The boat gained momentum fast and scurried along at 17 knots, past Norfolk, past Fisherman's Island, toward a new morning sky. We dived around 0600 without any interference and floated into the open sea far below surface.

That evening at 2230, *U-230* rose to the surface again. Siegmann chose a southwestward course and raced the engines high, leaving the scene of our secret gift far behind. The following day we were back in our old routine—diving three or four times daily before aircraft. The exultation over our performance did not diminish our alertness. Since our Metox had not helped us much to detect enemy planes, we relied on our eyes as the guarantors of our survival. On July 30 we received three consecutive distress signals, all giving the same position in the Bay of Biscay as the place of attack. Riedel, visibly shocked, handed me the messages:

ATTACKED. BOMBS. SINKING AT 46N 10W. U-504

ATTACKED BY AIRCRAFT. SINKING 46N 10-W. U-461.

AIRCRAFT. BOMBS. SINKING 46N 10W. U-462

We realized these boats had used the same formation conceived so ingeniously by Headquarters, but quickly abandoned by us. Knowing that they were large, unmaneuverable U-tankers, we could easily picture the uneven fight. Unable to repond quickly or to support one another, they had probably lost the fight before they stopped waving flags as the Phoenicians did 3,500 years before. Not only had three boats died; their destruction drastically reduced our chances of being refueled at sea.

The British air victory in the Bay of Biscay was matched by another one over land. For the third time, we heard on short-wave radio that Hamburg had been repeatedly bombed. The report said that the heaviest attack came during the previous night, when half of the city had gone up in flames. I saw Siegmann's face turn dead white at the news. He never touched his food that day; he stayed closed up in his nook behind the green curtain. We grieved for the Captain. Every man aboard knew that his whole family lived in Hamburg—his wife, his children, and also his parents. When the flames in Hamburg finally subsided, 41,000 people had died and over 600,000 were left homeless.

August 1. Having put some 400 miles between us and the Chesapeake coast, we risked sending a report to Admiral U-boats: SPECIAL MISSION COMPLETED. REQUEST NEW ORDERS. LOW ON FUEL AT 27N 68W.

Three hours after our transmission, two four-engined aircraft fell suddenly out of the sky. We crash-dived in confusion. Depth charges exploded all around us. That day we dived four more times, and it was obvious that our radiogram had sparked a massive U.S. air hunt. After dark we received orders to continue south through the Caribbean to waters east of the Windward Islands; there we would refuel from *U-459,* one of our U-tankers.

Two hours later Riedel deciphered a personal message from Headquarters: U-230. SIEGMANN. FAMILY SAFE. ALL WELL IN THE COUNTRY. DOENITZ. This signal did more for the Captain and the crew than a decoration for the mining mission.

We continued our march to the South with caution. The crash-dives were routine, and so were the bombs. Then, on August 3, we received a message from Headquarters which had a greater impact upon our lives than any since the beginning of the Allied offensive. ALL U-BOATS. ATTENTION. ALL U-BOATS. SHUT OFF METOX AT ONCE. ENEMY IS CAPABLE OF INTERCEPTING. KEEP RADIO SILENCE UNTIL FURTHER NOTICE.

This warning reached *U-230* in time, but it came too late for some 100 boats that had been sunk before the discovery. We were suddenly aware that in our very effort to survive, we had used a device that revealed our position just as clearly as a lighted Christmas tree. For weeks and months, we had been sending out invitations to our own funeral. The knowledge was maddening, and it made our survival all the more incredible.

We turned off the Metox with a sigh of relief and continued south. However, our hope of reaching port again diminished when we learned that our tanker had not answered Headquarters' repeated calls.

During those early days in August '43, *U-230* was shifted three times for refueling. Each time the expected U-tanker failed to arrive at the rendezvous, and we were left stranded. Whatever caused the mysterious failures of the U-tankers, our situation grew steadily more perilous as the days passed and our fuel supply dwindled. On August 9, our long, desperate wait was interrupted by a new tragedy, once again involving three of our boats. It began with a signal released from a boat that floated helpless some 400 miles east of Recife, Brazil: ATTACKED BY AIRCRAFT. DAMAGES. UNABLE TO DIVE. U-604. In an attempt to save the ship's company, Headquarters ordered *U-172* and *U-185,* which were in the vicinity of the stricken boat, to go to the rescue. There was radio silence for about 30 hours. Then on August 11, a signal crossed the Atlantic: ATTACKED BY AIRCRAFT. DAMAGES. U-172. Only minutes later: LIBERATOR. ATTACKED. SINKING. U-604. In about an hour we received a third message: RESCUED CREW U-604. DOWNED AIRCRAFT. DAMAGES. U-185.

Subsequent signals revealed that *U-172* had also

taken aboard survivors of *U-604*, and was hastily repaired with the help of *U-185*. Then the remaining boats began their 3,000-mile march to home port. *U-185* never arrived. She was lost on August 24, herself a victim of air attack.

By August 13, *U-230* was floating along with only two tons of diesel oil. Our position: about 300 miles east of Barbados. That afternoon, we received a fourth date to meet with a newly appointed supply boat, *U-117*, in grid square DP 64. The rendezvous was set for August 17. In an effort to be both saving and secretive, we submerged during the day, sailing at low speed to conserve our batteries; and at night we traveled on surface at moderate speed, parting with every liter of fuel that went into the diesel engines as if it were a drop of our own blood. Nevertheless, we arrived punctually in the designated area. We cruised slowly in a search pattern until we exhausted our fuel. Then, drifting helplessly, we sighted a black speck miles away. It came cautiously toward us. But instead of meeting with the tanker, we said "hello" to our old friend Dahlhaus of *U-634*, whose boat was also to refuel that day from *U-117*.

U-117 never arrived. After almost two days of strained waiting, Dahlhaus and Siegmann decided that *U-634*, which had almost 15 tons of fuel, would dash 150 miles westward and then inform Headquarters of our dilemma. Thus we would be safe even if Allied forces picked up the signal and converged on its source.

U-634 left us. We lay there motionless for hours, a sitting duck for any passing enemy. After 10 hours of suspense, we intercepted Dahlhaus' SOS signal to Admiral U-boats. Then we waited with even keener suspense for Headquarters' answer. It came at dawn on August 20, sparking new hope: U-634 TO SHARE FUEL WITH U-230. BOTH PROCEED INTO DF 91. REFUEL FROM U-847 AUGUST 27. RETURN TO BASE BY SHORTEST ROUTE.

Dahlhaus finally returned after an absence of 46 hours. Rather than running the risk of refueling by daylight, both boats submerged and waited until the sun had curved across the sky. After dusk we surfaced, received our share of fuel from *U-634,* and laid plans to meet Dahlhaus and the U-boat tanker again in five days. Then the two boats separated.

The nights were calm on our march eastward. During the day, we traveled submerged until we had reached the center of the Atlantic, where the air traffic ceased. During the night of August 27, we entered the square of our new rendezvous and began scanning the surface for familiar silhouettes. But it was morning before we spotted three conning towers in the quiet sea. As we converged, the superstructure of the huge supply boat, *U-847,* emerged from the ocean, increasing our number to five. We waved to *U-634,* greeted *U-415,* and sent our compliments to *U-172,* the boat that had rescued half of the crew of *U-604.*

Any assemblage of U-boats was extremely dangerous, and we could only hope that the enemy had not learned of our meeting. *U-634* and *U-415* did not waste any time; they pulled alongside the supply boat and began sucking their allotment of fuel. Three hours later, Dahlhaus relinquished his hoses to us and we began to draw aboard 15 tons of the precious liquid. Soon *U-415* had received her share and made way for *U-172.* As *U-415* turned away we wished her a safe return to Brest. I would have added a prayer if I had been prophetic, for I was to become the Captain of *U-415* seven months hence.

Knowing that we were helpless while taking the heavy oil into our tanks, our boys manned the guns and stood ready to cut the hoses instantly. Not so the crew of the supply boat; they simply stood around the large superstructure like street-corner idlers. In disgust, I yelled to the Exec of *U-847* through the megaphone, "What's the matter with you people, don't you have any respect for aircraft?"

"We haven't seen any since we passed Greenland," he shouted back.

"You better change your attitude. Tell me, where do you fellows sail from here?"

"To Japan," he replied nonchalantly. "But after giving away 50 tons of fuel, I guess we'll only make it to Surabaja."

Skeptically I wished him good luck. Soon afterward, our hoses were disconnected and *U-230* withdrew from the uneasy meeting. After a brief trim dive we proceeded cautiously on surface and followed in the wake of our predecessors, on a straight line toward port. Two hours after our departure, the supply boat broke radio silence and reported that she had completed the refueling of all four boats. By sending that message, *U-847* not only jeopardized the four boats she had supplied but also sealed her own fate. Within minutes, the British direction-finding service had pinpointed her position. Three hours later she was attacked by U.S. aircraft and sent to the bottom, a large iron coffin for every man aboard. That afternoon I heard the reverberation of many bombs some 60 miles astern, and I knew that *U-847* had died a needless death.

Like the other three U-boats, *U-230* did not have sufficient fuel for any elaborate evasive maneuvers, and we were obliged to take a short-cut through the Azores. While clearing those islands on the afternoon of August 30, we overheard a signal from Dahlhaus up ahead: CONVOY COURSE NORTH. HUNTED BY CORVETTE. U-634. Only minutes after we had received his call, we heard a terrible depth-charge barrage originating at Dahlhaus' approximate position. The pounding continued with increasing violence for over four hours. After that, *U-634* did not report again. She had been sunk with all hands.

After *U-230* passed the 20th Longitude West, air attacks increased. Now we were penetrating "Death Valley." We decided to stay submerged throughout the night and to travel on surface during the day, though only when the sky was clear. But the British ruled the sky, and the Bay of Biscay trembled under their constant bombardments. We thrust through falling bombs and blazing gunfire and a boiling sea, and managed to gain a few pitiful miles each day. The nights brought some relief, but not much. We slipped through cordons of corvettes and frigates, evaded their long-range Asdic pings and their endless supply of depth charges. After seven cruel days, we finally saw the rocks of Brittany emerge from the sea. It was the

eighth day of September, almost 10 weeks after we
had left port.

We met the minesweeper outside the entrance to
the harbor of Brest. That was the moment when the
men below changed into fresh fatigues and struggled
wearily onto the deck to smoke their first cigarettes in
weeks. That was also the time when our doctor rose
from his bunk and displayed his grayish, suffering face
to those who had long since forgotten him. Siegmann
stuck a big cigar into his full red Viking beard and
puffed away contentedly. Sailing under our magic um-
brella, we had once again defeated the enemy's best efforts to lay us on the ocean floor next to our dead comrades.

As soon as *U-230* had moored in one of the concrete berths, Friedrich came climbing down the bridge,
a straw hat over his long hair, a black beard framing
his pale face. He was carrying a porcelain cup in his
hand.

The Chief saluted and presented the cup to Siegmann. "I wish to impress on you, sir, that this is all I
could squeeze out of the tanks. A few drops of fuel
oil, no more."

Siegmann grinned. "You see, Chief, that is how ef-
ficiently I operate lately. You have got to give me
credit, I always provide a margin of safety."

14

Our reception in Brest reflected the strained state of
affairs and was overshadowed by the general dismay
over our endless string of losses. The pier inside the
large concrete bunker was dotted with a few men in
Navy blues, and two girls had found the time to greet
us with flowers. The ceremonial meal at the compound

was well prepared, but the mood of the feast fell far short of our former joviality. I soon retreated into my room and found my belongings neatly stacked on the floor. I withdrew my testament from the pigskin suitcase and tore it to pieces. So ended my longest patrol.

Then came the ritual of reincarnation: I was reborn in a hot shower and fully grown by the time I was shaved and barbered. It was my intention to call on Vera, in my weeks at sea I had plenty of time to make big plans for the evening and even greater ones for the weeks to come. I was just remembering how to knot my tie when Fred Schreiber, my confederate in many a land battle, walked unsteadily into my room carrying a half-empty bottle of champagne. "Well, well," he said boisterously, "I see someone is preparing himself for a comeback. How long were you at sea? Ten weeks, you say? May I make just one bet?"

"Go ahead, Fred, what's on your mind?"

"I bet that she has run away with another fellow in blues. You can't desert your girl for ten weeks and expect to find her waiting. Here, have a drink with us who have swallowed our chagrin over the infidelity of our girls."

I resisted the temptation to tell him that things were different in my case, that a girl was waiting for me right here in the compound.

Fred continued, "Why don't you join us this evening? We are going to have a great party in the photographer's atelier, with plenty of girls, champagne, a band, and much more. Burk's girl is giving her birthday party and everybody is invited."

Had I heard right? "Fred, who is the girl giving the party?"

"Oh là là, you won't have a chance. It's Vera, the photographer. She and Burk have been going hot and heavy."

That was the end of my fine plans. I took a glass of Fred's champagne and used it to swallow my chagrin. I told Fred I had made other arrangements; and as he left, I lit a cigarette and tried to dismiss my disappointment. After all, I had no claim on Vera, and a pretty girl in port was the target of many men who had the luck to be available. Vera probably never expected me to return. A U-boat man's estimated life span on the front was but six or seven months—no more.

Instead of going to Vera's, Riedel, Friedrich and I celebrated our return with a gala dinner in the "See Kommandant," the restaurant that offered everything a hungry seaman could want.

During the overhaul of our boat, great improvements were supposed to be made aboard. *U-230* was to be equipped with two two-barreled and one four-barreled anti-aircraft guns, a measure long awaited. The fire power of those eight barrels would undoubtedly make any pilot think twice before diving close to drop his bombs. A new radar receiver, known as the Bug, was to be installed, replacing the obsolete Metox. I was told that the Bug would register wave lengths in the centimeter range. If so, it should give us ample warning against sneak attacks, especially at night; for already our elimination of the Metox had forced the enemy to resort again to the detectable use of his radar. In addition, new torpedoes had been developed and were ready for use. These and other new weapons promised to change our luck in the U-boat war.

And the time for a change was long overdue. Thirty-seven boats had been lost in July. Ten out of the 17 boats that had tried to cross the Bay of Biscay in the latter part of that month never finished their dash. Then in August, 16 more boats had been destroyed. In a four-month period, over 100 U-boats had been sunk—almost 60 per cent of the entire operative fleet. As a consequence, our destruction of Allied shipping had fallen from a high of nearly a million tons in March to a mere 96,000 tons in August. Many friends and familiar faces had vanished; the mess halls had many empty seats and little of the laughter of earlier days. We, who had so far been spared, had good reason to think that our faces might also be missing soon.

Harbor routine swiftly replaced stress and strain. Our men kept busy, attending to their boat and to their girls with equal dedication. The Captain departed for the obligatory report to Doenitz and for a whirlwind tour through several classrooms to keep himself abreast of the rapid developments. Our doctor was released from U-boat duty and sent into the Austrian Alps to recuperate from his near-fatal adventure. Headquarters had finally abandoned the idea of staffing U-boats with physicians. Most of the submersible doctors had perished in vain with their boats, and medical skills were desperately needed elsewhere.

The new torpedoes promised for the next patrol meant that I would have to take a brief course in Gotenhafen on the Baltic. I accepted the unexpected interlude with relief. Before my departure I found time to visit my tailor. He was surprised to see me again, for our calamities were no secret to the French. My suit was hanging on a rack. It was perfect. To complete my wardrobe, I purchased a gabardine coat, silk shirts, and smart, sporty shoes. It was the fourth year of war, but the French still could supply everything—for the right price. I could afford to pay that price: there were no girls, no bars, no parties at sea.

Five days after *U-230* had returned from her mission, I was on an express to Paris, my civilian suit carefully folded in my pigskin suitcase. Upon my arrival, I returned to the hotel near Place de Vendôme and transformed myself into a civilian. It was the first time that I had put aside Navy blues in four years.

Now Paris lay at my feet. It pulsated with life as I thought life should always be. My desire to bathe in an atmosphere of peace had grown steadily as the war dragged on. I wanted to join the fortunate ones who did not have to worry about tomorrows filled with roaring diesels and exploding depth charges and death in an iron coffin. I wished to forget that I was a cog in the war machine that had spread disaster far and wide; I wished to see life again not as a warrior but as an innocent bystander, and to taste the feeling of complete independence from duty—if only

for a day between trains. Only one place seemed to
transmit the overwhelming sense of freedom and tranquillity that I desired—Paris.

Paris did not disappoint me; it was, as ever, en-
chanting. I felt the city's spell as people of many nations and eras had felt it. Free of the restrictions a
uniform enjoins, I strolled contentedly through the
streets and wide avenues, and I knew my disguise was
a perfect one when I felt the furtive glances of those
Parisian beauties who never condescended to look at
a man in uniform. I was entirely divorced from the
war for 12 pure hours.

I arrived in Frankfurt in blues and spent the evening
with my parents and sister. Mother and Father showed
no sign of strained relations despite his romance and
the ensuing trouble with the Gestapo. But all was
not well with Frankfurt. The destruction of the city
had assumed grotesque proportions since my last visit
in June. Large sections were now as mutilated as
Berlin. Father's plant, too, had suffered damages during a recent air attack, and had been only sketchily
repaired. I was told that the sixth fire in the attic of his
warehouse had been put out only two nights before
and that our apartment building had a minor blaze
too. All these disclosures were depressing, and I felt
vaguely responsible for our failure to stop the ship-
ment of American-made bombers that were now pul-
verizing German cities.

I was secretly glad that my schedule permitted me
to spend only a few hours at home. I departed the
same night on a train without lights. We stopped several times in woods and open fields, giving me the
dubious opportunity to listen to the deep, long roar of
hundreds of Allied bombers traversing the nightly sky.
The trip to Berlin became a long, drawn-out affair
and I arrived eight hours late. I crossed the Capital
underground, thinking of happier times with Marianne.
Since her death, Berlin had lost all its attraction. I departed from the city on my familiar route to the Baltic
seacoast, but only after another delay of six hours.

A second miserable night in a railroad car. The only

lights were flashing matches and the glowing tips of cigars and horrible-smelling cigarettes. Smoke and smell filled the overloaded cars. Discussions of the war smoldered everywhere and kept soldiers and civilians awake. I took careful note of the spirit of our people at home, and especially the attitude of our soldiers from the Russian front as they talked of their campaigns. Their belief in victory gave me a certain reassurance that we who fought in the Atlantic could depend upon their holding the Eastern front. The Allied landings in southern Italy, expected as they had been after the collapse of the Cyrenaika front in North Africa, seemed not to disturb our general belief in winning the war.

The express pulled into Danzig station 10 hours late. I switched trains and eventually arrived at the naval compound in Gotenhafen one full day late. There was suspense among the submariners who had congregated there to study the first fundamental change in U-boat warfare since the innovation of radar. A seaborne demonstration of the new weapons was arranged for the evening.

The Bay was black, the night was lukewarm. I had boarded a medium-sized motorship which had seen better days as a pre-war transport between German and Swedish ports. When she had reached the middle of the Bay of Danzig, the Commanding Officer of the torpedo arsenal addressed his guests: "We are going to demonstrate the performance of two new types of torpedoes which will revolutionize the U-boat war. First, we shall show you the destroyer killer T-5, an acoustical torpedo of great potential. Thereafter, we shall demonstrate the new LUT torpedo with its various applications. All torpedoes are battery driven. For demonstration purposes they are equipped with luminous dummy heads so that their course can be followed at night."

The motorship increased her speed sharply. Minutes later I spotted a greenish, iridescent light in the dark waters, moving rapidly toward our ship. The vessel turned to port—the light followed. Then we turned to starboard—the light chased after us. The luminous torpedo came closer. The ship was then thrown into a wild zigzag maneuver to escape the homing weapon. But the light in the sea followed persistently, reduced distance, then suddenly dashed below her stern. That was the moment when a warhead would have detonated. In our case, the dummy torpedo continued on its track, shot ahead of its target, turned in a circle, and attacked the ship a second time, passed below her keel, executed an elegant loop, repeated its snake-like movements and made still another pass before its batteries were exhausted. Then it surfaced like a dead fish, its bright headlight glowing in the black water.

This was a stunning performance. Here, I realized, was a weapon that could make the fight against fast destroyers and corvettes a pleasure. Then followed an equally impressive performance. A number of luminous torpedoes traversed the sea, screening and looping. The dark waters were mysteriously swept with numerous lights criss-crossing the mean track of the ship—departing, turning, approaching again and repeating the cycle until the torpedoes' batteries were drained.

Excited by the demonstrations, I pursued the three-day course like a young cat eager to try out its new-grown claws. The escort-killer torpedo was equipped with a homing device that guided it toward the sound of the target's propeller, or, if a vessel lay motionless, toward her auxiliary engines. It was sufficient to launch the torpedo in the general direction of the target; the homing device found its own way, no matter how violently a vessel tried to outmaneuver it. The second addition to the arsenal had a different purpose. It had become increasingly difficult to approach targets as closely as we had in previous years, and the new LUT torpedo was designed to overcome our inability to shoot at close range. It could be released at a great distance from a convoy and directed to pursue the target along its mean track, describing a number of predetermined loops, of any chosen size, at any chosen depth. A few of these torpedoes, released in a screening pattern, could form an effective barrier ahead of a convoy without forcing us to penetrate its tight defense.

I departed from Gotenhafen excited by these new weapons and by reports of others. I had heard of miracle U-boats that were being built in all available shipyards. They were supposed to be capable of staying submerged indefinitely and of performing submerged at very high speed—a speed close to that of our present boats operating on surface. These new submersibles had a retractable tube-like mast with a float, a Schnorkel, which would permit fresh-air intake and the charging of the batteries while submerged. This device seemed so vital to success and survival that I resolved to find out, upon my return to base, if one could be installed aboard the conventional U-boat. Continual submergence was the only answer to our problems. For the first time in months, I believed that we were beginning to get the weapons to survive and to risk our lives intelligently. We might yet be around to see the turn of the tide.

The sirens were screaming when I arrived in Berlin, and the stench of exploded cordite and smoldering fire was in the air when I departed. The night express to Paris was again unlighted and again packed with people on the run. Europe was burning—Europe was in hectic motion. The front was everywhere: in the cities, in the small towns, in the hearts of frightened people riding the trains.

When we were five hours east of Paris, I met Marguerite. She had entered the train in Châlons-sur-Marne. Since the compartment was darkened I saw little of her face, but smelled a perfume that was sold in almost every store on Boulevard Haussmann in Paris. At first it was mere courtesy when I offered to stow away her luggage. Then, during brief seconds when the lights of a small station flashed into her face, I saw that she was pretty enough. We fell into a casual conversation which led to her not-so-casual offer to show me St. Denis, her suburb north of Paris. "Paris without St. Denis," she said, "is like wine without spirit."

Marguerite showed me St. Denis—and a great deal

more. We spent two wonderful days together in Paris. I wore my civilian suit and Marguerite said she was happy with my French appearance. We walked through the bright streets, through parks redolent of the sullen smell of autumn leaves. Then another night —perhaps my last in Paris ever.

I arranged to meet Marguerite the next time I came to Paris. We parted and I went back to my war.

The compound in Brest was in a state of shock when I arrived. The surrender of Italy had just been announced over the radio and was the topic of heated discussion in the mess halls and the flotilla bar. After the British-American forces had established a beachhead at Salerno, the new government of Marshal Badoglio had ordered the Italian soldiers to lay down their arms, leaving our troops to resist the enemy alone. Fortunately, our battle lines seemed to hold strongly against the northward-marching foe. But it was evident that the ring of steel around fortress Europe was closing ever tighter.

The day of my return, the shipyard completed its work on *U-230* as scheduled, and I began to fit her out for our imminent patrol. The delivery of new-type torpedoes, however, had been slow, and we received only one of the escort-killers, eight of the looping torpedoes, and three of the conventional types. I investigated the availability of the Schnorkel, but met only astounded faces; no one had ever heard of such a device. However, the martial look of our boat and the heavy armament of eight gun barrels inspired new confidence. These fast-shooting guns, the wonder-working torpedoes, and the newly installed radar detector gave us a fair chance to return to old glory—and to port.

15

Monday, October 4. *U-230* set out to sea at dusk. We took advantage of a moonless night and separated from our escort as soon as the cliffs receded into the darkness. We steered a southwesterly course, a straight line into "Death Valley."

Minutes after we had separated from our escort, our new radar detector recorded the first enemy contact. Instead of diving instantly, we continued running surfaced at high speed, kept our new anti-aircraft weaponry at the ready, and resorted to a new diversion tactic which, we had been told, would be very effective. Riedel, in charge of the scheme, filled a balloon with helium gas stored in bottles affixed to the railing. Then he attached a string of aluminum foils to the balloon, and its loose end to a float, and tossed the arrangement overboard. The float came to rest on the surface while the balloon rose and stretched the string with the foils until it stood like a full-sized Christmas tree. The decoy rapidly disappeared astern in the ominous darkness. Five minutes later Riedel repeated the drop, and a second tree floated erect over the waters of the Bay. These aluminum trees were supposed to create a stronger image than a U-boat tower on the enemy's radar screen, allowing us to escape in woods of our own making. Unfortunately, two more balloons became entangled in the railing and three others blew up while being filled with the gas; and in the commotion, the snarled foils made our position amply evident on enemy radar screens. But our luck stayed with us. While Riedel fought with the foils and the balloons, we infiltrated a large French fishing fleet, which gave us more protection than the decoys and the guns. In fact, we discarded the aluminum trees and never used them again. They were more of a hazard than a help.

We zigzagged between the wildly scattered vessels for most of the night and made excellent headway. Then we were on our own again with Death waiting for us with a huge harpoon. But the Bug worked perfectly. Several times it registered aircraft approaching, giving us ample leeway for our crashdives. Each time the Tommies were left hanging perplexed in the air.

As soon as the British realized that we had been equipped with a new radar-warning device that actually warned us of their approach, they timed their flights along our projected track so as to force us to dive at ever-shorter intervals. As a result, our batteries were down to 70 per cent of capacity at the end of our first night. But, knowing now that the Bug was a reliable instrument that gave us a good chance to evade the bombers, we reversed our summer tactic and never exposed our boat to daylight again.

The instant we surfaced the following night, the British reacted briskly. Using their radar only occasionally, they surprised us with well-calculated strikes. Hour after hour we repeated the diving-and-resurfacing game, night after night we escaped their canny pursuits and ferocious attacks. On the seventh night, the assaults diminished, and on the eighth night we were able to breathe again. U-230 had broken the blockade and sliced her way westward in a phosphorescent sea. During the ninth night we received orders to head to AK 64 and take up position in an advanced patrol, remaining submerged until the convoy had been sounded out by one of the participating boats. Surfacing was permitted only briefly, for the secrecy of the undertaking had to be maintained at all cost. It was the key to success.

At 2035, October 15, we intercepted a signal with our new antenna, designed to pick up radio waves at a depth of 30 meters: CONVOY AK 61 COURSE WEST. SURFACE FOR ATTACK. U-844. One of the wolves had made contact with the enemy. The trap had sprung.

2100: *U-230* surfaced in time to catch the last faint shimmer of a dying day that we had not seen. Somewhere in the dark north rocked the convoy earmarked for a concentrated assault. As ever, we carried great hopes into battle. A surface attack at night, when all enemy aircraft were grounded aboard their carrier, promised a revival of the old patterns of pursue-and-destroy. The night was moonless and black. The sea was medium and the wind came out of the west. Occasional showers brushed us on the bridge.

2230: We disregarded feeble radar impulses which went on and off, sometimes disappearing for minutes. Nearby escorts were scanning the surface.

2250: Radar impulses increased in volume and in number. The Bug made us nervous, and the reports from below interfered with my firing instructions. I ordered the gear turned off. It was now obvious that we had been detected by the escorts, but the danger of being intercepted was not greater than in any other convoy battle. According to Prager's plottings, we should have made contact with the enemy already, yet there was not a shadow of an escort, not a trace of the convoy. With muttering diesels we raced diagonally into the long rolling waves, listened and sniffed the air in hopes of smelling the convoy's smoke before we spotted the ships themselves. It was as if the old times had returned—as if there had been no destructive May, no decimating July, no frustrating August. Once again I savored the excitement of speeding toward a clash with the enemy in ominous darkness, the sensation of fusing with the ocean and the forces of nature, the drama of defying danger and death.

2350: Borchert detected the first shadows: "Escort, bow right, three thousand meters."

The corvette exposed her broadside but soon disappeared in the nightly haze. Suddenly came the mate's vibrating voice, "Corvette, two thousand, bow zero!"

Siegmann shouted. "Both diesels three times ahead!" Then: "Chief, sit on all the pots!"—an order to Fried-

rich to squeeze the last fraction of power out of the
strained engines. There was not a word about shooting
the corvette with our killer-torpedo. We had been in
tight spots like this many times before.

Another shadow emerged from the dark background, bearing 100. Corvett bow left. She moved
gradually between our boat and the pursuing destroyer.
Siegmann grabbed his chance, turned *U-230* to port,
and we escaped to the north at nearly 20 knots while
the two escorts engaged in wild maneuvers to avoid
colliding. This tactic freed us long enough to make
contact with the cargo vessels. It was 0015, October 16.

Two, three adjustments for target speed, range, angle. Siegmann drove the boat on a collision course toward the starboard column of the shadowy phalanx of
steel, relying on the mate's ability to judge the situation in our wake. I aimed, corrected values, aimed
again, and moved the cross-hair of the TBT into dead
center of the biggest vessel—then waited. Ten seconds,
20 seconds, 30—then two fan shots. Four torpedoes
escaped their tubes. Siegmann swung his boat around
and chased parallel to the convoy, throwing the escorts
off the scent.

One torpedo hit the larger shadow squarely amidship. A huge flame streaked into the sky. Then a loud,
sharp report. Seconds later the shock wave brushed
our whiskers. This was the opening signal for the
battle. Star shells rose, flares curved and lit up the
armada. I waited for the vessel to disintegrate. I waited
for other torpedoes to hit. But at the moment of impact
the convoy had made a customary turn. Then there
was a flash—a second boom tore the night. A volcano
erupted. New commotion among the vessels. The sky
was turned red and golden by the flames and the slowly descending parachute flares. It was a holocaust such
as we had not experienced for all too long. I asked
the Captain for permission to shoot the killer-torpedo.
It meant stripping ourselves of emergency defense,
but targets did not always come so easy.

"All right, Exec, and make it fast!" Siegmann then
sent the watch below.

I gave the decisive order: "Tube five ready. Angle starboard ninety. Ready, fire!"

"Alarrrmmm!"

U-230 plunged into the depths to avoid being hit by her own homing torpedo. As she balanced out at 120 meters, there was another explosion. Hell broke loose. The swishing of speeding propellers criss-crossed the agitated, fuming surface as escorts attempted to catch the attacker. A series of depth charges detonated nearby. Asdic pings surged through depth. But the thrashing of the many cargo vessels' screws and the pounding of their engines covered up our escape and provided the music for our excitement. While the turmoil slowly subsided, torpedo mechanics and seamen worked feverishly to reload the tubes.

0310: We surfaced and reloaded. The night was impenetrable, the sea had increased in strength. U-230 bounced hard to regain contact with the fleeing convoy. Suddenly there was a light on starboard, three miles ahead. We turned and crept forward. As we drew cautiously closer we realized that it was the white beam of a searchlight directed against a sinking vessel. I spotted the corvette lying alongside the doomed ship, taking aboard survivors. We stole toward the scene at low speed and observed it with interest. The incapacitated escort was the easiest target I had had before the tubes; she lay there, only 800 meters ahead, offering her full broadside for a *coup de grâce*. But Siegmann bowed to a merciful impulse and an unwritten rule, and hollered, "The hell with these tin boxes, let's get some freighters. Left full rudder, both small ahead."

U-230 turned slowly so as not to divulge her presence. I detected a red light, small and perfectly round, moving from behind the stricken vessel, then floating around her. The spot grew rapidly into a glowing red balloon. We suddenly realized that another destroyer had spied us and was in full pursuit, using an infra-red searchlight to track us down. Immediately we threw our diesels into high gear and cut into the waves headon. The escort slapped strongly in the mounting sea. Although she listed and bounced severely, she closed

the gap with maddening persistence. Siegmann, however, had the slight advantage of dictating the course,
and he zigzagged in irregular patterns, driving his boat
through the onrushing water walls. From time to time,
Siegmann howled into the growing storm, "What's the
escort doing, Exec?"

"She is holding steady," I screamed over my shoulder, unwilling to admit that I should not have fired our
killer-torpedo. But she was gaining and had grown to
the size of a battleship. As the chase went on, however,
the wind increased in violence and the rising waves
gave the destroyer a heavy lashing, retarding her more
than us. After 90 minutes of desperate maneuvering,
we had lost her in the black, mad ocean.

0445: Two hours before daylight, a new shadow
surged into our aft section. We shot forward at high
speed, course north—and crashed into the convoy. The
shadows were dead ahead—three—five—ten; I whirled
around and picked out my targets without glasses. Then
everything went very fast. I had had the tubes ready to
shoot, aimed at a Liberty ship, pulled the lever, moved
the TBT into a second shadow, pulled the lever
again . . .

That was as far as I could go. A corvette scurried
from behind one of the cargo ships and dashed at us
head-on. U-230 swerved and surged into the waves on
our only getaway course. We had almost completed
our arc when a fire column flared into the night. Shock
wave and boom hit us simultaneously. The sky was
suddenly dyed red. The second torpedo never hit.

A new race was on. The destroyer astern surged after
us, apparently in a bold attempt to ram us if all else
failed. Again I regretted having used the homing torpedo too early. We repeated our escape maneuvers for
the second time that night, and shook off the threat after an hour of near-deadly sailing. As Siegmann intrep-
idly steered his boat toward a new attack, I ordered the
tubes reloaded; the fight was not over yet. But when a
grayish shimmer finally spread over the eastern sky
and the new day separated the water from the clouds,
we realized that we were all alone.

During the early morning hours, the operation took

a sharp turn. Our nightly victories had alarmed the British. Predictably, they sent up everything that could fly—from single-engined aircraft to long-range bombers—to engage in the hunt for the raiders. A ponderous assault from the air was in the making.

0825: I saw a four-engined plane flashing out of a cloud bank and called the alarm. The boat tilted drastically and plunged into the depths. In the next moments of uncertainty, four savage bursts twisted our boat and reminded us that, in the heat of the battle, we had forgotten to turn on the Bug. We outwaited the aircraft and surfaced after 40 minutes, then sailed after the lost targets, our eyes fixed to sky and horizon.

0915: We picked up a signal: ATTACKED BY DESTROYER 57N 24W. SINKING. U-844. No one could help our friends in this raging sea, but by transmitting the site of the tragedy, *U-844* gave us a clue as to the position of the convoy.

0923: Crash-dive before a Liberator. The hull responded fast to the urgent demands of rudder and hydroplanes. Four depth charges detonated on port.

0945: We surfaced; the sky proved to be empty.

1020: Alarm before a Liberator. Four more fiendish explosions followed us into the depths.

1050: Again we surged to the surface and resumed our effort to cling to the convoy.

1112: We intercepted the last call of another of our boats: ATTACKED BY AIRCRAFT. SINKING. U-964. My compassion for her crew was replaced by alarm as a plane registered on our radar warning gear. We tumbled into the depths, underdiving the closest blows, then rose again to surface and dashed in search of the convoy. Again and again the pattern was repeated, until the alarms became a blur of countless concussions and exploding bombs. In the late afternoon, another boat flashed the word of her demise: AIRCRAFT. BOMBS. SINKING. U-470.

When night settled over the battleground, three U-boats had been destroyed for the four vessels we had torpedoed the night before. It was a close fight—eye for an eye, tooth for a tooth. Ironically, the British had slain the innocents. We, the culprits, were still hunting strongly when a storm forced the aircraft to retreat. Almost three hours after midnight we intercepted a fresh signal from one of our wolves biting into the flanks of the armada: ATTACKED BY DESTROYER. SINKING. U-631. A frustrating night ended with four losses on each side.

On October 17, daylight saw the Allies renew their frenzied air attacks on the convoy hunters. The battle raged from dawn to dusk and it was a totally one-sided affair. We surfaced and dashed ahead in desperate attempts to gain a few miles, only to be forced over and over again into the protective depths. At the end of the second day of the operation, two more U-boats were bombed and sunk. *U-540* and *U-841* reported being attacked by aircraft, then went down to the bottom. The hunt was over and the toll was great. In all, six U-boats had been lost against four enemy vessels sunk. Ours was the only U-boat of our group to survive. This was the general average of life and death for U-boats in the fall of 1943: only one out of seven returned from patrol.

Since we had lost the convoy while escaping air attacks, Headquarters instructed us to sail into BD 62 and await further orders. As we marched toward that southerly position, the weather improved considerably. We traveled with greatest caution, staying submerged as long as there was a trace of daylight and surfacing only in total darkness. In the early morning of October 22, we reached our designated square. The temperature had risen almost 20 degrees centigrade in 24 hours and the night was uncommonly calm. The stillness was deceiving, but not to us. We had learned to sense danger like an old bear that had survived the bullets of many a hunter. We had learned that one second of carelessness resulted in death, that danger and the enemy were everywhere.

For several days our patience was put to a severe test. Lurking under the cover of darkness we zigzagged across the surface, observing an area large enough to hold three convoys; and when daylight forced us below, we hid at 40 meters, sounded and listened and probed. Then in the evening of October 26 came the break: the soundman detected tunes that only a convoy could produce. It was 2140 when we surfaced. A half-moon shone much too brightly in a cloudless sky. There was no wind. Our boat flew with ease across the smooth silvery surface, diesels roaring.

Dead ahead rocked the convoy, distance less than 6,000 meters. The horizon was strewn with black dots, moving at rigid intervals westward. Three corvettes roamed on port; one was silhouetted on starboard, one glided through the aft quarters. Distances varied greatly. Incredibly, we had surfaced inside the security cordon. Moments later, the escorts swung around one by one—funnels fuming, flags of sparks trailing—trying to cut off our assault. Siegmann chased his boat ahead at highest revolutions in a bold attempt to reach the fringe of the convoy before the wildly swerving destroyers had a chance to combine forces. Our irregular dashes from side to side retarded the pursuers, but three hostile shadows drew slowly closer, throwing big bow waves. Soon it looked as if we were trapped, but the firing line was still open, unobstructed, and *U-230* leaped forward, reducing the gap to the black monsters rapidly.

Suddenly there was the Captain's scream, "Exec, I give you just forty seconds to shoot!"

That was short notice, but I was ready. I corrected range, aimed, counted, then released the four bow torpedoes at short intervals. Our boat listed sharply as she swung on opposite course, and an instant later I lowered the lever a fifth time, firing our last torpedo. That was the fastest attack we had ever made.

As five torpedoes propelled westward, *U-230* ran away to the east with three escorts in wild pursuit. Their gray superstructures shone white in the glow of the moon. After several hundred pounding heartbeats, there was a series of flashes along the western horizon. Two vessels had been hit, possibly three. Time was 2225. At once, to our amazement, the escorts—only a stone's throw in our wake—swerved around and steamed after the stricken convoy.

U-230 continued at high speed for another hour before Siegmann ordered the crew to secure from bat-

tle stations. Three hours after the British had given us
another reprieve, Riedel informed Headquarters of our
situation: CONVOY BD 64 COURSE DUE WEST.
THREE HITS. SINKING NOT OBSERVED. FOUR
SUNK PREVIOUSLY TOTAL 26,000 TONS. ALL
TORPEDOES EXPENDED. RETURN TO BASE.

Following the transmission, we set course toward the
Bay of Biscay. Before the first sunrays could unmask us,
U-230 withdrew from the surface.

The sailing in permanent darkness continued. As
we proceeded on surface against the invisible barrier that the Allies had laid across the Bay, aircraft
attacks increased by the hour. We ran with our decks
awash, our bow and stern buoyancy tanks preflooded
for instant diving, and our hearts in our mouths. Every
hour we spent in our nightmarish passage through these
dangerous waters was likely to be our last one.

During the third night after our clash with the convoy, we shook off a total of 16 bombs. On the fourth
night, we dived six times and evaded 24 well-placed
packages of destruction. On the fifth night, we were
strafed and tormented by 28 bombs. On the sixth night,
we dived five times and 20 bombs missed. On the
seventh night, the attacks diminished, but we ran head-
on into a hunter-killer group—with our tubes empty.
We circumvented the threat, moving slowly, silently,
with motors making barely a whisper. Then, clear of the
danger, we roared noisily eastward into the night. By
the end of the night we were able to signal that we
were only 10 hours west of our assigned pick-up point.

On November 5, at 0930, *U-230* surfaced, and for
the first time in 18 days we saw daylight. Two mine-
sweepers lay waiting for us in the rolling sea near the
cliffs of Brittany. One of the vessels blinked us a message by lamp: AIR ALERT. MAN YOUR GUNS.

We promptly accepted the advice. Evidently our
mission was not yet completed. The hell from above
followed us right into port.

16

U-230 eventually came to rest in the concrete shelter
in Brest. Only then, with seven meters of reinforced

concrete over our heads, were we safe. As I crossed the gangplank and took my first hesitant steps on solid ground, the concrete walkway transmitted a feeling of security through my salt-caked boots into my bones.

I took a deep breath, heaved a great sigh of dismay. That was all I could do about our sinking fortunes in the U-boat war. Nowadays nothing went right for us; even our new, highly praised looping torpedo failed to perform as well in battle as it had when demonstrated under ideal conditions. We now had little ground to lose. Two years before, our battle line had been far out at sea. Last spring, it had moved east to the Continental shelf. Now the front had settled at the very coast of France. Many a U-boat which had somehow managed to stay afloat through the weeks of her patrol was sunk in clear view of the shore, just moments before her crew was to step upon the concrete pier.

The difference between then and now was dramatically evident in Brest. I noticed many empty berths in the bunker. Back in the spring, three U-boats had been crowded into each one of the bays and others had to wait their turn outside at the open jetty. I noticed the unusual calm that engulfed the shipyard. Not long ago, the yard had bustled with activity as our many boats were serviced 24 hours a day. Not that the boats were off chasing convoys; only a few remained out there in the Atlantic, and each was conducting her lonely hit-and-run operations merely to force the enemy to maintain his far-flung defensive system. In October, 24 U-boats had been sunk, most of them under a hail of bombs, the rest under the pounding of new and deadlier depth charges. The result of our own patrol was a surprisingly large contribution to the small total of enemy shipping destroyed by our boats. But the many empty places we found in our mess halls subdued all pride over our accomplished mission. The smell of death was everywhere.

My first dinner in port provided me not only with the first fresh vegetables in weeks, but also with more unhappy news. Strohmeyer, one of the staff officers, told me that three of my classmates and close friends had died at sea. Another had perished aboard his boat when an explosion ripped the forward battery compartment. The boat had made it back to port, but my friend had been buried in the Atlantic. Then Strohmeyer slashed me with the news that Gerloff and Goebel, my partners aboard *U-557*, had gone down with their boats during the summer months. Feeling the brush of death, I wished Strohmeyer a good evening and walked into the adjoining room.

At the bar sat a good group of our indestructibles. The night was still young, but their spirits were already soaring high. There was Riedel, sporting a moustache that he had kept as a memento of our many shaveless patrols. There were von Stromberg, Burk, and some others. I joined them, and drank and sang. We went through a whole repertoire of chanteys, some of which we had modeled after Linke's "Glow-worm" melodies. Then we bawled the refrain of our version of a popular song while Burk hammered the tune on the piano:

> ". . . Should we sink to the ocean floor,
> We still shall walk to the nearest shore,
> To you—Lilly Marleen,
> To you—Lilly Marleen . . ."

As so often happened when we ran out of champagne, patience, or ingenuity, we then decided to visit Madame and the girls of the Casino Bar. Without changing my battle fatigues, I piled into the crowded car, and we drove into the blackened city.

The Casino Bar was noisy, smoky, and gaily illuminated. Several friends of the 1st Flotilla were already there; they roared greetings and jibes at our boisterous arrival. Madame was charming, as always, and her merchandise was still of a certain quality which had long distinguished her place from others. Madame greeted me pleasantly but with a tinge of reproach: "Monsieur, we have not seen you for much too long. I hope you have not been mistreated by my girls."

"No, it was not their fault, it was . . ." I halted, recalling that her house was possibly an Allied information center. "It was the tide that had carried me away, Madame."

She tried to induce me to make my selection, but I had no special plans for that night. I sat at the bar, sipped a drink, listened to the loud phonograph music, watched my friends select their partners. The many girls, the sweet champagne—these stimulated me not at all, yet stimulation was all we wanted in these unhappy days. I realized that the Casino Bar had lost all its appeal for me.

As the clock finished ringing the midnight hour, the air-raid sirens began to scream, and my comrades hastened out of the Casino Bar. They were not intimidated by the bombs; they simply did not want to be trapped in the CB, which would have resulted in less-than-desirable fame. The sirens were still going strong when a group of us started out through the dark streets of Brest, listening to the heavy flak bellowing in the countryside in the direction of Quessant.

Lacking the time to return to the compound, most of my friends took shelter before the bombers arrived over the city, I gazed at the exploding shells in the sky and observed that the main thrust of the Allied assault was directed toward the south of Brest. In the next few minutes, I saw six or seven planes catch fire, fall out of formation and descend in exquisite sweeps, leaving trails of sparks. The greatly improved heavy flak around Brest put on such a spectacular show that I suddenly realized I had forgotten to seek shelter. By then there was no more need for it; the remnants of the air fleet had disappeared.

Stirred as we were, nobody thought of going to bed. We joined a group of friends in a taproom for more champagne. But as I settled on a high stool, the door flew open and someone shouted, "The Americans are coming."

We jumped from our stools in disbelief, though after the Allied landings in Sicily and Italy, anything was possible. However, the young staff officer who had brought the news hastened to add, "Don't get nervous, men. I only meant that they are bringing in the American flyers we shot down. Most of them are wounded. Don't you want to see them?"

The night became more interesting. I rushed over to the nearby naval hospital to see the strangers from overseas. The hospital yard was drenched in daylight by numerous bow lamps. Trucks and ambulances pulled into the parking lot, two and three at a time. Orderlies, nurses, and onlookers crowded around the vehicles at the entrance. The victims of our flak, some of them badly burned, were delivered on stretchers. Inside the hospital, a doctor I knew permitted me to enter the anteroom. New arrivals were rolled in as soon as some of the Americans were moved out for emergency operations. One of the Yankees, still wearing his leather flight jacket, seemed to be in a better condition than his comrades, but he rolled his eyes and turned his head in agony. As I stepped toward him I noticed that an ugly but superficial wound ran from his forehead to the neck, neatly dividing his scalp. His haircut was very short, in the Prussian military fashion. Seeing my first enemy at such a close range, I could not resist talking to him and asking him questions. I said in English, "You see, that's what you get for trying to hit our U-boat bases."

The American preferred to remain silent.

I tried again: "Does it hurt?"

He still did not answer. I continued, "Tell me, how did you receive this kind of a wound?"

Now he moved his head slightly, as if surprised that an enemy could take an interest in his condition. Then he said, "Well, it happened as I bailed out of my cockpit. My plane was hit, it was burning. The crew had already jumped. But I couldn't get out of the cockpit, the canopy was jammed. I banged my head against it until it broke and flew off. That's how I must have cut myself. How I got to the ground, I can't remember."

I was intrigued by his broad American accent, for I had been taught "English" English. "So," I remarked, "that finishes the war for you. Aren't you glad about that?"

"Well, the war might be over for me, but it will be over for all you Germans pretty soon."

"How do you mean that?"

"You heard me. We are going to pulverize your bases and your industry and in a few months—never mind . . ."

"Yes," I continued where he had left off, "in a few months we will pay you back. Look, I don't know what they have told you about us and our war potential. But one thing I assure you, one day all your planes will fall from the sky and that's the end of your war." I was thinking about our much-discussed new weapons, including death rays and atom bombs, which were now in the development stage.

"Oh, sure," the American said sarcastically. "What happened to your U-boats? Within six months we destroyed most of them. It'll all go the same way. You can't last much longer."

I was impressed by his knowledge but also angered by his arrogance. "What you said is nonsense. Who told you that there are no more U-boats?"

"Isn't that the truth?"

"No, it isn't. I am living proof. I just came back from patrol, and I can assure you there are many more boats still at sea, and soon there will be hundreds available, faster and more powerful ones than those at the front. They will sweep your sailors off the oceans." I was somehow relieved by what I had told him.

But the Yankee put on a skeptical smile and said, "Listen good to what I am going to tell you. One day you will remember it and that day isn't too far away. Whatever you Germans do, it will come too late. Time works for us—only for us."

Convinced that he was a typical victim of Allied propaganda, I clapped his shoulder and said, "You will find us Germans not as bad as your newspapers say we are. I wish you a speedy recovery, and one day you will have to concede that I was right."

We both smiled at each other, and I left. The Yankee's next stop was the operating table and, thereafter, a long rest behind barbed-wire fences.

When I returned to the compound, it was daylight and too late to go to bed. Instead I emptied my suitcases, hung my uniform and civilian suit in the closet, and arranged my books on the desk. I selected one of them and tried to read. The effort was not successful, for I heard the American pilot telling me that time worked for them, only for them. I became restless. I turned to the letters I had received from home and read them again. But the voice of the American spoke right out of the lines on the page. The air raids—my parents wrote—had greatly increased, and one of Father's business friends had been killed in an attack. The letters also revealed that Trudy's husband had come home on furlough and that the two had spent a week in the Black Forest where the nights were still calm and free of raids. These letters reflected the whole truth, the bitter fact that even at home things were deteriorating fast. I heard the American saying that time would work for them, only for them.

Early that morning, I sailed *U-230* into the Bay of Brest to conduct various tests. The flotilla's Chief Engineer was quick in determining and scheduling the bare minimum of repair work to be performed aboard, for the front demanded a fast turnover of the few boats still afloat. Our old workhorse was to be cleaned, gassed, painted, and fixed within two weeks, which meant that there was no time to send anyone on leave. For the second time I investigated the availability of the Schnorkel, but there was no man on base who could give me an intelligent answer. Instead, I was informed that we were to receive two improved radar receivers which were to detect wave lengths in the lower centimeter range, thus keeping us abreast with the enemy's rapid progress in the war of electronics. In our cruel duel at sea we had been forced on the defensive to such a degree that the Allies dictated the terms and the weapons.

On the first weekend ashore, I turned my back to port and boat and boarded the Brest-Paris express late Friday evening. During the night I went into the washroom and slipped into my civilian suit. By previous arrangement, I met Marguerite under the Eiffel Tower. She wore a blue silk dress with embroidered flowers. I embraced her, then met the eyes of German soldiers jealous of this indiscreet Frenchman. Paris was warm and fragrant. The strong scent of turning leaves, the smell of the waters of the Seine, the breeze-blown traces of perfume—all mingled in the limpid air. And above me shone the sun, which I was so often forced to abandon at sea. These were the hours when I imagined that all the bombing and killing was already over, and that I had been spared my inevitable voyage to the bottom of the Atlantic.

Shortly after my return to Brest—I was again in blues and nothing indicated that I had been on a brief journey into another world—the Captain was unexpectedly instructed to report to Senior Officer West. We assumed his trip had something to do with our next mission. After a day's absence, Siegmann returned and promptly asked Friedrich, Riedel, and myself to join him in his room. He wasted little time, "Gentlemen, I am going to make it brief. We have been ordered to break through the Strait of Gibraltar into the Mediterranean."

Siegmann paused to observe our reaction. I forced a smile; my partners were grim. It was common knowledge that any attempt to breach the narrows of Gibraltar had only a slim chance to succeed. But what difference did it make where we sailed? It was all the same everywhere—furious efforts to destroy combined with desperate attempts to avoid being bombed, mutilated, and sunk. It was like committing slow-motion suicide. The end was the same, only the name of the sea would change.

However, there was one consolation: if we should be lucky enough to break through the Strait, we would be operating in the calm waters of the Mediterranean. To ease the tension I suggested, "It reminds me of some places I'd like to see. The problem is getting there."

The Captain took the cue speedily: "If you, gentlemen, keep the mission an absolute secret, there is a good chance of lying on the beaches of Italy in January."

The ice was broken and our conversation grew animated. But then Siegmann took the wind out of our sails. He revealed that two of our boats, *U-732* and *U-340,* had been intercepted in the Strait and sunk by the British early in November. Other boats sent out to break through the blockade had been lost even before they had reached Gibraltar. *U-566* had been sunk by aircraft on October 24 near the Spanish coast, and the same fate overtook *U-966* on November 10. Nothing had been heard from *U-134* and *U-535,* which presumably had been sunk without a chance to signal. These recent casualties presented us with a clear picture of what we had to face.

As we prepared to sail, the odds against us continued to rise. The losses we sustained during the month of November had jumped again. As of November 25, fully 15 more boats had been destroyed, which nearly ended the existence of our once-great-and-proud Atlantic fleet. All that we had to stack up against the British-American achievement in November was a mere 67,000 tons of Allied shipping that our torpedoes had wrenched from small convoys.

17

On the evening of November 26, *U-230* slipped out of Brest Harbor for the last time. She followed in the wake of an escort, passed the submarine net and the narrows, then continued out to sea at high speed. We knew that our departure had been kept a secret, for the omniscient British broadcasting station "Calais," which delighted in transmitting bad news in German, had no special wishes for us when we sailed.

It was near midnight when we changed course to due

south and followed the French coast along the 200-meter line of the Continental shelf. Instead of sailing into "Death Valley," we raced south toward the north shore of neutral Spain. Through the night we were forced to dive three times, but managed to see the first rays of daylight without having received serious blows. Shortly after diving for a day-long submergence, Siegmann, speaking over our intercommunication system, informed the crew of our risky mission. Their reaction was a mixture of surprise and cautious acceptance. They had gone through hell long enough to know the rules of the game.

There were other predictable reactions. Many a man who had left a sweetheart in Brest suddenly realized that he would not be able to see her again. Disappointment over the forced separation expressed itself in amusing demonstrations. As I entered the bow torpedo room on one of my regular inspection tours, I noticed a seaman sitting on his bunk with his friends crowded around him. He held up a bra and panties, begged, borrowed, or stolen from his girl. His buddies smiled lasciviously and made insinuating remarks. I entered the circle and joined in their laughter. Men with that kind of humor made good sailors.

On our cautious voyage to the Spanish shore, we passed badly damaged Lorient during the first long submergence, and in the second night we had La Rochelle on port. When we sighted the lights of San Sebastian, we broke surface, turned westward, and followed the black contours of the high mountains at a distance of four miles offshore. Our track along the Spanish coast remained undetected, and we were treated to a view of the glowing cities of Santander and Gijon. On the fifth night we circumnavigated the dangerous cliffs of Cape Ortegal, and 20 hours later we passed Cape Finisterre, the area where four of our boats had recently been lost. The following night we saw the shimmer of a million lights reflecting in the sky—Lisbon. While its citizens went about their nightly amusement or slumbered peacefully under their quilts, we traversed Lisbon Bay. During the eighth day of our mission we frequently rose to periscope depth and took bearings on Cape St. Vincent. Shortly before midnight on December 5, as we approached the Bay of Cadiz on surface, Riedel stepped on the bridge and said nonchalantly, "There is a radiogram on your desk. It's still uncoded. Why don't you decipher it? Must be important."

With Riedel standing relief, I lowered myself into the narrow drum, took up the code books, then sat down to begin my task. But the message was already decoded. I read Headquarters' congratulations to Werner and Riedel on our promotion to *Oberleutnant*.

We soon had left Cadiz astern and sneaked ever closer toward the concentrated British defense of the Strait. Two hours after midnight, December 6, we penetrated the Bay of Barbate—the limit of our advance on the European side. We dived and settled *U-230* on sandy ground. During the day, frequent depth-charge explosions only a few short miles to the east reminded us that the Tommies were determined to prevent passage through the narrows. While some of the crew rested and others pretended to do so, I sat with the Captain in his corner, plotting the plan of assault. After hours of weighing various approaches, Siegmann finally decided to cut across the triangle toward the North African port of Tangier and proceed from there into the hangman's noose.

In the evening of December 6, the men were ordered to action stations and instructed to stay there for the next three days. At 2100, *U-230* broke through the face of a smooth sea, then hammered with both diesels toward the African coast. Above us spread a dark clear sky full of brilliant stars. As we emerged from the protective shield of the Spanish shore, radar impulses hit us in rapid successions. Trusting the man at the radar receiver, we continued our dash—with beating hearts.

"Detection—volume threeee!" The cry cut through the night like breaking glass. We fell into the tower and the boat plunged into the depths in a single motion. After the roar of the emergency procedure had subsided, there was only silence. Encouraged, we surfaced. But after an eight-mile run, a stubborn impulse forced us below again.

At 2300, we again surfaced and, when no planes appeared, we drove forward. During our run, we packed our batteries with enough electricity to last for three days submerged. We traversed a broad stretch of sea, casting up sparkling fountains which foamed around our hull and left telltale bubbles for miles behind. And yet, incredibly, we remained undetected. We surged ahead until the lights of Tangier became visible, then changed course toward the east and the narrow gap between the two continents.

Soon we ran into a fleet of African fishing boats and snaked through the flotilla in daring zigzags. Steadily we steered our boat ever closer to the Strait. After 40 minutes, we had passed the unsuspecting fishermen and were coming dangerously close to the narrows, where radar impulses screamed unbearably loud. There was no need for forcing our fantastic luck. We submerged.

December 7. At 0045, *U-230* began her silent run through the depths. The boat was perfectly balanced at 40 meters and floated noiselessly at a slight down angle, but with a rising tendency. Her speed was set at only one and one-half knots, just enough to keep her afloat; but the current, estimated to be three knots at the point of submergence, would boost our speed over ground to four and one-half knots. The current was expected to grow stronger the closer we came to the narrows, at which point the peak flow into the Mediterranean was supposed to reach eight knots per hour.

I settled myself in the control room to await a day of action. Kaestner, our best sound operator, soon detected faint propeller noises and Asdic pings dead ahead. There were also strange impulses he had never heard before. With Friedrich at the controls, I stole into the radio room to study the new phenomenon. I put another pair of earphones over my head and listened. I clearly distinguished the familiar insolent Asdic pings from the new sound, which Kaestner suggested came from a new detection apparatus. The impulses sounded like the whistling and squealing that rubber toys pro-

duce when they are squeezed. Suddenly it struck me:
"That's not a new British gadget, Kaestner, those are
dolphins talking to each other! Listen carefully, you can
even distinguish their voices."

Fascinated, we listened intently to the conversation
of the many tumbling dolphins enjoying themselves
in the underwater current. Some were at a distance,
others nudged our hull, but all of them seemed to like
the giant steel fish that had come to join their games.
Their palaver increased as we floated deeper into the
Straight, and so did the Asdic pings. When the first
depth charges detonated far off, our squealing companions hastened back into the Atlantic.

Above us a number of British destroyers busily cut
the surface in search of intruders. Their activity
reached its peak around 1000. Asdic pings showered
on us like hail, but fast-moving layers of water of different thermal density laid a protective cover over our
boat. Unable to make contact, the destroyers resorted
to the old game—throwing depth charges at random.
By noon, when I assumed my watch in the control
room, the pings had lessened somewhat and wandered
off astern. It was evident that we had passed the blockade and the narrowest part of the Strait. The turbulence decreased gradually and by 1600 Siegmann's patience had run out. He ordered, "Chief, bring the boat
up to periscope depth and let's see how we have made
out. Will be interesting to see Europe and Africa in just
one sweep. Care for a look, Exec?"

The Captain swung himself into the seat at the
scope. He quickly drove around its axis, checking the
immediate vicinity. Then he trained it on one spot on
port for a while, swiveled to starboard and back to port
again. Finally he said, "I think we have the Rock already far astern. Let me see the manual."

I handed him the heavy volume of the Maritime
handbook of the Spanish coast, which contained a pho-
tograph of the Rock of Gibraltar as seen from the
sea.

"Yes, we have passed it. We've been going considerably faster than anticipated. Call Prager, I want to take
some bearings."

The navigator soon gave us an accurate fix. The result of Prager's diagram was surprising. We had Gibraltar seven and one-half miles astern, and had penetrated the Mediterranean for that distance. A quick calculation revealed that we had made a submerged speed over ground of 14 knots, of which the current was responsible for 12½.

Siegmann relinquished his seat and I aimed the scope at the Rock, which rose iridescently from the green water into the azure blue sky. Through the low-lying haze, I counted at least six British warships guarding the entrance into the Mediterranean. I trained the scope to starboard and spotted the North African coast rising almost perpendicularly out of the ocean. On top of the high cliffs near Spanish Ceuta, a Civil War Memorial projected still higher, and the coast on either side of the monument melted away in the afternoon haze. I was so captivated by the view that I spotted the airplane almost too late to shout, "Dive fast, dive to sixty meters, aircraft!"

I retracted the long scope shaft, then ducked my head and waited. But *U-230* arrived at the designated depth without interference from above. I freed the Chief from his duty at the controls and took over his task of recording the detonating charges, which by then was purely academic. The boat was engulfed in wonderful silence. The chances of being detected diminished with every mile. At 2200, the small light bulb over the Captain's bunk was turned off for the first time in 12 days, and the dark green curtain surrounding his berth was closed.

Almost 24 hours later, at 2130 the following night, *U-230* surfaced—and had the lights of Malaga dead ahead. As I emerged from the hatch I saw the dark mountains looming up behind the illuminated city, against a pale sky. The night was so mild that I removed my leather jacket. Then the diesels resumed their wild hammering and *U-230* followed the black mountain range. We ventilated the boat and proudly transmitted our first radio message to Admiral U-boats: SPECIAL MISSION COMPLETED. REQUEST NEW ORDERS. U-230.

We expected our vital signal to produce enemy action within the hour, but it did not. Shortly before day dawned we received Headquarters' answer: WELL DONE. ENTER TOULON HARBOR. FOLLOW ROUTE WITH GREAT CARE. EXTRA PRECAUTION IN FRONT OF PORT. EXPECT ENEMY SUBMARINES.

We had been prepared for a brisk encounter with the Allies, who had established a flourishing supply business between the North African ports and the occupied southern Italian coast. To disrupt that traffic and relieve our front in Italy from the Anglo-American pressure was the ultimate objective of our mission. Therefore I could not understand Headquarters' decision to call us into port unless we were earmarked for a special mission which required briefing.

It took us three nights of fast surface runs, and a number of crash-dives to escape aerial bombardment, before we floated into the Gulf of Lions in the vicinity of Marseille. At 0100 on December 15, we informed U-boat Headquarters South of our imminent arrival. At daybreak we dived, and Siegmann soon spotted our escort through the scope as she crawled over the horizon. One hour and 20 minutes later, we surfaced 30 meters off port of the nervously cruising trawler. Her skipper requested us to follow her, and a signal by flags told us to be on maximum alert, for British subs had sunk one of our vessels and one of our U-boats two weeks previously. We raced after the zigzagging escort with all hands on deck, wearing their life jackets. At the harbor entrance, a tugboat admitted us, then shut off the entrance by dragging the submerged antisubmarine net from one pier head to the other.

We sailed into full view of Toulon. The bright sun shone on green mountains, on the red and green tile roofs of whitewashed houses, on the rusty superstructures of several damaged and grounded French warships. *U-230* carefully maneuvered through the harbor basin, past two sunken French destroyers, past three U-boats which lay unprotected alongside a quay. The Captain, spotting a small assembly of men in blues, steered his boat toward the empty place at the quay, and *U-230* came to rest parallel to land. What was regarded as a suicide mission had turned into a smooth sail. Our incredible luck still held.

The representatives of the 29th U-boat Flotilla treated us well. Our luggage had arrived from Brest and even the mail had been rerouted. Nothing was forgotten to make us feel at ease. I was about to clean out my suitcases when I was called to the Captain's room.

"Have a seat and a cigarette, Exec," said Siegmann casually. "I've received a teletype from Headquarters which tells me that our association has come to an end. You have been ordered to Neustadt to begin your training as commander. Let me congratulate you." Before I could fully comprehend, Siegmann rose and shook my hand and expressed his regrets that he was losing me. He wished me a better future at sea aboard one of the modern U-boats than he would have with his old *U-230*.

Still surprised, I muttered thanks for my 20 months of service under him, and wished him luck and a new boat, too. Then we briefly discussed the immediate problems arising from the changed situation. The greater portion of the boat's company was due for an extended leave, including Friedrich and Riedel. Since my training was not to begin until January 10, 1944, I was more than willing to take care of boat and crew as a last service, and also to spend two weeks in a port which invited exploration.

I returned to my room a different man. I thanked the Fellow Upstairs for having allowed me to survive to this point. I pondered my double promotion and what it would mean, and vowed that as a Commander I would do all I could to help achieve victory.

On December 18, two days after the end of our patrol, the crew was presented to the Commanding Admiral, who showered us with praise and medals. As he fastened another Iron Cross to my chest, it reminded me of all my friends in their iron coffins. By that sunny day in December of 1943, nearly all of the old guard of the Atlantic front had been eliminated, and many

newcomers from the German ports were being hacked
to bits in the Norwegian Sea before they could achieve
their operational goals. The Mediterranean, too, was a
deadly battleground. The latest boat to fall victim was
U-593 under the command of Kelbling, the one-time
"guest commander" aboard *U-557*. His successful career was terminated just after he had torpedoed a British escort near the North African coast. American
destroyers caught up with his boat and sent her down
to the bottom.

What our U-boats had not achieved in four years—
supremacy on the seas—the Allies had attained in a
matter of seven months. Their all-out drive to sweep
the seas clean of U-boats was almost an accomplished
fact. Only a small force of U-boats was afloat after the
bloody massacres in summer and fall. As of that December, the Allies had destroyed 386 of our boats, of
which 237 had been sunk in 1943 alone.

Siegmann and most of the crew departed that day
after the medals had been distributed. I became acquainted with the officers in the compound, who shared
the same way of life and the same doubtful future. My
new friends introduced me to the city and to their
hectic activities in this exotic port. We celebrated all
the parties as they came; they came in rapid succession
and were welcomed with desperate abandon. One evening I attended an exhausting fête at which boys and
girls bathed in a huge punch bowl of wine and champagne. At another wild affair, a spectacular scene was
created by a young Italian girl who, rejected by her
Navy lover, threw herself nude into the arms of an
Army *Leutnant*.

Just when the mild climate of the Côte d'Azur had
convinced me that spring was coming, Christmas arrived. The meager imported evergreens, garnished with
lametta and angels' hair, contrasted oddly with the
palm trees and made the holiday seem unreal. During
the week after Christmas, a bus provided by the flotilla
took us few northerners on a tour of the southern
French shore. An abundance of semi-tropical flowers,

as well as tall cypresses and luxuriant pines, graced our
sight-seeing route between the resort towns of La-
vardon, Saint Tropez, and Saint Maxime.

New Year's Eve was highlighted by a theatrical pre-
sentation and wild celebrations in the flotilla's mess
halls. I danced through the night with the young girls
from the ballet and forgot that the oceans were rever-
berating from a thousand depth charges and our cities
crumbling under the Allied bombings.

My days in Toulon ended when Riedel returned
from his short leave. He had not had much luck with
his traveling. In the wake of great, disruptive Allied
air raids, he had been unable to make it all the way
home to Bohemia, and had spent most of his furlough
on trains and in Munich. I turned my business over
to my friend, who now succeeded me as Exec aboard
U-230. For a last farewell, I reminded him, "Keep
your eyes open and your ears stiff, old fox."

It was indeed my last farewell to Riedel. One year later, he was lost on his first and only mission as Captain
of *U-242* in the final battle around England.

18

My journey to commanders' school in Neustadt began
in the evening of January 5, 1944. I was chauffeured
from Toulon to Marseille by one of my new friends
who drove at suicidal speeds over the winding, cliff-
side road. I checked into a small hotel on the Cane-
biére at midnight, slept till noon, then rushed out in
my civilian suit to sample the most notorious city of the
Continent. Sailors, beggars, former French soldiers still
wearing their old uniforms, thieves, prostitutes, Arabs,
Chinese, Blacks, and Whites—all milled about in furtive
harmony. I walked through the crooked alleyways

of the old section, along the smelly piers, past the fishing boats and old rotting vessels of yesteryear. I boarded a small motor boat which sailed across the bay to the ancient Chateau d'If, known best as the prison of the fictitious Count of Monte Cristo. That night I strolled through the elegant quarter and surrendered to a quiet evening in a cozy restaurant where I was served an excellent dinner in old-fashioned splendor.

At 0800 on January 6, I climbed the wide staircase to the Station Saint Charles and boarded a train to Strassburg. While I was carried peacefully through the summery hills and valleys of southern France, in Russia, Soviet divisions pounded the German lines as an overture to their winter offensive; in Italy at Monte Cassino, the Americans bombarded our front in an attempt to break through to Rome; and on the British Isles the engines of a thousand bombers were being readied for the night's assault of the Continent. My express arrived in Strassburg at 2230 and crossed the Rhine at Kehl around midnight.

In Mannheim we halted—and stayed halted. To investigate the cause of the delay I went out into the raw cold of the platform. A shadowy railroad employee told me that Frankfurt was under heavy air attack. "They say it's the worst. It looks as though we have to stay here for some time."

I had a sudden urge to run ahead of the train. Wild thoughts of what was happening to my parents and home raced through my mind. Only after a long delay did the express creep out of Mannheim and through its extensive freight yard; then it crawled with exasperating slowness toward burning Frankfurt. A gray, misty cold morning had replaced the agonizing night before the train edged cautiously into Frankfurt's damaged Main Station.

I grabbed my suitcases and ran through the stench of fire and cordite, through clouds of dust and heaps of broken glass to the street. The large Plaza in front of the station was a shambles. The gracious rotunda of stately buildings was reduced to smoldering ruins. An enormous smear of dark fumes lingered over the city. Fire engines, military trucks, anti-aircraft brigades, ambulances, and people by the thousands crowded the streets in a massive effort to fight the flames and clean the thoroughfares of debris. Stumbling over rubble and skirting bomb craters, I hurried across the Plaza, turned into Mainzer Landstrasse, made a left turn into Savignystrasse, circumnavigated a huge bomb crater in the midst of the street, noticed thousands of aluminum foils which the raiders had dropped to make our radars ineffective, and rushed on for another 50 meters.

Then I made a discovery that relieved my fears. Our house was still standing. I opened the heavy iron gate, walked to the entry, and rang the bell. There was no answer. Assuming the bell was out of order, I went to the rear to call. There, where a garden had been, lay a great pile of bricks, mortar, iron railing, window frames, glass, radiators, and pipes. The entire rear wall of the house had been sheared off by a bomb, exposing all five stories. Four of the five floors had already been evacuated; the exception was the second floor—our apartment. I recognized my parents' bedroom, the furniture still standing, the beds unused, neatly arranged but loaded with dust. There was the sewing room with the machine facing an imaginary wall. There was my sister's room with the turquoise décor. In one corner of the apartment hung a bathtub halfway in the air. There was no sign of my parents or my sister.

A woman appeared on the first floor and called, "It's good you arrived. We wondered whether anybody would come and take care of the furniture. It might as well be you."

Recognizing the woman as the landlord's wife, I said, "Can you open the apartment? I don't have keys."

"Can be arranged. I'll also get some neighbors to help you to clean up."

I assumed from her nonchalance that my parents were off on a routine visit. After the landlady gave me the key, I let myself in and surveyed the damages.

The doors to the rear rooms were split and out of plumb. All pictures had fallen off the walls. The floor was strewn with the items blown off tables and dressers. Relatively little had been destroyed—only glassware and some porcelain vases—but a thick layer of dust covered the furniture, beds, and floors. In order to tackle the clean-up task, I changed into some old clothes I found in my room, then answered a knock on the front door. Expecting several husky male helpers, I was surprised by the sight of four middle-aged women, all of them dressed in light gray fatigues like professional movers. They walked in as if our apartment were their own, and together we pushed the furniture around and cleaned and moved it into the vestibule and front rooms. It was late in the afternoon when the women rushed off—without accepting my thanks.

After changing back into blues, I went to the Army's information center, received food tickets, sent one telegram to my new command explaining my delay and several others in different directions to tell my parents, wherever they were, to return. Then I searched for a place to eat. Four restaurants of prewar splendor proved to be bombed-out ruins. In the fifth, a well-known spot on Kaiserstrasse, the fine linen had been replaced with paper placemats and the elegant waiters with morose matrons. The distasteful dinner came as a rude shock after the fine food I had been served in Marseille. It was an obvious irony that Frenchmen, having lost the war, ate like kings while we, the victors, lived on potatoes and *ersatz*.

As night covered the tragic city and its people trembled anew in fear of attack, I returned to our battered home and listened to the air-raid warnings on the radio until the danger of another assault had diminished.

I awakened bathed in sunlight and gazed about at my strange yet familiar surroundings. On the wall opposite my bed hung a drawing of a nude woman I had made when I was 18; Mother always wondered who had been modeling for me at that early age. Nearby hung a reproduction of Rembrandt's "Man with a Helmet" and next to it the gypsum mask of the "inconnue de la Seine," the unknown beauty who had been found floating in the river in Paris, face down. On the wall opposite the windows I had fastened my Navy trophies —the emblems, flags, and ribbons of my commands— and on the shelves along the walls were the books I had purchased in stores scattered through half of Europe. This was my room much as I had abandoned it in '39 for a war which, I had been told, would be won in a matter of months. Nevertheless, four years of constant struggle had propelled me to the heights in my chosen profession. I suppressed the feeling of pessimism that had been nagging me more and more of late. Soon, soon, we would bring this ugly war to a victorious conclusion.

It was dark when a key turned in our front door. My parents had returned. Mother and Trudy were bewildered, but Father said with a sigh, "Well, we have to get used to some missing floor space. It could have hit worse. We are together again and let us drink to that."

Father opened two bottles of Moselle wine. We toasted my double promotion, their narrow escape, and our belief that the Allies had to hit much harder to throw us off balance. We stayed together in the study till three o'clock in the morning, talking and listening to the radio warnings of enemy aircraft infiltrations. Then, since no Allied bombers were heading toward Frankfurt, we risked going to bed.

Late the following night, I stepped off the lazy train in the Baltic seaport of Neustadt, where an advanced U-boat training center had been established. I found a vacant bunk in one of the clean wooden barracks and flung myself onto a mattress filled with straw.

At 0800 the next morning, I found a small group of prospective commanders already practicing on a simulator. This complex mechanism, which resembled the interior of a conning tower, was mounted over a large pool and could be moved in every direction over scale models of freighters, tankers, and destroyers. The simulator allowed the student commander to familiarize himself with the techniques and tricks of submerged attacks until his choice of tactics became routine. Having had sufficient experience on the front, I managed with ease. After two weeks of intensive practice and a boring life in the compound near the small town, I welcomed my transfer to Danzig for active shooting.

One day in late January I boarded the train to Danzig. The station platform teemed with thousands

of infantrymen of every rank, and they all stormed
the express in a last-minute effort to find a seat for
their long journey to the Russian front. I accommodated myself in a smoky compartment with several
army officers. They were puffing cigarettes of Russian
machorka, a tobacco they had learned to smoke for the
lack of anything better. Soon I offered them my aromatic Turkish cigarettes, still available to us Navy men.
This gift considerably improved relations between the
Infantry and the U-boat Force—and also the air in the
compartment. While the express scurried east, we
talked about the war in general and the Russian campaigns in particular. These men from the front were
unanimous in their conviction that their lines would
hold against the vast and relentless Soviet onslaught.

Said one officer, "The few meters we give them here
and there are but tactical adjustments."

"The Soviets don't have our industrial capacity,"
stated another old fox from the Infantry. "They
haven't the material to maintain their attacks or to
stop ours."

Said a third, "Their clumsy equipment can never
stand up to our new weapons. Just wait till summer
comes."

I also talked to several of the fighting men and they
confirmed the general feeling that by spring our new
weapons and new strategy would drastically change
the somewhat embarrassing situation on the various
fronts. As we neared Danzig, I wished them luck on
the Russian steppes.

In Danzig, a streetcar brought me to the pier where
the large ocean liners of the Hamburg–America Line
had moored for years. I found the steamer which
housed the 23rd U-boat Flotilla in dilapidated elegance. My quarters: an antique stateroom finished in
plush and velvet. Although it smelled of moth balls
and cigars, I felt an immediate affection for the ship.

I found the Commanding Officer, *Kapitaen* Lueth,
in the bar with young officers who made up my group of
prospective captains. Lueth, a former commander with
over 230,000 tons to his credit, greeted me informally
and introduced me to the men. I learned that only two

of us student commanders had come from the U-boat Force, and none of the others had participated in a single war patrol, as was customary in previous years. They had been recruited from destroyers, minesweepers, capital ships, and desk positions to offset our terrible losses. The novices had been given one year of training to learn lessons that had taken me three years of active U-boat duty to master. They all lacked the essentials that only combat could provide: split-second reaction; the sensing of the enemy's next move; the experience to know when to crash-dive, when to stay on surface and shoot, how to handle the boat when depth charges and bombs came raining down, how to meet a thousand emergencies. These raw newcomers, who would be entrusted with a U-boat in just a few weeks, stood almost no chance of surviving, and neither did their crews.

Before dawn the next day, our shooting practice began with the sailing of seven U-boats and a contingent of surface vessels. Our torpedoes were propelled with compressed air, which left a clear wake for the grading of our performance during daytime, and were equipped with luminous dummy heads, which revealed our hits at night. Our teachers drove us through a long, exhausting schedule of hair-raising maneuvers that forced us to think and act instantaneously and soundly under emergency conditions. This grueling routine was kept up six days a week for four weeks, with very little time off for sleep or relaxation. At the end of the ordeal, the participants assembled in the mess hall, dressed in blues and white shirts and black ties, to be informed of their grades in the course. I learned that I had finished with top rating. I wanted only one reward—the command of a new wonder U-boat.

Two evenings later, I received the order that crowned my Naval career. We had gathered for our farewell party in the smoky bar of the liner. After the Commanding Officer ended his speech with commendations and good wishes, he reached for the bundle of teletypes from Admiral U-boats. "Mein Herren, here are the instructions for your future assignments aboard U-boats. I'll start with the only combat command I have to offer tonight. It's for the lucky winner of the top ticket, *Oberleutnant* Werner."

I rose to my feet. His voice suddenly seemed far away, as though coming through a thick wall of fog. I heard Lueth saying, "You'll report to the 1st U-boat Flotilla in Brest and assume command of U-415 as of April the first."

I walked toward him and accepted the order. It was as good as a death sentence, for the life expectancy of a boat on battle duty had been reduced to four months or less, and the obsolete *U-415* had already outlived too many patrols. This honor, this bright new command, was merely a matter of changing vehicles for an early ride to the bottom. I returned to my table, carrying the teletype and wearing a frozen smile to hide my chagrin.

As if to ease my disappointment, U-boat Headquarters allowed me a two-week furlough before I was to assume my new command. March was a good month for my favorite sport of skiing, and I headed for the Alps expecting much snow and fast slopes. Changing trains in Berlin, I closed my eyes to the vast destruction and continued on a slow express through smoldering cities and untouched country villages. I reached the small Bavarian town of Immenstadt around 1400 on the second day of my journey. I left the train to board a local to Oberstorf, the well-known ski resort. A second train had just pulled into the small station and scores of passengers were dismounting when I heard someone calling me. I turned and looked into the face of a girl I once had loved. I put down my suitcase and she, without hesitation, threw herself into my arms.

"What a pleasant surprise, Marika. What are you doing here?"

"Just passing through," she said, her eyes glistening with tears of joy.

"So am I. Where are you going from here?"

"I am on my way home. I've been at my parents' place for some time." I asked myself why she had insisted on this *wiedersehen*. She could as well have let me pass, just as she had eight years ago. Before I found an answer, Marika had already made up her mind for the both of us: "Let's skip the trains. We can't leave now after seeing each other only for seconds."

We investigated train schedules and discovered that we had almost three hours before we would have to part again. After depositing the suitcases at the luggage counter, we stepped into the snow-covered street. Marika clung to my arm and babbled happy questions and answers. She had beautiful blond hair, and her fine features had matured well. We found an empty café two blocks from the station and took a window-seat with a stunning view of the snow-covered peaks.

Eight years had blurred my memory of our youthful affair. We had met in the public rose garden of a small medieval town on the north shore of Lake Constance, where the roses blossom until December. We had both fallen in love for the first time in our young lives, and had not known what to do with our new discovery. It had been nothing but promises, kisses, and cautious embraces. When I had parted from the Lake we had vowed to treasure our love and to write often. But eight months later her letters ceased; our 12 months of separation had been sufficient to turn her from an innocent child into a bride. It was her colorful wedding announcement which had put an end to the role she had played in my dreams. Since then I had forgotten her almost entirely—until now when she crossed my path again.

Marika painfully explained why she had broken off our love so long ago. It was a classic story. Sometime in March of 1938, she had met a young law student who seduced her during the happiest and gaiest night of the carnival season. Soon she learned that she was pregnant. The result: a wedding and the birth of a child she had never wanted. Humiliations followed. Matrimonial rapes, she called them, filled the years. With a new life under her heart it happened that she met me again. This was all that was needed to make her feel sorry for the previous years. She pleaded, "Please, don't leave me again. Don't go away now that we have found each other. Let us make the most of it. Have your vacation with me."

I objected at first, but it was not hard to give in to her protestations of love and the stirrings of my old feelings for her. I proposed that she follow me to Oberstorf, where nobody knew us and where we could register as husband and wife. I bought a second ticket and claimed our luggage; then we boarded the old-fashioned train to Oberstorf.

The clerk in the hotel guided us to a suite. When the door fell into its lock, eight years and an endless war vanished.

Over our meager war-time breakfast, I broached the subject of skiing. Marika was not only lovable, she was also understanding. I rented a complete ski-outfit, and she accompanied me to the small station from which a lift ran to the peak of Nebelhorn, the highest mountain in the area. As the cable car carried me out over the steep slopes and ravines, I lost sight of Marika.

At the uppermost terminal, I mounted my skis and climbed to the summit. The day was remarkably clear. Around me spread the breathtaking panorama of the Swiss, Austrian, and German Alps. Those mountains conveyed to me the same feeling of immense power that I always experienced while sailing the Atlantic at the height of a hurricane; and I wished to defy them as I did the mountainous waves. I plunged into a headlong descent, down the steepest slopes, past the most dangerous cliffs, until the tree line forced me to reduce speed. Only after hours and several hair-raising descents could I return satisfied to Marika in our hotel suite.

The war had not yet touched the town in the mountains. One peaceful day followed another. During the morning hours I regularly rode to the peak of Nebelhorn and worked the slopes until it was time to meet Marika. In the evenings we enjoyed dinner and drinks, dancing or a movie. Apart from my violent exercise, the days and nights passed in perfect peace. Yet here, as everywhere, the war was a grim reality; all one had to do was turn on the radio. Day after day and night after night, broadcasts told us of infiltrations by Allied bomber fleets, warning the citizens of the Reich where attacks had to be expected and where raids were already in progress. The repetitious pounding reports soon cast a pall over the charming village; and as the week progressed and the time came closer for assuming my command, I grew more and more uneasy. The mountains, the snow, the skiing, and Marika too— gradually lost their allure.

Three days before I had planned to depart, the morning news revealed that Frankfurt had again been under severe attack the previous night, its worst since the raids had begun. With all communications into Frankfurt disrupted, I was unable to contact my parents. Now nothing could hold me in the resort.

Marika and I left the hotel and the town together, but parted in Immenstadt where we had met. Her train steamed toward the east. I boarded the express west to Lake Constance, Black Forest, Frankfurt.

My train climbed over the hills and wound its way through woods and valleys. It reached Lindau, the Island in the Lake, at dusk, and one hour later, in the dark and fog, it pulled in at Ueberlingen. Here my relatives lived, far away from screaming sirens. Their daily anxieties centered around their small problems. They knew nothing of the war at sea, had probably forgotten that I existed, for the fanfares which had heralded our successes had long since been silenced.

As the train stood still with its steaming engine I saw in the faint light of a feeble lantern one passenger boarding the express. He wore an Army uniform. In the second it took him to pass by the window of my darkened compartment, I recognized my uncle. As he stepped into my car, I said in a disguised voice, "There is a seat available at the window, Herr Major."

My uncle lighted a match, held it in front of my face and said, "What the devil are you doing in this part of the world?"

"I had a few days leave between two assignments," I answered. "I am on my way back to the front via Frankfurt."

There was a pause, just long enough to hint of trouble at home. Quickly I asked, "Have you heard from my parents?"

"They are alive. But don't return to Frankfurt, they've lost everything there. Your parents have found refuge in the Station Hotel in Karlsruhe. I talked to your mother just a couple of hours ago. . . ."

I pressed my lips together and held back a sudden wave of anger. Fortunately, it was too dark for my uncle to see the expression on my face. It must have been contorted with bitterness and sorrow as I thought of all my parents' wasted effort, of all the anguish and death my country suffered.

There was silence for a short time. Then my uncle began to talk about his new career as a commandant of a prisoner-of-war camp. He told me tales of a different war, in which insane violence was replaced by insane indolence. Uncle's appointment had come after a long string of bad luck. He had been at odds with the regime ever since January 1933. As a result of his opposition to the Party, which he had courageously made the policy of the newspaper he owned, the government had put him out of circulation. He had spent years in exile in the country, supported by his relatives. With the war had come the demand for men. As a previous officer of the Kaiser's army, Uncle had been reinstated in his rank, promoted, and soon put in charge of the POW camp.

One hour before midnight we bade farewell in the blackest part of the Black Forest, in a cold station house where a few female volunteers brewed coffee and soup for soldiers on the move; I sipped a hot bouillon until it was time to board the local to the lowlands and the Rhine. Eventually, after an interminable six-hour ride, the train slowed down in Karlsruhe Station. I rushed across the plaza into the hotel, and a clerk showed me to the room.

"Who is it?" Father's voice answered my knock.

"It's me," was all I could say.

Father was pale and his hair was suddenly quite gray. Mother and Trudy wept at the sight of me. To overcome the shock of grief and reunion, Father suggested that we go downstairs for breakfast. "It talks better that way," he said.

At the breakfast table, however, the conversation never really did get under way. Trudy, still disturbed, was very quiet. Mother, more resolute, regained her balance soon. Father told me that they had survived the air raid in the cellar, where they had been trapped for many hours, and that they had left behind a few suitcases that he was determined to salvage. He had already secured a truck for that purpose and to move their few belongings to his new plant.

We departed immediately by train to Darmstadt, met the driver with his truck, and then proceeded on the country road to Frankfurt. We entered the city from the south and passed many shattered, smoking buildings. Firemen were still digging out the dead, and we saw rows of bodies neatly laid out on the sidewalks and covered with blankets.

The truck crossed the bridge over the Main River, rumbled through the debris and past the blackened façades of broken buildings. We drove across the Station Plaza, around a few bomb craters, and into the devastated Savignystrasse. Large heaps of rubble and remnants of walls were all that remained of many stately apartments. The truck came to a halt before a mountain of mortar and steel that once had been our home. The first story of the attached building was still standing, piled high with the junk from the top floors. It was because the floor had held firm that rescue workers were able to dig through the basement, to cut a passage into our building, and drag my family and others to safety. Only that thin margin of luck had saved me from becoming an orphan.

I followed Father into the cellar of the neighboring building. His flashlight revealed a hole in the wall just about big enough to crawl through. I had the terrible feeling that the ceiling would come crashing down on us.

Father's hollow voice drifted back to me from our cellar: "Come over here, this is where we sat it out."

I crawled in and saw in the beams of our flashlights benches and cartons covered by a heavy layer of dust.

I said, "I guess you were frightened, waiting down here. Believe me, I know how it feels in a coffin like this."

"It was no picnic, son. It was like Flanders in 1916, when I was buried in an underground bunker."

We brought our last belongings to the surface and the husky driver heaved them onto his truck. Mother was again in tears. She had made the mistake of climbing the hill of debris in search of her belongings, and she had found some broken pieces of her former world. As Father led her away from the ruins, he professed optimism: "We'll get all new furniture, don't you worry. The Tommies and Yankees will pay the bills."

Army trucks and ambulances slowed our exit from Frankfurt, now no longer our home town, now a dying city. A generation of comfort and happiness ended as we escaped the heavy traffic and turned south onto the Autobahn.

Less than an hour later, the truck turned off the highway and drove into the small town of Pfungstadt, where Father had established his new plant. We jounced over old cobblestone roads and into the yard of a dairy, which Father had rented for the production of his patented foodstuff. We stored the boxes and suitcases in his new office, then Father proudly took us on a tour of his new place, which sparkled with white ceramic tiles on walls and floors.

My departure for Brest could not be delayed any longer, so we hurried by truck back to Karlsruhe Station. It was dusk when we arrived, and my train was on time. Hastily I embraced my parents and sister. I was confident that their ordeal was over and that they would be safe for the rest of the war. As the train pulled out, I saw them standing on the platform, waving. I watched them for a long time—till the darkness swallowed them.

PART THREE

DISASTER AND DEFEAT

19

It was April 4, 1944, when the train deposited me in the ancient, charming, but somewhat dilapidated town of Brest. An old bus took me through town, crossed the drawbridge over the canal, coughed uphill, and continued westward on the familiar approach to the 1st U-boat Flotilla. I noticed a number of barrage balloons floating gently over the harbor in the early morning breeze. They were a new defense measure installed to protect the U-boat bunker from low-level air attacks.

Dismounting at the compound, I found the executive offices closed, but a steward led me to the sundeck facing the Bay. As I stepped through the French door, blazing sunlight blinded me. The white garden tables were occupied by a dozen men in Navy blues. Not knowing the commanding officer by sight, I glanced around at the men's sleeves for the mark of a highest rank. One in the group said, "Are you the new captain of *U-415?*"

"Yes, I am."

"I am pleased to meet you," said the stocky officer with the three gold stripes and the Knight's Cross under his collar. "I am *Korvetten-Kapitaen* Winter, shake hands with my staff." He introduced me to the members of the breakfast party and told the steward to set another place. Winter himself needed no introduction; his reputation was known to all of us in the U-boat Force. He had compiled a remarkable record in the early years of the war, sinking more than 150,000 tons of British shipping. He was one of our last surviving aces.

While I ate breakfast, Winter and the others told me the latest news. On the positive side, Schnorkel assemblies had arrived in the shipyard to be installed aboard three U-boats for trial runs. But almost everything else was just an up-to-date version of our familiar recent troubles. British airplanes were now flying frequent missions under cover of darkness to drop magnetic mines in the harbor at Brest and in waterways leading out to sea. The U-boat war was still stagnating while we waited for the long-promised reinforcements of new weapons and modern boats. A few of our old diving machines were still lurking around the British Isles, the object of massive air-and-sea hunts. Even the "Black Pit" area in the middle of the Atlantic, which had long been free of Allied air surveillance, was now patrolled by planes from American aircraft carriers and by swift escorts. The current balance sheet: four out of five U-boats failed to return from their patrols—a casualty rate that far outweighed our meager toll of Allied shipping.

As the conversation veered off to the war in general, I noticed that officers expressed little concern about our battle line near Monte Cassino, or even about our Russian campaign, which was not going as the Army had predicted. Their talk was mostly about the threat of an Allied invasion of the Continent. Nobody knew when or where it would take place, but nobody seemed to doubt that it was coming. The men mentioned our recent efforts to strengthen even further our powerful coastal defenses, to repel the assault at the water's edge. Our leaders had said repeatedly that our Atlantic Wall was impregnable, and no one questioned their word. Defeat was impossible; the mere thought of it seemed treasonous to us.

Suddenly Winter rose to leave. *"Oberleutnant* Werner," he said, "you will meet the crew of your boat at fourteen hours. In the meantime, make yourself comfortable and prepare something to say to your men."

I took the advice of this impressive, sympathetic officer. I moved into a large corner room in the southeast wing of the complex, and soon I was splashing in my private shower, trying to compose a little speech. However, nothing sensible came to mind, and I eventually sat down at the desk to write a draft. That did not work either, so I followed an urge to inspect the compound and bunker.

At 1400, I met *Kapitaen* Winter and my boat's company in the courtyard of the Flotilla. In my impromptu speech, I told the men that I was an old friend of *U-415*, that we had met last year at a fueling rendezvous in the middle of the Atlantic. I told them I was proud of their accomplishments and honored to become their captain, that nothing would be changed to upset their routine, and that as long as I was aboard *U-415*, she would not be defeated. I shook hands with every man, and by 1420 I had taken over boat and crew.

At 1425 I gave my first order, instructing the Exec to have the boat ready in 30 minutes for exercises in the Bay. I was determined to train the men according to my own conception of U-boat warfare. The Exec led the crew downhill. I followed with the Chief and the Second Watch Officer, and asked them about their background. At it turned out, the Engineer had been with *U-415* since she had been commissioned, but the Exec and the Second Officer had had only limited front experience. Clearly I would have to assume a good portion of their duties at first.

U-415 lay waiting in her berth. I lowered myself through the bridge hatch into the conning tower and experienced an unpleasant surprise. The periscope in the tower was one of the earliest designs. I was accustomed to a fully automatic tube equipped with swivel seat, electric drive, numerous gadgets, and an integrated computer system. But to use this prehistoric scope, one had to squat to look through its eye-piece; and following the up-and-down movements of the long shaft would be an acrobatic exercise. A thorough inspection of the boat revealed no other discrepancies except her age: she was an old workhorse. Nonetheless, the large new arsenal of radar detection gear, plus two 20 mm. two-barreled guns and a sophisticated 37 mm. automatic, compensated for the lack of an advanced periscope.

All that afternoon and the following three days, I sailed *U-415* through the Bay of Brest, drilled the men in diving maneuvers, and let them practice on the antiaircraft guns with live ammunition. I added a few innovations that I had found extremely valuable and which the men accepted with a well-developed instinct for survival common to all hunted creatures. I drove the men hard, bringing them to peak performance and deepening our relationship. By the fourth day I was confident enough of boat and crew to report to Winter that we were fit for patrol. From that moment on, everything went according to routine. Duties that had been mine for years were now taken care of by my officers, and I had time enough to steel my nerves and fortify my spirit for the mission.

On the third day of the fitting out of *U-415*, I received my first operational order and met with Winter in his office shortly after breakfast. He was nonchalant as he briefed me on my assignment: "We have temporarily suspended our long patrols into the Atlantic in favor of shorter operations into areas where the convoy routes converge. Observe." Unfolding a large yellow sea chart, Winter pointed out the area that Headquarters had chosen for my first battles as a Captain. "You will recognize that your square is in a strategic location, commanding the westerly approach to the English Channel."

Studying the chart, I realized that the bottom was at an average of 150 meters below mean water level; operating in such shallow waters had its advantages as well as disadvantages. I also realized that enemy air surveillance and hunter-killer groups were concentrated in the area, and that there would be little chance to surface for air and a charge of the batteries. Under such conditions, a U-boat without a Schnorkel could hardly be expected to survive a massive hunt by squadrons of aircraft and fleets of destroyers. Common sense told me that *U-415* was doomed, and yet I could not believe that I had survived this long just to become a victim of obsolete equipment.

I accepted the order, folded the paper, and stuck it into a pocket of my fatigues. Then I saluted my senior and withdrew.

Finally the hour arrived: 2130 on April 11, 1944. My crew had assembled aboard on the aft deck. There were no well-wishers at the waterfront, no music, no flowers. My commands echoed hollowly in the concrete bunker. *U-415* sailed quietly into the shallow inner harbor, stern first, then turned and followed the nervous minesweeper into the long, dark channel leading into the open Atlantic. I had taken this route many times before. However, there was a great difference. I was now in command, with the lives of 58 men in my hands, at a time when our prospects for success and survival were at the lowest.

At 2245 our escort swung around without warning and went on opposite course. As she turned, her skipper wished us "good hunting," a valediction that had long since lost its significance. His farewell reminded me that our sailing could not have been a secret, for the mounting threat of an Allied invasion had given the French population hope for an early liberation, and every dock-hand, barmaid, or girl in the *établissements* was eager to spy for the British.

With the escort's departure, I speeded ahead; we needed speed to dive and I had not the slightest desire to shoot it out on surface. But in addition to the threat from above, there were the barriers of British mines to contend with. Although I had a tremendous urge to dive, I had to continue on surface until we were in water deep enough to overpass mines and withstand bombs from either side. And all the while, radar impulses chirped ceaselessly all around us.

"New impulse bearing one forty, getting louder!" shouted the operator through the tube.

"Take depth sounding and report steadily," I called into the control room from the bridge.

". . . thirty-one . . . thirty-two . . . thirty-two. . . ."

That was not deep enough for us to dive and still pass over a mine safely.

"Radar impulses increase sharply," the voice came through the tube urgently.

". . . thirty-seven . . . . thirty-eight . . . forty meters. . . ."

"Impulses volume four!" screamed the voice from below.

"Alarrrmmm!" I waited a few more seconds, half-expecting to see the searchlight of an attacking aircraft, then leaped through the hole. The boat roared with the familiar crescendo on a downward curve to starboard, but she went down only slowly in shallow waters. As I made a mental note of the fact—for never before had I been forced to dive so close to shore—the ocean exploded. One—two—three—four detonations ruptured the sea and hammered against the portside of the hull, tossing the boat sideways each time. Then with a hard sudden shock, the boat hit bottom at 46 meters—without activating a mine. I doubted that there were any mines at all at this distance from port, and decided that hereafter I would disregard the standing order not to dive within the 80-meter line.

At midnight *U-415* was again on surface, alone with the elements and the searching British planes. I checked the phosphorescent dial of my watch in order to establish the interval between our last crash-dive and our next. Thirty minutes and nine miles later, we were again forced to dive by three stubborn impulses. The boat had fallen to 55 meters when 12 charges exploded in clusters of 4. The hostile bombardiers did not stint their bombs; they fully intended to destroy us.

We surfaced again and crash-dived again in a repetitious game of attack and defiance. As the day finally dawned, we dived an eighth time, and with this attack the bombs wasted on us mounted to 40.

U-415 floated, submerged and silent, toward the entrance of the English Channel. Soon our sound gear picked up faint propeller noises and Asdic pings far in the west. The hunter-killer groups had reacted fast, guided onto our general track by the trail of booms left by the pounding aircraft. I lay on my bunk, eyes closed but my mind racing. The sound of the destroyers' screws could soon be heard inside the hull without earphones. For long moments it seemed that the pursuers had made contact; their pings drilled through the steel like bits. But time passed, and every hour we floated two miles further north-northwest; by late afternoon we finally had the ships outdistanced. The moment to surface drew steadily closer. It was the moment when we defied maximum air surveillance, when our fears and our heartbeats reached their peak. However, it was also the time when we got the air and the battery charge we needed to survive.

At 2215, *U-415* surfaced into a clear night. Cool air cut into my lungs. A spanking breeze came in from the west. Sheets of spray brushed our faces. What followed was a duplication of the previous night. When the impulses reached unbearable strength, when the air was pregnant with roaming aircraft, we crashed below. The boat bent under the countless concussions, tumbled, listed, and went out of control, then leveled, balanced, and floated silently until we surfaced again into the hot exhaust gases left by our attackers. Throughout the night we played the deadly game, until our batteries were fully charged. With day, submergence relieved us from the nerve-wracking exposures.

For five days and nights, *U-415* braved the barrages of bombs and depth charges. When the morning of the sixth day finally dawned, we reached our destination—and met with more bombardment.

On our third day of cruising in grid square BF 15, the soundman merely whispered the discovery: "Sound band port ahead." This was the sound I wished to hear —the deep thrashing rumble of merchant ships, the rhythmic pounding of piston engines. It was 0915.

The width of the band indicated the convoy was a considerable distance away. I mounted my first attack with the order, "Both half ahead. On periscope depth. On battle stations. All tubes ready for action."

At once, seamen, machinists, and mechanics scurried through the hull in sneakers and stockinged feet, wearing nothing but their blue knitted underwear. I leaped into the radio room and pressed a pair of earphones against my head. A mechanical symphony—fast and slow propellers, turbines, diesel and piston engines—greeted my ears. The urge to stop those damned propellers overwhelmed me. I gave up listening and surged into the tower. The crew awaited my action.

"Up scope—stop! Right so." I bent my knees before the old, still unfamiliar instrument, peered through its ocular, but saw only light green water. All of a sudden, sunlight entered the eye—the scope had broken surface. "Down scope—too much. Up—up—up—down. Right so . . ."

The vessels' black superstructures came into view, framing themselves against the light blue sky like a shadow-play. They rocked and swayed eastward in perfect formation, totally unconcerned. No wonder—they had made the trip across the Atlantic in absolute safety. I swiveled around to check the waters to my back and counted seven corvettes zealously cruising at various distances. This display of power meant I had to act fast. I downed the scope, ordered the four bow tubes ready for a fan shot, then checked the surface again. U-415 floated on her clandestine path toward the masses of ships. Distance diminished gradually but distinctly. The black silhouettes grew into ships, then became full-sized monsters. Four destroyers raced into our immediate vicinity. Then I realized I would not have enough time to get as close as I had anticipated: "Correction. New range, two thousand. Up scope—up—up—down—right so . . ."

"New range two thousand stands. Cover—cover—cover . . ."

"Fan shot—ready—fire!"

One by one the torpedoes jumped from the tubes, streaked toward the imposing array of cargo ships, escorts, and trawlers. Fifty-eight men counted to the rhythm of their heartbeats. Two minutes went by—no hit. I fixed the scope at the columns far ahead, almost hypnotized by the panorama. Then, one—two—three booms in quick succession. Three black clouds mushroomed within the herd. Then the view was sharply cut off by a huge gray bow.

"Emergency! Dive to one hundred and fifty."

The helmsman moved the handle of the machine-telegraph up and down three times. We braced for the impact. *U-415* fell away clawing for depth, her screws churning violently. Only I knew what had happened on surface—that an escort had found us because I had left the scope exposed for too long. The spread from above exploded just short of the conning tower. Six times in quick succession the boat was beaten and savagely shaken. For moments only the thrust of our propellers was felt, then a fresh series slammed against the hull, driving the boat further into the depths. The Chief leveled her off seconds before she would have rammed into the sand. This noisy maneuver brought down a new salvo. We heard the canisters splash into the water, and as they floated down we had little chance to escape them. A dozen detonations—a shattering roar. Somewhere a valve blew, and a fountain of water, thick as an arm, spurted across the aisle. The escorts above us—we heard them with the naked ear —assembled for the kill. A third barrage bracketed our trembling boat. Then the devilish grinding of propellers heralded another spread.

Though the sun sank into the ocean and night covered the attackers, they still hurled their cans, and the concussions kept crashing our boat into the sandy bottom and blowing her off again in repetitious sequence. By 0600 the next morning we had taken 18 hours of constant beating. The Chief had managed to keep the boat afloat in spite of the countless leaks, defects, blow-outs, and loss of compressed air and power. At noon, the attacks had not lessened. The British attackers quite obviously took turns; we had heard new escorts arrive and take over the chase with a fresh supply. Evening came and the bombardment continued with savage strength. We had long gotten used to the hammering pings and the threshing screws which came and went, stopped, grew nearer, stopped again, ground into reverse, came closer again, and then went into high gear. These were the seconds when the canisters tumbled down, when the explosions hammered against the coffin, when our heartbeats stopped and sparks flashed and water splashed. These were also the seconds when we were rammed into the ground and buried in silt, but found that we were somehow still alive.

Midnight once again. The British had pounded us for over 37 hours, dropping more than 300 charges, and were still unwilling to halt the pursuit. At 0215, however, an erratic movement of the killers led me to believe that they had run out of patience—or cans. Their propellers stopped, went on again, increased in revolutions, then grew dimmer. After interminable minutes the abominable sound faded out at the eastern horizon. The sudden silence hurt our ears. Everything seemed amplified into pounding blows: the beads of moisture dripping on the deck plates, the drops splashing in the bilges, the coughing of hard-breathing men, the ticking of wristwatches. Slowly, very gradually, stress eased and the crew realized that the barrage was over.

One hour later U-415 shot upward into airy freedom. I dragged myself onto the bridge, the diesels began to roar and the ventilators to sing, the boat gained speed and raced westward in the dark. Near dawn we dived. The Chief steered the boat at 25 meters, allowing us to receive our first radio communications in over two days. The messages came pouring in. Armed Forces communiqués disclosed that Berlin, Hamburg, and Hanover had again suffered heavy air attacks; that the front in Italy had been broken and that the Soviets had launched a broad offensive in the south of Russia. We learned from Headquarters that three U-boats had been lost while we had been hanging in the noose. U-342 had been bombed and sunk; U-448 and U-515 had failed to answer calls for days, and were presumed lost. We intercepted several radiograms directed to other boats, presumed to be afloat, and one intended expressly for us: U-415. DISCONTINUE ALL ACTIONS, REPORT POSITION. RETURN TO BASE AT ONCE.

Obediently we surfaced and transmitted to base our position and word of our score. Knowing that our signal would be detected by the British, we braced ourselves for attacks by their long-range bombers. Only minutes were left for us to replenish our batteries. Some 300 miles separated *U-415* from her concrete bunker in Brest; she could have reached it within 30 hours traveling at top speed on surface. Instead, she was forced to resume her sinuous dives into depth.

For four days and four nights we underdived and escaped the best efforts of the British to sink *U-415*. But finally we reached the reefs of Brittany, surfaced into a night illuminated by a sickle moon, clung to the wake of an escort, and sailed safely into the narrows of Brest. Close to midnight, our good old workhorse of a boat found her berth in the bunker. The pier was sparsely lighted. Only a few of the flotilla's brass had found the time to greet us. The boat's company stood in stony silence when Winter accepted my salute.

Soon I was seated in the mess hall next to the Commanding Officer, and I took the opportunity to ask him a question that had bothered me for five days: "Sir, why did Headquarters order us to return? Are we finally going to get our Schnorkel?"

"See me in my office tomorrow regarding these matters," said Winter. "For now, have your dinner in peace and tell me something interesting of your experiences."

"It's always the same routine. Get up on surface and catch a mouth full of air. Snatch a minute when Tommy isn't looking, duck as soon as he moves around, and surface again when you think he has turned his back. The trick is to find the right moment to take your chance." Between my bites of cold pork and my swigs of cool beer, I told him of the long British pursuit which had almost made that dinner unnecessary.

Long after Winter retired, the crew continued to celebrate their safe and victorious return. I spent another hour or so at the bar with my officers before I retreated into the solitude of my room. After a long hot soaking in the tub, I sank luxuriously into sweet-scented linen.

20

At 1530 the following afternoon, I entered Winter's office. Immediately he expressed concern about my men, and I told him they were well taken care of.

"Good," he said. "Now to the reason for your being called from patrol. As you probably have heard, the Supreme Command is expecting an Allied invasion in the near future. All indications point to a landing on the Continent in May."

"Everybody has a theory of where they might strike," I ventured. "Does anybody know?"

"I don't. Norway is a possibility. Some think they might try to land on the Biscay coast. But most likely they will try to go ashore near Le Havre, the shortest distance from British ports. In any event, we have to be vigilant—and prepared. Your boat will be overhauled immediately. Only the most urgent repairs will be permitted. Have her in combat order in ten days. At that time your men must be on a six-hour alert. Instructions about your operation and tactical deployment will be given at this office by Senior Officer West as soon as all commanders involved have assembled for our counteroffensive."

Recalling his concern for boat and crew, I challenged him: "It seems likely, sir, that such an extraordinary mission will require a Schnorkel. Have any provisions been made for installing one aboard *U-415?*"

"Not that I know," he said evasively. "There is simply no more in supply. I am sorry, but you will have to operate without it, and so will most of the other Captains. We'll have to fight the invasion with what we have."

"Sir, Headquarters can't assume that we'll be able to reach the operational goals without a Schnorkel."

"I understand your argument fully. However, I am in no position to change the situation. I wish I could help you but there is a limit as to what I am able to do."

I left Winter's office determined to dig up a Schnorkel and have it installed aboard *U-415* before the Allies would strike. Measured by the great enemy power we had seen at sea, I was convinced that any invasion force would be so gigantic that none of our U-boats would have a chance to survive without a Schnorkel. It was disturbing to realize how little Headquarters had learned about the Allies' power, and how little our terrible losses had taught the men in Berlin.

I brought *U-415* to dry dock and arranged for her overhaul. Then I telephoned the shipyards in Lorient and Saint Nazaire about a spare Schnorkel, but with no success. Schnorkels were in such short supply that only seven boats operating from Brest were equipped with the underwater breathing device. For a moment, I saw a ray of hope: a shipyard engineer told me of having seen Schnorkel assemblies lying around in the freightyard of the Gare de Montparnasse in Paris. However, my efforts to requisition and transport the desperately needed equipment were drowned in a sea of bureaucratic confusion. I eventually resigned myself to the bitter fact that I again had to sail without a Schnorkel.

For a number of days, single U-boats sailed or limped into harbor. They amounted to only a fraction of those which had been ordered back to counter an Allied invasion. During the first four months of 1944, over 55 boats had been destroyed—about 80 per cent of those sent to sea. The meager tonnage we sank in that period did not justify the sacrifice of so many boats. Their survival alone should have been of highest priority, so that they would have been available when the Reich's existence was in gravest danger.

With the return of *U-821*, the thin trickle of U-boats ceased entirely. *U-311* was sunk on her run for port, and *U-392* failed to meet the escort near the rocks. *U-625* and *U-653* were lost in the Bay of Biscay, and *U-744* and *U-603* disappeared without a signal. In addition to these boats, which had sailed from Brest and were expected back to bolster the anti-invasion group, 20 boats had been sent out from bases in Norway. None of these newcomers had been equipped with Schnorkel, and they also lacked the experience needed to escape the British death traps. Only two boats out of the 20 reached their destination. In all, only 15 boats—seven with Schnorkels—lay in Brest to defend the Thousand-Year Reich against a million invaders.

The month of May had come with a fragrant explosion of magnolias and lilacs. These scents of new life were carried across the wide pastures of Brittany by a gentle breeze from the ocean, where death prevailed. When I had departed from the coast in early April, there had been only a presentiment of spring in the air: a warm wind from the south, a few opening buds here and there. During my absence the trees had sprung into full leaf, the grass had turned greener, flowers had blossomed, and the countryside had plunged into hot, summer-like weather.

Under the common concrete roof, the shipyard personnel worked around the clock to have the 15 U-boats repaired, equipped, and fitted-out for their most vital mission. Torpedoes, fuel, and food were stowed aboard simultaneously to reduce the loading period, and our machinists made scores of repairs on their own, helping to put the boats in fighting condition by the required deadline.

While the activity in the shipyards slowly subsided and the invasion jitters mounted in the compound, the enemy completed his immense preparations across the English Channel. He also increased his air strikes on Biscay ports, harassing us at any hour, keeping our flak crews chained to their guns. Night after night, groups of Allied aircraft swept over our U-boat bases, seeding harbors and waterways with magnetic mines. Day after day, our minesweepers searched for the hidden menace, and the sound of explosions echoed occasionally from the cliffs in the Bay of Brest. Large Anglo-American bomber fleets penetrated France, systematically hammering, disrupting, and obliterating roads, rails, stations, depots, airfields, barracks, bridges, villages, and cities—devastating the beautiful France which had been virtually untouched by the war.

On one of those sunny and portentous days in May, Senior Officer U-boats West, *Kapitaen zur See* Roesing, made his expected appearance in the compound of the 1st Flotilla to brief us on Headquarters' plan to sink the Allied invasion fleet. *Korvetten Kapitaen* Winter played host to the high guest, as well as to the commanders of the 9th Flotilla from the other side of town. As we settled around the conference table, I took note of my colleagues in this extraordinary operation. My friend Hein Sieder, Commander of *U-984*, was seated to my left, and to my right was Dieter Sachse, Captain of *U-413*. There was Teddy Lehsten, Captain of *U-373*, Heinz Marbach of *U-953*, Boddenberg of *U-256*, Uhl of *U-269*, Hartmann of *U-441*, Stark of *U-740*, Bugs of *U-629*, Knackfuss of *U-821*, Matchulat of *U-247*, Stahmer of *U-354*, Becker of *U-218*, Cortes of *U-763*, and finally myself of *U-415*. We were all young, faithful, and determined to win the fight for which we had suffered so long. Eight of us, including myself, were skeptical of the immediate mission and our future deployment. Admiral Doenitz, however, had neglected to ask the opinion of those who had to do the impossible—to reach and halt an invasion fleet without benefit of Schnorkel.

The group grew quiet. *Kapitaen* Roesing patted his silvery hair, which seemed to interfere with his thinking. Not until he had caressed it into submission was he ready to speak. "Gentlemen, as you know, the Allied invasion is expected momentarily. You must be in the position to sail at any hour. Because our Intelligence has been unable to discover the exact date and location of the landing, I have only general instructions for you. We shall be prepared to counter the blow wherever it falls. In Norway we have twenty-two boats on alert. The Biscay ports of Lorient, Saint Nazaire, La Pallice, and Bordeaux are staffed with another twenty-one boats. Most likely, however, the invasion fleet will simply cross the Channel and try to land some twenty to fifty miles from England. This is where you gentlemen step in. Headquarters' directive is short and precise: ATTACK AND SINK INVASION FLEET WITH THE FINAL OBJECTIVE OF DESTROYING ENEMY SHIPS BY RAMMING.

Deadly silence gripped the room. Fifteen Captains, all experienced U-boat men, could not believe what they had heard. This was sheer madness. We had battled ferociously to preserve our lives and our boats through months of defeats and mounting losses. Now, with only a few of each left, Headquarters had ordered the sacrifice of all survivors without a thought for continuing the war. It was ludicrous to use a U-boat to accomplish what a torpedo should do. Was suicide the purpose for which we had been trained so long? Was this futile gesture the greatest glory and satisfaction we were permitted to take down with us into our wet graves?

I regained my composure and asked our executioner: "Sir, does that mean we have to ram our boat into an enemy vessel even if we are able to return to port for more torpedoes?"

"As the order stands, it means ramming. That is the directive I have been given to relay to all of you. Gentlemen, I have to be frank. You may not get a chance to repeat the attack. That's why total assault is ordered, even though it means deliberate self-destruction."

That was very clear. He was indeed precise in his interpretation of the order, and he left us no choice but to perform a German version of the Japanese Kamikaze sacrifice. It occurred to me that this order might represent Headquarters' admission that the war was already hopeless. But I did not dare to think further along these lines.

Hein Sieder, whose boat had been equipped with a Schnorkel, ventured to say, "I respectfully propose that the Schnorkel boats be dispatched into the Channel at this time, sir. It would be advantageous to hit them early and often within hours after they sail and before they strike."

"We cannot afford to expose our boats to the Allied defense before the invasion begins," countered our guest. "You will get the order to sail sufficiently ahead of time. We have a well-functioning alarm system established along the coast. Detailed orders will be released the instant you leave port. If you have any further questions, *meine Herren,* now is the time to ask them."

What was there to question? We had been trained to execute orders without question. For a while, however, we 15 Captains engaged in a rather one-sided discussion of points not covered explicitly in Headquarters' directive. Our conclusion was that we were free in our tactical maneuvers, but once we had the invasion forces in front of our tubes, we would exhaust our torpedoes—then ram.

The group dispersed; each man went his own way, struggling to reconcile his own grim thoughts. I retired to my room, tuned in the radio, and tried to relax in the easy chair. I calculated that Schnorkel-less U-boats would be prevented by Allied air-and-sea vanguards from reaching any given point in the English Channel once the invasion had begun. I knew that seven of my friends would come to the same conclusion. That would leave a grand total of seven U-boats equipped with the Schnorkel which had a fair chance of actually confronting the Allied invasion fleet. Thus, at best, seven U-boats were all that Headquarters could muster to head off an invasion in the Channel; and they would be facing—if my experience with Allied sea power was any index—an invasion fleet of virtually thousands of cargo vessels, warships, and landing craft, not to mention the numberless aircraft that would blanket the scene. Of course seven U-boats could not hold off such a vast armada. Even the notion that they could inflict noticeable damages was an infantile illusion. If our Armies and the Luftwaffe were not able to halt the vast onslaught on the beaches and drive the Allies back into the sea, Good God have mercy on our souls and on Germany.

The establishment of a six-hour alert denied our 15 doomed crews any excursions in the city. Landpasses had been cancelled. I took special care of my men, trying to make them forget that their bell would soon toll. Bus rides, hikes, games, and plays kept the men in motion and in competition. Classes were held to further their education. *Kapitaen* Winter did his best to make our last weekends happy and rewarding. We Captains spent sunny hours in the flotilla's resort, Le Treshier, swimming in the ocean, sunbathing, playing chess or bridge with the girls from the Naval Administration, who had no notion of our fatal mission. We never talked about the invasion, but we thought of it incessantly—and of our death.

Everything reminded us of death, especially a device that preserved life. On weekdays we could see those U-boats equipped with Schnorkel training in the blue waters of the Bay of Brest. We non-Schnorkelers, men and officers alike, followed their submerged maneuvers with intense jealousy; as we watched the small Schnorkel heads grazing the surface, leaving only a short, white foamy streak in their wake, it seemed that they guaranteed life, and that without one we would surely die.

On Sunday, May 28, we 15 commanders were invited by an SS Division to see for ourselves the defense measures installed along their particular section of the Atlantic Wall. We were driven by truck to the Channel coast, were shown the most sophisticated weapons, armored pillboxes, and mobile reinforcements. Groups of soldiers put on impressive maneuvers, displaying various techniques for repelling invaders. The division was composed of very young troops; the "men" were boys not yet 18, and their officers were only a little older. However, it seemed that the Army, Luftwaffe, and SS were capable of thwarting a landing in its infancy, and we returned to Brest somewhat relieved.

During that night, we registered seven infiltrations by single enemy aircraft in the sky over the Bay. The next morning, May 29, I was advised by the *Adjudant* that all U-boats were confined to their berths until further notice. "The Tommies have planted one of their mines right in front of the bunker," he explained.

"A gunner on our rooftop spotted the drop. Our mine-sweepers will take care of the matter quickly. The basin should be cleared by nightfall."

"Those Tommies," I said in disgust. "Soon they'll be laying their eggs in our beds." The *Adjudant* knew exactly what I meant.

For the rest of the day, two sweepers circled in the inner harbor, concentrating on the approaches to our bunker, where 15 U-boats were held captive. However, the vessels were unable to find the mine. By evening the search was ended and the harbor opened for traffic. The matter was closed: the gunner had been a victim of the pressures that were building up inside us all.

Days of tense waiting alternated with sleepless nights. The increasing air raids, the sporadic activities of the French underground, the mounting aversion we felt in our dealings with the French population, the aggressive German-language propaganda of the British radio station "Calais," the fact that we soon would have a full moon in perigee and a spring tide in early June—all these things pointed to the strong likelihood of an imminent landing. And on June 4, when a British fleet of four-engined Liberators came falling out of the noonday sun and down upon our concrete bunker in an attempt of unparalleled daring to destroy our boats, I knew that the hour for our last performance was very near.

Then came June the 5th. In the early morning hours, before the chirping birds grew lazy and silent in the day's rising heat, I took my men on the road again. We marched through the suburbs singing cheerfully, awakening the French. The seven-kilometer hike was welcomed by my men as a departure from routine.

In the afternoon I left the crew in charge of my officers and went into town with Hein Sieder, Captain of *U-984*. Around 1800 we checked in the office for any word of the Allied invasion. Since nothing was new, we decided to have an elegant dinner in town instead of the thinly sliced sandwiches served in the compound. We entered one of our favorite places, selected two large live lobsters, and had baked snails as appetizers. Sieder and I enjoyed the classic Breton dinner but missed the pretty girls of Brittany who had recently become so shy and retiring. I thought of Marguerite in St. Denis and regretted that I probably would never again be able to see her or Paris.

The compound was silent and darkened when we returned. All the lights had been dimmed, all the men seemed to be sleeping. Only the night watch and some operators in the radio room were on duty.

In the middle of the night, I was awakened by the sound of fists hammering against my door. The steward's voice cried frantically, "Emergency, the Allies have come, emergency!"

I was at the door within a second. "Where have they landed?"

"In Normandy, the invasion is in full swing." Away he sprinted to awaken my friends.

I turned on the light and looked at my watch. It was 0347—the date, June 6, 1944. I thought with disgust: while the Allies had boarded their ships and landing craft, had warmed up their fighters and bombers, had sneaked across the Channel to hit in surprise, we had been asleep in white linen 200 miles from the place where we should have been.

Strangely tense yet calm, I slipped into my battle fatigues without a shave. Little remained to be done. Methodically I collected my belongings, bundled and stored them in my closet. Secured my toothbrush and a small tube of paste in the chest pocket of my green blouse. Put on my lambskin jacket and locked the room. Walked downstairs, out of the building, down to the bunker. My call had come. I would not return.

My crew was already assembled on deck for the roll call when I crossed the gangway. The Exec saluted: "All men are on board, sir. Boat is ready for patrol."

I touched the peak of my cap and faced the file. "Stand at ease. Men, you all know that the enemy has landed, or is in the process of doing so. We are no longer able to prevent that. But what we can do is cut off his supply and stop more troops from crossing the Channel. We shall try our best. Prepare for immediate sailing, man your action stations." There was no need of telling them the whole fatal truth. As far as my men were concerned, the mission would be just another normal one.

I paced up and down on deck, awaiting the signal to sail. Alongside lay *U-629* commanded by Bugs, with whom I had emptied many a bottle of wine in Le Treshier when the accent was on life and recreation. Although we sensed that our last battle was but a few hours away, we nonetheless managed to exchange a smile and good wishes. Then I continued to pace the deck. The minutes ticked away. An hour passed without action. Another hour. Then the decisive night slowly died.

A new day dawned hesitantly over the coast of Normandy, where the greatest invasion of all time was in progress. A prodigious fleet—over 4,000 landing craft with 30 divisions of Allied troops, 800 destroyers, cruisers, battleships, warships of all sizes and classes —was about to reach the Continental shore, which was being pulverized by the bombardment of over 10,000 enemy planes. Meanwhile divisions of paratroopers rained down behind our coastal defenses, and countless gliders landed laden with men, tanks, guns, and supply.

While the French soil rocked under millions of exploding bombs and grenades, while the first waves of the intruders were decimated by the concentrated fire of the defenders, while only a few hundred of our own planes found their way into the sky, while the resistance of our tanks and guns and human walls slowly crumbled under the ponderous assault from the air and the sea—while all that happened, 15 U-boats waited under the protective cover of the concrete bunker in Brest, 21 more lay in other Biscay ports, and another 22 remained safe in Norwegian fjords.

At 1000, still no order to sail. Not a single word of command had reached us. Our men brought radios up on deck to listen to the news. Our networks flooded the Reich with reports of the Allied landing. They told of our Armies' heroic resistance and of how they threw the waves of intruders back into the sea. Fanfares and military marches were interspersed to confirm that the nation's greatest battle would certainly end in victory. The crews of the 15 boats on top alert cheered the news and tapped their feet to the martial tunes.

Now orders were issued and cancelled within minutes. Confusion grew as more time passed. The boats were still at the pier at noon. Rumors and false alarms chased each other like steers in a stampede.

At 1440 we 15 Captains were told to report in Winter's office. There was silence all around as Winter gave each commander sealed orders. I opened my blue envelope and unfolded the red paper which contained the Lion's long-delayed instructions. As I peered at the teletype I froze. The bold letters fused into one another. But I managed to read: U-415 TO SAIL AT MIDNIGHT AND PROCEED ON SURFACE AT TOP SPEED TO ENGLISH COAST BETWEEN LIZARD HEAD AND HARTLAND POINT. ATTACK AND DESTROY ALLIED SHIPPING.

The message was even more insane than our present standing order from Headquarters. It required me and seven of my friends, all of us without the Schnorkel, to remain on surface and race unprotected toward the

Corvette

southern English coast at a time when the sky was black with thousands of aircraft and the sea swarmed with hundreds of destroyers and corvettes. Clearly we would not survive long enough to commit suicide by ramming cargo ships in the English ports.

The seven boats equipped with the Schnorkel were more fortunate. They were ordered to proceed submerged into the area where the invasion was taking place. The slow underwater voyage would postpone somewhat their inevitable annihilation.

Kapitaen Winter was pale and grim. He pressed the hands of his Captains who had become his friends. He had done all he could to make our last days worthwhile. There was nothing more he could do before madness would triumph.

21

It was past 1700 when I returned to the bunker. The radios had been silenced. Instead, the huge vault-like structure resounded to the songs of our 800 crewmen, who remained eager to sail against the enemy even if it meant sailing straight to their deaths. At 2100, as night descended upon the Normandy battlefields, 15 U-boats slipped out into the Bay. The night was clear. The stars glittered faintly in a still light sky. Soon a full moon would rise and light up our way into the Atlantic.

2130: The seven Schnorkel boats began diving in the Bay of Brest and one by one they disappeared at five- or ten-minute intervals. Their departure was undetected by the enemy aircraft lurking offshore, ready to strike at anything that crawled on surface. As they marched submerged in single file through the narrows into the Channel, we, the underprivileged, lay in the black bay near the escorts, waiting for the huge red ball of a moon in perigee to rise and show us the way.

2230: The Coast Guard vessels began to float toward the harbor mouth. As they sailed into navigable waters, our diesels coughed to life and the black silhouettes of the eight U-boats swerved into single file astern of the leading minesweeper. First came *U-441* under Captain Hartmann; as the senior among us, he assumed the lead. *U-413* with Sachse followed closely. Teddy Lehsten sailed his *U-373* into the line. Then came *U-740*, Stark; *U-629*, Bugs; *U-821*, Knackfuss; *U-415*, myself at the helm. *U-256* with Boddenberg closed the long chain. The moon had risen fully above the horizon in the southeast. Standing like a giant lantern in the sky, it illuminated the long row of U-boats and was sharply reflected in the calm sea. Contrary to common procedure, all the men had put on their yellow life jackets. The bridge had been stacked with piles of ammunition, the conning tower turned into an arsenal. The gunners hung at their automatics in tense expectation of the first enemy plane. I stood in my nook trying to keep my boat directly in the wake of *U-821*, and to hold the distance to a prearranged 300 meters.

2310: The first radar impulses were picked up by our Bug and the Fly as the coast receded. The report from below—"Six radar impulses, all over forward sector, increasing in volume fast!"—alarmed every hand on the bridge. All ears turned into the wind, all eyes searched the quarters ahead. I kept my gaze circling above the armored superstructure, but the intense moonlight revealed no winged black monsters.

2320: The head of our procession reached the open sea. With the escorts still in line, the eight boats sliced the silvery surface and drove ever deeper into the enemy's defense. The scream of high-volume radar impulses and the stream of emergency messages from below never ceased.

2340: Sudden fireworks flared up in the forward port quarter, five miles ahead. We had been warned that several of our destroyers were en route from Lorient to Brest, and we should not mistake them for the British. I focused my glasses on the disturbance and sighted seven destroyers in an athwart formation, fighting off a British air attack. Thousands of tracers were exchanged, and brilliant flares parachuted down upon our vessels, adding their white light to the yellow moonglow. The sound of gunfire and howling aircraft engines increased as we drew closer to the battling forces. The Tommies, noting our approach, halted their wild attacks to avoid being trapped in the crossfire between U-boats and destroyers. The destroyers raced eastward past our long file, and our trawlers, seizing the chance for a protected trip home, swerved out of formation and fastened onto the destroyers' wake. Their sudden maneuver left eight U-boats at the mercy of the British. At that moment all eight U-boats acted in concert, and I ordered, "Both engines three times full ahead. Shoot on sight."

June 7. At 0015, our long chain of boats was racing at top speed toward the Atlantic. The diesels hacked, the exhausts fumed, impulses haunted us all the way. I found myself glancing repeatedly at my watch as if it could tell me when the fatal blow would fall.

0030: Radar impulses chirped all around the horizon, their volumes shifting rapidly from feeble moans to high-pitched screams. The Tommies were obviously flying at various distances around our absurd procession. They must have thought we had lost our minds. Sometimes I could hear aircraft engines at fairly close range, but could not spot a plane. The hands of my watch crept slowly ahead while the British waited for reinforcement; our eyes sharpened and our hearts beat heavy under our breasts.

0112: The battle began. Our leading boats were suddenly attacked. Tracers spurted in various directions, then the sound of gunfire hit our ears. Fountains reached into the sky.

0117: One of the enemy airplanes caught fire. It flashed comet-like toward the head of our file, crossed over one of the boats, dropped four bombs, then plunged into the ocean. The bombs knocked out Sachse's *U-413*. With helm jammed hard-a-port, the boat swerved out of the column. She lost speed rapidly and sank below surface.

0125: The aircraft launched a new attack, again directed at the boats in the front. Three boats, brightly lighted by flares, concentrated their gunfire and held the planes at bay. A spectacular fireworks erupted,

engulfing U-boats and aircraft. Suddenly the Tommies
retreated. Radar impulses indicated that they were circling our stubborn parade, regrouping for a fresh attack. I raised myself over the rim of the bridge, strain-
ing to see and sound out the roaming planes.

0145: The boat at our stern, the last one in the
column, became the target of a new British tactic.
Trying to roll out the carpet of fire from the rear, a
four-engined Liberator came roaring down on starboard, diving for the bow of U-256. Boddenberg's
men opened fire. But the aircraft veered off in front of
the boat, where her guns became ineffective. That
was our chance.

"Open fire!" I screamed.

Five barrels, all that we had available, blazed away
at the Liberator as it dropped four depth charges
ahead of U-256 and roared past us. Four giant water
columns leaped skyward behind the riddled aircraft as
it tried to escape our fire. But some shells from our 37
mm. gun hit the plane broadside. It exploded in midair,
then plunged into the sea.

U-256, beaten and mutilated by the depth charges,
lay stopped and helpless in our wake, slowly falling
out of line. That was the last we saw of her. Realizing
that her demise left us the first target in any new attack
from the rear, I called for more ammunition. Radar
impulses increased rapidly. For a while, however, the
British held back.

0220: Impulses now from starboard. I presumed
several planes were approaching. Suddenly, a Sunderland shot out of the night from starboard ahead. I
yelled, "Aircraft—starboard forty—fire!"

Short bursts from our two twin 20 mm. guns followed the sweep of the plane. It cleverly flew in from
dead ahead, making our guns ineffective, and dropped
four barrels in front of our bow. Simultaneously, a
Liberator attacked from starboard bearing 90, firing
from all its muzzles. An instant later, four detonations
amidships. Four savage eruptions heaved U-415 out
of the water and threw our men flat on the deck plates.
Then she fell back, and the four collapsing geysers
showered us with tons of water and sent cascades

through the hatch. This was the end. Both diesels stopped, the rudder jammed hard-a-starboard. *U-415* swerved in an arc, gradually losing speed. Above on starboard floated a flare, its treacherous glare enveloping our dying boat. *U-415* lay crippled, bleeding oil from a ruptured tank, slowly coming to a full stop—a target to be finished off with ease.

Bewildered, I peered down through the tower hatch into the blackness of the hull. All life below seemed to have ceased. I feared the boat might sink at any moment and ordered, "All hands on deck! Make ready dinghies and lifebuoy."

Not a sound came from below. The men must have been knocked out by the blows. Interminable seconds passed. From the distance came the drone of planes regrouping for a new assault. It had to be fatal. Suddenly, some men came struggling up the ladder, shaken, mauled, groggy, reaching for air, tossing inflatable rubber floats to the bridge. As they jumped on deck and prepared the dinghies, the gunners raised their barrels toward the invisible airplanes circling their disabled prey. The speed of the attack and the resultant damages prevented us from sending a distress signal. This, I thought grimly, was the way many of my friends had died—the silent way, leaving no word.

U-415, hopelessly damaged, lay waiting for the *coup de grâce*. Since the boat did not seem to be sinking, I told my men to take cover behind the tower instead of lowering the dinghies into the water. I was determined to remain on board as long as the boat would float and to shoot as long as there was ammunition and men to handle the guns. It turned out, however, that we would not die unreported: the radio mate managed to patch up our emergency transmitter and sent Headquarters news of our destruction.

0228: Increasing engine noise heralded a new attack, a fresh approach by Sunderland from starboard ahead, guns blazing. Zooming over our bridge, it dropped four canisters. Four deafening booms tossed the boat aloft. At that moment a Liberator attacked at low altitude from port ahead. Our men on two 20 mm. guns started firing at once and emptied their magazines into the plane's cockpit. The black monster swept across our bridge, dropped four charges, then zoomed away, blowing hot exhaust fumes into our faces. As the boat made four violent jumps to port and as four white mushrooms soared high alongside our starboard saddle tanks, the gunner at the 37 mm. automatic sent a full charge of explosive shells into the bomber's fuselage. The flaming aircraft plunged into the sea. Somewhere, the sound of the Sunderland's engines faded in the distance.

Then all was very quiet. The flare still flickered on surface next to our boat. *U-415* was near death, but still afloat. The Fly and the Bug had been shot away; we were without a warning device. The bridge was punctured by many projectiles. A gunner lay scalped by a shell. Other men had been hit by steel fragments. The Exec moaned in pain, his back badly lacerated by countless splinters. In the aftermath of battle, I felt hot. Assuming I was sweating, I wiped my burning eyes. But my hand came away red, and I realized that blood was streaming down my face. My white cap was punctured like a sieve, and the tiny fragments had torn my scalp.

Then I heard the Chief's voice from below: "Boat is taking heavy water through galley and bow hatches. Strong leak in radio room. I'll try to keep her afloat, if you keep the bees away."

"Can you get her repaired for diving?" I shouted back.

"Can't promise. We have no power, no light. We'll do our best."

I lowered myself to the slippery deck. It was split in several places by the impact of depth charges which had hit the planks before falling into the water where they had exploded. One barrel had bounced off the starboard saddle tank and had left a deep dent. Far more serious, the starboard aft ballast tanks were split wide open. Diesel oil escaped in a thick stream, spreading rapidly over the surface.

With each minute of truce, the danger of a new assault increased rapidly. The boat swung softly in the breathing ocean, paralyzed, seemingly dead. The next

20 or 30 minutes had to bring the finale. With every heartbeat we expected another attack or the boat to slip away from under us.

Suddenly the Chief's creaking voice escaped the hull: "Boat is ready for restricted dive. Twenty meters —no more. Only one motor good for eighty revolutions."

"Can you hold her at twenty meters or will she go to the bottom?"

"I can't tell, we ought to try."

I tried. Quickly the men climbed up the bridge and dropped one by one through the round opening into their iron coffin. I watched the deck gradually sink below surface. As the water crept up to the bridge I slammed the lid shut. Seconds later the floods engulfed the boat.

The interior looked as if a tornado had struck. In the shimmer of emergency lighting I saw that the floor plates were strewn with pipes, ducts, cables, glass, hand wheels, bunks, tables. Water gushed from the leak in the radio room and poured through the bow and galley hatches. Both drive shafts were bent, the starboard shaft so severely that it could not be turned. The forward batteries were cracked and the acid had flooded the compartment. Our radio room was a shambles and the gyro-compass was wrecked. The depth finder was shattered, the electric and diesel compressors were demolished, both periscopes were out of order, the starboard diesel was knocked off its foundation, and the main centrifugal pump was ruined. Since the rudders and hydroplanes were jammed, I ordered them operated manually.

Gentle silent running. Only the fine humming of the one electric motor and the muffled clanking of tools could be heard. The stress, the terrible strains on body and mind, slowly faded. For hours we glided along, myself at the control and the Chief supervising the repairs. We traveled almost blind, steering only by an inaccurate magnetic compass, always aware that the boat might suddenly fall away.

1027: A sudden shock rocked the boat at 27 meters. Two more shocks followed. She had hit the reefs off the coast of Brittany. It was a terrifying situation, for I had no scope to use to orient myself.

"Right full rudder. Blow buoyancy tank three. Steer two-seventy."

Another shock, and another, then a piercing sound. The drum made a violent jerk and lunged up to 15 meters. One—two—three sharp clanks, an unearthly grinding—and the boat shuddered under a new collision. The force of impact almost tossed her to surface, where we would not have lasted longer than a few minutes. Then the boat swung lazily onto a westward course which I thought would carry her clear of the deadly rocks.

1045: The Chief dropped from the conning tower and reported the upper scope repaired. I took his position in the tower. When the eye of the tube finally cleared the water, I was shocked to see black rocks looming up all around us. Atop one huge pinnacle to the northeast stood the lighthouse of Quessant. We had been caught in the current, which would soon dash us against the sharp rocks. Recoiling from the terrible vision, I cried, "Chief, what's the highest revolution for port shaft?"

"One hundred and twenty."

"Make it one hundred and fifty or we'll crash into the cliffs." Through the scope, I spotted a squadron of low-flying planes, then focused on the lighthouse to check our progress against the current. There was no forward motion. I hollered, "Chief, give me another fifty revolutions."

"I can't take that responsibility, the motor is going to bust," he screamed back.

"The hell with responsibility. Give me two hundred —and make it fast." Soon I felt the increased vibration. I focused on one of the threatening rocks. The boat made some headway westward; with agonizing laziness she crept toward the exit of the trap. Forty minutes later we had outflanked the westernmost rocks, and I mopped my sweaty neck in relief. After the tide had turned, I swung *U-415* on her previous south-bound course and reduced the revolutions of the shaft to a safer 100.

1300: The Chief brought me the shattering news that we would run out of power in less than two hours. If so, we would have to scuttle the boat. But I was not ready to give up the ship; I hoped to reach the usual pick-up point with a bold surface dash.

1330: Periscope depth. The sky was alive with aircraft flying in formations of four and six. Land was nowhere in sight.

1345: Periscope depth. A squadron of two-engined planes skimmed the surface a mile to the north.

1358: Two Liberators flew in from the east. I retracted the scope and waited.

1410: Up scope. An unevenness at the southern horizon convinced me that we were nearing the outermost cliffs of Brest. A quick check—three two-engined aircraft had sneaked in from astern. I downed the scope as fast as its motor allowed.

1418: There were no black dots defacing the blue sky. It was our chance to try the dash to the point of rendezvous and radio for help.

1420: The boat broke surface. As I reached the bridge, the brilliant sun blinded me. The one diesel coughed and the sluggish boat gained speed slowly. I nervously scanned the sky while the radio mate fumbled with the dials of the emergency transmitter trying to send the vital signal for air cover. Then minutes of solitude on the bridge. The boat limped through the hostile sea trailing a flag of heavy oil. For inexplicable minutes the sky remained empty; after improbable minutes we arrived at the calculated intersection with the escorts. I turned the boat east to reduce the distance to land. But then our time expired: five two-engined planes appeared over the horizon astern. We dived instantly.

Disaster. The boat, drained of electric power, went out of control, drove her stem into the bottom, then settled with a hard jolt at a depth of forty-two meters. Long seconds later, a spread of explosions bellowed above. Water gushed into the boat and splashed over the floor plates, filled the bilges, and threatened to flood the electrical compartment in the stern. The water increased the weight of the boat tremendously, and if the enemy kept us submerged too long, *U-415* might never be able to lift her weight off the bottom.

1935: High water short-circuited the power supply for our only working pump. The chance to lift the boat grew dimmer fast. The hull was as silent as a tomb. Only the soft trickle of water was heard. I closed the green curtain around my bunk and considered the few alternatives left to me.

2300: I expected action from base at any time now —if anyone had heard our call. I ordered the sound gear turned on, but the only noise the mate distinguished was our own.

0100: There was still no trace of a sound in the east where port and rescue seemed so close. I decided to risk waiting another two hours, then try a lonely breakthrough.

0150: "Faint propeller noises dead ahead," the mate's voice electrified me. I joined him, putting on an extra pair of earphones. The escorts' sound did not increase. It soon diminished completely. I felt the entire weight of the masses of water above the boat physically resting on my own body. Had the escort stopped? Was our fix inaccurate? Had they been attacked by planes and been sent running back to port?

0307: The sound reappeared and grew louder quickly. The threshing noise of two propellers stood out clearly. I had to act fast or the vessels would turn away from the empty surface.

0308: "Blow all tanks." The air swished into the tanks, but *U-415* lay motionless.

0309: "Stop blowing one and three—all men to the rear." No movement from the boat.

0310: "All men to the bow—blow all tanks!" I cried.

0311: "All men aft . . ." I broke out in a cold sweat.

0312: "All men to the bow—run, fellows, run!" The compressed air ceased to flow.

0313: "All men aft again." Then, very gently, the boat began to sway. She listed, shuddered, then rose —and rose. *U-415* had worked herself free. With a distinct shock she broke through the surface and lay abruptly still.

I flipped open the lid and popped into darkness. The two shadows short of our bow swung around. I signaled by lamp that we were incapacitated and could make only five knots. At once, one of the escorts turned and set herself in our wake. Thus taken between the two vessels, *U-415* began her slow march into port.

0445: Maneuvering with difficulty on our one lame diesel, I aimed my ship toward the illuminated square in the bunker, where I saw a few black figures waiting on the pier. The bow bounced off the concrete head wall, but the lines, already fastened at the pillars on land, held the boat steady.

The moment the gangway was down, *Kapitaen* Winter rushed aboard and pressed my hand. He was visibly moved: "I am glad to see you and your men again. You better get your face cleaned—you look like a pirate. Send the boys to their quarters and let them rest. See me later, whenever you are ready to talk." He turned toward my men, saluted, then returned to the pier.

As I crossed the gangway I was greeted solemnly by Sachse and Boddenberg, who had made it back the previous night. Their boats had been towed into port by the escorts which had fled in the destroyers' wake when our column of U-boats was attacked.

I dragged myself up the hill and into my room. With deep appreciation I thanked my lucky star. I believed that *U-415* had made her last patrol. She was so badly wrecked that I did not expect to get her repaired. Now Headquarters would have to give me a new boat with a Schnorkel. Solaced by this conviction, I showered, washed off the blood and sweat, then rolled between soft white sheets and fell into a death-like sleep.

Heavy pain wrenched me back into the world at noon. My head ached from the shrapnel wounds, the pain drilled through my flesh in the rhythm of my heartbeat. The blazing sun hurt my eyes. I dressed in agony and labored to the compound hospital two blocks away.

A young doctor inspected the wounds and said,

"I'll have to shave your head to get down to the root of your problem."

I argued until the doctor agreed to remove only small patches of hair. He iced my skull, then probed and cut and stitched for nearly an hour before releasing me. Relieved of my pain, I visited my wounded Exec and gunner. Both had been well cared for and would mend without difficulty. They were in good spirits and asked me not to look for replacements.

I soon discovered that the Allied invasion of Normandy was still touch and go. American beachheads on the Cotentin Peninsula and British landings near Bayeux might yet be wiped out. Our lines had taken punishment, but they had not been broken. Meanwhile, however, the pitiful remnants of our U-boat Force had been decimated once again. In the month preceding that fateful sixth day of June, 25 boats had been sunk, raising our total casualties to the incredible number of 440 boats, and leaving us with less than 60 operational U-boats to counter the invasion. Most of this complement had been kept in Norwegian and southern Biscay ports; the only boats which saw action were the 15 that sailed from Brest. Of the eight Schnorkel-less boats which had been sent out to commit suicide, five never returned to base, and we three survivors—*U-415*, *U-413*, and *U-256*—had escaped only by accident. As a result of our heavy losses, Admiral U-boats rescinded the mad order to march on surface and ram enemy ships, thereby postponing the final destruction of the U-boat Fleet. As for the seven Schnorkel boats which had left Brest with us on June 6, their fate was not yet known. But five other Schnorkel boats had been sent from the Atlantic into the Channel to offset our losses, and only two arrived there. Thus we had lost at least 12 boats in the first phase of the invasion.

U-415 had been put into dry dock. Practically everything aboard needed fixing or replacement, from our badly dented hull to the two useless drive shafts. My Chief had itemized nearly 500 important repairs, but the list was cut down to 55 because of the shortage of parts and time. Every available boat had to be sent back to sea as soon as possible, even if she were barely capable of fighting. Somehow *U-415*, with all of her woes, was to be patched up for another patrol within two weeks.

While the work went forward, I kept demanding a Schnorkel but was repeatedly turned down. The explanation was that our supply trains were being sabotaged en route by the French underground. In desperation I tried to hire a truck to conduct my own hunt, but I was forbidden to risk a cross-country trip. Even common equipment and parts were in such short supply that it was decided to cannibalize *U-256* in order to outfit *U-413* and *U-415*. Boddenberg, the commander of *U-256*, decommissioned his wrecked boat and departed with his crew for home and a new command.

With Boddenberg's departure, Sachse and I became the last U-boat captains in Brest. We realized that the men who gave the orders had lost their good judgment and even their common sense. But we were trained to obey orders, sane or otherwise, and so we would die in *U-415* and *U-413*. We never voiced our thoughts, never disturbed each other with any reference to our imminent, senseless deaths. We tried to concentrate on our duties, and we listened with growing concern to the news from Normandy, including the official Armed Forces communiqués and the more accurate reports direct from the battlefields to the north.

During the second and third week of the invasion, the Anglo-Americans gradually consolidated their hold on the Cotentin Peninsula, then broke through our front in two places and began driving west. However, new German divisions were rushed into battle, and we still were hopeful that our lines would hold firm. In the same period the U-boat war continued to deteriorate. *U-247*, a Schnorkel boat, was savagely beaten by destroyers and was forced to return to port before she entered the Channel. *U-269*, another Schnorkel boat under Uhl, was sunk off the southern coast of England. Five Schnorkel-less boats finally sailed from Norwegian ports and were sunk in quick succession. By June 30, U-boat operations since the invasion began were a full-fledged disaster. We had sunk only five allied cargo ships and two destroyers, and we had lost 22 U-boats.

During the last days of June, Headquarters sent me an unwelcome surprise. Three young and very inexperienced officers arrived to replace my veterans; they were to get their first—and probably fatal—taste of submarine warfare. My crew viewed them with obvious skepticism, and the loss of my experienced officers left a huge vacuum that only I could fill. As I staggered under the weight of this added burden, U-415 was declared fit and seaworthy on June 30.

On the eve of my new patrol I received a letter from home. It told me that my parents and sister had moved into an apartment in the center of Darmstadt, the capital of Hesse, and that Trudy was expecting a baby in the fall. News of the baby delighted me, but I heartily disapproved Father's move back to a town, into constant danger of air attack. I told him so in my last letter home. I did not tell him how death was coming ever closer to me. In a grim mockery of my prospects, I finished the letter with a cheerful wish for an early *wiedersehen*.

22

It was July 2, late evening and very dark. The crew strolled aboard in small groups, as inconspicuously as possible, so as not to suggest to the French dockhands of the night shift that we might be sailing. At midnight we removed the lines from the pillars. I brought the boat out of the bunker and navigated her into the wall of the night. It was not quite 0200, July 3, when U-415—still without Schnorkel—began her final voyage.

As soon as we had a safe depth of water under the

keel, *U-415* submerged. To conserve power, we floated with minimum revolutions, riding the outgoing tide westward. My instructions were to operate in a 200 square-mile area approximately 80 miles west of the coast, and to keep the entrance to Brest Harbor clear of enemy destroyers and landing parties. *U-415* was now the ghost of a boat. With her movements greatly curtailed, with her combat readiness doubtful, with her basic needs to surface and replenish air and electric power challenged constantly by British planes, she had become a floating coffin, poised for the attack that would send her down to her grave.

When the tide broke and a new day dawned, I put *U-415* aground to await high water at noon. Her stem touched the sandy soil like a grazing horse. I had all motors and auxiliaries turned off, sent all hands to their bunks. With the renewal of the outgoing tide, I lifted the boat off ground, floated further out to sea, then put her aground again. I repeated the pattern at regular intervals. During the second night, we risked five endless minutes on surface, replenishing our air. We dived under a clamor of radar impulses and continued our silent run close to the bottom. Occasional detonations, originating in the English Channel, reminded us that the British all too often caught up with a target.

After 40 hours, *U-415* reached her allotted area. With lowest revolutions, we proceeded north 30 meters below the surface. No trace of propeller noise was picked up by our sound gear. As the day dwindled and the moment for surfacing approached, our hearts beat faster, harder. Then we surfaced into a quiet night.

For a little more than 20 minutes the Tommies left us unmolested. Then they came in large numbers. We crash-dived. The moment that the sea laid its cover over our boat, a hail of bombs and depth charges came thundering down. The sudden impact was too much for my new Chief. With the boat out of control, he sent us on a roller-coaster ride which threatened alternately to ram her into the bottom and to throw her back to surface for the final blow. Shouting commands, I leaped into the Chief's position, tamed the boat's wild motions, and trimmed her until she floated quietly on even keel. Then, with a deep sigh, I told my stunned Chief, "Take it from here, Selde, and kept it this way."

Still shaken by the explosions, he took over control. This had been his first bombardment, his first brush with death. I knew that I had to tolerate his inexperience and would have to give him many more chances to adjust.

With this opening barrage the danse macabre began. Throughout the night we fought fanatically for the surface, for power, and for air. An hour before dawn, on our final trip to the surface for the night, we almost completed charging our batteries. After the last deafening spread, we remained in protective depth, weary, exhausted, fatigued.

The third day at sea—and the fourth—did not bring the Allied destroyers we had been sent to destroy. On the night between, I put the boat aground, and only the breathing of the crew and the soft grinding of the bow rotating in the sand was heard. But the next night, our need for air and power dictated another series of struggles to the surface and crash-dives in the teeth of exploding charges. Through it all, *U-415* waited in vain for naval units to attack. While the Royal Air Force spared no effort to sink us and other lone wolves, the British Navy ignored us completely. Not a single ship entered our area. I operated precariously in the square for an entire week without seeing or hearing a destroyer or an Allied landing craft. During the ninth night of the fruitless operation, I challenged the Tommies' aircraft by signaling base: NO TRAFFIC IN AREA. SEND NEW ORDERS.

Immediately after transmitting the message, we dived and floated at a scant 25 meters, awaiting Headquarters' answer. The reply instructed us to return to Brest. We made the journey back into port in just 42 hours, hopping and floating with the rising tide into the narrows of Brest. It was late evening, July 13, when we arrived at the pick-up point. A quick rise, a fast answer to the escort's challenge, and *U-415* made her last dash into port.

At 2235, I maneuvered my boat into the bunker, under the protection of a concrete ceiling seven meters thick. The engines stopped. The eery light cast dark shadows on the yellow faces of my men as *Kapitaen* Winter walked over the gangplank. He accepted my report and welcomed the crew with a smile, but was unable to conceal his grave concern. After he had passed the files, he turned toward me and said with a subdued voice, "You've been called back to prepare for a special task. Get together with my Chief Engineer to determine the major problems, those which require immediate attention and can be taken care of quickly. You have to be equipped for patrol in three days. That's all the time we can give you."

I saluted and climbed to the bridge. Here the flotilla's Engineer was talking to my Chief, and I heard him say, ". . . and I suggest taking the boat out to the Bay as early as seven. Any objections?"

It was I who had objections. I had not slept for 10 days, and the crew also needed rest and a chance to see the sun. To my Exec I said grimly, "Have the boat ready for maneuvers at nine sharp, and have cook awake me at seven. Any more questions?"

"None whatsoever, sir."

"All right, dismiss the men. And make sure that there are no drinking parties tonight, or I'll have to withhold some special privileges."

Through the nebulous veil of my slow awakening, I heard the boom of many depth charges. The last booms forced my eyes open. I realized that I was not at sea but in my quarters in port, and that someone was hammering on my outer door. Still groggy, I staggered across the room, opened the inner door, and shouted into the vestibule, "That's enough, I've heard you!"

A steward's voice penetrated the outer door: "Sir, you were supposed to sail at nine, and it's already ten. Since seven this morning we've been trying to get you out of bed."

"Thanks. Please call the bunker and tell my Exec I shall be down in ten minutes."

Angry at my slip-up, I dressed speedily, rushed down the staircase five steps at a time, into the blazing sun and down the serpentine path to the bunker. As

I made the turn into the large doorway I spotted my boat. She was sailing stern first into the inner basin, with diesels fuming. My temper flared. The Exec had no right to take the boat out without my specific instruction. Just as I thought about setting him straight, a thunderous explosion rocked the air. A huge fountain shot skyward out of the spot where my boat just had been. Then—it had to be a hallucination—the stern of U-415 was lifted out of the water like a log, heaving two of my men through the air. The geyser collapsed and showered the boat. U-415 had been hit by a mine. She swerved to starboard and reached for the long stone jetty which enclosed the inner harbor.

For a moment, I was the paralyzed witness to the killing of my boat. Recovering, I jumped into a motor launch and chased after U-415. She floated toward the pier head, then smashed head-on into the stone wall. At that moment I came alongside. Machinists and seamen poured out of the conning tower hatch, bleeding, pale, and shaken. Some were limping, others crawled dragging their legs. The boat began to list to port. I ran against the stream of outpouring casualties, climbed to the bridge, and hauled the struggling men through the narrow hatch.

"There are more in the aft compartments, dead or unconscious," said a machinist.

"Move them into the control room," I ordered. The man did not respond—he had blacked out.

The parade of the wounded continued to come up the aluminum ladder. Some men had their arms broken, others their legs. As the flow from below ceased, I dropped into the control room, followed by two uninjured petty officers. The boat was a ruin. Overhead pipes, ducts, conduits, switches, hand-wheels, and equipment lay piled on the floor plates and in the bilges. Dirty, stinking water flashed through a large crack in the hull into the aft torpedo room, flooding the boat rapidly. Three men lay near death on the deck plates in the diesel room. Two more were sprawled unconscious, jammed between the motors in the aft compartment. While the boat filled with oily water and slumped gradually to port, the three of us dragged the heavy machinists to the bow compartment. Someone had opened the forward hatch, which was still above water level. With the help of many hands, we hoisted the machinists out of the drum and placed them into one of the several launches which had come alongside.

U-415 listed dangerously, her stern already swallowed by the sea. As I crossed over into a launch, the good old workhorse slipped off the stones and spun to port. Her deck disappeared in the murky waters. Then, with a last convulsive heave, the conning tower and bridge flipped over and the whole boat disappeared below surface. *U-415* was dead.

I was still staring at the spot above her grave when the motorboat touched the pontoon and my Exec approached, limping and badly shaken. My temper rose again over his unauthorized and unorthodox maneuver, and I said angrily, "I'll put you on the carpet for this, Exec."

"Sir, the flotilla's Chief Engineer ordered me to take the boat out of her mooring. He had waited an hour for you. He got impatient."

"The Chief isn't your superior, Exec. He can't give you any orders as far as the boat is concerned. You should know better. Now, get all the uninjured together and count them. I'll accompany the wounded to the hospital."

"Sir, I think we've lost two men."

"Yes, I saw them flying through the air. Take a boat and cruise around, you might find them floating. Take care of their bodies and notify me at once."

The great explosion had attracted men from other U-boats as well as dockworkers, shipyard personnel, and staff officers in blues. Helping hands were many. As we carried the serious cases into waiting ambulances, I had a chance to inspect their injuries. All of them had broken legs; their feet dangled backward, their toes pointing in the wrong direction. Some had obviously received internal injuries and they moaned in pain. Others, unconscious and bleeding from the head, seemed to have fractured skulls.

I settled in an ambulance beside a severely injured electrician's mate, and we raced through the streets of Brest with sirens screaming. It dawned on me then that this was July 14, Bastille Day, and that *U-415* had died as a British present for the French people. My boat had become the victim of the mine dropped during the night of May 28; her pounding diesels had activated the mine's acoustical timing device. Yet, I suddenly realized that her fate had been merciful. *U-415* had not been sunk at sea, where all of us would have been entombed; she had perished in port, where our chances for survival were the greatest. Why had I failed to awake in time? Why had the Exec given in to the Chief Engineer, and why had he used the diesels instead of the quiet electric motors? Those questions rose in my tortured mind. And why had I survived thousands of blows at sea while others had to die? It seemed that neither Hell nor Heaven wanted any part of me.

When I arrived at the hospital, some of my men were already on the operating table. The five we had rescued from the aft compartments were still unconscious. The broken legs and arms were not serious, but the doctors said that two men had broken backs. Others had skull fractures, concussions, various head cuts —injuries received when they were thrown against the plates. When I departed, I left 14 of my crew behind.

Back in the compound I met a distraught *Kapitaen* Winter. His Chief Engineer had told him that he had delivered the fatal order. Since the flotilla's Engineer was second in command of the base, Winter found himself in an awkward situation. I was in no position to press charges against a superior under the circumstances; I could only effect my Exec's dismissal. However, I forgave the Exec, reasoning that he lacked the confidence to contradict the Chief Engineer, telling myself that he had only executed the order of a Higher Authority.

The loss of *U-415* soon became just another statistic in the dismal obliteration of our U-boat force. During the first two weeks of July—the period of my last patrol—we had lost 11 non-Schnorkel boats, almost the entire complement then sailing. Two more Schnorkel boats had been sunk in the Channel, reducing the anti-invasion group to a mere five. With the death of *U-415*, *U-413* was the only survivor out of the eight Schnorkel-less boats that had sailed in the evening of June 6. *U-413* still lay in the shipyard awaiting completion of repairs.

In the meantime, the five remaining Schnorkel boats used their air masts to remain submerged and to avoid destruction from above. They continued their missions in the Channel and even achieved some success. *U-953* sank three destroyers; *U-984* sent three freighters and one frigate to the bottom; *U-763* sank three cargo ships and one corvette.

During these disastrous two weeks, no more than three or four U-boats at a time were attacking the convoys ferrying invasion supplies between the southern English ports and the Normandy beaches. Close to 100 U-boats would have been there if they had not been senselessly sacrificed. With the U-boat collapse matched by the failure of the Luftwaffe, the Allies lost very little of their supply at sea; and new Allied divisions, fully equipped and with thousands of tanks and vehicles, poured ashore over huge pontoon piers that had been floated to the coast of France. Cherbourg was soon taken by the Allies, thus securing a major base for their gigantic operations. Our Armies had been unable to prevent the Anglo-American forces from driving deep wedges through our lines and into the French interior. Avranches had fallen, and American units were advancing along the north shore of Brittany, coming ever closer to Brest.

The day after the destruction of *U-415*, I made the first of many trips to the hospital to look after my injured men. I found most of them in fair condition, their arms and legs in casts. The five most severely injured lay entirely enveloped in plaster; two of them were still unconscious 32 hours after the blast. I distributed a large supply of cigarettes and tobacco. It was all I could do for the innocent victims of an ignorant mistake.

When I returned to the compound, one of my petty

officers told me that the British radio station "Calais" had made a broadcast about us that morning. "Sir, the announcer said that you sank *U-415* yourself, so that you wouldn't have to sail again with an obsolete boat."

I smiled and said, "Now you see how fast the English get their information and twist it around. It should be a warning to all of you."

I spent day after day waiting impatiently for my new command, preparing the remainder of my crew for an imminent train ride to Germany. While Headquarters struggled to decide my fate, I saw Hein Sieder return from his mission, greeted Marbach at the pier, listened to Cordes' homecoming report. We four celebrated their successes, trying to recapture the good old days with much champagne and a sumptuous seafood dinner. If any one of us celebrants feared that the war would come to a horrible end, he never admitted it, not even to himself. As of then, we remained hopeful and convinced of eventual victory. I was certain that the war would take a dramatic turn once our wonder U-boats were available in great numbers, and I believed that I would soon be sailing one of them.

Then came July 20. That afternoon, after I had returned from a visit to my men in the hospital, a steward told me to meet *Kapitaen* Winter in the officers' mess hall. To my astonishment, I found the flotilla's entire contingent of officers and warrant officers assembled there. Everyone realized that only an event of far-reaching consequences could have sparked the meeting. The guesses were many and tensions high when Winter entered the mess hall with his staff. Winter's face was stony as he demanded attention. *"Meine Herren,* I have the duty to inform you of the contents of a teletype I have received from Admiral U-boats. This morning, an attempt has been made on the Fuehrer's life. However, he escaped injury. The would-be assassin, an Army officer, has been captured. I can assure you that the Navy had no part in the plot. Gentlemen, there will be no change whatsoever. The war will go on until final victory."

The disclosure shocked the crowd. The fact that

someone had tried to kill the idol of the nation was beyond comprehension. Our reactions ranged from disbelief to deep concern. The assembly dispersed in confusion and anger. The news soon echoed throughout the compound: the crews were told immediately before they could be surprised by propaganda on the British radio station "Calais."

I retreated into my room bewildered. Of course I knew that there was a certain amount of discontent at home; that was only natural during a long hard war with many casualties and widespread devastation. But I had never thought that there was an organized opposition that would plot treason and attempt open rebellion. While I feared that German morale would suffer as a result of the assassination attempt, we soon found out that it produced only one visible change in Navy life. The military salute was abolished and the Party's manner of saluting was made obligatory in all branches of the Armed Forces. As a result, a perplexing and amusing situation often arose as the traditional salute was quite frequently executed to return somebody's new-style greeting. Otherwise, the war went on as usual—deteriorating steadily.

Then began a time of sad farewells. On July 21, two tugs dragged *U-415* along the bottom of the harbor into dry dock. I was instructed to secure her valuable instruments and confidential material. Taking my officers and the available crewmen, I went to the dock. We found the boat lying on her starboard side. The rear of the hull was split wide open, ribs were cracked, the aft tanks were torn apart, the shafts were bent, and rudder and hydroplanes were cut off at the hull. All that remained of *U-415* was scrap. I left the supervision of the work to my deputies and turned my back on the boat.

Two days later, the sea released the bodies of our two seamen who had been killed by the blast. A minesweeper on perpetual clean-up duty brought them into port. On July 25, we buried our dead in the small cemetery of a suburb nearby. My battered crew came in Navy blues, some with their arms in casts, to pay their last respects to the two who had to die for no reason at all. Winter laid down his wreath. Then, under a volley from 24 rifles, the wooden coffins were slowly lowered into earth.

Before the day came to an end, I addressed myself to the difficult task of writing to the parents of the dead. What could I say to parents who, if their sons must die, wanted them to die as heroes in combat? I unfolded the fine letter paper with the thin, black line around the edges and the black Iron Cross in the upper left-hand corner and began to write. I was still struggling with my sentences long after midnight.

23

I was not sorry to see July come to an end. As usual in recent months, conditions were worsening at an accelerating rate. Strong Allied forces, spreading out from Normandy against only light resistance, threatened to cut Brittany off from the rest of France, thus denying us access to Germany. Our most important U-boat bases on the Atlantic coast came under greater peril every day. These bases—the once-lively ports of Brest, Lorient, and St. Nazaire—were practically dead already, along with their U-boat flotillas. In July alone, 18 more boats had been sunk, most of them by air attack. Among this number were the obsolete, Schnorkel-less *U-212* and *U-214,* which had sailed from Brest to keep our front yard free of Allied naval units. British destroyers, which had begun to tighten the noose around our port, had sent the pair to the bottom.

In July, too, I had bade farewell to my friends Sachse of *U-413* and Sieder of *U-984.* Their patrols were lone-wolf affairs, but both boats—with all hands—were destroyed on one and the same day.

With the departure of my closest friends, I felt increasingly superfluous. Headquarters still had made no decision as to the future of my crew or myself; in vain *Kapitaen* Winter had intervened in our behalf. With nothing else to do, I prepared myself for a war on land. A siege of Brest was impending. As American tanks rolled south through the highlands of Brittany, our troops began to withdraw into Brest, which was declared a fortress. The feverish work of building up the city's defenses went on everywhere. My men were issued rifles and machine guns, and I was told to train them for ground fighting. Our prospects of being trapped and captured in Fortress Brest seemed all too good.

One day in early August, I was returning from field exercises with my men when word came that I was to report to the Commanding Officer. Winter received me with a rare smile on his face: "You are a lucky man, you have been appointed Captain of *U-953*. Congratulations."

I was stunned and elated. Marbach, the boat's Captain, had journeyed to Headquarters in Berlin to accept the Knight's Cross—that much I knew. I discovered that his return had been prevented by the Allied advances.

"You'll take over her crew in an hour," continued Winter. "The boat, as you know, is equipped with a Schnorkel, and her repairs will be completed in about ten days. Prepare yourself for an exciting job."

"Sir, I am delighted." The new order completely reversed the outlook for my immediate future. Instead of being trapped in Fortress Brest, instead of being killed on land or humiliated in an Allied prison camp, I would at least be able to fight and die on the seas. This was what I knew and where I belonged.

At the designated hour, I took over the helm of Marbach's boat. Most of the crew already knew me or had heard of me; and this, together with the mounting Allied threat, prompted the men to accept their new Captain with relief and with hope. Since a portion of the crew had gone on leave and presumably would be unable to return, I filled the ranks with machinists and seamen of *U-415*, who had taken a jealous interest in my new boat. In preference to fighting on land, they would gladly have sailed a dinghy to sea to fight British destroyers.

The days now passed rapidly in preparations for our sailing. My composite crew worked desperately to beat the clock and to offset the increasing shortage of reliable, experienced shipyard personnel. More and more of our French workers were encouraged by the Allied advances to abandon their conquerors. Some of them actually ran away during lunch time. Worse, those who remained behind were more hostile than trustworthy, and they had to be watched constantly. Moreover, the remainder of my crew from *U-415* were sent to the outer trenches of Brest, and those left at my disposal were pestered constantly by German civil employees, who offered large bribes to be smuggled aboard when we dashed out of the trap. Under these hectic conditions, it was impossible for us to meet our sailing schedule.

Brest awaited the enemy. More and more of our troops poured into the city as fast-moving Allied units fanned out from Normandy, threatened Paris, surrounded Lorient, and reached for St. Nazaire. The citizens of Brest now stayed in their houses and waited developments with a mixture of fear, eagerness, and stoicism. Too late, Headquarters ordered all U-boats to evacuate Brest, Lorient, and St. Nazaire. By then the British had anticipated Doenitz's command and had sealed off our escape routes. Strong destroyer forces had steamed south, surrounding and besieging the three ports. Night after night, Allied aircraft dropped their mines into navigable waters, stopping all surface traffic and making the U-boats' comings and goings a fatal proposition. In addition to the hunt at sea, the Royal Air Force attacked all bases repeatedly and in great strength. The tragic remnants of a glorious Fleet that once numbered several hundred U-boats now postponed their destruction by lurking in bunkers, under cover of seven meters of concrete.

On August 13, at 1045, the air-raid sirens howled through our compound in Brest. I took cover in the tunnels carved into the hill. Fierce shooting erupted almost at once. From the entrance of the tunnel, I stared out at a swarm of about 20 four-engined Liberators. They were flying at medium altitude into the

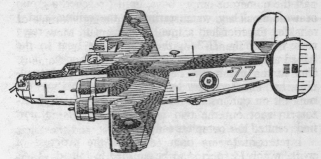

Liberator

concentrated gun fire of our heavy flak. They drew closer, disregarding the black mushrooms bursting around them, stubbornly holding course and altitude. Suddenly, a wing sheared off a plane and glided through the air. The aircraft followed it, spinning and tumbling toward the Bay. The white dots of four parachutes unfurled in the sky just before the crippled plane crashed into the water. The British kept flying straight toward our U-boat bunker, aiming carefully. A second Liberator caught fire, swerved out of formation. A third plane exploded in midair. At that moment each of the remaining aircraft released a single huge bomb; the bombs, clearly visible to me as I edged back further into the tunnel, angled toward the bunker below. Then the world was lifted off its hinges. Volcanic explosions rocked the hill and made the air tremble. The hard pressure waves hit us with staggering force and took our breath away. Tall fountains of dust and debris rose toward our anti-aircraft barrage balloons, blotting out the entire panorama. A few more blasts from our A-A guns, a low roar in the sky in the north—then silence.

I dashed down the hill, concerned about my new boat. Climbing over masses of stone and broken cement, I rushed into the dark coolness of the bunker and found *U-953* completely untouched, rocking gently in her berth. I continued down the long alleyway, past the numerous empty bays, until I reached a group of workers. They were staring at the ceiling, and I saw that the roof had a small fracture with reinforcing rods protruding. *U-247*, the only other boat in the bunker, had been thinly covered with cement dust. The six-ton bomb, the heaviest the Allies had available, had spent its fury harmlessly. Since this was the only hit on our installation, the enemy's enormous effort to root out the two remaining U-boats in port had resulted in a complete failure.

I returned to my boat to check the progress of work, which I expected to be finished in four days. As I boarded *U-953*, the Chief, who had served under Marbach, called me into the bow torpedo room. I lowered myself into the drum—and stared into the yawning tunnel of a torpedo tube. The inner door had been broken away. The round cover, the only safety door besides the outer door, lay on the deck plates. I was puzzled and worried.

"That," said the Chief, "is from the shock wave of a bomb that exploded in the basin some fifty meters away. I am sure that we have lost some of our boats this way. With their outer tube doors open and a faulty inner door, a single depth charge would do it. They never lived to tell what happened."

"Listen," I said, "if our outer doors weren't tight, our boat would be lying on the bottom right now—and you and I would have to walk a long way back home. Check all doors and have this broken one replaced. And do it in a hurry. I don't want our sailing delayed any more."

As in Brest, the Allied air attacks upon the U-boat bunkers in Lorient, St. Nazaire, La Pallice, and Bordeaux produced little or no results. However, the Allied advances overland spread consternation. Everyone who could flee was scrambling from our threatened northern bases toward La Pallice and La Rochelle. These ports, having a common entrance between Ile de Ré and Ile d'Oléron, were as yet unbesieged by British naval units and still offered an escape route through France for those thousands of Germans who had been ordered to retreat. The twin ports had been selected by Headquarters as a refuge for U-boats from the northern ports. Here our boats would receive whatever supplies and repairs they needed for their next mission.

But the British Navy now ruled the waters off our northern ports, and our crews, leaving base in lame, half-repaired U-boats, stood little chance of reaching the twin ports safely. Those boats which were not sunk by blockading destroyers were destroyed by aircraft or shattered by mines. *U-736,* sailing from Lorient, was sunk on August 6. *U-608,* following her, was destroyed at almost the same spot on August 10. One day later *U-385* was blown to bits under a depth-charge barrage. On August 12, *U-270* was sunk near Lorient and *U-981* struck a mine while trying to penetrate La Rochelle harbor. On August 14, *U-618* was crippled by air attack and subsequently sunk by destroyers. On August 18, *U-107* succumbed to bombs and *U-621* fell victim to one of the most experienced killer groups to sail the Bay of Biscay.

During those days of German decline, the collapse of our Atlantic defenses was almost matched by defeats on other fronts. Soviet armies had recaptured the cities of Prezcemisl, Bialystock, Kowno, and Preskow, and were pressing their powerful offensive deeper into the old Russian territories. In Greece, our forces had suffered great setbacks, and Rumania had gone over into the Allied camp. In Italy, our troops had withdrawn from Rome and were battling to hold new lines further north. To top off these defeats and the ensuing confusion, a strong American-French-British invasion force had landed on the Mediterranean coast between Nice and Toulon on August 15; and Allied armored units, racing north from this new front, threatened to cut off our divisions in western France. The U-boat base in Toulon was eliminated by the bombing and sinking of eight U-boats, among them the old *U-230*. As a result, the U-boat war in the Mediterranean ceased. The dismal picture was rounded out by our loss of all destroyers, Coast Guard vessels, and mine-sweepers in French waters.

With our retreats came confusion and even panic, and the atmosphere in Fortress Brest neared the ex-plosion point. The city had been declared off limits for our troops. A strict curfew had been imposed upon the population. The shipyard had been secured by marines. All anti-aircraft guns were relocated in strategic positions to reinforce the defense perimeter. Navy units, armed to the teeth, patrolled the city and its suburbs. The Naval College, the home of the once-illustrious 1st U-boat Flotilla, was chosen to serve as the center of the defense of Brest because of its vast underground tunnel system. The 9th U-boat Flotilla was dissolved and its commander was ordered to leave port for Norway. As his last gesture, he succeeded in the nearly impossible task of refloating Boddenberg's *U-256*. This old boat, put in running order and even equipped with a Schnorkel, eventually slipped out of port and broke through the British blockade near the rocks.

Now *Kapitaen* Winter faced his finale. He trans-ferred vital units of the 1st Flotilla into the under-ground caves, managed with bravura to hold off the invasion of the German military. A large number of arrogant Army officers, who had escaped the battles for the Reich's existence and who miraculously main-tained their easy life in France, arrived in port with their French mistresses and baggage-trains of personal belongings, wine, and champagne. Some of the officers demanded U-boat transportation for all their posses-sions, and they were very indignant when Winter turned them down. The situation assumed riotous pro-portions when the first shots were fired at the front lines and the first American Sherman tanks rumbled into view of the outer trenches.

During these chaotic days, when the Navy was the only defender of Brest and nobody knew where the front lines were, or when the Allies would attack, only two U-boats remained in the beleaguered port, *U-953* and *U-247*. The repairs that would permit them to make the run for freedom were nearing completion. *U-247* was finished first and tried to make her break. She was lost with all of her crew. Now only my boat survived.

Sherman Tank

On August 19, *U-953* was finally declared seaworthy—with limitations. The diesels were in poorest condition. The batteries should have been replaced some time before, but there was no material, no replacements, no time or opportunity to make any kind of major repairs. Certainly we would have no chance for trim dives or Schnorkel exercises. With the tireless effort of every hand aboard, we doubled our watch to prevent any attempt by the French underground to sabotage our boat at the pier, and we managed to fit her out with some food and fuel. I had been ordered, to my consternation, not to take aboard any torpedoes, but to load boat and tubes with all the engineering equipment and valuable instruments and key personnel that we could carry out of the trap. This precious freight we were then to transport south to La Rochelle, where the civilians might yet make a run across France for home and safety.

I took a critical look at the situation and concluded that what was good for civilians was even better for the remainder of the crew of *U-415*. After obtaining Winter's permission to take them on board, I collected my loyal seamen at the trenches, drove heavily armed to the hospital and said farewell to those crewmen whose wounds kept them there to face a long siege. Then I instructed my two crews to abandon all unnecessary items and supervised their exodus from the compound. As we arrived at the pier, I was confronted by a large group of weeping and gesticulating civilians, French and German alike, who tried to force their way aboard. My men pushed and tossed the frantic people back to the pier. Some were so desperate to escape that we had to keep them away from the boat at gunpoint.

The crew quickly fell into line for roll call on the aft deck. Six civilians stood on the bridge, tense and seemingly lost. My Exec reported the oversized crew for inspection. Together with the six civilians and myself, we were 99 heads—45 more than our normal complement. Hoping to discourage the people on the pier, I gave my grim instructions to the crew in a loud voice: "I want to emphasize that this patrol will be one of our hardest. We'll sail with all hands on battle stations from pier to pier. The regular crew will maintain the controls while the crew of *U-415* will help out in their normal jobs. You'll work, eat, and sleep on action stations. There will be no walking, no unnecessary talking. Cans will be placed in convenient places for sanitary use. I want you to know that the coastal waters are crawling with enemy ships and our chances of surviving are very poor. The odds are ten to one that we won't break through three British blockades to reach La Rochelle, so don't have any illusions. You must be prepared for instant sailing. No one steps off the boat for any reason."

I dismissed the men and turned toward the six civilians. For the first time they realized with horror the dangers they faced, and two of them grabbed their bags and hurried off the boat. I was amused and glad to see them go; it gave us just a little more room to breathe. The four courageous civilians followed me below deck. The center aisle and all the compartments except the control room were piled high with large, bulky equipment, wooden boxes, suitcases, and cartons. In the forward torpedo room, material had been stored in the bilges, spare torpedo racks, and tubes. I told the four guests that this was their place to stay, and I left them standing there bewildered.

Then I set off to report to Winter that we were ready to sail. As I climbed the serpentine path toward the compound, I heard the windblown bellowing of machine guns to the north and saw Winter's *Adjutant* racing down the hill. He told me breathlessly that I had to take four more technicians out of port—men whom the Reich could not afford to lose to the Americans. Since these indispensable men could not join us before morning, our departure was postponed for 24 hours. I walked back to the boat thoroughly disgusted, for the longer I stayed in port, the harder it would be to break through the blockades to La Rochelle.

Soon the aroma of goulash permeated the boat; the men, perching on boxes and suitcases and pipes and bunks, ate the dinner they had thought would be their last in port. Our radio played low and pleasant tunes. I was sitting at the small desk in my nook, planning our escape, when the music subsided and the announcer began to report the news:

"This broadcast is intended for our U-boat friends in Brest. The time has come to relieve you from fighting. If you sail out of port with a white flag fastened to your scope, we will treat you with respect. But should you choose to fight, you will face quick extinction. I say this expressly for you, men of *U-953*, who have to sail once again. I can tell you that dozens of our British destroyers are waiting to receive you, and they will sink you should you decide to continue your war. I warn you, it will be your last. . . ."

I had heard enough and shouted angrily into the radio room, "Tune that fool out and play some music!"

"But sir," said a mate, "it's the only station we receive inside the bunker."

"Then turn it off and put on some records."

In the forenoon of August 21, our last four tourists
arrived with large quantities of luggage and instruments. I refused to allow them more personal gear
than my men, and after a heated argument the newcomers parted with their private possessions. I confined them in the aft torpedo room, and told them that
they had to stay there—had to eat, sleep, and possibly
die there. Then I had the hull closed tight, the radio
shut off, and the batteries charged to top capacity. As
I stepped off the boat, both diesels fumed and resounded in the hollow berth.

I walked from the cool, dark bunker into blinding
sunlight and summer heat and proceeded uphill to
make my last report. The huge rock was swarming
with men in Army uniforms. A large number of officers wore dress uniforms fit for a gala evening at the
Paris Opéra but not for the defense of Fortress Brest.
Disorder and nervous tension were apparent everywhere. Army ambulances stopped in front of the underground tunnels, unloading the first casualties of the
battle for Brest. Fierce fighting now raged along the
outer trenches, and some American tanks had broken
through into the vicinity of the compound. I rushed
through the tunnel in search of Winter, but was told
that he had gone to the compound. Following the
booms of heavy anti-aircraft guns, I reached the deserted base just as a black mushroom cloud rose no
more than 700 meters to the north. On the flat roof of
the southeast wing, I saw some Navy men with their
glasses trained north toward the scene of action. I
dashed up the staircase and found Winter; he and
his staff were elated by the success of our guns. One
American tank had been demolished as it made a run
for the college. Winter was resigned to the fact that
the defense of Brest and his one-boat flotilla had been
assumed by an elderly, nervous, monocled General. I
approached my commander and reported U-953 in
sailing order.

"You may leave port at your discretion," said Winter. "When do you propose to sail?"

"After sunset, sir, at twenty-one thirty."

"I shall be there to see you off. But no commotion, please. I don't want to stir suspicion among the dockers."

As we walked down the hill, the air-raid sirens started screaming. We ran toward the entrance to the underground facilities. Moments later the hill began to shake under an endless chain of terrific explosions. I followed Winter into the vast network of tunnels, past the many bunks already occupied by the first wounded of the battle. I had a glimpse of pale German nurses, whose future was gloomy; the dishevelled French girls, nervously awaiting their terrible fate as collaborators; their vain cavaliers, haughtily stalking around in jackboots and splendid uniforms with red-striped trousers; the bewildered sailors and infantrymen, flitting about executing frantic orders. The bombardment went on relentlessly. Everything in the catacombs—the ground, the beds, the running men—was drowned in the fierce bellowing of the flak and shook in the continual vibrations of ponderous explosions. It was the beginning of the end of the Fortress Brest.

After almost 30 minutes, the violent attack ended. When all had been calm for some time, the sirens announced the departure of the raiders, and I returned with Winter to the compound. There we were struck dumb with dismay. What only a short time before had been a stately complex of granite buildings was almost demolished. With the fall of the College, the fate of the 1st U-boat Flotilla was sealed, and Winter stood amid the ruins of his work. There was nothing he could do but send his last boat out to sea. I realized that he wished to be left alone and began my slow walk back to my boat.

24

Time: 2120, August 22, 1944. Only a few seamen were on deck to handle the lines. I stood on the bridge awaiting Winter's farewell.

At 2129, he walked over the gangplank. Returning my salute, he said, "Take good care of the boys and the boat—and good luck."

"The same to you, sir, I hope we meet soon under better conditions."

"Never mind, you get out of here before it's too late."

A few commands, and the lines were removed from the pillars, the gangway pushed back to the pier. *U-953* slid silently out of her berth. She glided toward the middle of the Bay, cautiously, noiselessly, so as not to activate any acoustical mines. I brought the boat to a standstill, lowered myself into the hull, then the Chief dropped her routinely for a trim dive.

Conditions inside the narrow drum had made a mockery of good seamanship and the regulations for safety aboard a submarine. The center aisle was blocked by our tourists' precious equipment. Communications between the various compartments were seriously impaired. The heavy weight of the additional cargo, plus a company twice the normal size, created extraordinary problems for the Chief to master. It took him over an hour to establish the buoyancy and balance that he required to handle any emergency.

U-953 surfaced and crept into the shadow of our escort, probably the only one still afloat. The night was moonless and pitch black. The escort began to move; *U-953* followed. When we passed the submerged net I switched to diesels. As the cliffs receded and radar impulses came sparking toward us from dead ahead, I knew that we had already been detected. Suddenly a flare shot into the night 200 meters ahead. At the same moment, the escort began signaling us by small lamp: WARNING. ENGLISH TORPEDO BOATS IN ATTACK POSITION. PREPARE YOUR GUNS.

I had not thought of meeting the British that way. With my calculations suddenly wrecked, I alerted my men at the guns: "Search the surface for small boats—shoot on sight."

The flare died down and the water was black again. The escort had stopped, forcing me to do the same. We were now exposed to a menace that we could not see, and that we could not fire at because our guns were ineffective against attack from dead ahead. To put up a fight, I would have to turn U-953 around, pointing her bow toward Brest and her guns toward the tiny boats. But how could I possibly sail out to sea stern first?

I signaled the escort to move forward slowly and shoot flares continuously to force the torpedo boats into deeper waters. But as soon as we got under way, I spotted a dozen shadows launching a swift attack from about 800 meters. I shouted, "Both diesels full ahead—left hard rudder!"

U-953 swerved reluctantly, exposing her full flank to the attacking enemy for interminable seconds. As my boat completed her turn, our guns began blazing. We raced back into port at high speed, denying the torpedo boats their first chance to aim and release their explosive loads. The small British boats, far superior to us in speed, drew closer quickly in the light of the flares. But then, just as suddenly as they had appeared, the little devils turned and headed out to sea.

The incident demolished my hopes for sailing that night—or perhaps any night. These small torpedo boats were not only deadly in themselves; their unexpected appearance indicated the presence of a strong supporting destroyer fleet. It seemed that our return to Brest was irreversible, and that we were condemned to blow up our boat and share the fate of the beleaguered garrison.

It was near dawn when *U-953* sneaked back into port. I told the crew to stay away from the dockers and keep silent about our night's adventure. Then, for the second time, I closed the green curtain around my nook and tried to figure out a way to escape. Only one possibility remained: to risk a submerged exit. This maneuver was imperiled by shallow water, mines, and heavy current, and it had never been attempted before. But I calculated that if we sailed at high tide, without a telltale escort, we could float toward the narrows undetected, then dive as soon as the water was deep enough to cover our bridge. Then we would have a slender chance to float out of the trap on the outgoing tide.

I rose quietly from my bunk while 100 men slumbered in full confidence of my ability to sail them to freedom. On my way to report to Winter, I walked through a completely deserted bunker and yard. I found him with his staff in the underground networks. Winter looked disturbed, grave, and weary as I reported the torpedo-boat incident and described my plan to outsmart the Tommies. He wished me Godspeed, then asked, "Will you join me on an inspection tour of the trenches?"

"Sir, I'd like to. But I have to prepare myself for tonight. Haven't had any sleep for days."

Winter said grimly, "You may miss something that no one else will live to hand down to posterity." Then, concealing his emotion with a casual toughness, he added, "Never mind, keep your ears stiff and your head high. I can't come to see you depart. My duty holds me here."

Again we shook hands. I turned away with the positive feeling that I would never see him again.

At 0255 on August 23, I shoved back the green curtain, put on my leather jacket, stepped into the

dimly lighted control room, reminded the Chief to sub-
merge very carefully whenever I called for a dive.
Then I took my place on the bridge.

At 0305, I sailed *U-953* out of the bunker on a voyage of no return. As she silently glided into the night
and toward the narrow channel leading straight into the
enemy's teeth, I took a last glance at the city astern.
The harbor with its vast docks and shipyards was a
mere shadow. The College on top of the hill, bombed
and devastated, cut a bizarre silhouette into the nightly
sky. And above all was the vague contour of the sky-
line of Brest, a city chained to the cruel history of war,
awaiting destruction and surrender. Now I sensed fully, perhaps for the first time, that all was irrevocably
lost—the glory, the successes, the triumphs. The past
could never be rebuilt.

U-953 floated by the abandoned underwater net
and sailed like a ghost into the narrows. The dark
background of the hills and cliffs covered our escape.
At 0345, the height of the tide, we slipped through
the shallow waterway. I sailed by memory, managing
to keep the boat in the navigable channel. When the
sky in the east showed the first light streaks, we spotted
the enemy boats ahead, lying motionless, mere black
dots in a purple sea—and the water was not yet deep
enough to dive. I continued with low revolutions,
avoiding noise, and presented our smallest silhouette
to the enemy. A soft hint of color in the sky heralded
dawn as we glided on the outgoing tide toward the
blockade. Then I saw sudden motion in the boats'
rigid formation. They began to flit across the lazy surface, then headed for the rocks on either side of the
passage. At that instant we reached the limit of our
surface advance.

At 0423 we dived—and emitted a strong sigh. The
boat's bow dipped slowly into the sea. For long seconds
I watched the motions of the small boats, then the
water gushed into the horseshoe of the bridge. I shut
the lid and listened to the water gurgle as it enveloped
the boat. Loud, high-pitched propellers beat the surface as the many torpedo boats scurried in various di-

rections through the calm sea. The moment the Chief had finished trimming *U-953*, I made my calculated moves: lowered her to 15 meters and rigged her for silent running. Three depth charges detonated harmlessly at a distance.

0440: *U-953* sank to twenty meters. A greater number of the racing boats criss-crossed above our overloaded drum, dropping hand grenades to scare us.

0508: Six depth charges exploded starboard ahead. Countless high-pitched propellers skimmed the surface and kept us sweating and guessing in the moist coffin.

0520: A spread of twelve canisters detonated seaward. Asdic pings began to flash through the shallow depth. A new series erupted starboard ahead, thundered through the coastal waters and echoed long after.

0645: The boat floated at 40 meters. The torpedo boats cruised resolutely far astern, still throwing hand grenades. Across the forward section, from Quessant to the southernmost cliffs of Brest, the ocean vibrated from depth charges dropped at random.

0730: I changed course to south-southwest and lowered the boat to 50 meters.

0810: We had floated 20 miles over ground, had hit sand banks several times, but always the current had lifted our drum gently over the uneven floor. Several miles ahead four destroyeres zigzagged at medium speed. On starboard, another killer group sounded out the depths for the fugitive. By now, our civilians were dying a slow death of fear and tension.

0900: We steered a new course of 200 degrees. Unable to see or to orient myself by instrument, I was governed by intuition. With both motors off, I let the boat float and slide above ground on a cushion of air in the southbound current. Asdic pings hit the steel hull with intensified force as action on surface increased.

0940: Low tide had arrived. The Chief put the nose of the boat into the sandy bottom, 85 meters below the hunters. All around us were the nervously churning propellers of a dozen destroyers. They constantly drew circles, stopped, sounded, dropped their charges, regrouped, raced ahead, stopped again, probed, dropped charges which drove us against the rocks and turned our hull into a torture chamber.

Noon: *U-953*, her bow turned into the current, swayed gently like a pendulum. Explosions and propeller noises kept every man on alert, yet the water—gray, muddy, warm water full of algae and ocean debris—seemed to protect our boat from detection.

1630: The tide began to fall, the current reversed and headed out to sea. *U-953* lifted her nose and resumed her motion over ground. Enveloped by a rattling, chirping, booming veil of sound, the boat slowly glided into the Bay of Biscay. As the noise slowly faded, it became apparent that we had evaded the British ships and slipped out of the trap. We were free—but the captives of our own smells. A horrible stench filled the narrow steel drum, emanating from the many sweating bodies, from fuel oil and grease and the overflowing sanitation cans. Some of the shipyard engineers vomited.

August 24. 0300: It was high time that I used the Schnorkel to ventilate the compartments. The process required us to run the diesels while sailing submerged —a novelty that had long intrigued me. The Chief raised the boat to 14 meters, had the mast erected and drained, and the valves opened. With a long sigh, fresh air streamed into the sweating drum. One of the diesels began to mutter and draw more cool sea air into the hull. As the boat gained speed, she stabilized and floated rigidly through the depths. What a sensation! The impressive performance convinced me that the total U-boat had been born. There was no longer a need to risk extermination on surface. Life in a German diving tube had become bearable again.

We charged our batteries and floated in secrecy through the eastern fringes of the enemy-infested Bay of Biscay. We stopped our engines and made our sound checks at irregular intervals, so that no pursuer could plot our course and intercept us with a deadly barrage. When a new day dawned, I suspended our submerged breathing exercise; periscope and float were withdrawn, and *U-953* balanced out at a depth of 40 meters.

While the sun made its daily circle, *U-953* continued blindly on her submerged run southeastward. This cruising without any navigational fix became a greater challenge the longer we stayed below surface. When midnight came again, we stuck our float and scope into the air. None of the aircraft patrolling the Bay detected the head of the air mast or the tip of the scope, even though they flew low enough to graze the water.

By dawn on August 26, we had succeeded in reaching the southernmost point on our route; from here I had decided to make the run east for coast and port. Five hours later, *U-953* gently touched ground at a depth of 48 meters. I had her raised to periscope depth and discerned a thin line in the east—land. Searching the horizon carefully, I spied the mastheads and funnels of destroyers lurking in the north. We had circumvented the trap by chance.

1320: The next time that the eye of the scope broke through the slimy surface, the coast stood like a wall ahead of us. We were overwhelmingly close, too close for safety. I acted fast to avoid being washed ashore: "Hard left rudder—steer three-forty."

Soon I could almost reach out and touch the slender lighthouse on the northern tip of Ile d'Oléron. A formation of six two-engined aircraft flew into view at low altitude; I downed the scope and let them pass. Three minutes later I found the sky clean, took several bearings on the lighthouse, while Hennecke, my navigator, did the plotting. We detected a strong northbound current and I realized that I could not maintain the boat's position until nightfall, when I could risk surfacing and proceeding into port. I had the boat put aground in an area where some of my friends had been slaughtered only days before, stepped down into the eery light of the control room and studied the chart that contained all details of the coastal waters around the two islands. Ile de Ré in the north, with the small town of St. Martin in its center, had attained dubious fame. The ancient fortress dominating the landscape had been the intermediate station from which the French sent their hardened criminals and political prisoners to Devil's Island.

Two hours after sundown we surfaced. The lighthouse had disappeared. Assuming that the current had carried our boat northward, I headed into the current toward the tower in the south, running on quiet electric motors to avoid attracting the destroyers' attention or activating the acoustical mines. Seven minutes later my binoculars picked up a tall, thin tower. I identified it as the lighthouse and sent a stream of information to my navigator, relying upon his skill to guide the boat through the waterway into the anchorage of La Rochelle.

"It's time to turn east, new course one-one-five," Hennecke advised.

"Left hard rudder—steer one-one-five," I ordered.

As *U-953* turned silently toward land, it looked as if we would sail straight into the ground. Suddenly a grinding and a light shock indicated that the boat had indeed hit ground. She slid into soft silt and came to an immediate stop.

"Blow all tanks—all back emergency!" I screamed.

The boat rose, and the wildly churning screws pulled her out of the mud and back into deeper water. Disregarding the destroyers, I ordered the depth finder turned on, found the groove in the narrow channel, and continued cautiously east, occasionally hitting ground. Something was positively wrong. The lighthouse gradually dissolved astern as we groped ahead for four hours, unable to spot any recognizable point; and I grew ever more suspicious as the bottom again came steadily closer to our keel. Then came the moment when there was simply no more clearance. After swinging the boat around in a circle and hitting ground several times, I conceded that we were trapped. At that moment day dawned and fog rolled in. I dropped anchor to ride it out until the sun burned off the white fluffy mass.

At 0740 the fog settled, exposing the higher portions of the nearby coast. Then abruptly the blanket evaporated and the land lay fully exposed. So were we. I weighed anchor in a hurry and was comparing charts and handbook when an explosion rocked the air, barely 100 meters on port. The low bellow of a cannon followed. We were being attacked by our own artillery.

"Challenge from land, sir, they request identification."

"Give them our number by lamp, Exec, and tell them to inform base that we will be in port by twenty-three hours."

As I realized that I had sailed into the wrong bay, I ordered the Chief to dive at once. U-953 settled with a light jolt in soft silt; a mere three meters of grayish, sandy water covered the rim of the bridge—and high tide had just occurred. My promise to reach port before midnight was far too optimistic.

It was now all too clear that I had mistaken the lighthouse on the northern end of Ile de Ré for the one on Ile d'Oléron. Since I had definitely identified the proper lighthouse the day before, I concluded that we had been dragged north by the strong current for the incredible distance of 17 miles, and had unknowingly passed the mine-infested entrance into port where three U-boats had been destroyed the previous week. Since all lighthouses look alike at night, I had had no reason to assume that I had taken my bearings from the wrong tower. Besides, the bay that I was trying to enter had physical features almost identical to those of the waterway leading into La Rochelle harbor.

Now, riveted to scope, I was obliged to watch the water fall and wonder how long we would be permitted to live. Beyond the lighthouse, three British planes kept scanning the surface—while our bridge rose higher and higher out of the muddy lake. Two hours after noon, the tide stopped falling, but I was so hypnotized by the arrogantly flying aircraft that I did not realize the water was rising until the bridge was fully swallowed by the bay. Then, vastly relieved, I dropped into the control room and played cards with the Chief and a few mates until nightfall.

2130: U-953 rose to surface, sped with thundering

diesels out of the unfriendly bay, passed the light-house, raced one-half mile out to sea, turned south, and surged parallel to the shore of Ile de Ré toward port. We saw the shadows of the British destroyers following us, as if confused by our reckless self-exposure; and after an interminable hour of listening to shrill radar impulses, we reached the channel leading into La Rochelle. Then, halting our noisy diesels, I switched to silent electric drive.

In a short time we spotted the silhouette of a small minesweeper sent out to our rescue. After we had answered her challenge, the vessel hurried back into port with her minesweeping gear rattling loudly. Six acoustical mines detonated at various distances in an arc ahead of the trawler. The concussions drove our whole company out of the hull.

At 0230 on Monday, August 28, *U-953* finally glided into her berth in the concrete bunker in La Pallice. She was the only boat that had survived relocation from the northern ports.

When my men passed through the center aisle with their aromatic morning coffee, I shoved back the green curtain and turned on the light. Soon, refreshed by a strong brew, I left the boat to report my arrival to the Commandant of the 3rd U-boat Flotilla. I spotted only two U-boats—old submersibles, their conning towers battered and streaked with rust. Signs of desolation were apparent everywhere. Reaching the end of the cool, dark bunker, I stepped into the humid morning air. A short ride in a Citroën brought me into the ancient walled town of La Rochelle. The car stopped in front of a three-story building, and armed sentries directed me to the Commandant's office.

A short, stocky officer, well over 15 years my senior and wearing a washed-out khaki uniform, rose from his desk. "I've already heard of your arrival," said the Commanding Officer. "We are open all weekend, you didn't have to wait until today to enter port. You are lucky that our artillery understood your signal. They usually don't. They have orders to shoot at anything that approaches land. At first they thought you were a British submarine discharging saboteurs. You see, we are well prepared for a landing."

"Do you think the assault is imminent, sir?"

"Yes. They might very well try to penetrate from the sea side, but our guns will keep them away. We have some advantages over Brest and Lorient." He informed me briefly of the efforts the combined Armed Forces made to reinforce the city's defense. The German front along the Biscay coast was slowly falling back, and the naval defenders of La Rochelle expected a great influx of heavy artillery, tanks, and infantrymen, which would relieve them of their unfamiliar land duties. The Commanding Officer urged me to send my supercargo—the extra men of *U-415* and the stowaway technicians—to the *Adjutant* for immediate repatriation to Germany. All equipment wrenched from the Allied grip in Brest was to be loaded on trucks and shipped to ports at home.

The Commandant concluded, "Your boat must be ready for patrol by the weekend. Four days in port is all I can allow you."

"But sir, I need more time than that. My batteries and the diesels should have been replaced months ago. I was told I would get new batteries here, that's why I made the trip in the first place."

"You were misinformed," he said firmly. "We have no supply of any kind. I am sorry, but you will have to wait for replacements till you arrive in Norway."

I swallowed my anger, saluted and marched out. In four working days, we could not even make repairs essential to the boat's safety, much less prepare her for a long patrol. The short trip from Brest had already revealed countless deficiencies; they would grow rapidly more dangerous the longer they went unserviced.

On my return to La Pallice, I instructed the two former officers of *U-415* to disembark their crew and arrange for their return to Germany. Then I told my officers of *U-953* about our blitzkrieg schedule. We soon discovered to our dismay that German shipyard personnel was already fleeing homeward to escape another approaching disaster. I therefore put all my machinists to work to get U-953 into fighting condition. At once frantic activity sprang up along the pier and around the cubicle where our boat had found temporary refuge. The bulky cargo which had hampered shipboard operations was brought to daylight and loaded on trucks. The drivers fidgeted impatiently, eager to make their getaway to the east.

The situation in port reflected the confusion which spread throughout the French countryside. The Allies, attacking in all directions with strong armored columns, had made considerable progress during the days we had been at sea. In Brittany, American forces had overrun Nantes and were continuing along the coast with great speed. Paris had fallen into Allied hands on August 24, to the joyous frenzy of the French population. Along the Côte d'Azure, the Allied invaders took Toulon and Marseille and terminated our losing struggle in southern France. Everywhere in German-held areas, teams of saboteurs in the French underground gained enormous strength; supplied by Allied air drops, they cut our communications and supply lines and harassed our escape routes through the French hinterland. Rails and highways were also the targets of Allied bombers, while fighter planes machine-gunned the long columns that streamed out of the western ports. Thousands of men untrained in land warfare—civilians, technicians, garrison clerks, sailors, shipyard hands, supply workers, auto mechanics—could not fight back against ambush and air attack, and were slaughtered wholesale. Some columns were reduced to pitiful handfuls of refugees who hiked and foraged their way back to Germany.

Twenty-five thousand men escaped La Rochelle and nearby ports during these days of general retreat in late August 1944. Among them were my former crewmen of U-415, along with hundreds of seamen from other U-boats which could not be made seaworthy. In Bordeaux, the crews of U-123, U-129, U-178, and U-188 had to blow up their veteran boats before they took to the roads. Their flight across a hostile France lead those men through a hell of hardship and humiliation. Only a few reached the German border. The rest ended up dead in ditches or interned behind barbed-wire fences.

In La Rochelle, the U-boat tragedy lasted a little longer. One boat, *U-260*, sailed for Norway at the end of August. She was one of the few boats to succeed in breaking through the blockade, but she later was lost in a minefield near the southern coast of Ireland. With the departure of *U-260*, my boat was the only one remaining in the vast concrete structure which had housed well over 40 U-boats during the peak year of our power at sea. *U-953* was also the last of our boats to lay in any French port. Sixty-six U-boats had been destroyed since the day the invasion had begun, as against only 170,000 tons of enemy shipping sunk by us during that period. The Allied defense had been so effective that more than three-quarters of the Schnorkel boats sent out to attack the invasion convoys had not returned. During the crucial days of August, the British defenses were expected to be weak along the convoy routes through the Irish Sea and the North Channel, but by then only a few boats survived to exploit the weakness.

With the extermination of at least 90 per cent of our operational fleet at sea, and with the foreclosure of all Biscay ports as U-boat bases, Headquarters was forced to cease the U-boat war in the English Channel. The last act of the tragedy would be played out further north—and my boat lay stranded in La Rochelle.

Realizing that France was irrevocably lost, and that we had only a few days left to spend our last pay, I allowed my crew a three-hour shopping spree in the downtown stores during a Saturday afternoon. My pockets were filled with francs, but I found little to buy and less that attracted my fancy. Finally I surrendered my bundles of francs for a colorful housecoat for Mother and silk stockings for my sister. At curfew, the crew returned promptly to their temporary quarters in town, for our safety at night could no longer be guaranteed. Just that morning, two half-dressed naval officers had been found dead in a side-street gutter, throats slit and penises cut off.

U-953 was not in running order by our weekend deadline. My mechanics worked all of Sunday to complete the most important repairs, but it was not until Tuesday evening, September 5, that the Chief declared the boat ready for patrol—with certain restrictions and limitations. I scheduled our seagoing for Wednesday night.

At 1000, September 6, I entered the Commandant's office, wearing my washed-out fatigues, to report *U-953* ready for sailing. Informally, he accepted my notice and wished me luck. He then disclosed that Senior Officer West, who was about to escape the siege by plane, had asked me to report to him. I wondered what *Kapitaen* Roesing had to tell me. I had never quite understood his function, since the tactical deployment of U-boats was decided at Doenitz's Headquarters. I jumped into the waiting armored car and raced through the city with screaming tires. Minutes later I arrived at a stately villa. Everywhere were signs of hasty departure. Marines were burning piles of documents on the lawn, loading cabinets and office machines on trucks. I was led to the Senior's elegant room.

Roesing, wearing snow-white trousers, finished packing tennis balls and rackets in a valise, then began speaking in his staccato manner: "Had time to leaf through your logbook. Noticed you managed well in shallow waters. Is that your specialty? You seem to have no difficulty breaking blockades."

"Sir, it can be done," I answered, annoyed on two counts. First, it was he who had told us, back in May, to ram our boats into enemy ships. Then, too, the compliment meant little coming from a man who had only shortly been in command of a U-boat, and probably had never heard a depth charge explode.

He continued, "Well, we'll give you a hard nut to crack this time." He unfolded a map and Headquarters' plan for my patrol. I was to operate in the North Channel, in a dangerous area tucked between the northern Irish coast and the minefields west of Scotland. Detailed orders would follow by radio. He handed me some charts containing data on the minefields, advised me on how to avoid disaster at La Rochelle, how to circumnavigate the British blockade, and how to reach my operational area. Then he snapped, "Any more questions?"

Since I had my own ideas on how to navigate, I simply said, "No questions, sir."

Roesing's salute ended the peculiar meeting. I ran to the car and raced alongside armored columns to the compound. I packed my meager belongings and took the armored car back to the bunker. En route I saw a few heavy tanks rumbling by, and infantrymen and light artillery streaming through town to take up their field positions. From beyond came the low rolling thunder of the approaching battle. In less than one week La Rochelle had turned from a sleepy medieval town into a strong garrison determined to make a last-ditch stand.

Reaching La Pallice, I paused at the entrance to the U-boat bunker and raised my face toward the sky and the sun. I savored that moment, knowing that I would dive that night and live in obscurity for many weeks, that I would not see the sun again until I surfaced in a Norwegian fjord after an underwater voyage of some 2,000 miles, after summer had gone and fall or even winter would have arrived. Or I might never see daylight again and sink instead to my grave in eternal darkness.

As I approached my boat, I was strangely startled by the wooden containers of fresh vegetables that stood on deck. For a moment it seemed as if nothing had changed since the days of glory when I began my service aboard U-boats. Of course, nothing was the same. Like our great land victories, our few hundred U-boats had all but vanished. But at least one would die fighting.

My Exec, who was overseeing the loading of the fresh food, came to my nod and I told him of my decision: "We leave this trap one hour after midnight, without an escort. Keep that to yourself. And no roll call either, please."

"How about notifying the artillery, the coastal batteries?"

"I don't want them to know that we sail. The Tommies have too many ears. I'll take the risk of being shot at." Then I lowered myself into my coffin

At 2030, after dinner, the lights went out. I closed my curtain and stretched out on my green leather mattress. The lonely pressures of command gripped me like a cold fist. With the departure of *U-953*—with the sailing of our last U-boat from our last port along the Biscay shore—the battle in the Atlantic came to a bitter yet defiant finale.

25

September 7. 0100: I was studying the charts in the eery light of the control room. My planning absorbed me so deeply that I was startled to hear the Exec's low voice: "Boat is ready to leave port—crew is on action stations."

"Thanks. Have all watertight doors shut and all men put on their life preservers. Only two or three should be in the hull while we traverse the harbor."

The watertight doors clicked and the crew slipped into their yellow inflatable jackets. I put on my lambskin coat, followed the last man to the bridge, and said quietly, "Let go bow and stern ropes. Both motors slow astern—rudder amidships."

The boat silently cleared the pier and glided, stern first, out of the concrete structure, 300 meters into a dark night. No one took notice of our escape.

"Both stop. Both small ahead, port twenty. New course two-eighty."

I directed the boat into the center of the narrows

between the two islands. For the last time I glanced at the shadowy city of La Rochelle, which would soon face the fate of Brest and the other ports under Allied siege. The sleek boat sailed noiselessly through the dark waters—the last of the wolves deserted his lair. It was a bitter pill to swallow, abandoning this shore from which we had carried our flag across the seven seas. I felt as if all my previous patrols, all our great sacrifices, had been vain endeavors.

As the faint strip of land receded and the bay overflowed into the ocean, the tide was at its highest. The lean tower of the lighthouse of Ile d'Oléron on port ahead showed us our way through the nightly haze.

"Shadows on starboard. Destroyers, bearing three-forty. . . ."

At that moment we were confronted by six enemy surface vessels, only vague images seaward. Yet there were no radar impulses; we remained undetected even by our own artillery. When we had the shadowy lighthouse on port 120 degrees, I changed course to due south. I proceeded noiselessly and slowly, using the black coastline as a cover. After the lighthouse had vanished I risked switching to diesels. As the worn-out engines began to mutter and spout black exhaust fumes, U-953 gained speed. We sailed southward in close proximity to the shore for a distance of 10 miles, always prepared to be intercepted by the enemy. But, just as I had expected, the watchdogs slowly retreated before the first sign of a dawning day and the renewed threat of our coastal batteries. Then I turned the boat toward the open sea. When the stars were extinguished, U-953 withdrew from the surface. The Biscay shore would never see her again.

After sundown on our second day at sea, a storm blew up. High winds swept heavy waves over our Schnorkel float, cutting off the air supply every so often, creating a vacuum which took our breath away and made us feel as if our heads were exploding. Notwithstanding the raging storm, I felt comfortable. With the boat protected by 14 meters of water and by high waves, radar detection of the float and scope was almost impossible. It had been a long time since I had felt so secure, and the unpleasant side effects of the Schnorkel routine were evened out by the relative ease with which we evaded the enemy aircraft.

During those hours of clandestine activity and highest vigilance only a few meters below the lethal surface, our radio operators kept busy decoding signals from Headquarters concerning *U-953* and the few other wolves which were still afloat. In the stream of messages that reached me in the control room was a precise order for a new operation. I was to form a patrol line together with *U-484, U-743,* and *U-925* along the western entrance to the North Channel. *U-953* was to assume the southernmost position.

After the regular transmission time for signals with tactical contents, Headquarters flashed out the latest Armed Forces communiqués. They told us of raging battles and of our serious losses in western and southern France. The British had made a spectacular advance into Belgium, and the Americans had reached a line from Namur to Orléans. We also heard that French-British forces were pressing north along the Rhône, and that the Soviets threatened to overrun our eastern provinces. More news, all bad, told about air attacks by huge bomber fleets which leveled our cities and turned them into incinerators. There was not a single encouraging sentence, not the faintest hint of a halt in the declining trend.

On the night of September 10, a cable fire in the control room brought us to the verge of disaster. Only the quick reaction of the Chief, who extinguished the flames with his gloved hands, spared us an unscheduled ride on the surface—to our annihilation.

U-953 maintained a steady northwesterly course across the vast plains of the Bay of Biscay. Strong fall gales whipped the surface and made the use of the Schnorkel difficult. During the early hours of September 11, just after we had passed the eighth Longitude West, our centrifugal pump stopped working. The breakdown presented a grave danger, since it was the only pump capable of keeping us afloat in

sudden emergencies. Berger, Warrant Officer and top
mechanic, dismantled the pump and worked until
dawn to put it back in service.

Shortly after midnight September 13, the bad news
from Headquarters contained a personal shock. What
I long had feared had finally happened: Darmstadt,
my parents' new home, had been under heavy air attack. The raid during the previous night had wiped
out the center of the city, tens of thousands had died
and many more thousands were left homeless. My
parents, who had moved into the center of town against
my advice, had surely lost all their belongings once
again—and I hesitated thinking any further. I hoped
they had found protection in a public shelter nearby.

The next day I set U-953 on a north-northwesterly
course, continuing along the Continental shelf. Our
submerged voyage had been unmolested since we had
sailed out of port. We owed our lives to the Schnorkel
just as surely as hundreds of U-boats owed their deaths
to the lack of it.

September 16. Forty minutes after midnight, the
starboard diesel stopped abruptly. The breakdowns began to haunt me. When the Chief returned from the
stern, his frown meant trouble: "Diesel bushing busted
—the hell with this old junk."

Then a sudden vacuum prevented me from questioning him. The float of the Schnorkel had jammed in
closed position, and with the air intake cut off, the port
engine had sucked most of the air out of the hull before the diesel could be halted. The Chief's orders died
in the thinned air. The men gasped for air, their eyes
bulging. The Chief lowered the boat, bringing the
Schnorkel head below surface in an effort to loosen the
float. To no avail. Breathing became ever more difficult; suffocation seemed imminent. The Chief gesticu-
lated wildly, trying to tell his men to lay down the air
mast, which might result in unlocking the float. With
agonizing effort, the mechanics turned handles, lowered the mast by cable, then erected it again with the
primitive winch. Painful minutes passed, but then the
mast drained and the seawater gargled down into the
bilges. The float cleared with a snap and air was

sucked into the boat with a long sigh. The sudden change in pressure burst many an eardrum. Some of the men covered their faces in pain and sagged to the deck plates. Others swallowed violently to equalize the pressure.

Bad luck and mechanical failures continued to dog the boat. On the night of September 17, the sea was rough, and holding the boat at Schnorkel depth with our one operative diesel was a nerve-wracking task. The Chief had tried for hours to get the batteries fully charged, but his progress was retarded by the high seas and a continually jamming float. Then, without warning, the boat slipped out of the hands of my skilled engineer. The sound of gushing water emerged from the diesel compartment. The boat flipped away astern and sank at a severe down angle, totally out of control. The Chief's frantic emergency measures finally caught her at 285 meters, and after a few wild curves she was tamed.

The reason for the waterbreak was a puzzle, but somehow the air intake duct had allowed the ocean to enter the boat. There were well over 20 tons of water in the diesel room bilge and five more in the duct. After the water had been drained, we again tried to Schnorkel. But instead of air, tons of water again surged into the boat and forced her into another near-disastrous plunge.

No doubt about it, our Schnorkel was out of order, and the situation was desperate. Our only choice was to face suffocation below or destruction above. I chose the surface, where we had a slim chance to reach the Irish coast, hide in the cliffs, and repair the damages. I swung the boat east and surfaced into a raging storm. The gunners raced to their automatics. Two machinists loosened the deck grates and disappeared into the cavity between hull and superstructure to investigate the cause of our difficulties. The port diesel howled loudly, the boat began to run before hurricane winds and mountainous waves and driving cascades of rain. It was an abominable night, but one that would keep pursuers in port.

Since the weather seemed to favor us, I extended

the run for shore and fully charged the batteries. We dived just before dawn without interference. The Chief reported the findings of his machinists: a ruptured blind flange at a "Tee" in the air intake system had been torn off its seat. A new flange would be fabricated and ready for installation by evening.

Another violent night on surface fit only for U-boats protected us from harassment. Finally, after two hours of battling the elements, continually bathed in breakers, the two machinists had installed their new flange, and our batteries were fully charged. Without stretching our incredible luck any further, I dived *U-953* into a 20-meter wave.

At 2318 the following night we sighted the first beacon light of Ireland which was burning in peace-time fashion. From the description of the Exec at the scope, I identified it as Loop Head, at the mouth of the Shannon River. Forty minutes after midnight, during a routine sound check, we heard detonating charges out at sea in the area we had crossed one night before. The British had returned to their hunting grounds.

The machinists went to work dismantling and repairing the starboard diesel bushing, and we in the forward compartments concentrated on the task of keeping the boat on Schnorkel depth. Short signals and news reached us during those hours of danger and apprehension. Headquarters repeatedly advised the few lone wolves to travel along the 200-meter line on their march to Norwegian ports. My observations of strong Allied defense activity along that line made me suspect that a leak in our security system had sent the British destroyers there first. A mere half-dozen boats were running the gauntlet of overwhelming Allied sea power, and all but two of them were doomed. A distress signal, repeated by Headquarters, was handed to me in the control room: BOMBED. SINKING. 62N 01E. U-867. Not much later, another distress signal came from the same area: SCHNORKEL DEFECT. AIR ATTACK. UNABLE TO DIVE. U-865. This was the boat's final message. Before dawn she was sunk by aircraft.

Later that night, word came that Fortress Brest had fallen after four weeks of siege. My thoughts wandered back to *Kapitaen* Winter, who must have done all he could, and then further east to Darmstadt. What was the fate of my family? I would have had an answer a year ago, when Doenitz still kept close contacts with his Captains, informing them of good and bad news from home. But those days were gone beyond recall.

A sudden cry came from the helmsman in the conning tower: "Can't hold course—compass out of order..."

I cursed in helpless rage at this latest breakdown. Without gyro-compass, our mission was in dire jeopardy. The auxiliary magnetic-compass was of no help; it had not been adjusted since the boat had left Kiel a year before, and was totally unreliable. Taking no chances, I ordered *U-953* aground. Berger dismantled the gyro-compass, repeatedly threatening that he had not the slightest notion how to put it together again. All day long, the busy screws of Allied hunters cut the water around us. But finally, after 19 hours of ceaseless effort, Berger managed to fit the parts together.

By dawn on September 20, I had taken bearings from Inishbofin lighthouse. Then, expecting enemy action soon, I discontinued Schnorkeling and rode at periscope depth in search of the foe. Asdic pings and propeller noises reached a hideous crescendo. But all I observed was one airplane and the cliffs of Clare Island. Then I realized that we had been fooled by a new British device. Floating sound buoys had been planted in coastal areas to drive lurking U-boats out to sea where water conditions had no adverse effect upon the detection gears of British hunters gathered for the kill. Reassured by my discovery of the rattlers, I ordered normal speed.

The following night, the sea was calm and the rattlers were many. *U-953* turned around Erris Head and proceeded toward Donegal Bay. At 0308 the port diesel stopped. A quick report from the rear: "Diesel clutch jammed."

I swore like a corsair, leaped forward and relieved

the Chief from the controls so he could investigate.
He soon returned with disgusting news. The clutch was
frozen solid; it had to be dismantled. With both diesels
now out of order, I continued for another three hours
on electric motors, then laid the boat aground in Sligo
Bay. The machinists, thickly smeared with grease and
oil, labored frantically in the dwindling air for an
entire day. Frequent booms of exploding charges at
the western horizon, and the fake pings and engine
noises, were our constant companions. The work on
both diesels was finally completed one hour after midnight, and *U-953* separated from the bottom.

The hard rumble of detonating canisters followed us
along the rocky coast. By early morning I spotted Aran
lighthouse sparkling in the sun, and at nightfall I took
bearings from Tory Island, whose soaring cliffs rose
like a cathedral from the ocean. During the night,
U-953 entered the North Channel. It echoed with the
British activity along the 200-meter line. We Schnorkeled cautiously from beacon to beacon and reached
Inishtrahull Island by dawn. *U-953* had arrived in her
hunting ground. It was 0600, and I laid the boat in
ambush on the rocky Channel floor, preserving power
for the attack.

The thunder in the west never ceased. The Tommies dropped their costly canisters as if they were
cheap marbles. The intensity of their barrage again led
me to suspect that the British had been informed of our
mission and had amassed great forces to catch up with
my partners and myself. At one time, late in the evening, a destroyer passed within two miles, heading for
Londonderry harbor. Close to midnight I moved east,
Schnorkeling and penetrating deeper into the Channel, where the convoys had but a narrow path to travel.
For three hours we patrolled the narrows, cautiously
maneuvering, listening, probing. Then we settled again
to the floor, 13 miles east of Inishtrahull. It seemed a
perfect spot to hide and strike. Continuous underwater
thunder rolling in from the west and weak propeller
noises of fast-moving destroyers told us of fierce fighting seaward. None of the British captains, though, ever
thought of searching the narrows. They could have

easily trapped us between the coast and the nearby minefields.

During our third day in the Channel, two destroyers sped toward the Irish Sea. I ignored the killers in favor of bigger game, which was supposed to come along. A premature attack would only have disclosed our presence and closed the route to all shipping. That day and two more passed with plenty of activity along the 200-meter line, but no convoy cut through the Channel.

On September 29, after seven days of fruitless search, the mission of *U-953* reached a sudden end. The Schnorkel routine had become a nightmare. A wild storm drove high waves from the Atlantic toward the Irish coast. The Chief worked frantically to hold the boat below surface, but at times the mast extended three and four meters into the air, allowing the Tommies to take proper aim. I saw no reason to continue the risk of getting bombed or wrecked in the cliffs, so I called off the torture: "That's enough for tonight, Chief, bring her down."

"Mast doesn't move," called the man activating the winch. "Cable is broke, sir, the damn thing is broken..."

The new breakdown was a deadly matter. If the boat assumed a sharp down angle, the mast would collapse, and no power could have erected it again. It would have meant the end of our submergence—and of our existence. It was vividly and painfully clear that we were put out of action. And yet, my luck still prevailed: the mast was stuck in an upright position, allowing us to make further use of the Schnorkel, provided we could keep it erect. However, its bulky and conspicuous float, protruding above surface when on periscope depth, ruined all hope of launching a secret attack.

The crippling damage to the Schnorkel was the last straw in a long mission devoted to nothing but coping with our endless mechanical deficiencies. Although the crew deserved at least one victory as a reward for their endurance, I decided that I had to break off the patrol. With the Schnorkel mast standing foolishly erect

at a depth of 40 meters, I set *U-953* on a course for
our new home base—Bergen, Norway. We diagonally
traversed the Channel, fighting a strong current, and
steered between the minefields and the British killer
groups toward the Outer Hebrides.

Midnight October 1. The diesels pushed the boat
forcefully ahead. Leaning over the chart table in the
control room, I composed a signal informing Admiral
U-boats of our mishap and planned a quick escape
from the point of transmission. At 0100 our message
flashed from the antenna mounted to the tip of the
Schnorkel. It took only four letters in code to say: NO
ENEMY TRAFFIC. STRONG DEFENSE. DAM-
AGES. RETURN TO BASE. U-953.

My communication prompted Headquarters to request other boats in the area to report their findings.
But the call was not heard by our three companion
boats on the North Channel mission. *U-484* and *U-743*
had been destroyed northwest of Inishtrahull on the
same day less than 20 miles apart, and *U-925* had
been sunk off the Irish coast.

My signal produced other obnoxious results: at
daybreak our sound gear detected three destroyers approaching from astern. I swore to myself never again
to use the radio transmitter and to leave the guesswork
up to the fellows at Headquarters. At 1030 a new
hunter-killer group was picked up by our gear, this time
port ahead. We counted six destroyers screening the
sea, and they probably had squadrons of aircraft supporting their search. The pinging and throbbing din
soon filled all compartments. Some men listened with
wide-open eyes while others turned in their bunks
pretending not to hear a thing. The six Tommies
searched and probed unaware that we were but three
miles to their east and only 20 meters below surface,
sailing along the outer edge of their minefield. By
nightfall the noise had wandered gradually astern and
out to sea. At midnight there was but a hint of sound
in the gear. Two hours later the spook had disappeared, and at 0300 we breathed fresh air and resumed our noisy routine.

For several nights and days, *U-953* traveled past the Outer Hebrides and into the northern regions. Here strong fall gales whipped the surface and threatened to break our precarious life line. Constantly hunted by destroyers, constantly shadowed by countless aircraft, *U-953* somehow remained immune. During these weeks of perpetual submergence, the men lived with their shattered eardrums, their impaired eyesight, their abused lungs and, worst of all, their private thoughts. One could think of youth, school, the glorious early advances on land, our hundreds of sinkings and victory celebrations, women and love. But once the plug of memory was pulled, a bitter fountain rose to mind—our lost battles. Our defeats at sea. Flights out of ports. Memories of friends now dead on the bottom. Retreats on land. Disintegrating cities. And above all for me, the uncertain fate of my parents and sister.

While *U-953,* floating on her eastbound course, furtively passed the Shetland Islands in the second week of October 1944, the obliteration of our U-boat Force was nearing completion. Since we had escaped beleaguered La Rochelle, 17 U-boats—almost the entire contingent at sea—had been destroyed. All but four of these boats had sailed from Norway on their first patrol; they were perfectly equipped with the Schnorkel, their crews were well trained but badly prepared and ill advised. They had become easy kills for the Allies.

Forty miles northeast of the Shetland Islands we ran into a killer group which had sealed off the Norwegian Sea. Then came 28 hours of cruel pursuit, nerve-wracking pings, chasing screws, circling destroyers, detonating depth charges. In the throes of this last ordeal, we floated just below surface, prepared every minute to shoot and die, and yet *U-953* managed once again to slip out of the devil's grip. For many hours after the ordeal, the sound of hell followed in our wake until, after six weeks of unprecedented submergence, the soaring mountains of Norway stopped us from sailing further east.

Some two hours after daybreak, I spotted the planes on duty, and also the low lighthouse on a forlorn rock in the middle of the passage into Bornjefjord. The sea broke on the naked stone, creating a foamy circle around the tiny island. Trusting the mast no longer, I changed to electric drive. *U-953* worked hard to overpower the current and gain a position from where we could surge into the fjord. The iron drum shook under the broadside attack of the sea. A sudden thud, then a rumble and a bang—the mast had fallen on deck. The force of the rising tide threatened to drive the boat into the outer cliffs. *U-953* thrust forward at 10 knots, all she could produce submerged, fighting like a salmon against the turbulence. Meter by meter she crept ahead. As she floated past the lighthouse, she was caught in the violent whirlpool and forced toward a mountain wall that rose perpendicular from the water's edge. I made a quick adjustment, and the boat was pushed into the fjord. And yet again we had survived.

26

A trawler, a Coast Guard vessel, lay quietly in the center of the fjord, oblivious to our submerged arrival. When I was able to see the faces of her crew clearly, I lowered the scope to make the surprise complete. My command to surface ended the long submergence. Compressed air hissed through the pipes. With a low moan, the boat rose into daylight—and into a broadside of gun muzzles.

The startled captain shouted through his megaphone, "What the devil are you doing?"

Pleased by the success of my little trick, I shouted back, "This is a raiding party. Do you have contraband aboard?"

"No, just a harem. But not for your boys." And, as if he were indeed afraid we would have a closer look at his ship, the Captain ordered his vessel onto opposite course. Meanwhile, all my men poured out of the bridge hatch; some manned the guns, others brought ammunition to the platforms, and the rest swung through the railing on deck putting white cigarettes into their pale faces.

After breathing the fresh sea breeze for some time, I choked on the beastly stench of rot and decay which escaped the hatch. The aromatic scent of tobacco, missed for so long, did not disguise the horrible smell of six weeks of slow decomposition. On the contrary, the first cigarettes left a bitter taste in my mouth. But two hours later, as *U-953* turned the Bergenfjord, I had rediscovered their old spicy savor.

The Coast Guard vessel had signaled our arrival in advance, promoting a meager reception. A handful of men in blues or gray leather suits had come down to the waterfront. It was a rare opportunity for them to witness a U-boat's return from patrol; for months boats had sailed but none had returned. However, my men hardly fit the heroic role in which we were cast. We had filthy hair, long beards, green faces, hollow cheeks, and eyes as big as golf balls. We looked more like undernourished and fatigued jungle fighters.

Our lines were thrown ashore. The Commanding officer stalked aboard, nodded at my brief report, hailed the crew for their accomplishments, told us that greater sacrifices were expected, but warmly assured us that the worst lay behind and that things would improve fundamentally almost at once. He then invited us for cocktails and dinner. The drinks were strong and the food was heavy. We were asked about our last days in Brest and our stopover in La Rochelle, and the crew responded with tales as fantastic as *The Thousand and One Nights*. When it appeared that my men had had too much liquor to stop their yarns, I rose from the table and ended the party. We were billeted in a building of our own. Soon one could hear the bearded seafarers singing loud chanteys in tubs and showers.

After a good night's sleep, I launched a campaign to acquire a new boat, for *U-953* was virtually disintegrating. She not only required a new Schnorkel system, but also two new diesels, a whole new complement of batteries, and a thousand other pieces of equipment not readily available. My conference with the flotilla's Chief Engineer went in the right direction; there was not a single part that I needed in the base, nor were there facilities to put my boat into dry dock for a long, exhaustive overhaul. I seemed to have won my case.

More was missing in Bergen than parts and replacements. There was no mail waiting. I had expected a letter, a telegram—anything to tell me that all was well at home. But our mailbags had been lost somewhere, either in the gigantic rerouting snarl in France or in supply vessels sunk by enemy aircraft in the Skagerrak and in the fjords. We were cut off from the homeland, and uncertainty over the fate of our loved ones rested heavily upon every man's mind.

Through gray layers of thin low clouds, I sailed U-953 into the arsenal to unload our torpedoes. There we saw a few dilapidated hulls in the process of being cut up for scrap. I had expected revived U-boat activity in Norwegian ports after the bases in France had been lost, and the quiet was depressing. I searched in vain for new type U-boats which we had long been promised.

In the compound, evening dinner was very small and exactly apportioned, a fair index to our fortunes in the fifth year of war. I was informed that the Commandant had arranged a party in our honor; there would be drinks and snacks, music, and some Norwegian girls to dance with. Returning to my room, I retrieved my blues from the lone suitcase I had brought with me. The suit was clammy and full of wrinkles and rank with mold. The odor accompanied me as I was driven to a lodge in the mountains, the flotilla's resort.

In the morning of my third day on land I met an old acquaintance—Senior Officer U-boats West. *Kapitaen* Roesing had succeeded in escaping his La Rochelle quarters by plane only hours before the Americans moved in. He had already established offices near the compound for a renewed campaign against England.

After briefing him on my patrol, I made my plea: "Sir, I appeal to you for a new boat—one of the new types if possible. *U-953* is simply falling apart. There are no facilities in Norway to repair and put her into fighting condition."

"I see no opportunity for you to take over a new boat at this time," replied the Senior. "As a matter of fact, we are making special efforts to restore every conventional type U-boat for a massive offensive in spring."

"Sir, rehabilitating our boat may take as long as building a new one."

"That is not for you to determine. We are making the decisions. You will get the orders." That was clear enough, and also the end of our conversation. I was dismissed.

The decision to reconstruct *U-953* in a German shipyard was reached the same day. My future was inseparably intertwined with that of *U-953*, and I realized that I had better stop dreaming of a perfect new boat and concentrate on extending the old one's life.

The order to rebuild the boat completely was received by the crew with stoicism. There was other news pouring in over the radio which aroused far more concern. The British, we learned, had reached the lower Rhine, and the Americans had penetrated the first German city, Aachen. There were reports that Stuttgart, Munich, and even Innsbruck had been the targets of huge Allied bomber fleets. The situation was very serious, but—we were told—it was not hopeless. The voice from Berlin assured us over and over again that new weapons would soon strike, and final victory would then be ours. We believed, we trusted, and we continued to sail.

At dusk, on a misty day late in October, *U-953* was ready to leave port. A small Coast Guard cutter guided us into the fjord just before nightfall. It was a silent march through unfriendly waters in which British torpedo boats were already operating. At the end of the first night we sailed into Haugesund harbor, hid the boat behind a pier-end shed for the day. By nightfall we followed our escort through the cliffs, rapids, and narrows along the rocky coast to Stavanger. Another strained day at an utterly unprotected pier. At sundown we started a night-long run through fjords and dangerously narrow waterways to Egersund; here we fastened our lines to the crippled pines growing out of the cracks of a huge rock and pulled our boat under the branches. Next night, we raced alone into the open sea and, using the cable temporarily repaired in Bergen, Schnorkeled our way around the southern heel of Norway into the Skagerrak. Two nights later, we met a German convoy in the Baltic and sailed around Kiel Lightship just before daybreak. It was a gray cold morning when *U-953* came to rest alongside the Tirpitz Pier. We were in Germany at last.

Our arrival caused no celebration; in fact it went entirely unnoticed. Dressed in my old, wrinkled leather suit, I stretched my legs on the pier and walked over to the old steamer which had been moored there since the war began. I searched for the 5th U-boat Flotilla's offices, for the tender *Lech* had disappeared. I was told that they had been relocated ashore. Stalking over the familiar tarred planks, I saw evidence of great decay since my last visit 22 months ago. An old tender lay aground, bombed to wreckage, her decks spilled over by heavy oil and scummy water. In the distance stood the blackened walls of demolished houses. The hills of rubble and steel that dotted the shore had once been the elegant Bellevue district. I eventually found the flotilla's new quarters among destroyed barracks, and the Commanding Officer accepted my report with indifference. I was advised to sail to Leubeck. Here the overhaul of my boat could be guaranteed, whereas a stay in Kiel would only jeopardize her existence.

One hour after we had fastened our lines we removed them again. *U-953* scurried out of Kiel harbor and chased eastward under the evening sky. When the morning fog lifted, *U-953* steered into the mouth of the Trave River, and shortly before noon came to rest at a flimsy pier of the small naval base Luebeck-Siems. My attempt to report my arrival to the Commanding Officer met closed doors. A guard advised me that the

Commandant had gone for lunch and that it might be hours before he would return.

There was no activity in the small compound, and it seemed that the Navy had made little use of the facilities. *U-953* was the only boat at the pier. The men sat on the rim of the bridge or squatted on deck enjoying their lunch. It was little enough, but we all felt grateful. At mid-afternoon, I was told that the Commandant was inclined to receive us. We assembled in the small square at the base, and I presented the crew to the well-fed officer. It mattered little to me that he had found a perfect place to serve the country, preserving his habits and family life; but I bitterly resented the look of distaste that crossed his face as he inspected my seafarers, unkempt and exhausted after months and years of front-line service.

Our rehabilitation began at once. I sailed *U-953* into the shipyard, where she was to remain for her own rejuvenation. Returning to the compound, I noted with satisfaction that the Exec had taken possession of a barracks and was about to settle the men in their places. My suitcase had been delivered into a corner room which was to be my home for some time. I unpacked and sent my few clothes to the laundry and cleaner. Then, finally, nervously, I tried to get in touch with my parents. But telephone service to Darmstadt was still out of order—this two months after the air raid. I sent a telegram instead, asking them to reply at once by wire.

It was soon made known that the overhaul of *U-953* would take eight to 10 weeks. The news, which meant a longer furlough for all hands, came as a godsend to the men, whose desire to rush home and search for their loved ones had grown ever more desperate since we landed in Norway. Since my parents had not answered my urgent telegram, I arranged for my own departure somewhat earlier than I had planned. I was about to leave the compound when Headquarters informed me that it was necessary to transfer my Chief Engineer and my Executive Officer. The loss of the Chief, an outstanding technician, was a great disappointment, and it became a serious blow when his re-

placement turned out to be my inept former Chief
aboard *U-415*. To make matters worse, I was also
presented with a very young ensign who knew nothing
of U-boats. Since he was to assume the Second Officer's
place, I had to raise the incumbent, Ziemer, to Executive, even though he lacked the experience to fill this
position. The dangerous shuffle of personnel demanded
strong action, but I decided to do nothing until my
return from leave.

It was a cold misty day in early November when I
departed from Luebeck and headed for Darmstadt by
way of Berlin. The express was packed with people
who spoke with a hard Baltic accent, people who had
fled their homes ahead of the advancing Russians. The
refugees—mostly women and children and old folks—
wore threadbare clothes and carried humble house-
wares; they stood in trembling groups beside their
boxes, bundles, valises, and bedding. Along this pitiful human chain, alarming war news and rumors
flashed through the train from compartment to compartment. The eastern front was moving west fast and
Koenigsberg was in gravest danger, and the western
front was moving east almost as fast.

I leaned at the window in the passageway, deep in
forlorn thoughts. At my feet lay the suitcase with the
presents for my parents and Trudy. The landscape
rushed by, desolate and gray. In time, the monotonous
North German plains were broken more and more often by larger and larger clusters of blackened walls,
craters, rubble, and cut-off chimneys. Then the ruins
themselves became a vast plain of destroyed city
blocks, a whole civilization in ruins. We had arrived in
Berlin.

People on the move, people in flight. Thousands
filled the station. Women in Red Cross uniforms distributed food and a black gravy they said was coffee.
Thin young infantrymen, heavily burdened with guns
and knapsacks, wearing faded and patched uniforms,
moved about like worn old men. I shoved my luggage
through the crowded platforms and headed crosstown
for the Anhalter Station. The subway ride spared me

the sight of the ruins above, but not the human ruins below; the thousands of homeless who lived in the underground, the hollow-cheeked women and children on the run, the bewildered soldiers on their way to shattered homes or battered fronts. Privation, hunger and lack of sleep, indifference and resignation marked the faces.

Night had fallen over the city when my darkened train left behind the devastated world of Berlin and shrieked and clanked its way south. I passed the hours smoking, waiting, dreaming. I calculated that I would be home—if not in Darmstadt, then at Father's new plant—by noon the following day, provided all went well.

One hour after midnight. A girl in the uniform of the Luftwaffe's Woman Corps had taken an opposite seat in the compartment and was showing a more-than-casual interest in me. To escape her annoying curiosity, I stepped into the corridor and lighted a cigarette, but moments later the girl followed.

She asked hesitantly, "Aren't you Trudy's brother?"

Involuntarily I said, "No, young lady. You must be mistaken."

"I'm sorry," she said, "but you look just like him. You see, my girlfriend's brother is also in the Navy, and the resemblance is striking."

At this, I confessed: "All right, I am Trudy's brother. And who are you?"

She began to smile, her memory had not tricked her. "Don't you recognize me at all? I am Clara Ehinger. I was a classmate of Trudy, maybe her best friend."

No, I did not recognize this woman, but I remembered her as a little girl when I was a boy of 15. Ten years—a whole lifetime—had passed since then. Now that she was here, I welcomed the opportunity to shorten my trip with pleasant memories of our happy youth. We talked about our years in school and recalled long-forgotten episodes. She had indeed been my sister's best friend when we had lived near Lake Constance. Then Clara told me that she had always liked my parents, that the long article about them in the local paper had been so well written.

A sudden chill clutched my throat, and I demanded, "What article are you talking about?"

Her eyes widened, her mouth opened in horror. "Don't you know?" she stumbled. "No you didn't know!" She covered her face with both hands. She did not have to tell me any more.

Everything around me began to turn, very slowly at first, then with a rush, as if a giant wheel had gone out of control. I heard the girl sobbing and saying far away, "Oh, forgive me, poor Trudy and your parents died in the air raid on Darmstadt two months ago."

In my sickening dizziness, I pressed myself against the glass wall of the compartment to stay erect. The window, the wall, the people faded before my eyes. I clenched my teeth fiercely and fought back my tears; no one should ever see me crying. I closed my eyes and drew a deep, racking breath.

Eventually—I did not know how long it took me— I reawakened to my surroundings and to the news I had heard. Clara must have been wrong, yet I knew it had to be true. It was all over now. I never would see my beloved ones again, never hear my sister's laughter, never again have Mother's care or listen to Father's plans. They had simply vanished, and by some terrible mistake. It was I who should have died, I, who had prepared a thousand times to leave *them* behind. I had gone to sea to fight for their lives and safety, and I had failed them completely. Why had God taken their innocent lives instead of my guilty one?

Clara, too, recovered slowly from the shock. She was gloomy and sad about her role as death's messenger. I tried to calm her and told her that she had spared me much anguish and a trip in the wrong direction, and then I altered my plans. There was no need for traveling toward Darmstadt.

In Eisenach I changed trains together with Clara and headed south toward Lake Constance. The night was long and our conversation moved tediously. I could think of nothing but the loss of all I had loved and the pointlessness of all that remained. When the train rattled into another gray November morning, and when I wiped the foggy moisture from the window, it came as a crushing irony to read the slogan painted on a wall of a station house: OUR CITIES CRUMBLE, OUR WALLS COLLAPSE, BUT OUR HEARTS NEVER BREAK.

As the night fell on the eastern spur of the Black Forest, the train reached Clara's home town. She said good-by, bewildered and shy. I traveled into another night and I did not stop until I saw the moon reflected in the waters of Lake Constance. I dragged my luggage from the car in Ueberlingen East, where my relatives had sought refuge from the war. As I started for their house, I had a sudden urge to turn and take another train and return to crew and boat. That was where I belonged. But I kept on going, the suitcase with the presents hanging heavy in my hand. I did not know what to do with the gifts. I did not even have a sweetheart to whom I could give them. Marianne had died in the early ruins of Berlin. Yvonne had disappeared years before. I had lost Marguerite and Paris to the Americans, and Marika was the wife of another man.

My appearance at the door of Grandfather's house caused consternation. My numerous relatives, living more or less in harmony under a large roof, had not expected my return from the depths of the Atlantic. They thought I had been lost in the turmoil of the invasion; that was about the time my parents had received my last letter. Their shock at my resurrection immediately gave way to disturbed looks and nervous whispers behind my back. To put their minds at rest, I said firmly, "I've heard. You don't have to explain."

"What do you intend to do?" they asked with worried looks.

"I don't know."

"Do you wish to stay?"

"No, I just came to say hello. I'll leave my books and some other things. . . ."

Soon I learned that my cousin, Lore, had found refuge in the Black Forest, and I phoned her immediately. Lore told me that there was much snow there and that the skiing was good. At last, I found an escape, a place to go to forget.

Early next morning, relieved of books and presents, I departed from the Lake. The slow-moving train carried me into the mountain ranges, which turned from dark green to brilliant white in an hour's time. Winter had come earlier than expected. At a station-stop deep in the forest, I mounted a horse-drawn sled which brought me upland to Schoenwald, where my cousin had reserved a room for me in a hotel.

Lore was an excellent skier. In the next several days, we met when the first sunrays touched the white tips of the evergreens, and we climbed into the woods, then slalomed down into the valleys. We repeated the exhausting tour many times each morning, ate lunch from a canvas bag I carried attached to my belt, then continued skiing over the white meadows and frozen streams until the sun set. My depression gradually relaxed its grip.

Lore did all she could to cheer me up, but she could do only so much. She could not blot out the sound of artillery, and every evening we could hear the thunder of heavy guns rolling in from the Vosges only 60 kilometers to the west. We could not close our ears to the radio broadcasts, which told of staggering losses on all fronts. The Soviets had captured Riga, overrun Lithuania, bitten off half of Poland, and pocketed the Balkans. The fighting was fierce on the west bank of the Rhine, and American bombers had leveled Cologne and Aachen. I listened to these reports with increasing nervousness. No, I could not stay here in moody idleness while the Reich's defenses crumbled and her cities vanished in fire and smoke. I belonged —once again—with my boat and my crew; they were all I had left.

One cold November afternoon I said good-by to Lore and took the sled bound for the train station. As we descended into the peaceful valley, I asked myself where in God's name we were going. What had happened to all the wonder weapons we had been promised over and over again? Without them, how could we possibly stop the Russians, the Americans, the British, the French—the whole world?

I arrived at the U-boat base in Luebeck-Siems on a cold, blustery day. Selde, the young Chief whom I had left in charge of the skeleton crew during my absence, reported that air raids and missing parts had slowed down work on our boat; that, far from making our deadline, we would be lucky if we left port by New Year's Day. Yet despite the bad news, I settled in my cozy room with a feeling that I had finally found refuge. The room smelled of cedar woods and resin. I knew my men in the adjoining rooms, heard their talk, recognized their voices and their laughter. I felt comfortably at ease. Their presence gave me confidence and purpose.

I joined and talked with my comrades that night and soon learned that all too many of them had also tasted personal tragedy on their leaves. Berger had found his home town of Cleve, a stone's throw behind the western front, in ashes. His wife and only child perished in the flames. Someone had led him to the grave and told him that they were buried there; that very hour he had turned around and set out for base and boat. A machinist's mate had found his parents' home in ruins and his family gone without leaving an address; he, too, had hurried back to port. Others had spent their furlough on trains and buses, tracing their families' flights from town to town. For those who had finally made a reunion, there was little time left to spend together. Some of my men had returned without even reaching their destination; the front had already rolled past their towns and homes in Silesia. For all of them, as for me, the road led only one way— back to boat and comrades, back to the men with whom they had shared their gravest hours.

Not all my dealings with my company were pleasant and comradely. December had arrived with snow and cold, with biting winds from the east that announced a long winter, and my continuing problems with three officers made my mood as grim as these gray days. My Exec, my Chief, and the Ensign were immature and inexperienced. They not only gave me more trouble than help, they also disaffected the crew. The men, decorated professionals with long and distinguished combat records, had little use for the unskilled Chief, and they viewed the very young Ensign with distinct disdain. These problems were too difficult and dangerous to cope with on a frontline U-boat, so I had regretfully called the personnel department to ask for replacements for the Chief and the Ensign. This routine request, which a year before would have been honored automatically even if the Captain's reasons were capricious, was summarily rejected. I protested that I was trying to save the life of boat and crew. The reaction: a shrug that seemed to say, What difference did it make? The life expectancy of a U-boat was too short to worry about, even if she had a perfect crew.

My troubles with the Ensign merely began with his general incompetence. To make matters worse, he had been assigned by the Party to indoctrinate my crew with official theories, ideals, and never-say-die slogans. Such Party meddling in U-boat affairs had a brief but stormy history, dating back to the attempt to assassinate Hitler. Before then, the U-boat Force had been free of political interference. Even afterward, when the power of the Party had increased everywhere else, the U-boat Captains, myself among them, had successfully countered the infiltration of politically trained officers by passive resistance. But with the Reich's accelerating decline, the Party grew ever more powerful and dogmatic, to the increasing dismay of our U-boat veterans, officers and men alike. My comrades had complained to me from time to time of the Ensign's blatant approaches. Their reaction was perfectly normal: they had proved their loyalty and courage with deeds, and they needed no Party preacher to tell them how to fight and die.

Whether or not I could get the Ensign transferred out, I was determined to stop his harassing sermons. I called for a conference and made it clear to all three, the Chief, the Exec, and the Ensign, that they had not yet qualified for their positions aboard U-953, and that they might not have the jobs long if they did not follow my strict training program to make themselves fit for patrol. In addition, I gave the Ensign so many minor duties that he had no time for Party speeches.

By the second week of December, activity in port had increased dramatically, pointing to a spring offensive for our forces at sea. Within a 10-day period, five conventional U-boats arrived from the Baltic. The barracks spilled over with new life; the shipyard resounded with hammering and riveting. But the boats in port bespoke no drastic change; they had everything in common with our ancient *U-953*. And all the renewed activity promised no halt to our precipitous decline.

But suddenly, a brilliant thrust lighted the dark horizons in the west and stirred new hope in Germany. In the early morning hours of December 16, our armies in the Ardennes had launched a massive counteroffensive against the Anglo-American forces. The nation's radio networks proclaimed smashing victories and major advances in the first hours of our assault. The great offensive, long promised, had finally materialized. We were moving westward again, and our divisions would not halt until the last Allied soldier was driven into the sea. I listened to the news and to the fanfares with a mixture of hope, anxiety, and caution. Though the assault had produced spectacular early results, it had been confined to a front too narrow for deep penetration. My hopes faded and my anxiety grew as the days passed and the good news dwindled. One week after we had been agitated by fanfares and military marches, the voices which had told us of a quick victory went silent. The offensive had been slowed down by ice and snow and mud, and it was stopped by the fresh Allied divisions that rushed in to reinforce the bulge in their lines. By Christmas Eve our chances for a major victory had vanished.

Christmas Eve in port was solemn and calm—at least until midnight. I made my evening rounds through the various rooms, talking quietly with my men, offering them reassurance they did not need. Each man had grown his own hard shell to protect his spirit from the torments of our dissolving world. I retreated into my quarters after sharing too many drinks with my officers, mates, and enlisted men. I brewed coffee on my hot plate, sank into the armchair, and read for a while. The room was filled with the sweet aroma of the evergreen that my men had erected in a corner; it brought to mind memories of happier Christmases. The compound grew silent. I went to sleep little dreaming that the high jinks had already begun.

Hours after midnight, I was roused by loud knocking on my door. It was the political Ensign, who was on watch duty. "Sir, I beg to report that there are girls in the men's quarters."

I laughed. "Do you suffer from hallucinations?"

"No, sir, I saw one of the seamen sneak through the fence with a female and disappear into a room."

The matter became interesting. I began a cautious inspection tour at the far end of the barracks, where many of the men shared a single room. I opened the door quietly; all was dark and peaceful. I switched on the light, but discovered that the boys had taken the precaution of removing the bulbs.

"Get your flashlight, Ensign."

"Jawohl, Herr Oberleutnant," he said, full of excitement and enterprise.

I remained at the door, listening. The slow, rhythmical breathing of sleeping men was all I heard. I regretted the Ensign's meddling in this matter, and my own. At this point in the war, what difference did it make where the boys made love? Surely none of us had long to live and love. Still, orders were made to be enforced. . . .

The Ensign returned with the flashlight and I played its beam over the first man's face and blanket. All seemed natural. The next face woke up and big eyes blinked in the cold light. The third blanket was suspiciously bulky, and I lifted one corner of it. The small face of a frightened blond girl appeared. I realized how rude I was, and guiltily dropped the blanket. Then the barracks lights came on, and I discovered two other girls hiding in beds.

I halted my investigation then and there, trusting that the men in the other room had heard the commotion and would get their sweethearts out of the barracks in a hurry. As for the three men already exposed, I could not avoid the old conflict between military discipline and personal loyalty. However, I postponed a decision until after the holidays.

On the second day of Christmas, the earth began to tremble and there was a steady rumbling in the distance. I knew the sound well: it meant that a city was being bombed into dust—in this case, Hamburg. I took my powerful binoculars and posted myself on the nearby highway which commanded an excellent view of the countryside.

The sky was pale blue and cloudless, the air cold and clear. A white winter sun shone over Hamburg, and from where I stood I could see the glint of the sun on the wings and fuselages of Flying Fortresses coming in from the sea. They glided out of the sky and moved relentlessly forward. Flight after flight pushed through the haze in the distance and droned over the dying city. Tiny gray and black flak clouds popped up among the hundreds of bombers and their countless fighter escorts. Through my glasses I saw the bombs raining down upon Hamburg, aircraft exploding, red and yellow fireballs erupting in the silken sky, burning planes tumbling through the air, our Messerschmitt fighters plunging upon the bombers like hawks, filling the sky with debris. The ground shook under my feet, many kilometers away from the target. Thousands of innocents, who had prayed on Christmas Eve, were being roasted alive and turned into ashes. And I thought that my loved ones must have died the same way.

What a miserable, obscene war, where able-bodied men and sophisticated machines were employed to exterminate the helpless and harmless. I told myself that my war was quite a different kind of struggle, that it was a war in which ships were engaged to sink ships, weapons, and supplies before they could be used to destroy. But whichever way one fought the war, the total results were indivisible and hideous beyond the powers of men to comprehend. Death on a gigantic scale had become so routine that life itself seemed rather odd and irrelevant, and all the once-commonplace

joys of life seemed abnormal, ludicrous, and weird.
Even the love of a generous woman came as an unreal
interruption in the normal nightmare of survival.

My bitterness toward the war—my revulsion over
the blunders and incompetence that made our sacrifices meaningless—became intolerable in early January. After spending the days between Christmas and
New Year's trying to speed up work on our boat, I
was summoned—without explanation—to meet with
Admiral Doenitz at his Headquarters outside Berlin.
It was a puzzling command in that the Lion had
steadily drifted further and further away from his Captains. In the years of glorious victories, he had visited
them and their crews regularly in port. Later, he had
stopped making visits and instead required his commanders to call on him in the cool atmosphere of his
Headquarters in Paris. Then, after the Allies had captured Paris and sunk most of our U-boats, meetings
with the Lion had ceased almost entirely.

In Berlin, I took a room in the Hotel Fuerstenhof,
showered and shaved, put on a fresh white shirt and a
new tie, rode the S-bahn to the eastern suburb of
Bernau, boarded a small bus that had been waiting
for me, then rolled over a deserted highway, through
the pine woods, to the closely guarded Headquarters
complex, known by the exotic name *Koralle*. After a
sentry had scrutinized my papers, I was ushered into
the inner sanctum of the mighty naval establishment.
Its maze of sterile hallways and its legions of immaculate white-jacketed officers created the impression of a
huge hospital; only the smell of ether and antiseptic
was missing. At once I felt out of place and wished to
return to my sweaty, grimy men.

I was told that the Admiral had not yet arrived and
was invited to join the staff at lunch. The decorated
tables, the fine linen, the exquisite china, the ornate
silverware, the serried ranks of distinguished officers
in tailored white jackets—all this seemed to me ex-
cessively grand and self-indulgent. I found myself
thinking that most of these men should have spent the
war years to better advantage. If they had enjoyed

themselves a little less and worked a little harder to supply us with the means to fight, Germany would still have many of the crews that went down in the 203 U-boats sunk in the previous year. We might even have a fleet as large as our ghost armada—the 682 U-boats which had been sunk since the start of the war.

As the elegant diners departed, I was left with five officers whose blues set them apart from the white-jacketed permanent staff, and whose lack of U-boat decorations marked them as new men who had never tasted battle. We struck up a conversation, and I learned that they were captains of new boats of a series that was already obsolete when commissioned, and that they had been ready to set out on their first patrol when the Admiral summoned them. I looked at them, and I saw dead men; they stood little chance of surviving without experience even if they were intelligent, capable, well-trained officers. If they had heard of the enemy's vast and sophisticated defense system, they did not know how to cope with it. And, I suspected, they had not been advised of what they would soon face.

After some time, we six were told that the Lion was ready to see us, and we were guided into a large, bright room. Doenitz stood at the window, the wintry sunlight touching his pale face. He had aged considerably since I saw him last in Lorient in 1941, on that hot autumn day when he fastened the Iron Cross on my chest. Now he looked thinner, smaller, less dynamic.

The Admiral pressed our hands and gestured toward a row of chairs facing his desk. He walked up and down before us and then began to speak. He talked slowly and quietly—a sharp contrast to his energetic, fiery manner of earlier years. But he seemed confident and determined. He spoke of the need for our continued sacrifices and of the great improvements in U-boat warfare that would come very soon. He told us that the purpose of our latest mission was to tie down Allied naval units in their own waters and prevent them from reaching toward territories still controlled by our forces. We were the gallant ones who would keep up the good fight until our revolutionary new U-boats would turn the tide of the war; and we would have one of those new boats when we returned from this patrol. Finally Doenitz made the shocking announcement that, to achieve our present objective, he would send every available conventional U-boat to the front, even those which had been relegated to training use.

The Admiral's talk was brief and altogether impressive. Doenitz, though he seemed worn and weary, still transmitted that same spark of enthusiasm which had galvanized us when he spoke in our years of triumph. Yet nothing he said was really new, and I had the feeling that he was convincing only because I wanted so desperately to believe him. From what I knew of Doenitz, his tactics which once had led us to victory were now causing the senseless death of thousands of trusting men in outdated diving machines. His latest order I could only interpret as a frantic attempt to delay inevitable defeat. Yet I wished with all my heart that I was wrong.

After a two-day absence, I returned to the base. At breakfast the next morning, the Exec reported that the overhaul of U-953 had indeed been completed and that our boat had been towed to the pier the previous day. Then, brimming over with excitement, he told me that two of the newest-type U-boats had come alongside ours just before dusk. I cut short my breakfast, changed into my leather suit, and went down to the riverfront. U-953, freshly painted, deck scraped, guns greased, lay at the foot of the pier. My men assembled on the aft deck for the roll call, glancing at me with one eye and with the other at the monstrous new boats to either side. I stepped aboard our revived workhorse, returned the Exec's salute and the crew's friendly "Good morning, sir," then told the old seafarers that we would have to sail once more in our old boat before we would get a new one of the sort they saw swaying nearby. I made that promise in the hope that Doenitz would be able to keep his pledge to me.

From what I could learn in my dockside inspection of U-953, the shipyard had done an excellent job.

Our boat, which had suffered from all the ills of old age, displayed a rejuvenated fitness and all new equipment. A hydraulic Schnorkel with a much improved float had replaced the primitive one that had caused so much hardship and a near disaster. The stink of decay had been routed by the clean smell of fresh paint. *U-953* seemed to be ready.

I then went to inspect one of the newest type submersibles. Crossing the gangplank to one of the big whales, I asked the seaman on guard, "Is the Captain aboard?"

"Yes, sir, he is."

"What's his name?"

"Kapitaenleutnant Siegmann."

My old Captain of *U-230*! I climbed up the huge superstructure to the bridge, dropped through the hatch into a highly sophisticated conning tower, then lowered myself into the control room, which looked like a power station. I saw Siegmann in his nook with his back turned toward me, and I said, "Good morning, I wish to report aboard."

He spun around. "What the devil, it is you! What brings you into this lousy port?"

"I have come from Norway with an old jalopy to have a new one made out of it."

"You're still sailing one of those old coffins?" he asked with surprise.

"Yes, I don't have your connections. Congratulations on your new boat."

"Thanks. Come on, I'll show you around, or have you seen such a ship before?"

"No, I have never had the pleasure."

As we walked to the bow he told me that he had exchanged *U-230* for this boat in the spring of the previous year, that the *U-230* under the command of *Oberleutnant* Eberbach had been scuttled by her crew on August 21 when the Allies landed at Toulon, that most of our old comrades had been captured and imprisoned, that Friedrich who had also left the boat in the spring was still his Chief, and that Riedel had become Captain of *U-242*. We arrived in the bow torpedo room. Six tubes, instead of the conventional four, extended into the large compartment. Special storage magazines for 14 spare torpedoes were located alongside the hull.

"We charge all tubes hydraulically within ten minutes," Siegmann explained. "We push a few buttons and all goes very quietly. We don't touch the torpedoes anymore."

The compartment was equipped solely for storing, servicing, and reloading the torpedoes; and crew, which on old boats slept crowded together among the steel fish, lived in a roomy compartment of their own. Officers' and petty officers' quarters were like first-class staterooms on a passenger liner. The boat's displacement was nearly three times that of *U-953*.

Siegmann continued, "You will be astounded to hear that we are faster below surface than above, and can maintain a top submerged speed of seventeen knots for quite some time."

"Then you can revive the convoy battles from a submerged position."

"More than that. We are not only faster, we have more torpedoes and can shoot them at a depth of fifty meters without seeing the targets. We dive almost twice as deep as you with your old tube, and we run away from every pursuing escort with ease."

"That makes you practically invulnerable."

"You're right. The high speed allows us to attack and escape below surface without detection. A new computer guidance system gives us a one hundred per cent accuracy of fire. Our new Schnorkel is managed pretty much the same way you handle your scope; it goes up as quickly and permits faster recharging of the batteries. This boat is the total submarine."

What we had been told for many months was true: the new boats indeed existed, and the evidence was overwhelming that they were truly wonder U-boats. Sent out in sufficient numbers, they could force the Allies onto the defensive at sea. If only the fronts in east and west could hold out long enough. . . .

Siegmann declined my invitation for lunch; he was spending the weekend with his family. We separated warmly, wishing each other luck and success. But we both knew that a barrier had come between us. His magnificent new boat gave him a reasonable guarantee of living to see the end of the war. My antique boat, however, condemned me to almost certain death in the British shooting gallery.

With growing bitterness in my heart and great concern for my crew, I prepared myself for an early sailing.

27

On the morning of February 8, *U-953* slipped out of Leubeck harbor and headed north. After 12 hours of rocking in the waves, it was as if we had never been on land; and our boat, despite all the unkind remarks we had made about her, seemed fit and well behaved. *U-953* sliced at high speed through the narrow, shallow waters between the Danish islands. A whole arsenal of new electronic equipment protected her from sneak attacks. A sensitive new radar, small and handy, turned steadily to scan the sky and the waterway.

We reached the open Skagerrak on the eve of the second day of our mission. Our arrival in deep water coincided with the appearance of fog and with increased enemy air activity. Feeble radar impulses flashed from various sources, but the dense fog shielded our boat as cotton protects a fragile glass jar in a box. Despite the white blanket I did not intend to risk remaining on surface just for the sake of making headway. As our radar picked up the images of two aircraft, I ordered, "Dive, Chief, dive cautiously."

I heard the long sigh of blowing air and felt the boat falling away. My last thought before I closed the lid was that the British would have a hard time finding the spot of our submergence in the fog. *U-953* dived for a submerged run which I had intended to last until we completed our patrol, seven or eight weeks hence. As the hiss of escaping air ceased, there was a cry: "Diesel loading hatch cracked—boat takes heavy water!"

"Not again," I groaned. "The hell with this old ship." Then I yelled, "Close vents, stand by to surface —level off, Chief."

All of a sudden the boat tilted sharply astern. Concluding that the leak was serious, I ordered both bilge pumps started up. But before the pumps became effective, *U-953* fell away quickly. I gave my instructions as routinely as possible: "Blow all tanks. Both full ahead. Surface. Don life preservers!"

At the Chief's cry, "Bridge is clear," I rushed to the platform, followed by the gunners. Dusk had replaced daylight. The fog was so thick around the boat that she seemed to have lost her bow and stern. We had but one way to go—north into Oslofjord. There I expected to find facilities to repair the leak at Horten, a small naval base—if we survived the night.

"Aircraft, bearing one-two-five, distance five hundred, approaching!" came a cry through the voice tube. Then a scream in the air. The starboard 20 mm. two-barreled gun started to blaze, the 37 mm. automatic followed suit. In a split second, a faint shadow passed over the boat and disappeared before my men could swing their guns. Somewhere two bombs detonated almost simultaneously. The engines of a second attacker roared closer fast. Our guns sent up a barrier of metal into the fog. Then the plane was above, bellowing, spitting. Bright light showered from the sky. The fog glared like a sheet of fire. The Tommy had dropped a parachute flare that hung somewhere in the fog.

A new attack came from starboard aft. A wall of tracers spread through the glare. A second flare unfolded. While the two planes circled, our radar picked up a third image. Soon, four aircraft circled around us like hungry vultures. We awaited the next assault with a new supply of ammunition and a wary glance at the ice-cold water of the Skagerrak. Then, one by one, the planes dived down on us. But their strafing missed, and our gunfire held them outside of bombing range. As the attack concluded, our radar picked up the images of only three planes.

Our diesels hammered in concert with the engines in the air. Our guns moved in circles, following the radar's directions. For over two hours there was no new attack. Then at 0220, our radar went dead. With the blinding of our eye in the sky, we had no defense, no accurate fire. The end of our boat seemed nearer than Oslofjord.

We spent another two hours under closest surveillance by the British. Then the improbable, the incomprehensible occurred. One by one the planes gave up pursuit. At 0440, the air was free of aircraft. Shortly after 0600 the fog rose and disclosed the Norwegian mountains. An hour later we sailed into Horten harbor.

To my great disappointment I found that the small base was not equipped to repair the diesel hatch, and I was told to try in Kristiansand, where the flotilla had a sizable floating machine shop. However, I managed to find a clever electrician who replaced the scorched radar cable. After a restless day in port, I sailed *U-953* into another frustrating night. Creeping along the rocky coastline, feeling our way ahead with radar between cliffs and through a small fishing fleet, we again escaped detection by the British, who were busy scrutinizing the southern horizon. One hour before daybreak we snaked into Kristiansand harbor. But here I learned that the only place we could have the leak plugged was Bergen. I had no choice but to continue on surface, trusting in my luck and the heedlessness of the British flyers. There was absolutely nothing I could do to avoid disaster if the enemy struck in a mass assault.

We sailed out of Kristiansand one hour after dusk, hammered through a moderate sea, surged by menacing rocks, dashed into and through the fjords in the shadows of the mountains. We wound around cliffs and ambushes at night and hid our boat under flimsy screens in ports during the day. When I finally turned the bow of our boat into Bergenfjord at sunrise on February 16, we had completed a trip that had been considered virtually impossible. We had traveled all the way from Luebeck to Bergen on surface without receiving a single scratch. I was convinced I could not do it again.

We found the 11th U-boat Flotilla in a state of terrible anxiety. The tension was caused in part by the disappearance of *U-1053* the previous day; ready for war patrol, the boat had failed to surface after her last deep-dive maneuver; and, despite a frenzied night-long search, no trace of her had been found. Then, too, the radio had announced the distressing news that the Red Army had broken through our Eastern front and had driven our troops to the west bank of the Oder River. Incredible as it seemed, the Russians had succeeded in establishing a bridgehead near Wriezen, only 60 kilometers east of Berlin and just 40 kilometers from Doenitz's Headquarters. Clearly truth was stronger than hope and desire; it was brutally impartial. I realized that Germany's very existence was in deeper jeopardy than we had the courage to admit.

Nonetheless, I continued my work as if the war would go on forever. With grim energy I concentrated on running my boat as I had pledged, and on sailing her as I had been ordered. In the afternoon of that vexatious day, I steered *U-953* into the shipyard to have the loading hatch riveted and welded shut; I had all equipment stowed aboard and did not intend to use that hatch again as long as I remained at the helm of *U-953*. I retired early, for it was my last chance to sleep in linen and in peace before weeks of submergence.

At noon the next day I sailed *U-953* out of the shipyard, assured that the seam of the hatch would now withstand the severest depth-charge attack. In order to test the boat's tightness, I followed the path *U-1053* had taken to her death. The same small trawler which had attended her descent awaited the start of our deep-dive maneuver. I brought *U-953* into position, locked myself and the crew into the hull, then ordered the Chief to lower the boat below surface, slowly, cautiously. We listened for a bolt to blow, a seam to crack. All remained calm. *U-953* reached the limit of her test, stayed tight, behaved well, and obeyed all orders willingly.

It was late in the evening of February 17 when we finally left Bergen. The night had fallen quickly over the fjord and the mountains closed in as if to swallow us. The wind chased heavy clouds from west to east, occasionally covering the moon and providing a curtain to help us escape detection. After two hours we reached the northern exit of Bergenfjord, where bizarre cliffs, reflecting in the pale moonlight, broke the foamy onslaught of the ocean.

"Radar impulses all over forward quarters," shouted the mate through the voice tube.

I knew we could not stay on surface for long, but I needed more time to clear the boat from currents and cliffs. As she crossed from the silvery surface of the fjord into the rough waters of the Norwegian Sea, I called the Chief to the hatch. "Listen carefully, Selde," I said as if to a child. "When I call for alarm, I want you to bring the boat very cautiously below— no rush, no excessive down tilt. No more than thirty meters, you understand?"

"Yes, sir, no more than thirty meters."

"Target twenty-five hundred, bearing zero," cried the mate.

That was the end of our surface run. The bell shrieked, air escaped the tanks piercingly. Before I lowered myself into the hatch I noticed that the bow fell away somewhat too fast and hollered, "Hold the boat above thirty meters, Chief, watch out."

As I slammed the lid shut, I felt the boat sink at an increasing down angle: *"Verdammt,* catch the boat and hold her nose up!"

The bow dipped toward rocks which could slice her hull wide open. Within seconds, a violent jolt threw me from the tower onto the deck plates. Then the boat leaped like a wild horse and shot toward the surface. I seized the controls; a few hard rudder maneuvers, fast trimming and adjusting, and the boat calmed down. Shaken and outraged, I called the Chief to attention: "What in the devil's name were you doing?"

"The trim must have been disturbed, sir," Selde mumbled apologetically.

"Nonsense, you established trim just a few hours ago."

"It could have been also the frontal impact of the sea."

"Come on, Selde, no more of that. I guess I'll have to teach you diving again when we return into port—if we ever return." I grabbed the microphone from its overhead cradle. "Attention bow torpedo room. Check all tube doors and linkage. Check outboard valves. Report at once."

After minutes of strained waiting, the calls came in. The Exec in the bow room reported everything in order. Although the shock had been extraordinary, we had escaped damages. For a while, U-953 floated peacefully at the designated depth, course northwest, direction Atlantic. But soon the Chief again demonstrated his inexperience and, worse, his lack of aptitude. Incapable of holding the boat level on Schnorkel depth, he repeatedly exposed her to the watchful Tommies and allowed her to tumble down toward the floor. Each time the Chief disturbed the buoyancy, it sent the whole company through new tortures. The vacuum it created set the men twisting and vomiting in agony while they were tossed about wildly by the boat's pirouettes. Each time the punishment became unbearable, I again assumed control and again tried to teach my Chief the fundamentals of Schnorkeling.

We continued our tumultuous progress, though the mission seemed futile. By the time of our sailing, the Allies had called in vast dispersed naval forces and concentrated them in the waters around the British Isles. Destroyers in overwhelming numbers were posted near the Shetland and Faeroe Islands to catch our few lone wolves, whose comings and goings had been reported beforehand to the British Admiralty by Allied sympathizers or agents. None of our preparations for a spring offensive had remained a secret. During the first days of February, six U-boats had been sunk, all on their first patrol. One by one they sailed into the enemy's bristling defense; they were too slow to evade his skilled air-and-sea teamwork, and most of their officers were too inexperienced to know the tricks of survival. The seas around England had become a sort of private pool in which the British eagerly played their game of killing off a helpless U-boat now and then; and if the hundreds of aircraft and surface vessels failed to sink our boats, then the hundreds of square miles of minefields did.

Such were the conditions when *U-953* approached the first line of Allied defense. For days the crew had suffered the painful maneuvers of our incompetent Chief; yet despite their shattered eardrums and their blurred vision, they lost none of their spirit or humor. When calm sailing replaced the cruel Schnorkeling routine, the crew immediately relaxed and engaged in optimistic pursuits. Some wrote letters—letters they knew might never be mailed or never reach their destination. Others read and wrote poetry. I occasionally received copies of their literary endeavors along with the typewritten sheets of daily Armed Forces communiqués. The poems made up in authenticity for what they lacked in grace. "The Schnorkel Lament," written by machinist Hagemann, joked about the terrible suffering we endured every night:

Since we sailed from Bergen on our tour,
Much anguish has fallen on us sailors poor.
With jitters and fears and lamentation,
We drag ourselves often to "Schnorkel station."
When the vacuum happens to rupture our ears,
We writhe on the deck in torture and tears.

Our eyes go jumping from out of our heads;
To see, we take them in our hands instead.
To ease our pain and distorted poses,
We equalize pressure by squeezing our noses.
Everyone swears—it will go down in history—
"The Schnorkel float should have stayed a mystery."

But we were born to Schnorkel till very late,
And we were chosen to suffer this nightly fate,
And we will depend for the rest of our lives
On the eardrums and eyeballs of our faithful wives.

Mechanic Mueller, a good-natured fellow, chose to
versify on a more cheerful theme:

A sailor often wears a tattoo—
For decoration, not as a taboo.
A confession of his every sin
Is also found on his martyred skin.
Among the anchors, ropes and sawfish,
Turtles, butterflies, and starfish,
Reigns—as lovely as a pearl—
His once beloved, naked girl.
He holds her safe and strong and warm
On his lower left and hairy arm.
On the right one is etched a pair of hands intertwined,
Inscribed: Rosy, I'm yours with all the money you find.
Some other names of dames of late
Are all stricken out, including the date.
Yes, a deceived sailor never loses face;
His faithless girl is easy to erase.
A cross through her name, and another tatoo—
And Rose becomes Susy from Timbuktu.

After one week spent cautiously circumventing
hordes of hunters, we received our order of operation.
It came one hour after midnight on February 23, while
U-953 was rocking severely in a storm which came
rolling in from the west. The inept Chief tried frantically to hold the boat on Schnorkel depth, but she rose
and fell like a see-saw, forcing the men to cling to
pipes and wheels as they tried to perform their duties.
In despair I took over again and said, "How often,
Chief, must I show you how to control the boat and
lay her on even keel?"

He replied, "The storm is getting worse, that's why
I can't hold her."

"Don't tell me that story again, Selde, you see her
steady now. Just hold her at thirteen meters."

Within a few minutes the boat again lost her stability. The men gasped for air and slid around on the wet deck plates as if on ice. They rolled their eyes in despair, silently begging me to put an end to the senseless torture. Then the boat tilted up sharply and shot to the surface, exposing her superstructure and offering a splendid target.

The hawks had detected us already. "Radar impulses, volume threeee!" yelled the operator.

Resisting the urge to open the hatch and send the gunners to the bridge, I shouted, "Both diesels emergency ahead! Open all vents. All men to the bow, you included, Chief."

The diesels knocked wildly, the boat rocked hard. For a few seconds that lasted a lifetime, the sea held the boat in a crazy position, then she sank, slowly, steadily. As she swung into a 40-degree down angle, the surprised men struggled to their stations, crawling, pushing, pulling themselves toward the stern sections. The electric motors took over from the diesels. Schnorkel and scope cut under, and the boat plunged into the depths. At 80 meters I managed to level her off and establish her trim. Only then did we realize that no bombs had followed us.

Twenty minutes later, as *U-953* Schnorkeled her way smoothly westward, I closed the book on the Chief once and for all. Clearly Selde would never learn. Clearly, too, I could not justify giving him another chance to kill 54 men. I requested him to stay out of the control room and spend the rest of the patrol in the ward room as my guest.

I remained at the control for the rest of the night. When the first Asdic impulses bounced against the hull and a number of propellers throbbed above in typical search pattern, I had the engines stopped, the air mast lowered, and the boat prepared for an encounter.

Headquarters' signal had been lying untouched on the plotting table since shortly after midnight. I held the paper to the small lamp and read: U-953 OPERATE IN PLYMOUTH BAY FROM LIZARD HEAD TO START POINT. TRAVEL ALONG TWO HUNDRED METER LINE. INFORMATION RE NEW MINEFIELDS FOLLOW.

The order was astonishing for two reasons. Headquarters had terminated U-boat activity in the English Channel in October of the previous year because our losses there outweighed our successes. Why did Headquarters now decide to send us back to an area which had proved to be a U-boat wrecking yard? And why this insistent demand that our boats travel along the 200-meter line? Headquarters had been informed often enough about the strong enemy defenses along that line; there, too, our losses provided grim confirmation. Determined not to commit suicide, I disregarded the latter part of the order and continued on my established route.

U-953 advanced well on her march through the depths. I navigated her along the western edge of the huge minefields south of the Hebrides, avoided the herd of destroyers near the North Channel, then sliced through the calm coastal waters of western Ireland, passing the familiar beacons. During this leg of our clandestine journey, Headquarters' attempt to revive the U-boat war in the English Channel produced more casualties. *U-480* was sunk near Land's End, and *U-927* was bombed by aircraft at the Eddystone Rocks. *U-927* was the thirteenth boat to go down to the bottom in February.

For 17 days of submergence, I alternated at the controls with Berger, my top machinist, in a rigorous routine. *U-953* left the southernmost tip of Ireland near Fastnet Rock Lighthouse to cross over into the English Channel. During these days we studied the Armed Forces communiqués, desperately seeking the faintest glimmer of hope. All in vain. The news grew ever more hectic and crushing as our fronts collapsed completely under the Allied onslaught. On March 5, American troops marched into Cologne; two days later they crossed the Rhine at Remagen, and soon the entire length of the Rhine from Holland to Koblenz had fallen into Allied hands. In the east, Soviet armies had stormed into Germany all along the front from the Baltic to Silesia, driving before them hundreds of thousands of soldiers and civilians. As we waited for a miracle to save our homeland, the home town of many a crewman was overrun by the enemy. And all the while, our spring offensive at sea died aborning. Inadequate boats and inexperienced young officers and helpless crews were bombed and depth-charged to the bottom in a steady procession, like ignorant animals filing to the butcher's block, and the music for their funerals was played by thousands of sound buoys shrieking false warnings of enemy destroyers poised for the kill.

This diabolic concert accompanied us day after day, and the explosions which had sunk *U-683* were still echoing through the depths when we cautiously approached Lizard Head, the southwestern spur of England, on a clear sunny morning. The screams of the sound buoys followed us to the edge of Falmouth harbor, where I spotted three real destroyers on a routine check. The vessels zigzagged throughout the forenoon, but the water's density protected us like a shield, and the strong current, which tossed us further into the Bay, helped to conceal our presence.

For several days we cruised in the coastal currents in search of worthy targets, sometimes having no more than five meters of water above the rim of the bridge and two meters below the keel. We floated secretly up and down waiting for our chance, wedged between Eddystone Rocks and Plymouth harbor, haunted by surface vessels and screening aircraft and screaming buoys, which kept us from reaching for air and charging our batteries.

On March 19, we came very close to sharing the fate of our friends. *U-953* was lying aground, waiting for the tide to break, when faint propeller noises swelled into loud rotations with inexplicable speed. Before we had time to lift the boat off the ground, three destroyers had caught us in only 38 meters of water, and a series of depth charges made the boat take six quick, convulsive jumps. However, the thunder of the barrage was not nearly as frightening as the noises that preceded and followed the attack. At first it sounded as if something like a chain or an iron net were being dragged along the hull; then came a wild clattering, as if a great load of pebbles were being dumped upon the boat. These were brand new sounds to all of us—and a terrifying, tortuous experience. What was all this scraping and clattering? It could have been just another sound-effect designed to torment us beyond the limit of our endurance. But I concluded—correctly, as I later learned —that the British were using a new search device akin to the Asdic.

The reverberations of the first barrage had not yet died out when the destroyers launched a second attack. The ocean burst under new eruptions, shaking the ground, beating the boat, rupturing our eardrums, bending the steel to its limits. But *U-953* still held tight. Asdic impulses kept hitting the hull in relentless repetition, but the third series of canisters exploded further away. It now seemed that the destroyers had come upon us by accident, and that their various search devices failed to record a clear image of our hull. Soon the tide swept the hunters out to sea, and for over three hours we heard them continuing their random attempts to kill.

March 20. *U-953* cruised with the strong current on periscope depth. At 0920 I identified several mastheads at the easterly horizon. There was no sound detection. Ten minutes later the tips had grown and the smoke-stacks of seven cargo ships and four destroyers became clearly visible above the silvery surface. I was intoxicated by the view, gleeful at the thought of sending some of the black monsters to the bottom. I ordered speedily, "On battle stations, both half ahead."

Weeks and months of waiting and taking punishment would now be rewarded. I set the boat on a collision course with the small convoy and calculated my chances. Two escorts swept ahead of the bulky ships and two secured their wake. Their starboard side was open for attack. Berger, who was at the controls, handled the boat like an old professional; I was pleased with my choice of a new Chief. While *U-953* lay solidly in ambush, the small convoy made no evasive move. It plowed toward Lizard Head or Falmouth harbor with unbelievable frivolity. I was exultant over these easy kills and commanded, "Starboard ten, right so—hold her steady . . ."

I took a quick sweep of the horizon. A few tiny aircraft dotted the sky. Hennecke plotted the course and the first seaman's mate adjusted the dials of the computer.

"Open tube doors. Ready for firing. New distance two thousand. Both full ahead."

U-953 raced at high speed, well concealed against the targets, momentarily ready to shoot and destroy. Then came a report that wrecked the attack: "Tube doors don't fully open."

A string of oaths escaped my teeth. "Try again, you must open the doors."

Seconds passed and the boat surged forward.

"Can't get the doors open all the way—linkage is bent!" shouted the Exec through the voice tube.

"For the last time—you must get them open!" I hollered.

"They don't move at all," cried the Exec, climbing into the tower in consternation.

"Didn't you check them after we hit the rocks?"

"Yes, sir, I did. They functioned then."

Enraged and frustrated, now knowing that he had not checked the doors according to prescribed procedures, I put the boat aground. Then I rushed into the bow compartment hoping to solve the problem. Several hands were still trying to turn the linkage, but the doors and bow caps remained locked in half-open position. The breakdown deprived us not only of our victories but also of all chances of continuing the patrol. In fact, the situation was worse than anything we had previously experienced. With the outer torpedo doors frozen ajar, the inner doors were our only protection against the sea, and they were too frail to withstand the shock of a depth-charge explosion. I recalled the air raid in Brest, when a single bomb, exploding 50 meters from our boat, had broken off an interior door even though the outer door was closed perfectly. I felt an icy chill run down my back; an encounter such as the one we had had the previous day would easily knock in our interior doors and drown all of us within seconds.

Blaming myself for having taken my Exec's early finding at face value and not having checked the tube-doors' mechanism myself when we were still near a shipyard, I now faced the dim prospect of making the long haul back to Norway. With but one tube in firing order, I grimly prepared for our silent run to home base through the deadly waters between England and Ireland.

After the tide had broken, I lifted the boat from the bottom and steered her westward. Death stood up before our eyes when a raging depth-charge barrage—the one that destroyed *U-327*—thundered on our starboard side near Lizard Head. That day was doomsday for two other boats. *U-1003* was sunk in the North Channel and *U-905* was destroyed near the Hebrides. The battle continued to be a one-sided affair; our boats were sunk methodically at the rate of one a day. The thunderous receptions our newcomers received in the

North Channel and in traps near Lands End and Lizard Head seemed to me a clear indication that the British had been informed of our assignments.

It was during those weeks of our frenzied self-destruction that I lost one of my last old friends and classmates. Riedel, in command of *U-242* and on his first mission as a Captain, was lost somewhere around England. He sank quietly. No one knew exactly where his coffin went down.

We cleared the North Channel, maneuvered around

the Hebrides, and Schnorkeled cautiously in the satin
sea. We circumvented countless destroyers along the
way, and more near the Shetland Islands, and escaped
a last British threat in the Norwegian Sea. As *U-953*
approached the majestic mountains, the Allies gave up
their hunt in the anticipation that we would return.
I entered Bergenfjord submerged, without signaling for
an escort, then surfaced in utter despair and frustration. We had nothing to show for our long and agonizing voyage—nothing at all except our lives.

28

Gray clouds hung low in the sky when *U-953*, once
again old and rust bitten, fastened her lines at the quay.
It was 1610 on April 7, 1945. No one expected us;
no one was there to greet us. It began to drizzle as the
crew entered the compound. Bergen and the hills disappeared in the chilly squall. It was a sad sundown—
full of misgivings.

The Commandant 11th U-boat Flotilla speedily arranged a dinner reception. I reported our mission un-
completed and said that we were lucky to get back
alive. I told him of the convoy that had passed safely
in front of our blocked torpedo tubes.

"There is always a next time," said the Commanding
Officer confidently. "The British don't simply vanish.
You will have plenty of targets to shoot at on your next
patrol." He assured me that success lay ahead of us,
that the newest type U-boats were expected any day,
and that conventional boats, used in training flotillas,
were now pouring into port in greater numbers.

Our conversation dragged on. We kept talking shop,
never touching on the war at home. I had been awake
for five consecutive days, and without rest for seven

weeks, and I felt an insuperable desire to go to sleep. When I noticed that the drinks had begun to affect my men, I rose abruptly, ending the party.

The following morning I delivered *U-953* into the shipyard for a thorough inspection. Her damages proved to be more severe than we had thought. Since she required a dry dock for these extensive repairs, it was decided to transfer her to our base in Trondheim. Armed with the report, which provided new reasons for ridding ourselves of the Chief, I gathered up my logbook and charts and went to see Senior Officer West.

I was greeted by a nervous man in meticulous blues. Worry had replaced the ruthlessness he displaced back in May 1944 before the Allies had struck. Without mincing words, I asked him to replace my Chief.

"We don't have an engineer with the qualifications you wish," he declared. "They are in limited supply. I suggest that you train Selde in the fjord before you leave for your next patrol."

"Sir, I have been patient and have tried many times to teach him to handle the boat. He just doesn't have the aptitude. It was my Chief Warrant Officer who did the Chief's job. Selde would never have brought us back into port."

Grudgingly the Senior said that he would look into the situation. I left his office with the feeling that the matter was not yet settled.

The showdown came the next day while I was preparing boat and crew for the transfer to Trondheim. Around dusk I was summoned by the Senior.

"Your Chief has seen me," the Senior began. "He complained that you confined him to the ward room for most of the patrol. Why did you have to take this drastic measure, and why didn't you tell me about it?"

"Sir, it was necessary for the boat's safety. I did not mention it because I thought it irrelevant."

"Quite the contrary. The matter is serious enough. It changes the entire concept. I now understand your situation. I certainly do not approve of your action, is that clear?"

"I beg to remind you, sir, that the Captain's responsibility begins with the safety of ship and crew. If that is jeopardized, he has standing authorization to take any measures he sees fit. The Captain is the sole judge of a situation and of the steps needed to meet it. As Captain, I did what I judged was necessary to save boat and crew."

"I grant you all that, but you should not have resorted to such a solution. I see the matter clearly now. Your Chief will be removed."

Despite the urgency of my departure for Trondheim, the Senior engaged me in a lengthy conversation. He said that close to 60 old-type U-boats were in process of being fitted out for the front. More important, 80 large and 40 small type submersibles of the newest design were nearing the end of their training and would be ready presently—in two weeks at most—to strike in an unprecedented offensive. Soon we would have more than 150 U-boats sailing around the British Isles, cutting off the Allies' supplies for their Continental front. I listened to the news with fascination and excitement. Yet it all seemed too simple. According to Roesing, Germany would be resurrected in just a matter of weeks. I wondered whether he had heard the latest Armed Forces communiqués.

The same evening, April 11, I sailed *U-953* out of Bergen harbor. Aboard was a pilot, a *Leutnant* from the Coast Guard, who was familiar with the tricky water ways inside the fjords. The boat hammered northward through the dark waters, defying the British torpedo boats and submarines which had infiltrated the fjords and had sunk several of our ships. For three nights we snaked through narrow channels in inky darkness. We slid past cliffs by the margin of a hair; escaped death at Hellisoey, where *U-486* had been torpedoed the night before; ran aground near Aalesund but slipped off the rocks in the rising ride with diesels screaming in reverse; roared around lofty mountains out to sea; challenged radar impulses for an eternity; then swung into a hole in the mountains which turned out to be another fjord; barely missed ramming the cliffs at Smoela, where the Norwegians had changed the

beacon light to trap us; and finally arrived—at the
end of the third night—in Trondheim, where I
moored the boat in the concrete bunker. It was 0600
on April 14.

Since it was too early to arrange with the 13th U-
boat Flotilla to quarter the crew and dry-dock the
boat, I settled for the morning coffee. We tuned in a
German radio station and soft music traveled
through the compartments. I was sipping my first cup
in my tiny nook when the announcer interrupted:
"Stand by for a special bulletin. We will bring you
important news."

As the music resumed, my tiredness vanished, for
a special bulletin always meant good news. What the
good news could be was beyond my imagination. Just
the previous night we had heard that our Ruhr industrial region was surrounded by the Allies, that the British were on their way to Hamburg, that the Americans had occupied Darmstadt, Frankfurt, and Stuttgart,
that the Black Forest was being swept by the French,
that the Russians had occupied Vienna and were
storming Berlin; and if a miracle could save Germany from downfall now, it would have to be a gigantic miracle.

Now the music cut off and the voice came on again:
"This is a special bulletin. Franklin Delano Roosevelt,
the President of the United States, died on April the
twelfth. Providence has removed one of the fiercest enemies of our country. Providence is with the German people. Roosevelt's death is of far-reaching significance. The unity of the Allies will soon break down
and the war will turn in our favor. I repeat—Franklin
Delano Roosevelt has died in the United States. . . ."
The announcer's voice was drowned in the brassy
chords of a military march.

My men, who had listened silently, continued their
breakfast. Quite obviously, the news did not seem important enough to them to divert their attention from
their boat, their homes, their families. As for myself, I
could see nothing in Roosevelt's death that offered Germany any encouragement. Someone else would step
into his place and continue the same remorseless

course. Victorious armies do not simply turn around and walk off a battlefield.

The compound of the flotilla, though at one time an important base of the U-boat war in the Arctic, was small and I did not meet anyone I knew. I reported our arrival and had the crew accommodated in the barracks. The move from boat to quarters was easily accomplished: a toothbrush, some underwear, U-boat fatigues—these were all that we had to call our own. To keep myself informed, I took the short-wave radio from the boat into my room. The war news sent my thoughts wandering back to the places where I had spent my youth, to Frankfurt and the Black Forest, where German people and German soil were already under Allied rule. Now the rest of Germany was being crushed between two giant forces, and the fighting was so desperate that young and old, women as well as men, were told to make a last stand to fight with tooth and fingernail and a "Panzerfaust" against the mighty invaders.

Panzerfaust

My war plunged downhill along with the nation's. On April 17, I received notice that our boat had suffered almost irreparable damages. The bow tubes had been knocked out of alignment by the blow, and they had to be realigned. This long and difficult procedure would delay our next mission considerably. To make matters worse, the dry dock would not be available for some time.

I became increasingly irritated. With sudden and terrifying clarity I now saw that the war was lost; I accepted what I saw, and I pictured all of us ending up in an immense prison camp at the mercy of our merciless enemies. We would be reviled and brutalized, and there would be no way out except death by starvation.

Yet there was one way out of the horror that would engulf us, one way to escape intolerable humiliation. Down at the waterfront lay my boat. When she was fully equipped, I could sail her to South America— to Uruguay or Argentina, perhaps. Absconding with the boat seemed suddenly the only means to survive the catastrophe. How lucky I was that I had been able to preserve her for a final task!

Instantly I put the wild impulse into practical planning. I sent Hennecke to secure the necessary charts without telling him of my intentions. For days on end I stayed in my room, pouring over the maps and plotting escape routes. I reckoned and calculated my chances for reaching the Rio de la Plata. I planned on reducing the crew to a skeleton, taking only reliable, loyal, unmarried men, thus reducing the risk of being betrayed. I knew that I could count on most of my men, but was wary of including my officers. The Chief had been transferred and a new one not acquainted with the crew would be a heavy burden. The same applied to the Exec and the Ensign, both too young to grasp the situation. In my mind I selected the few key men whom I would first draw into my conspiracy. No more than a few, for I was playing a dangerous game. I would not only be flouting naval authority, but also a strong group of die-hards who advocated turning Norway into a fortress and starting a war of their own to achieve some obscure victory.

In the meantime, German resistance fell apart in Italy, Austria, and inside Germany. Now only a madman could speak of recovery. But German oaths and patriotism and discipline were so deeply rooted that many a sane man threw his life into the fires of a lost cause. Among them were the captains and crews of our boats at sea. U-boats were sunk at the rate of two and three a day as they sailed from Bergen, Kristiansand, and Kiel on their first and final mission. Hundreds of good men died futilely to honor their pledge to duty and country.

On April 27, *U-953* still lay at the pier, and it seemed that she would never be repaired in time for me to execute my plan. Then I was taken by surprise by an order to report to Senior Officer West in Bergen. Puzzled by the urgent call, I prepared myself for a long train ride through half of Norway. Because I owned nothing but U-boat fatigues which were unsuitable for the trip, I requisitioned a ski outfit from the supply laid in for those who had taken their leaves in the Norwegian mountains during better days. Dressed in blue ski pants and a light gray anorak, with food for four days in a knapsack, I departed from Trondheim and began the journey through the snow-covered mountains. Late in the afternoon of April 30, the train pulled into Bergen station. I managed to find the compound by memory. Someone led me to a room. I felt like a stranger in a hotel.

Tuesday May 1. At 0830 I knocked at the door of the Senior Officer's sanctuary: "I beg to report as requested, sir."

"You were expected yesterday," was *Kapitaen* Roesing's dry reply.

"Sir, I made it as fast as I could."

"Never mind. Your boat will not be ready in time for the great offensive. We need every experienced man on the front, and you are going to take command of another boat which is ready for patrol. The boat is about to arrive in Kristiansand from a German port."

"Yes, sir."

"You are going to sail against England with vigor and determination. Admiral Doenitz has ordered all conventional U-boats to leave Germany for Norway, and we will continue our war at sea from here. We shall never surrender. We'll hold out and our U-boats will force our terms upon the enemy." He handed me an order to report to the 27th U-boat Flotilla, then continued: "It occurs to me that you might as well act as a courier. I'll give you some top secret papers which I want you to deliver to our bases in Oslo, Horten, and Kristiansand. I expect to have them ready this afternoon."

I was too stunned to make any reply. There was no limit to insanity. I clicked my heels, turned and left the room. Once outside, I gritted my teeth because my marvelous plan to escape was suddenly put beyond execution. But then it dawned on me that a new boat, already equipped for patrol, would give me an even better and quicker chance to reach South America. My determination to flee was strengthened by Headquarters' irrational decision to force the battle at sea until the last man in the U-boat Force would lie on the bottom.

The effects of Doenitz's order were immediately apparent. In the compound and along the waterfront, last-minute preparations were made to send still more old type U-boats to their deaths. Mechanics and dockhands labored violently, hectically, as if the Reich's existence depended upon their efforts alone. Meanwhile, bewildering news spread throughout the compound. The latest Armed Forces communiqué had revealed that the Battle for Berlin was nearing its climax. Hitler himself had taken command of the troops defending the capital.

At 1900 I received the secret papers for which I had been waiting. By that hour it was too late to depart, so I had a meager dinner in the officers' mess hall and left to get a good night's sleep for my trip to Kristiansand harbor.

I tuned in the radio and waited for news stretched out on my bed. The music stopped. The announcer's voice, first stuttering, then loud and harsh, broke the brief silence: "Attention, I have an important announcement to make."

Instantly I was wide awake. I looked at my watch. It was exactly 2130. The music was a slow-moving passage from a Wagner opera, heralding a grave disclosure. I guessed that Berlin had fallen into Soviet hands, or even that a cease-fire had halted the senseless massacre. Then the announcer spoke again, low and solemn: "Our Fuehrer, Adolf Hitler, fighting to his last breath, fell for Germany in his Headquarters in the Reich's Chancellery. On April the thirtieth, the Fuehrer appointed Grand Admiral Doenitz to take his place. The Grand Admiral and successor to the Fuehrer now speaks to the German People."

This was the end, the end of the torture, the end of the war and of German history. The one impossible disaster was an accomplished fact. Hitler's death could only mean final recognition of defeat. Vaguely I heard Doenitz's voice, far in the background. He was saying that the military struggle had to go on to save the lives of millions of refugees, that we must continue to fight and defend our rights. His statement was drowned in the tunes of the national anthem.

An immense sadness overpowered me. Along with tens of millions of Germans, I had given everything I had owned, loved, and cherished. I had sacrificed home and family for the sake of my country and victory, and had blindly believed in the cause, and had fought and hoped and suffered and waited for the miracle in deep devotion. Now, it was all over, simply over. The end.

Heartsick, I struggled to the mess hall. There sat the Commanding Officer and a few others, pale, grief-stricken, confused.

One said, "He died on the barricades, we have to go on."

Someone else declared, "He gave us an example. We must hold out and continue here in Norway. The Allies will have a hell of a time smoking us out of the mountains."

Others, voicing their opinion cautiously, suggested that this was indeed the end. Hopelessness soon silenced the exchange. We dispersed.

The next morning, May 2, I took the express to Oslo and arrived late in the evening.

On May 3, I delivered one envelope of secret papers to the given address, then boarded a train to Horten. In Horten, I handed over a second envelope to the *Adjudant* of the Naval base and continued by rail on the final leg of my last assignment.

On May 4, after a sleepless night on a wooden bench in an unheated compartment, I arrived in Kristiansand around 0700. A blue sky spanned the city. I hiked down a narrow, dusty road that led to the compound, strolled through pines and crippled firs into the extensive complex, and entered the executive offices of the flotilla at 0830. A youthful *Adjudant* showed me into the Commanding Officer's elaborate room. Before me rose a decorated officer in blues who had been a U-boat commander when hunting and shooting had been a pleasure. *Kapitaen* Juergensen was one of the lucky few who had been withdrawn from the front just in time to escape the holocaust.

"I beg to report for duty, sir," I saluted.

"Oh yes, naturally, I've been informed of your arrival. You're supposed to take a new command. Your boat hasn't arrived yet. I assume she'll sail into port any time. Why don't you accommodate yourself in the meantime. I'll let you know. That's all for now."

This short, cool reception gave me a strange premonition. Something was odd about Juergensen's behavior, something that went beyond the strain that had signed his face. He seemed to be absentminded and flustered. I walked out of his office convinced that he knew of some calamity that he had been unwilling to divulge.

I hurried down to the waterfront. Two old-type U-boats lay alongside the pier. Poking up beyond them was the strangely formed conning tower of a smaller boat of the new class. As I approached to examine the new weapon, I spotted her Captain's white cap, then his face, above the rim of the bridge.

"Angermann, is it really you?" I shouted across the water.

"Hello, I see you're still alive," he called back.

"Ill weeds grow apace."

"Is one of these old jalopies yours?" He pointed toward an old diving tube.

"No, I am waiting to take command of another one, still to arrive."

"I don't want to discourage you. But out there is hell, and she may never get here. We have just crossed the Skagerrak and I know. Aircraft all over. The sky is black with them. And the devil is loose in Germany. Berlin is taken by the Soviets. The Americans have met them at the Elbe, and we escaped Kiel under direct fire from land." He wiped the sweat off his face and continued: "The Tommies have captured Kiel. The first tanks reached the Tirpitz Pier when I was in the middle of the Bay, and they began firing their big cannon, and God, it's a miracle that we made it here. We lost at least seven boats in the crossing, and I stopped counting this morning. I tell you, it can't last much longer."

Angermann was reciting still more horrors when another small new boat plowed up to the pier. A man threw a line. At that moment I recognized another face below the Captain's white cap. My good friend Fred Schreiber had also escaped the massacre in the Baltic.

Fred raised his right hand in salute. His flashing eyes had lost their vividness. His skin was ashen. I knew that disaster had struck.

As soon as the gangplank was laid down I rushed aboard to greet him. We pressed our hands in silence. He pulled a crumpled paper from his pocket and handed it to me and his eyes grew moist. I unfolded the sheet. It was a deciphered signal from Headquarters:

ALL U-BOATS. ATTENTION ALL U-BOATS. CEASE FIRE AT ONCE. STOP ALL HOSTILE ACTION AGAINST ALLIED SHIPPING. DOENITZ.

As I stared at the message its letters blurred. I heard Fred saying, "We received it a half-hour ago. It's the finale."

I felt a sudden pain welling up in my heart. I turned around and fought back my tears, for I had never been taught to lose.

As of May 5, 1945, hostilities came to a halt. Doenitz, the head of the new government, had agreed to a preliminary surrender to the British Armies involving all of our Armed Forces in the northern region of the Continent.

The next day, every seaman on base was electrified by another radiogram from Doenitz. The Admiral who had led the U-boats to glory and to disaster mourned for the faithful who lay on the bottom and gave thanks to those few survivors of the monstrous battle:

Submariner's Badge

MY U-BOAT MEN, SIX YEARS OF WAR LIE BEHIND YOU. YOU HAVE FOUGHT LIKE LIONS. AN OVERWHELMING MATERIAL SUPERIORITY HAS DRIVEN US INTO A TIGHT CORNER FROM WHICH IT IS NO LONGER POSSIBLE TO CONTINUE THE WAR. UNBEATEN AND UNBLEMISHED, YOU LAY DOWN YOUR ARMS AFTER A HEROIC FIGHT WITHOUT PARALLEL. WE PROUDLY REMEMBER OUR FALLEN COMRADES WHO GAVE

THEIR LIVES FOR FUEHRER AND FATHER-
LAND. COMRADES, PRESERVE THAT SPIRIT
IN WHICH YOU HAVE FOUGHT SO LONG AND
SO GALLANTLY FOR THE SAKE OF THE FU-
TURE OF THE FATHERLAND. LONG LIVE
GERMANY.
YOUR GRAND ADMIRAL

This was the message that put an end to the suffering. It admitted defeat for the first time. The mur-
dering had finally come to an end. Henceforth we
would be able to live without fear that we had to die
tomorrow. An unknown tranquillity took possession of
me as I realized fully that I had survived. My death
in an iron coffin, a verdict of long standing, was finally
suspended. The truth was so beautiful that it seemed
to be a dream.

Epilogue

Nominally, the war ended on May 5, 1945, but I had
to fight for almost six months more before I won my
battle for survival. At first, Germany's surrender left
me feeling deceived and betrayed; I concluded that it
relieved me of my sworn obligations to Folk and Fatherland and military discipline. Since everything I
held dear was dead, my only concern was to be free.
But between me and freedom lay the vast, creaking
apparatus of the Allied occupation. I assumed, quite
correctly, that all who had fought for Germany faced a
slow, painful, humiliating process of internment and
interrogation and grudging repatriation; and I refused
to subject myself to the whim and convenience of Allied military officials who were at best bewildered by
their enormous task, and at worst vindictive and cruel

to their former enemies. I was determined to flee and to find my own peace; I vowed that nothing would stop me from doing precisely as I pleased.

In the days after Germany's capitulation, I found no cause for confidence in the victors. The British went on attacking those last U-boats which fled German ports for Norway, and I thought that they were merely continuing their policy of extermination. I spent most of my time at the waterfront with my old friend Fred Schreiber, watching as a few other Captains dashed into Kristiansand in their battered, shell-punctured U-boats. Eckel of *U-2325* and Wex of *U-2354* told us that five of their companion boats had been sunk while crossing the Danish Sea and the Skagerrak. This brought our U-boat casualties since war's end to 16, and to 779 the grand total of U-boats sunk since the start of the war.

May 7 was a day when hysteria reigned supreme all around us. The Norwegians wildly celebrated their liberation. Three of our seamen, who were found drunk in the company of Norwegians, were put in chains by Juergensen, the Commanding Officer, who grimly planned a court-martial as a warning. And last but not least, the British came ashore in Kristiansand, stirring speculation about an imminent seizure of our compound. Against this hectic backdrop, I persuaded my good friend Fred Schreiber to escape with me to South America. Reluctantly, he fell in with my plan. We would abscond with his small boat and men, Schnorkel all the way to Trondheim, where my larger *U-953* lay waiting, then sail her with a select crew to Argentina.

That night, just as we were about to put our plan into effect, every one on base was ordered to report to the repair shop for a "show" being staged by *Kapitaen* Jergensen and his aides. Fred and I recoiled in horror when we entered the dimly lighted square where the U-boat crews had formed a human horseshoe facing the white-walled shop. There, suspended from a makeshift scaffold, hung three nooses. Below stood a large table, with three high stools lined up on top. In front of the gallows was a crude bench, covered with a huge Navy war flag. A ship's lantern, placed on the red cloth, cast an eery light on a Navy saber and a copy of Hitler's book *Mein Kampf*. A band of armed marines took up position behind the stage. Staff officers rushed back and forth. *Leutnant* Lange, Juergensen's young *Adjudant,* shouted frantic orders.

As the crowd stirred uneasily, Juergensen began speaking: "Soldiers, I have called you together to demonstrate how we will avoid another 1918. I am going to make an example of these three deserters—an example that will strike fear into the hearts of any men with revolutionary tendencies. We will protect and nourish those ideals instilled in us by our martyred Fuehrer. Guards, bring these men to justice!"

What followed was a perfect nightmare come to life. The captives, their hands tied behind their back, were led into the square. Momentarily they were paralyzed by the sight of the nooses; then they broke away and fled. Lange shot one man repeatedly in the back. As the fugitive fell on his face, the two others surrendered. Then all three were brutally dragged back to the scaffold.

Lange shouted a long list of trumped-up charges. He then demanded the severest punishment: death by hanging. No one in the crowd dared to protest in the face of the many rifles.

Juergensen pronounced the three men guilty on all counts and condemned them "to be hanged by the neck until death has separated body from soul."

The guards were then ordered to execute the sentence. But before the three doomed men reached the platform, they broke free again and began fighting desperately for their lives. Shots were fired. There was struggling, trampling; dust rose in the lantern's gloomy light. The three were recaptured, but with superhuman force they broke free once again. They fought, bit, kicked, and punched until they were surrounded and again overwhelmed.

Now Juergensen cried, "Shoot these men dead, don't hang them, shoot them!"

The marines heard the call, and all went very fast. One man raised his rifle and fired point blank. The mate's face flew off like a pancake. The two other prisoners collapsed and were riddled with bullets. The marines dragged the three bodies against the wall of the repair shop and left them there. The crews were dismissed; the guards marched away; everyone vanished.

Long after midnight, two petty officers helped me lift the bodies into a rowboat. We fastened heavy weights to their feet and neck, then rowed out into the middle of the fjord. Three splashes—and the dead seamen had at least received a sailor's burial.

The execution completely reversed Fred's decision to sail that night—or any other night.

For the next few days, the compound remained in the grip of a deathly calm; most of the men were stunned and guilt-sickened by the organized murder. The deed drained off my last lingering hopes: when Germans killed Germans without a qualm, there could be no future for me in my homeland, no mercy at the hands of the conquerors. To my surprise, however, the British ignored our U-boats at the base and did nothing to harm other boats which complied with their order to put into the nearest English port flying a black flag from the extended periscope. And my fears were further allayed by my first contact with a British officer.

It was mid-day when I was sent to see the British district commander in a small town east of Kristiansand. My mission was to arrange the evacuation of all naval personnel from the U-boat base. I made the trip by armored car with two seamen holding submachine guns at the ready, for we had been warned against an ambush by vengeful members of the Norwegian underground. I found the English commander, one Colonel MacGregor, dressing belatedly in his room in the village hotel.

MacGregor closed the door behind me and offered me a chair. "I've just taken my morning exercises," he said apologetically in an interesting Scottish brogue. "Running helps me to keep trim, you see. A man of my age must watch his weight." Then MacGregor poured me a glass of wine—"It's the best I could find in this damned town." And as he continued dressing, MacGregor told me a little about himself: he had parachuted into the mountains three months ago and had organized the Norwegian resistance. He then explained that his orders called for all German troops to leave Kristiansand within three days and go to the nearby island of Tromoey. I was completely disarmed by MacGregor's informality, and I decided that it was neither disgraceful nor dangerous to cooperate with such an officer.

In the heat of a May afternoon, thousands of Navy men poured over the bridge into the well-kept garrison of Tromoey, which had been a German coast-artillery base for years. Our enlisted men were billeted in barracks; Fred and I joined a group of officers and took over a neat farmhouse that had served as a club. The total absence of British troops, and our unharried settlement into domesticated groups, led us to think that our stay on Tromoey would be brief and quite tolerable.

It proved to be neither. Despite our strict, self-imposed routine, which included many organized activities and an early curfew, the hours dragged and the days inched by. The compound was agog with rumors and wild speculation about our future and that of our homeland. Our insecurity and resentment grew as the days became weeks—and still no word from the British. Some men were unable to maintain their equilibrium under the subtle pressures of our defeat and confinement. One officer hanged himself from a rafter in the attic, and we buried him between the red rocks of Tromoey. Three weeks after our arrival, a riot broke out in a barracks occupied by enlisted men who claimed to be non-Germans pressed into service. They barricaded themselves in their quarters and shot an officer who came to investigate. The mutiny was not put down until the commotion attracted British troops from the mainland.

Two nights later, the English returned for reprisals. We were awakened from a sound sleep, herded at bayonet point into a meadow, and ordered to strip. We marched forth and back between two rows of Tommies while their comrades ransacked our quarters searching for hidden weapons. Our nudity was a calculated indignity: it erased the distinction between officers and men, and informed us all that our subjugation was complete. The Tommies found little that interested them, and after shooting up our quarters in disappointment, they departed as suddenly as they had arrived.

In early July they came again, this time to set up a board of inquiry under the sky. We were informed that we had to register to get our discharge papers. Elated by our renewed prospects for prompt repatriation, I gladly gave a Britisher all the information he wanted. When he asked about my home town, I named Frankfurt as a likely place to start over again, though I now had no connection with the city except sad memories and a bank account of worthless currency. But the Tommies departed, and our hopes were soured by two more weeks of interminable waiting.

The break finally came on July 24. A small detachment of British troops arrived and collected those of us who had elected to be discharged in the American and the French occupation zones. We were marched down to barges waiting in the fjord, then ferried to the small port of Mandal. There we were surrounded by mixed British-Norwegian troops who displayed an alarmingly martial look. That night we slept in a field in British tents, with our bellies filled for the first time in weeks—with Irish stew.

In the morning, we went through a long ordeal of search and interrogation. To put us at a disadvantage and make deceit more difficult, the Tommies again ordered us to strip, then took us for questioning in a nearby barn. My inquisitor was a British officer about 15 years my senior. For the first time I was asked—and I honestly answered—questions that would be put to me often in the years to come:

"What was your last position in the Navy?"

"U-boat commander."

"I thought we had all of you chaps eliminated. How many Allied ships have you sunk?"

"I don't know."

"Come, now, didn't you report your sinkings?"

"Of course I did. But I had no interest in keeping count."

"Does that mean you hope to disown responsibility for what you've done?"

"Sir, I did my duty. I stand on it."

"Well, let's not argue that point. But we have cleaned up your ranks pretty well, haven't we?"

"There may be two dozen captains still alive. Besides me, two or three of them may have fought through most of the war."

"Have you been a member of the Nazi Party?"

"No."

"Have you been a member of the Hitler Youth?"

"No."

"Have you ever been a member of any of the Party's organizations?"

"No."

"Nonsense, that's what all you Germans say. You had to belong to at least one of the organizations. How else could you have become an officer in the Navy—especially a U-boat captain? Come on, at least admit that you were a member of the Hitler Youth."

"I'm sorry to disappoint you, but you are misinformed. The Navy did not recruit officers from the Hitler Youth, and membership in the Party was not a prerequisite for joining the Navy. We had only to meet the same sort of qualifications your Navy asks."

"I've heard otherwise. I must warn you to tell the truth. Any false statement will incur a heavy penalty. You had better admit your membership now and save yourself a lot of trouble. We've captured all the Party's records, and it is easy for us to find the truth."

"These are the facts, I have nothing to add."

The inquisitor broke off his questioning and consulted a heavy volume—the Allies' "wanted" list. Finding nothing, he asked me how I had managed to survive, and seemed startled by some accounts I gave him of my narrow escapes. Finally he stamped my discharge papers and handed them to me with a bleak smile. "Take good care of these. Without them, you're liable to end up behind barbed wire. And Captain, good luck."

Late that afternoon, I was at the rail of a grimy old freighter when she sailed for Germany. Several thousand discharged service men crowded the deck and watched the Norwegian shore fade away. There was no laughter, no rejoicing—just silence. We were all back on deck the next morning, July 26, when our vessel entered the wide delta of the Weser River and was shunted by two tugboats to a quay in Bremerhaven harbor. We were silent, too, as we set foot again on German soil. At once American troops took us under their command and collected our discharge papers. We were loaded on trucks, transported to a camp on the outskirts of Bremerhaven, fumigated and fed. Fred and I shared a small tin of sardines and a few biscuits of our own, then we rolled up in blankets and fell asleep under the stars.

At dawn on July 27, about 3,000 of us were herded onto a freight train bound for Frankfurt, where we were to be released. It was a long, slow, dismal trip. We passed wheat fields ready for the harvest, countryside stations and crossroads guarded by American soldiers, highways clogged with Allied armored columns, and mountains of rubble that once had been beautiful cities. We reached Frankfurt late the second afternoon of our journey, and as the train snaked through the suburbs and then along the Schaumainkai at the Main River, I bitterly accepted the fact that my home town, destroyed beyond recognition, had become an American garrison.

The train stopped on the quay amidst the once-flowering Nizza Park. I asked our guards what the problem was, and was told that we would have to stay in the open cattle cars until we had reached Hoechst, a city west of Frankfurt.

The train finally pulled out of Frankfurt. We rolled to Hoechst, then through it and further westward on and on without another stop. I felt that the Americans had double-crossed us and thought of leaping off the train. But before I could act, the train stopped at sunset in the valley of the Rhine. A few rifle shots, an enormous commotion, and our caravan was surrounded by French troops. Someone speaking fluent German in a French accent announced over a loudspeaker, "Keep your heads down. This is the French Army, and we will shoot at any sign of disobedience. Remain calm and follow orders."

Total consternation. I knew now that freedom was but a dream, that the reality would be imprisonment behind barbed wire. We cursed and complained that our transfer to the French was illegal. But there was no one to hear our accusations, our anguish. That night no one slept. We sat in the boxcars under a battery of truck headlights and threatening gun muzzles. The wolves had been entrusted with the care of the flock.

At 0500 on July 29, we were awakened by a recording of the "Marseillaise," followed by a candid Alsatian voice saying, "Leave the cars at once. Form ranks at the riverside. Make no attempt to escape—it would prove fatal."

Some 3,000 Germans dismounted and lined up as ordered. We were marched onto a swaying pontoon bridge, across the Rhine, and into the French occupation zone. Soon we were treated to an ironic spectacle; as the sun rose, its rays glinted on the huge victory monument atop the Niederwald mountain. Now the Rhine barred our way back to the relative security of the British zone, and hundreds of us would never return.

We continued our march through the morning heat, driven ahead by a shouting, gesticulating detachment of French troops. By noon, we were dehydrated and fatigued as we dragged ourselves into the notorious Camp Dietersheim, a maximum security camp for prisoners of war. As we walked beneath the ornamented arch into confinement, a horsedrawn wagon rumbled by, loaded with nude, emaciated corpses. Flashing bayonets separated officers from enlisted men and forced us into a huge cage already crowded with German prisoners. Our countrymen were walking skeletons, half-naked and filthy; their hair and beards were long and snarled, their skin leathery brown and ruptured by malnutrition. For months, they had lived in the open and slept exposed to the elements in holes in the ground. Every rain would turn this barren land into a sea of mud and bury men in graves they had dug with their own hands.

Fred and I selected a vacant hole, buried our few belongings in the dust. As we awaited further developments, playful Moroccan soldiers continually set off hand grenades and fired rifles for their own amusement. Shortly after noon, a cart arrived with aluminum cans containing our first formal meal since the Irish stew back in Norway. It was supposed to be soup, but it looked and tasted like greasy dishwater. I told Fred that I was not going to sit around wasting away into another skeleton. I would find an escape route that very night.

When night had fallen over the camp, I began a nerve-wracking trial run for my first escape. I cautiously crawled into the alleyway between our cage and the adjoining one, then snaked along the dusty ground toward the perimeter fences at a spot halfway between two guard towers. I moved slowly across the floodlit open stretch in full view of the lofty machine gunners. Then I wriggled along the inner fence until I reached a dimly lit zone. Now only a barbed-wire roll and another fence lay between me and freedom. Not far outside, a thicket of high ferns promised safety—if only I could reach it. Deciding that this was the way I would make my break the following night, I slowly retraced my wriggling path. By the time I had returned to my hole, most of the night was gone.

The blaring strains of the "Marseillaise" wrenched me out of my sleep. Immediately, I told Fred of my escape route. To my disappointment, Fred was not enthusiastic; he suggested that my chances would be better if I tried alone. If I succeeded, he would follow and meet me again at an address in Frankfurt.

I started crawling again that night at 2130; it was a long, heart-pounding trip. With utmost caution I crept into the shadow of a corner post. For minutes I paused there, steeling myself to go on. Then I fell flat on the ground. Teeth clenched and mouth dry, I slid into the alleyway, toward the two perimeter fences. I stretched my body to full length, buried my fingers in the dry soil, pulled and pushed and wriggled toward the barbed-wire roll. Sweat ran into my eyes, soaked my clothes. I touched the wire roll, slid into the entanglement, then I was at the outer fence. Taking a deep breath and a quick look at the towers, I lifted a wire cautiously, rolled under and away from the fence, through the fern thicket and into darkness.

Silence. I stole through meadows and rye fields to a small village in the Nahe Valley about three kilometers south of the camp. There I crept into a barn and fell asleep in a mound of hay.

A sharp sound awakened me. It was the farmer, harnessing his horses. I approached and told him outright that I had escaped from the camp and needed help. Amazed, he said that the only prisoners to escape thus far had accomplished the feat by signing up for the French Foreign Legion. He took me into the kitchen, where his wife and daughter fed me an enormous breakfast of eggs and fried potatoes. As I ate, he told me that he would arrange to supply me with papers for Fred and myself.

After a good night's sleep in a feather bed, I awoke with new vigor and a firm resolve to get Fred out of the camp. Though the farmer disapproved of the risk, he supplied me with necessities. After nightfall, I cautiously approached the camp carrying a sack of food for the skeleton men. While I was creeping toward the outer fence, two Moroccan guards spotted me. I rose to my feet, expecting to be shot on the spot. To my surprise, however, they were more interested in the contents of my bag. Speaking better French than they did, I convinced them that I was merely trying to smuggle food to a friend, and I promised them a large gift of American cigarettes if they allowed me to pass their post at will for a similar bribe each time. Greed triumphed. They accepted two packs of Camels and even lifted the wire for me. I found Fred asleep in the hole. Dumfounded by my reappearance but still unready to escape himself, he argued that he expected to receive his legitimate discharge papers by the weekend. He said that if he did not have them by Saturday night he would make the break then. Annoyed by the failure of my risky mission, I left Fred and the food with the dying and hopeless. Another pack of American cigarettes secured my retreat from the camp. An hour later I was back in the farmer's barn.

For two days I enjoyed my life on the farm. I helped the farmer in his fields, raked the hay, loaded wagons. I ate good food with an appetite long unassuaged and splashed after sundown in the tin tub in the barn. I was completely happy with my lot, for I had discovered that freedom could be won in a courageous moment.

On Saturday night I approached the camp again with more of the farmer's American cigarettes. The two Moroccan guards accepted the bribe and let me slip through the fences. As I approached Fred's hole, a number of shadowy figures loomed up out of the darkness. In a moment I was surrounded and overpowered. Only then did I realize that I had been seized by my own countrymen. It turned out that my name had been included in an afternoon roll call; afterward, the Commandant had announced that everyone on the list was to be shipped to France, and that five men would be shot for anyone who escaped. My comrades, finding themselves in a terrible dilemma, had hoped that I would come back again—into their trap. Perhaps my return had saved five lives, but at that moment I could not forgive the treachery of my fellow prisoners. I drew a sharp mental line between myself and my comrades of yesteryear.

Before sunrise on Sunday, August 5, Fred and I were lined up with a huge group of prisoners and marched off to a railroad siding. There stood a freight train of 42 cattle cars. We were packed on board, 100 men to each filthy car, and locked in. The train started out on a long journey to an unknown destination inside France.

Suffocating heat and the stench of manure turned the cattle car into a torture chamber. As the train rolled toward the French border, I sat at the rear wall, cutting and sawing at a plank in the siding with a knife that I had managed to secrete. I worked long

and furtively while all the others lay in a stupor, half
dead of thirst and hunger. By midnight, I had cut out
a portion of the plank, making a hole big enough to
slip through. When the train came to a stop, I stuck
my head through the opening, then my shoulders. Halfway to freedom, I was suddenly grabbed by my feet
and dragged back into the boxcar. A dozen of my
comrades fell over me like hyenas. Again I was their
captive.

The trip went on in misery all that night, the next
day and another night, without food or water, with
men suffering from dysentery and worse. One of the
skeleton men died the second night and another died
on the following morning. The stench of death and
decomposition became unbearable. To get a breath of
clean air, I pressed my face against the bars of the
only vent—and sniffed the ocean.

Soon afterward the train ground to a halt at an improvised platform in the middle of nowhere. Deployed
on both sides of the track were a great many French
soldiers of the regular army. They ordered us to dis-
mount and prodded us into a well-concealed prison
camp that resembled a fortified colonial outpost. I
learned that we were near La Flèche, a town midway
between Le Mans and Nantes.

The camp swallowed us up. As soon as the enlisted
men were separated from the officers, we were quar-
tered in crude shelters and issued food tickets. At once
I began to prowl the caged-in area in search of a way
out. But the camp perimeter was bristling with
machine-gun nests and barbed-wire walls more formidable than those in Dietersheim. Besides, the young
French regulars were not the kind of troops whom one
could bribe. Fred and I were forced to admit we might
be in for a long wait on short rations.

My days dragged on in heat and hunger; I made my
endless rounds through the cage, looking for an escape
route. For many hours I lay in the shadows of the
latrines, observing the guards' routine. At night, when
the heat had lessened, I crawled along the fences,
slipped out of the rotating beams of searchlights,
climbed the fences into adjoining cages—all in vain.

After two weeks in La Flèche, my cheeks were hollow and my ribs protruded. I scorned those who had given up, and even those who were carried out dead. Hunger was greater than friendship, stronger than prayers, deadlier than disease. Ruthless trading among the prisoners was as common as death. Rings, watches, clothes, and even gold teeth were bartered for food. Food rations were exchanged for the soggy butts of cigarettes. There were informers, thieves, religious and political fanatics, madmen and cowards—and a few with a flaming desire to escape.

It was not until my third week in camp that I hit upon an escape route. My plan was so simple that it could not fail. Every day a large detail of prisoners from the enlisted men's section went to our latrines, picked up tall metal drums filled with human waste and, marching out under heavy guard, dumped the contents into pits outside the north end of the camp. Fred and I would join the detail unannounced, walk out of the camp with a drum and then simply neglect to return.

The following morning our first attempt miscarried. The moment we left our cage with the column of coughing prisoners, a self-seeking Austrian prisoner recognized us as officers and alerted the guards. Fortunately, we were able to talk ourselves out of two months in solitary confinement. I quickly improved on the plan. The same evening after the camp was asleep, I slipped out of the barracks and across the yard to the fence separating our cage from that of our neighboring petty officers. I climbed the fence, jumped into the adjoining cage and disappeared in one of the latrines. Moments later Fred was at my side.

At sunrise the camp came alive, and two hours of uneasy waiting followed. Then the work crew arrived. Fred and I lifted a drum, mingled with the men, and marched out of the petty officers' cage fully unrecognized. With our hearts beating hard, we arrived at the pits, ducked behind the big drum. While the guards were nonchalantly palavering, we fell flat into the high grass and rolled and snaked away. Reaching the edge of the nearby woods, we crawled through low thickets until we were safe in the forest. At once we hastened westward through dense underbrush and across rivulets and paths.

After three hours of struggle, we fell exhausted into a thicket. Later we found some berries that quenched our thirst and took the edge off our hunger. By nightfall we took a road that led eastward, toward Le Mans. For hours we dragged along the pavement, jumped into the ditch along the road whenever a truck or a car passed, and took to the road again in sheer agony. Our stockings disintegrated, blisters formed on toes and heels, and the skin came right off our feet. For three nights we hiked along, passing French outposts and farmers on their way to town, always on the verge of being discovered, full of suspense and an unbroken will to succeed, subsisting on food that we found in farmers' gardens or scavenged from butchers' scrap heaps. During the days we slept huddled together in woods or culverts. When we finally reached Le Mans at the end of the third night, we spruced up our clothes, shaved our whiskers in a park, then walked into the center of the city with terrible hunger cramps in the stomach. We managed to find the station and discovered that the Paris express would not come through until well after midnight. We left the city and hid for the day in a field overgrown with mignonettes. Long after dusk we cautiously approached the railroad station from the rear, where the freight yard promised cover and a clandestine approach to the passenger platform.

At 0107, when the express clattered into the station, Fred and I hurried through the dark freight yard, into a throng of passengers and onto a crowded coach. As the train left Le Mans, we joined the passengers sprawled on the floor and feigned sleep in the hope that the conductor would not bother to wake us for tickets we did not have. But when the conductor appeared at the front of the car calling *"Vôtre billets, mesdames, messieurs,"* Fred climbed to his feet and headed toward the rear of the train. As expected, the conductor left us tired ones undisturbed. Then I waited for Fred to return. He never came back.

It was a magnificent Saturday morning, that first day

in September 1945, when the express rolled into
Paris and came to a stop in the Gare de Montparnasse.
I stood like an island amid the outflowing passengers,
looking for Fred. There was no Fred, and the fruitless
delay cost me my freedom. An attendant asked me for
my ticket. As I concocted a story that my luggage had
been stolen, I was suddenly confronted by two suspicious gendarmes, who demanded to see the contents of
my pockets. I fled into the streets of Paris. But my
painful feet slowed me down, and after a short chase
by police and civilians, I was again a captive. Unwilling
to be taken for a thief, I admitted that I was an escaped prisoner of war. As a result I was stripped and
put into a windowless cell.

All too soon, a corporal appeared at the police station, allowed me to put on my clothes but not my
shoes, then handcuffed me and prodded me with his
gun barrel into the streets of Montparnasse. We traveled through Paris by Metro to the Gare du Nord,
then by train through a sunny countryside to Cormeille
en Parisis, and finally on foot to the grim bastion
named Fort Cormeille.

A new search. A new interrogation. I refused to talk
to anyone but an officer. As a reward, I was flung headlong into a windowless dungeon. I groped around in
the inky darkness, found a pile of straw, and fell into a
deathlike sleep.

Later, much later, I was awakened and ordered out
by two guards. They dragged me down a corridor that
smelled like a morgue, up a staircase, and into an office. There an Alsatian sergeant offered me a deal:
a glass of water for a full confession. Wearily I agreed.
But naturally the truth was not to the sergeant's liking.
With great relish he described the penalty for such a
pack of lies—indefinite solitary, with all the privations
it entailed. However, he said, there was a way out:
officers with my training were needed to serve in the
French Foreign Legion, and if I "volunteered," I
would be a free man in four weeks, enjoying the food
and wine of legionnaires, as well as the talented prostitutes in Sidi-bel-Abbès. I told him that I was not his
man; he smiled maliciously and guaranteed me plenty

of time to reconsider my hasty decision. Soon the door of the dungeon closed behind me again.

Perpetual night surrounded me, and hunger consumed me. Yet the darkness was comforting, for it spared me the sight of my degradation and misery and also of the vermin which populated my cell. For long periods I drifted in a deep trance, haunted by the sergeant's advice to reconsider. I finally did reconsider, but only because there was no escaping this stone fortress; I had to be sent elsewhere to find some avenue of flight.

When the guards carried me out of my cell, I gasped to the sergeant, "I'm joining up." He put on his malicious smile and ordered a soldier to bring me food. Somewhat restored by a meal of goulash, bread, and coffee, I signed my life away and was promised a quick transfer to another post to recuperate. But my departure was delayed by a desperate bout with dysentery, which put me in the Fort hospital. For several days I clung to a thin thread of life and then, somehow, made a sudden recovery. On September 28, I was given back my few belongings, and a shabby brown uniform of the German Labor Service, which would mark me out as a prisoner in case I escaped. A friendly corporal took me on a trip back through Paris, and thence by express to a camp near Le Mans.

As a new Legionnaire, I was far from free. In fact, my situation was now worse than ever. I was still in captivity, in a maximum-security prison camp. In addition, as the French Commandant was quick to warn me, I would be court-martialed and shot as a deserter from the Legion if I attempted to escape again. And I was also weakened by my long ordeal and the loss of about 30 pounds.

On October 1, I was released from a temporary cell into the officers' cage, which was located in the center of the camp. Here I found some fellow prisoners from La Flèche, who had been transferred here as security risks because this camp was allegedly escape-proof. The same evening I began to explore the camp looking for a way out. Tall fences, complicated wire works and keen-eyed guards made my search difficult. Day after day I spent many hours studying the habits of the sentries on the machine-gun towers, the guards walking along the double fence separating our cage from the French compound. I climbed fences at night to examine the other cages and to probe for weak spots in the defense perimeter. I found no exit, and my search grew desperate as the day approached when I was to be sent away to the Legion.

On October 13, my lucky star suddenly rose again. I received a package from the International Red Cross for which I had signed while in the hospital in Fort Cormeille. The contents included cheese, biscuits, concentrated foods and—best of all—four packs of American cigarettes and a can of tobacco! Now I was a wealthy man, with valuable wares to trade for the civilian clothes I needed. Something still more valuable turned up two days later. While I was investigating the camp infirmary, a young medical student, who helped treat the prisoners, asked me what I had to sell. I gave him my wristwatch, which I had labored long and hard to conceal from my various searchers. The student said that he could get 1,000 francs for the watch and, much to my surprise, he delivered the sum the next night after supper. The money was sufficient for train tickets to Germany and for food for many days.

As I bargained judiciously for my going-home wardrobe, a plan of escape gradually took form. My fellow prisoners proved highly susceptible to my American cigarettes. For six cigarettes I acquired a leather brief case in which to stow my meager possessions. A dove-blue overcoat cost me ten cigarettes, a hat and shirt only three. My biggest expenditure was 20 cigarettes, plus my tell-tale uniform, for an inconspicuous blue suit belonging to a prisoner, Horst Bender, whom I trusted enough to ask for help on the night of the break. The last items I needed were a number of butcher hooks. I acquired these for 10 cigarettes from a young prisoner who worked in the shop, telling him I intended to use them to build a clothes rack. Actually, I planned to use the hooks to get through the barbed wire fences in a dimly lit area between the kitchen compound and the guardhouse. I reviewed my plan over and over again, and resolved to die fighting rather than be recaptured again. I decided to make my break around 2200, just before moonrise, on October 27.

Saturday, October 27. The morning roll call was routine. I enjoyed the thought that in another 24 hours the camp would be in uproar over my escape. I was in an altogether excellent mood, and made it a point to talk to the men I knew as a kind of farewell. I gave Horst Bender final instructions about the part he was to play that night. At supper time, I wrapped my coat around the briefcase, handed the bundle as well as my evening ration to Bender, and stationed myself near the cart which had brought food to our barracks.

It was raw and cold when the work gang picked up the cart shortly after 2000. I quickly mingled with the men and helped them push the wagon out of the cage, down the camp's main street, and into the kitchen compound. Under the cover of darkness I stole away and entered the latrine, where I waited until all the afterdinner strollers had left the adjacent prison yard. Then I stepped into the dark area next to the fence that separated me from my previous cage. A shadowy figure came forward from behind a tree—Bender. He flung a bundle over the fence into my open arms. I rushed back into the latrine, took out and put on Bender's blue suit, wrapped my brown uniform, went out and threw the package over the fence to Bender. He tossed me another bundle containing my coat and briefcase, then waved a white hand in farewell.

A few jumps, and I flattened myself alongside the inner fence, opposite the guards' watchhouse. I froze while a guard passed just six meters away, then used some of my hooks to gather several strands of barbed wire. After checking the watchhouse and the machine-gun towers to the right and left, I crawled through the fence in slow motion and continued on, pushing my bundle ahead of me toward the barbed wire roll, always remaining in the shadow that an evergreen cast across the firing line. I parted the roll, hung it up with a hook on the outer fence, used two more hooks to make an opening in the last barrier, tossed my bundle through and followed it into the outside world. In the shadow of the guardhouse I put on my coat and hat and stuck a cigarette in my mouth. When all the guards were out of sight, I walked into the soldiers' compound. As I entered the illuminated drill grounds, a number of soldiers crossed my path. I halted, lighted my cigarette, then continued straight ahead, through the yards, between the barracks, and finally out of the camp.

Strolling into Le Mans from the outskirts, I reached the station at 2310 and bought a second-class ticket to Paris. About two hours later—it was now Sunday, October 28—I boarded the express and took a corner seat in a smoky compartment. At 0700 in the morning I arrived in the Gare de Montparnasse, nonchalantly displayed my ticket to the controller, passed by one of the gendarmes who had captured me two months ago, took the Metro to the Gare de l'Est. After buying a ticket to Metz, I had fully 13 hours to kill before my train departed. All day I roamed through Paris in a turmoil, thinking that everyone was staring at me, certain that the very next gendarme would ask to see papers I did not possess. But I managed to stay out of harm's way and returned to the station in ample time to board my train.

The journey to Metz took nine hours and brought me to the brink of exhaustion. In Metz I purchased a ticket to the French border town of Forbach and planned my trip when darkness would again be a cover. Again I walked out into the city streets. My head was spinning, my stomach aching. The strain was almost unbearable. I needed sleep, but did not dare to rest. I needed food, but I hesitated to enter a store without having ration tickets. Yet I also felt that I was riding a lucky streak—that nothing could stop my escape.

Finally I went into a bakery and made some excuse for having no tickets. I bought two crisp loaves of bread and wolfed them down as I wandered through the alleyways of the old town. But the meal left me so hungry that I boldly went into a restaurant, explained that I had lost my ration tickets, and asked to be served anyway. I had a bowl of pea soup, a big portion of

Lyonnaise sausage, and potato salad. After the veritable banquet, I resumed my furtive, fearful wandering. But at dusk I was still free, and at 1845 I returned to the station.

Knowing full well that I faced an exacting border inspection at Forbach, I boarded the waiting train and worked my way forward looking for a place to hide. When I arrived at the locomotive, there were no trainmen with the cab. A quick decision—a fast move—and I buried myself in the coal pile on the tender. Moments later the stoker and the engineer returned, the whistle sounded, and the train pulled out of the Metz station.

After two hours, the stoker had shoveled his way dangerously close to my position. Cautiously I crawled to the back of the tender, saw a large metal box, opened it and removed a hose, then dived in and closed the lid. Suddenly, with brakes shrieking, the train slowed down and stopped in the Forbach station— amid a large contingent of French soldiers. The locomotive, uncoupled from the train, rolled into position to take on water. When the trainmen looked for the hose, they found me in the box instead. Speaking French, I mumbled an excuse that apparently satisfied them—that I was just going to visit some friends across the border. They ordered me off the locomotive. I hurried into the darkness of the railroad yard and hid under a boxcar. In time, the soldiers finished their inspection and withdrew. The engine moved into place, was hooked up, and the train started forward. At the last moment, I raced across the tracks, caught the rear bumper of the first car, climbed its flimsy ladder, and flattened myself on the roof.

The train rolled on through the night. I clung to the roof, scarcely aware of the biting cold or the clouds of soot brushing my face. When I glimpsed lights ahead, I descended the ladder and waited on the bumper until the train stopped. I was in Sarrbruecken. Again the platform was swarming with French troops. I hastily mingled with departing passengers and looked around for the local German railroad personnel. Spotting the stationmaster in his blue suit, I went up to him and whispered in German, "I am German, I've escaped from a prison camp. I need help."

The stationmaster only nodded and said, "Follow me, just act normal and pretend to be one of us." He led me out into the freight yard, to an isolated railroad car. With a knock at the door, he pushed me inside, into a group of off-duty railroadmen.

The workers plied me with excited questions, gave me soap to wash off my layers of soot, fed me fried potatoes and *ersatz* coffee. They told me that my chance would come in 30 minutes, when an American express en route from Paris to Frankfurt would stop to switch engines, with a German crew to continue the journey to Frankfurt. Then they pressed a railroad lamp into my hand to make me look natural, and escorted me to the platform just in time to see the express pull into the station. American military police dropped from the cars, inspected the axles for fugitives. The engines were quickly switched and the train was ready to leave. As I stood between the workers at the head of the train, everything, sight and sound, seemed to be as sharp as a knife. The panting of the locomotive. The Americans searching the cars. The French roaming the platforms. Commands shouted in English. Sentences spoken in French. With a great crash the locomotive lurched forward. I pressed the hands of my two friends, leaped onto the moving engine. Ten, twelve piston strokes, and the express surged into the darkness, away from the border and deeper into Germany.

As the sky turned purple in the east, the train rumbled over the Mainzer bridge across the Rhine, rolling eastward, always eastward. And when the first rays of the morning sun touched the tops of the pines in the woods south of Frankfurt, I knew that I was free. At exactly 0640 on Tuesday, October 30, 1945, the train came to a halt at a signal. I leaped from the cab and ran into the woods of my youth.

APPENDICES

Appendix I

U-Boat Losses, 1939–1945

	1939	1940	1941	1942	1943	1944	1945	
January		1	–	3	6	15	12	
February		5	–	2	19	20	22	
March		–	5	6	15	25	34	
April		7	2	3	15	21	57	
May		1	1	4	41	23	28	
June		–	4	3	17	25		
July		2	1	12	37	23		
August		3	3	9	25	34		
September	2	–	2	10	9	23		
October	4	1	2	16	26	12		
Noember	2	2	5	13	19	8		
December	1	–	10	15	8	12		
Totals	9	22	35	96	237	241	153	793*

*Includes *U-505* and *U-570*, which were captured on the high seas.

411

Appendix II

Balance Sheet of the Battle of the Atlantic

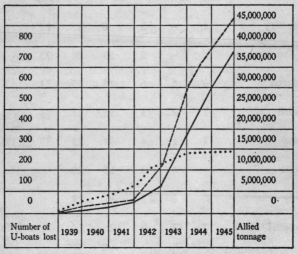

Number of U-boats lost	1939	1940	1941	1942	1943	1944	1945	Allied tonnage
800								45,000,000
700								40,000,000
600								35,000,000
500								30,000,000
400								25,000,000
300								20,000,000
200								15,000,000
100								10,000,000
0								5,000,000
								0

Legend

————————— German U-boats sunk
- - - - - - - - - Allied merchant ships constructed
• • • • • • • • • • • • • Allied merchant ships destroyed

412

Glossary

Asdic. Underwater detection apparatus by which surface vessels and submarines detect other submerged vessels or objects through the use of high frequency sound waves.

Ballast tank. Outboard tank aboard conventional U-boat. Several tanks were attached to either side of pressure hull and filled with diesel fuel at the outset of the mission. As the fuel was used, the tanks were refilled with seawater. Tanks were also used to regulate trim.

Biscay Cross. A German radar warning device in the form of a cross with a wire strung from top to bottom, creating an antenna capable of receiving radar waves in the upper centimeter range. The device, first used by U-boats in the Bay of Biscay, was soon obsolete because Allies were able to reduce radar wave lengths.

Bow left, angle 35. Term is used to identify the enemy's track in relation to the U-boat's position. The observer sees the target's bow pointing to the left and indicates the angle between the target's bow and the observer.

Bug. A revised German radar warning device, the fourth of a series, which detected radar waves in the lower centimeter range.

Buoyancy tank. Pressure-resistant tank of great capacity. Several were built within pressure hull for the purpose of effecting diving maneuvers, regulating buoyancy, and leveling boat.

Continental shelf. That portion of a continent submerged under relatively shallow sea, in contrast with the deep ocean basins from which the shelf is separated by the relatively steep continental slope. The break of the slope occurs at a remarkably constant depth of approximately 200 meters, or 600 feet below the mean water level.

Direction finder.   Antenna aboard a ship to locate the source of a radio beacon transmitted by a land radio station. The intersection of three or more beacons determined the ship's accurate position. A U-boat sending coded signals near a convoy was thus able to home other U-boats to the target.

Flak.   German term for *Flugabwehr-Kanone,* anti-aircraft gun.

Fly.   A much improved German radar warning device that was capable of detecting radar waves in the lowest centimeter range and of indicating direction of transmitting source.

Flying boat.   Aircraft whose main body consists of a single hull, or boat, that permits take-off or landing on water.

Grid Square.   A system of squares drawn on a nautical chart, arranged in a specific manner, and identified by letters and numbers to determine a particular spot at sea with ease in the shortest possible term.

Gyroscope.   An apparatus consisting of a rotating wheel so mounted that its axis can turn freely in certain or all directions; it is also capable of maintaining the same absolute direction in spite of movements of the mountings and surrounding parts. It is based on the principle that a body rotating steadily about an axis will tend to resist changes in the direction of the axis, and it is used to maintain equilibrium to determine direction.

Gyro-angle.   Angle at which the directional gyroscopic control of a torpedo is set prior to firing. A "zero angle" causes a torpedo to travel in the same direction as the heading of the submarine at the time of firing. The torpedo may also be set to travel right or left of the heading of the submarine after it leaves the tube.

Gyro-compass. A device used like the ordinary magnetic compass for determining directions, but employing a continuously driven gyroscope instead of a magnetized needle or bar; the gyroscope is mounted so that its axis constantly maintains its position with reference to the geographical north, thus dealing with true geographical meridians used in navigation instead of magnetic meridians.

Horizon. The line which forms the boundary between ocean and sky and extends or diminishes depending upon weather conditions and the observer's eye level measured from the surface. The horizon as seen from the bridge of a U-boat on a very clear day is at a distance of 16 nautical miles.

Kilometer. One kilometer is a unit of length, the common measure of distance equal to 1,000 meters, and equivalent to 3,280.8 feet or 0.621 mile.

Knot. The unit of a ship's speed of one nautical mile per hour.

Longitude. Angular distance east or west on the earth's surface, measured by the angle between the meridian of a particular place and some prime meridian, as that of Greenwich, England, or by the corresponding difference in time.

Maquis. Name of one of the French resistance movements (or any of its members) during the German occupation in World War II.

Meter. The metric system's fundamental unit of length, equivalent to 39.37 inches.

Metox. A German electronic radar warning device, replacement for the bulky "Biscay Cross," and capable of detecting radar waves in the ten centimeter range.

Mile—nautical mile. Officially fixed in the U.S. at 6,080.20 feet and in Great Britain at 6,080 feet; a unit of distance in sea and air navigation, equal to 1.852 kilometers.

Oscillograph. An electronic tube for recording radar waves and transforming them into visible images on the wide screen of the device.

Parallel. A circle on the earth surface formed by the intersection of a plane parallel to the plane of the equator, bearing east and west and designated in degrees of latitude north or south of the equator along the arc of any meridian.

Periscope. An optical instrument consisting essentially of a long tube with an arrangement of prisms or mirrors by which a view of the water surface is seen from below.

Port. The side of a ship left of a person facing the bow. Also, on the left side of the vessel.

Port astern. On the left side and in the rear quarter of a vessel as seen from the bridge.

Radar. An electronic device emitting high frequency waves for detecting objects on or above surface and measuring their range and bearings. The device was common before World War II on German and Allied ships, but was greatly improved during hostilities allowing detection of very small objects by means of very short wave lengths.

Sky-periscope. A periscope which allows a submerged submarine to view the sky directly above the boat. The head of this periscope is bulky and, therefore, not used for day attack.

Starboard. The side of a ship to the right of a person facing the bow. Also, on the right side of the vessel.

Target Bearing Transmitter. (TBT). A device mounted on the bridge of a submarine by which the bearing to a target is measured and transmitted to the torpedo computer in the tower for solution of the torpedo-firing problem. German term of the device: *U-Bootzielobtik* (UZO).

Torpedo computer. A high-speed electronic calculating machine for deriving a torpedo-control solution from data on the target's course, speed, and range integrated with data on the submarine's course, speed, and the speed of the torpedo. Computed gyro-angle is electrically transmitted to torpedo in tube permitting split-second release of torpedo onto calculated track independent of submarine's movement at the moment of firing.

Trim dive.   A diving maneuver; the daily requirement for conventional submarines to correct weight, buoyancy, and trim due to changes of the sea water's density caused by fluctuation in temperature, flora and fauna, currents and tides, and consumption of supplies.

Trim tank.   Tank or tanks inside pressure hull to regulate weight and level of submerged submarine.

THE AVIATOR'S BOOKSHELF

THE CLASSICS OF FLYING

The books that aviators, test pilots, and astronauts feel tell the most about the skills that launched mankind on the adventure of flight. These books bridge man's amazing progress, from the Wright brothers to the first moonwalk.

☐ **THE WRIGHT BROTHERS by Fred C. Kelly** (23962-7 • $2.95)
  Their inventive genius was enhanced by their ability to learn how to fly their machines.

☐ **THE FLYING NORTH by Jean Potter** (23946-5 • $2.95)
  The Alaskan bush pilots flew in impossible weather, frequently landing on sandbars or improvised landing strips, flying the early planes in largely uninhabited and unexplored land.

☐ **THE SKY BEYOND by Sir Gordon Taylor** (23949-X • $2.95)
  Transcontinental flight required new machines piloted by skilled navigators who could pinpoint tiny islands in the vast Pacific—before there were radio beacons and directional flying aids.

☐ **THE WORLD ALOFT by Guy Murchie** (23947-3 • $2.95)
  The book recognized as *The Sea Round Us* for the vaster domain—the Air. Mr. Murchie, a flyer, draws from history, mythology and many sciences. The sky is an ocean, filled with currents and wildlife of its own. A tribute to, and a celebration of, the flyers' environment.

☐ **CARRYING THE FIRE by Michael Collins** (23948-1 • $3.50)
  "The best written book yet by any of the astronauts."—*Time Magazine*. Collins, the Gemini 10 and Apollo 11 astronaut, gives us a picture of the joys of flight and the close-in details of the first manned moon landing.

☐ **THE LONELY SKY by William Bridgeman with Jacqueline Hazard** (23950-3 • $3.50)
  The test pilot who flew the fastest and the highest. The excitement of going where no one has ever flown before by a pilot whose careful study and preparation was matched by his courage.

Read all of the books in THE AVIATOR'S BOOKSHELF

Prices and availability subject to change without notice

Buy them at your bookstore or use this handy coupon for ordering:

Bantam Books, Inc., Dept. WW4, 414 East Golf Road, Des Plaines, Ill. 60016

Please send me the books I have checked above. I am enclosing $_____ (please add $1.25 to cover postage and handling). Send check or money order —no cash or C.O.D.'s please.

Mr/Mrs/Miss _____

Address_____

City_____ State/Zip_____

WW4—11/83

Please allow four to six weeks for delivery. This offer expires 5/84.

Join the Allies on the Road to Victory
BANTAM WAR BOOKS

These action-packed books recount the most important events of World War II. Specially commissioned maps, diagrams and illustrations allow you to follow these true stories of brave men and gallantry in action.

Join the Allies on the Road to Victory

BANTAM WAR BOOKS

These action-packed books recount the most important events of World War II. Specially commissioned maps, diagrams and illustrations allow you to follow these true stories of brave men and gallantry in action.

☐	23549	FLY FOR YOUR LIFE L. Forrester	$3.50
☐	20308	THOUSAND MILE WAR B. Garfield	$3.50
☐	22832	D DAY: THE SIXTH OF JUNE, 1944 D. Howarth	$2.95
☐	22703	LONDON CALLING NORTH POLE H. J. Giskes	$2.50
☐	20749	BREAKOUT J. Potter	$2.50
☐	23833	COMPANY COMMANDER C. MacDonald	$3.50
☐	24104	A SENSE OF HONOR J. Webb	$3.50
☐	23820	WAR AS I KNEW IT Patton, Jr.	$3.95

*Cannot be sold to Canadian Residents.
Prices and availability subject to change without notice.

Buy them at your local bookstore or use this handy coupon for ordering:

Bantam Books, Inc., Dept. WO, 414 East Golf Road, Des Plaines, Ill. 60016

Please send me the books I have checked above. I am enclosing $_____
(please add $1.25 to cover postage and handling). Send check or money order
—no cash or C.O.D.'s please.

Mr/Mrs/Miss _____

Address_____

City_____ State/Zip_____

WO—12/83

Please allow four to six weeks for delivery. This offer expires 6/84.